T0287508

INDUS
BASIN
UNINTERRUPTED

'The Indus has defined the subcontinent in myriad ways. Based on deep archival research, Uttam Sinha provides a fascinating narrative of its role and influence, with focus on the Indus Waters Treaty that was signed six decades ago between India and Pakistan. The treaty now confronts a fresh political and ecological challenge, which is what makes this book very timely. It is a valuable contribution both to the world of scholarship and to the larger public discourse.'—Jairam Ramesh, MP and former Union minister

'Drawing on a wealth of archival material and critically researched information, the book vividly takes readers through a historical tour de force of the Indus basin. Without obscuring facts, the author, with his easy narration, reminds us, through the past, of the contemporariness of the divided rivers between India and Pakistan. Very often, the Indus Waters Treaty is described as unfair to India. However, the effort should be to reduce cost on India by maximizing the storage and using the waters.'—Nripendra Misra, chairman, Nehru Memorial Museum and Library

'Uttam Sinha has written a most fascinating chronicle on how the lives and destinies of the Indus basin inhabitants were influenced by the designs of invaders, conquerors, kings, greedy Coy wallahs and the great games played by the canny colonizers. Traversing the maze of historical events, from long before Alexander and his army crossed the Indus, this writing presents an excellent exposition of the complex challenges which were met before the signing of the Indus Waters Treaty. The book, which contains valuable lessons for war and peace, must be read by security strategists, diplomats, economists and political leaders.'—N.N. Vohra, governor, Jammu and Kashmir (2008–18)

'This is a well-researched, historically grounded and carefully argued account of the Indus basin. Sinha, who has previously written with much authority on the politics of hydrology in South Asia, has distilled a significant corpus of literature into this book. As a consequence, it is a work of considerable sweep and deals with an issue of compelling contemporary political significance. Academics, journalists and analysts alike will benefit from reading this extremely topical book.'—Sumit Ganguly, distinguished professor, Indiana University, US

'This lucidly accounted history of the turbulent Indus basin will help in enhancing understanding of complex issues in water management, which is otherwise an emotive subject, causing disputes. The past impediments in the development of the basin and the possible options for its better management are clearly discernible from the narrative of the book. It is an excellent outcome of systematic and consistent research.'—Suresh Kumar, chief principal secretary to chief minister of Punjab, and policy fellow, Center for Science and Policy, University of Cambridge

'Sinha's book traverses through 3500 years of subcontinental history like the Indus itself—mesmerizingly and uninterruptedly. It is a pure master class on Indus's transformation from a cog in military strategy into a source of conflict and cooperation post 1947. A treasure for scholars and policymakers alike.'—Ashutosh Misra, South Asia expert and CEO, Institute for Australia India Engagement, Brisbane

'Civilizations have adjusted and transformed over thousands of years in the Indus basin, adapting to the magnificent river system which itself changed constantly. Yet, the society always craved continuity, and in that process created the largest public surface water irrigation system in the world. Uttam Sinha brilliantly describes the unceasing changes and the search for stability through wise development of the water resources network. With an eye for strategic dimensions, regional and local competition for water and related power plays, he discusses the history leading to the Indus Treaty. That the treaty itself had to decussate multiple objectives, needs, intrigues and strategic concerns is a lesson for reconciliations everywhere. This book will interest a wide array of readers.'—Junaid Ahmad, country director for India, World Bank

INDUS BASIN

UNINTERRUPTED

A HISTORY *of* TERRITORY & POLITICS
from ALEXANDER *to* NEHRU

UTTAM KUMAR SINHA

VINTAGE
An imprint of Penguin Random House

VINTAGE

USA | Canada | UK | Ireland | Australia
New Zealand | India | South Africa | China

Vintage is part of the Penguin Random House group of companies
whose addresses can be found at global.penguinrandomhouse.com

Published by Penguin Random House India Pvt. Ltd
4th Floor, Capital Tower 1, MG Road,
Gurugram 122 002, Haryana, India

Penguin
Random House
India

First published in Vintage by Penguin Random House India 2021

10 9 8 7 6 5 4 3 2

The views and opinions expressed in this book are the author's own and the
facts are as reported by him which have been verified to the extent possible,
and the publishers are not in any way liable for the same.

ISBN 9780670094486

Typeset in Adobe Caslon Pro by Manipal Technologies Limited, Manipal
Printed at Thomson Press India Ltd, New Delhi

www.penguin.co.in

For
Divakar (Mohan)
Our uninterrupted love

Map 1. North-Western Frontier of British India, 1844, by Herbert B. Edwardes

Source: John Brown, *Historical Maps of the Survey of India* (1700–1900)

Map 2. Trans-Indus Frontier of the Punjab, 1851, by Herbert B. Edwardes

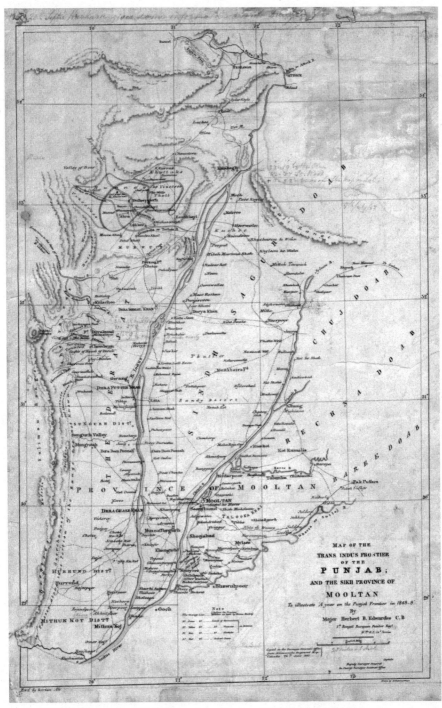

Source: John Brown, *Historical Maps of the Survey of India (1700–1900)*

Contents

Contents

Part III
Colonization, Canals *and* Contestation

Part IV
Partition *of* Land *and* Rivers

Part V
Making *of* the Indus Waters Treaty

Preface

It is a frightening acknowledgement that the Indus basin, with its richness and impetuosity, can be so all-pervasive, defining history, ordering territories, attracting invaders and in many senses, determining the way of life and the politics around it. Much, of course, is known of this vast basin, yet much is unknown. It is time, perhaps, as we mark sixty years of the Indus Waters Treaty, to 'talk of many things', as the Walrus said to the Carpenter in Lewis Carroll's *Through a Looking Glass*.

Many centuries after the great Indus civilization, Edward Gibbon, the historian, known to be a mute and indifferent backbencher in the House of Commons, reflected on the ravages of the Tiber on Rome and the efforts of the Roman emperor Augustus (27 BCE–14 CE) to prevent flooding. He observed with irony,

> The servitude of rivers is the noblest victory which man has obtained over the licentiousness of nature.[1]

Both in terms of 'licentiousness' and as a

> . . . lasting amelioration of nature . . .[2]

that the eighteenth century French political philosopher Montesquieu expressed, the Indus has remained a powerful symbol of the passage

of time, influencing and in turn being influenced by the sharpening
of the sociopolitical landscape, the institutional structures, the
technological interventions, the moulding of the legal and the
potential for commerce and peace, though not without its share
of dispute and conflict. These acquired dimensions continue to
influence the basin in the twenty-first century.

The past is always as inescapable as it is intriguing. An attempt
has been made to open the pages of history to the interlinked events
of the Indus basin. The book engages with history, not strictly in the
sense of historical inquiry but by identifying with historical figures,
like characters shaping plots, and their decisions. Often and not
unintentionally, the narrative takes a first-person account involving
the lived experiences or the position of the figures. The characters
that run along the timeline of the Indus right till the Indus Waters
Treaty in 1960 are influenced by concerns of pride, power, envy,
fear, desperation and many a time sheer greed. Their actions and
consequences have been momentous.

The book utilizes varied sources, from memoirs and biographies
to letters and diaries. The 'Nehru Papers' at the Nehru Memorial
Museum and Library (New Delhi) provides valuable information,
adding substantially to the volumes published of the *Selected Works of
Jawaharlal Nehru*. Substantiating these papers are the fantastically well-
documented telegrams, communiqués and notes on the canal water
disputes compiled by Avatar Singh Bhasin. Niranjan Gulhati's work
based on his experience as India's principal negotiator on the Indus
is a valuable source that details most extensively the negotiations for
its resolution. The World Bank archives and files on the Indus basin
dispute, which are now digitized, form another crucial primary source.
The new and unused material that has been indicated to the best extent
possible, one hopes, will help enrich the existing source of reference.

The book is an outcome of a two-year sojourn at the Nehru
Memorial Museum and Library (2018–20) graciously offered by my
parent organization, the Manohar Parrikar Institute for Defence
Studies and Analyses, New Delhi. Both are institutions of pride and
legacy, and one is humbled by being associated with them.

SETTLERS,
INVADERS *and*
SUCCESSIONS

Ageing of India's History

For all of Lord Curzon's unpopularity as the viceroy of India—not to mention his racist mindset and the infamous announcement of the partition of the undivided Bengal—his appointment of John Marshall, barely twenty-six years of age, as the head of the Archaeological Survey of India in 1902, was an act of prudence. Marshall encouraged archaeological studies and spearheaded excavations which were to change the chronology of ancient India.

Prior to the great unearthing of the mounds in the valleys of the Indus, it was thought that India's civilization dated back only to the time of Alexander's invasion. The history before that was in the realm of the unknown. In 1921, the epoch-making discovery of the site of Harappa and the following year at Mohenjo-daro brought to light the existence of a singularly uniform civilization (3300 to 1500 BCE), located in what is now Pakistan and north-west India up to the Arabian Sea. It was

. . . closely akin but in some respects even superior to that of contemporary Mesopotamia and Egypt.[1]

The discovery became a source for

. . . popular perceptions of India's ancient past . . .[2]

and inspired a nationalistic sentiment of a

. . . glorious golden age.[3]

3

Later, in post-Independence India, the Indus civilization became a revered reference for the nationalistic Hindutva cultural claims of the Hindu–Vedic society and the *Sindhhu Saraswati Sabhyata* (Indus–Saraswati Civilization).[4]

An intriguing aspect of the Indus Valley relates to the circumstances that brought an end to the civilization. It is largely evidenced that the civilization between 1700 and 1500 BCE witnessed widespread climate change in the form of rainfall deficiency and drought, and as one theory suggested, the numerous settlements on the Indus flood plains were engulfed by mud. The impact of it was undoubtedly telling but of significance also was the resilience of the society and the means of adaptation that the settlers practised until it became unsustainable. The Indus civilization—Harappa, along with Mohenjo-daro, Lothal, Dholavira, Kalibangan and numerous other sites—presents an intricate relationship of the monsoonal and fluvial changes, and their societal impact. The Harappans harnessed flood inundation irrigation (*sailaba*) and dry farming (*khushkaba*) in the arid plains.[5] Methods like storing rainwater and then channelizing it for irrigation was also extensively applied. Evidences of check dams and reservoirs, for example, in Dholavira,[6] confirm hydraulic interventions that helped the people to cope with decreasing rainfall and the eastward shift of the rivers.[7] Such knowledge many millennia prior to the development of the world's largest irrigation system in the Punjab remained instructive, none more so than the fact that the Indus basin, while extremely productive, is equally unpredictable with frequent changes in the course of the rivers and variation in flow.

Over 5000 years ago, the Indus civilization teemed with tigers, rhinoceros and elephants as they roamed the 'moister regions', a radical contrast to the ecology today. The river system also had a different profile. Mohenjo-daro in the Sindh Valley was flanked by two parallel rivers which flowed to the sea—the westward Indus and the eastward Mihrān. During the period of the Indus civilization, the Indus was a subsidiary branch of the Mihrān, which was possibly the Hakra in its upper reaches and dominated the hydrology of the region by channelling the waters of all the rivers of the Punjab to the sea. The courses of the two rivers in successive periods intermittently changed, at times being close and connected, and at other times, distant and independent. The existence of two rivers with an eastern flow and a western flow at the mouth of the ocean is noted by the chroniclers of Alexander of Macedon during his campaign in the Punjab. But the Indus or the western flow, as observed, had a greater volume. Many centuries later, the two rivers were recorded by the Arabs. Al-Baladhuri in the ninth century, followed by the tenth-century historian and traveller, El-Mas'ūdī, and the eleventh-century Persian scholar, Al-Beruni, all describe the domineering Mihrān while the Indus is actually referred to as the river Sindh— the classical Islamic geographers' interpretation of the basin. By the fourteenth century, there are fewer references to the Mihrān, possibly with the eastern flow merging with the western flow of the Indus. Later, as observed during the Tughlak period,

> . . . the western branch which flowed under Thatta was the mainstream so broad that you could not see from the left bank the battle that was being fought on the opposite shore.[8]

With the British colonial rule, the Indus as a nomenclature got firmly established. During 1808–10, the Englishmen in their diligent survey of the Sindh, Kabul and Lahore regions of the Indus basin, while referring to the accounts of the Arab travellers and the ancient texts, observed the contradictions in the descriptions of the rivers. Quite perplexed by the interchanging emphasis on the Mihrān and Indus, the British cartographers broadly concluded that the river Sindh was the Indus.

> Thus above its junction with the Chenab, the Indus was called Sindh; from this point to Aror it was the Panjnad; and from the city to its mouth it bore the name of Mihrān.[9]

The varying nomenclature and uncertainty over what was to be regarded as the main stem required a powerful expression of unification and, under the British administration, the Indus became the all-encompassing river—it was not only the Sindh but also the Panjnad and the Mihrān.

The Punjab plain made up of *doabs* or the land between rivers was a 'staging-point' for invaders as they descended from the wuthering heights of the mountain passes on the north-western side to enter India. There the exhausted invaders halted, organizing their army and preparing stratagem to capture the seat of power, whether it was Taxila in the fifth-century BCE, or Lahore till the thirteenth century and later Delhi. The defenders of power would pre-empt the invaders by meeting them at the entry points in the plains or at times greet them to form alliances. Several clashes and bloody battles were an outcome. The Punjab shaped India's destiny in profound ways and its location brought an interrelation of war and peace, and an intersection of race, language and culture that led to a variety of descriptions through different times—the 'sword arm of India', the 'gateway of India' and the 'seedbed of new ideas', to cite a few.

Rivers never failed to capture the imagination of the people and different cultural ages christened Punjab through its rivers—the *Sapt Sindhu* (land of seven rivers) in the Vedic time, the Persian pronunciation ('s' as 'h') being *Haft Hind*; the *Panch Nad* (land of five rivers) in the Mahabharat age; and when the Greeks came to Punjab they named it the *Pentapotamia*.[10] Punjab with its rivers was a great melting pot, and

> . . . beating and being beaten by hordes of warriors and invaders gave rise to a composite culture which bore the imprint of every age through which it passed and every race and culture with which it came into contact.[11]

Edward Gibbon's *The History of the Decline and Fall of the Roman Empire* is an indispensable source tracing western civilization from the height of the Roman Empire to the fall of Byzantium. In a grand narrative unmatched during the time it mentions, briefly, Alexander of Macedon in the Punjab with Greek references to the rivers that joined the Indus—the Hydaspes (Chelum/Jhelum), Hyphasis (Beyah/Beas), Ascesines (Chenab), Hydraotes (Ravey/Ravi) and Renney or Hesidros (the Suteldj/Sutlej).[12]

Alexander Thought Indus to Be Head of Nile

After decisively defeating the Persian ruler, Darius III, and marching eastwards to Afghanistan and establishing a series of outposts, Alexander came to the banks of the Indus through the Hindu-Kush range in the spring of 327 BCE. Beyond this, as the Greek understood, was the land of India. Alexander's army crossed the Indus on a 'bridge of boats' near a small village of Hund about 32 kilometres from Tarbela (now a dam site in Pakistan).[13] Ambhi, who ruled Taxila, the land between Indus and the Hydaspes, greeted Alexander with open arms and accepted his suzerainty without any resistance, as did many other smaller chieftains. The exception was the lone-standing and courageous Porus, who ruled the territory between Hydaspes and Ascesines.

In July 326 BCE, Alexander imperiously marched towards Hydaspes with a huge army that swelled further by the contribution of troops by Ambhi. The swollen river acted as an initial barrier to Alexander's naked ambition of conquering India. On the other side of the riverbank, waiting for him with his imposing army and perched on his elephant was a confident Porus, a 'child of the monsoon', familiar with every ebb and flow of the Hydaspes. Despite all the defensive value and strategic depth that a flooded river could offer him, Porus was defeated by the deception and daring of Alexander, whose soldiers crossed the Hydaspes at Jalalpur while the rest of the troops remained camped at Haranpur.[14] History recounts the romanticized description of the chivalry of the victor (Alexander) and the pride of the vanquished (Porus).

Rivers marked the territorial divide and the arrangement that followed the battle of Hydaspes.

> Alexander left Porus to rule over the entire territory between Beas and Jhelum and . . . Ambhi to rule to the west of Jhelum.[15]

Triumphant and emboldened, Alexander moved eastwards and captured the settlements between Ascesines, Hydraotes and Hyphasis. Beyond this the Greeks had believed was 'the end of the world' with the great 'Outer Ocean', only to learn that the world did not end but continued endlessly. Alexander was determined to march further eastward and explore the unknown, but his weary troops longed to go back home. Sensing disgruntlement in the ranks and possible sedition, Alexander spoke to his men with great emotion and inspiration, every now and then looking eastwards from the banks of the Hyphasis:

> . . . If we have driven the Scythians out of their deserts, and caused the river Indus, the Hydaspes, the Ascesines, and the Hydraotes to flow through our territories; why should we now delay to extend our conquests yet further and add Hyphasis also and the countries beyond it, to the Macedonian empire?[16]

Stillness prevailed after Alexander's invocation, none daring to express a contrary opinion until finally Caenus, his intimate friend, after having spoken at length, ended by saying:

> Thou art an emperor, and at the head of such an army, what enemy can terrible to thee? But consider once for all, that the turns of chance are sudden, and therefore to mortals, however prudent, unavoidable.[17]

Alexander sensed the mood and saw the heaviness on the faces of his troops, some shedding tears, and decided to return. Having remained the invincible conqueror throughout his short life, he was to be overwhelmed by the emotions of his men.

During his passage home, he moved to the banks of the Hydaspes, where he had emerged victorious over Porus, and built two cities on either side, the Nicaea (Victory City) and Bucephalous, the latter in memory of his illustrious horse. By then Alexander had planned to voyage southwards to the Indus delta opening to the ocean and then onwards home. In preparation, he built a fleet

. . . from the timbers growing upon the neighbouring mountains.[18]

With vessels sturdy and ready, Alexander and his army commenced their journey from the Hydaspes to the Ascesines where his ships encountered terrible turbulence before the conjoined rivers suddenly and seamlessly merged into the Indus, sighting as they journeyed southwards 'crocodiles' and 'beans' growing on the riverbanks. Alexander seriously assumed the Indus to be the head of the Nile which rose in India and, after travelling and getting lost in the vast Persian desert, emerged in Egypt before entering the Mediterranean. It was only after some inquiries from the locals that Alexander was convinced that

> . . . the river [Hydaspes] lost its water in the Ascesines, and the Ascesines its water and name in the Indus, which river discharged its stream by two mouths into the ocean, very far from the country of Egypt.[19]

As Alexander's army shipped down the Indus with the 'clashing of oars' and 'shouts of oarsmen', in a formation of soldiers on horses and foot on both banks of the river, the troops encountered several tribes and principalities. Some of them ceded while those who resisted were put to sword, like the country of Shogdi in which

> . . . 6000 Brahmins are said to have been hanged by Alexander in a row to cause panic in the whole region.[20]

Earlier, Alexander destroyed the provinces of Malli and Oxydracae, which had come together to fiercely thwart his advance. On reaching Pattala (the site of modern-day Hyderabad in Pakistan), an island formation on the Indus delta from where the river branched left and right to the 'ocean', Alexander, having spent some time here, took the land route westwards journeying home, which he never reached. Meanwhile, his fleet under Nearchus followed the Makran coast to the Persian Gulf.[21] But before Alexander set for home, he ventured twice into the ocean (the Arabian Sea), and as he did so, the description of the delta and the west and east branches of the Indus is vividly told:

> When he (Alexander) had sailed far down the left branch and was near the mouth thereof, he came to a certain lake formed either by the river spreading wide over a flat country, or by additional streams flowing in from the adjacent lands, making it appear like a bay of the sea . . . he, with some biremes and triremes, passed out at the mouth of the river and sailed into the ocean.[22]

Alexander's march in the Punjab was halted at the banks of the Hyphasis (Beas). His army never got to face the Sutlej (Hesidros) which was further east of the Beas. Not surprisingly, the accounts of Alexander's voyage describe the four rivers, instead of five, which merged into the Indus. Of the rivers in the Indus system, Sutlej has had a varied hydrological past often not part of the basin configuration. It could have been the 'lost' river re-emerging later in time or one of the 'other' rivers which followed a different route to the ocean and then subsequently, as widely presumed, because of tectonic shifts, the course changed and joined the Indus basin. An intriguing article on the 'lost river of the Indian desert' was carried in the *Calcutta Review* in 1874 which was followed by an equally interesting counterargument the following year. The article, based on detailed observations, argued,

> There can be no doubt that the Satlej, instead of turning nearly due west from Ropar to join the Biyas, as at present, originally flowed in a much more southerly direction; and that the Sotra or Hakra is its ancient bed.[23]

The response to this note written by Nearchus, an obvious pseudonym, noted that the

> Satlej did not flow out of its present course. But running to the westward, anterior to the thirteenth century and that the lost river

(the Sotra or the Hakra) did not reach the sea, but ended its course in the old Indus, near Rori.[24]

The point, without going into the 'lost and found' Sutlej debate, is that the Indus basin, with its complex hydrology system, has always remained difficult to comprehend.

The geographical narration, particularly in reference to the rivers, and the anecdotal observation that follow from the historiography of Alexander, remain invaluable in understanding the socio-politico-cultural ethos of the time as much as the psyche of Alexander. War was inseparable from Alexander and his search for fame and glory made him, like his hero Achilles, whose shield he purportedly used, a

> . . . stone cold killer.[25]

His conquest meant not only subjugating his rival but scaling the riverine terrain. Throughout Alexander's campaign, rivers played a specific part. The military planning entailed crossing the rivers, not in the parts which had the narrowest width, as it was more turbulent, but in those parts of the rivers

> . . . where the channel was the widest, and consequently stillest for the transportation of his army.[26]

Almost two centuries before Alexander, King Cyrus of Assyria (590–529 BCE) faced the difficult river terrains in Punjab and could only succeed in bringing under his control the tribes west of the Indus. Further in time, Semiramis (811–806 BCE), the legendary queen of the Assyrian Empire, while crossing the Indus with her troops, suffered huge losses and retreated. Alexander proved all the past wrong, set new benchmarks as a conqueror, and as he was wont to say,

> The end and object of conquest is to avoid doing the same thing as the conquered.[27]

Alexander's entry into the Punjab established a pattern to be repeated through millennia of successive invasions. Each subsequent conquest led to new socio-politico-economic dynamic that impacted human systems, including agriculture and irrigation. Each conqueror and his conquest, however, embraced the water methods of the previous regimes. As empires expanded, rapid agrarian development seeking intensive interventions on the river systems to water the fields followed. Water development became an exigent issue inextricably linked to prosperity and the legitimacy of the ruler.

Once Alexander left, after almost two years in India, the Mauryan dynasty under Chandragupta, having established power in the Indo-Gangetic plains, conquered the whole region of the Punjab, including the territory held by Seleucus Nicator, a Greek general of Alexander who had campaigned in India (305–303 BCE). It was for the first time that the conquest to such a far point in the west came from the east. A treaty was signed between the two in which Seleucus ceded the trans-Indus territories—Aria (Herat), Arachosia (Kandhar), Gedrosia (Makran) and Paropanishae (Kabul)—to the Mauryan Empire. In exchange, Chandragupta made a gift of 500 elephants to Seleucus and married his daughter. In their administration of the Punjab, the Mauryans were known

> . . . as the great managers of the distribution of irrigation waters as the question of irrigation was of fundamental importance to the people and the State.[28]

As Kautilya, the economist and adviser to Chandragupta, explains in his treatise *Arthashastra*, all water belonged to the one who governed, and the golden rule of 'no-harm to others' while irrigating one's own fields was emphasized. Some of the other rules prohibited obstruction or diversion of watercourses and the release of water from barrages without legitimate reasons, and where damage was caused, compensation was awarded. Almost two millennia later, the Indus basin came a full circle as India and Pakistan tirelessly negotiated the waters, balancing the principles of sharing with the imperatives of demand.

Qásim Crosses the Indus

In the early eighth century, 711 to be more precise, Muhammad-bin-Qásim marched his troops through the Buddhist city of Siraj-ji-Takri along the western limestone terraces of Sukkur in Upper Sindh down to the port town of Debal (later Karachi) on the Indus delta. It marked the advent of the Muslims into India and a landmark episode of Islamic history, bringing the territories west of Indus into the orbit of the political and cultural influence of Islam. The Umayyad Caliphate, which ruled the Islamic Empire from 661–750 with the seat of power in Damascus, had earlier made several incursions from its protectorate in Baghdad to deal with the pestilence of the sea pirates on the coast of Sind. But never had the expeditionary force crossed the river to the other side. Until Qásim, its finest and most obedient general, faced the descendent of the Hindu Chach family, Rai Dáhar,[29] the 'king of Sindh and the sovereign of Hind', on the banks of the Mihrān in Rohri (earlier Aror) and changed history.

History describes Dáhar throwing down the gauntlet at Qásim,

> Either you cross over or we will do so.[30]

Dáhar, proud and courageous, knew the river and was familiar with its impetuous turns. He said:

> Let them come down to the river from another place where the water may be deep and where there may be plenty of mud and slough. You must keep your boats ready to harass them, and subject them to losses when they attempt to cross the river.[31]

Qásim meticulously planned the crossing,

> . . . so that no harm may be done to the troops.[32]

When he crossed the river at Bet, shortest in breadth, less deep and with a river island in between, he sent round a crier, proclaiming:

> O army of Islám these waters of the Mehrán will be behind your backs, and the army of infidels will come in your front. Whoever wishes to return, let him go back even from this spot. If, after the coming up of the enemy and the commencement of battle, he turns his face, the soldiers will be disheartened, and they will run away, and our enemy will then be more pressing and powerful. Whoever so turns his face will incur disgrace, and die the death of a coward, and be liable to the torture of the next world.[33]

So powerful and motivating was the call that no one returned, except three persons; and when the 'bridge of boats' was ready, the army safely crossed over with just one casualty. In the ferocious battle that followed in 712, Qásim's intrepid and superior military skills, backed by a powerful cavalry, eventually prevailed over Dáhar's infantry with elephants. Dáhar died in battle and his head was sent to Baghdad. The young, swashbuckling Qásim, who was only eighteen years old, continued with his victorious procession, capturing Makran and then Multan. As he proceeded to Multan, a part of Qásim's army fought a ferocious battle for seventeen days to lay siege to a fort at Sikkha opposite Multan, while the rest of the army crossed the river Basmad (Ravi) and pillaged the city. It is recorded that

> . . . six thousand warriors were put to death and all their relatives and dependents were taken as slaves. Protection was given to merchants, artisans and agriculturists.[34]

An account of this expedition was described by the Arab traveller and chronicler Al Baladhuri.

Sindh was well known amongst the Arabs, and seafarers would come to Debal, which enjoyed a certain popularity as a port city. The geographical features of Sindh were similar to the great river-desert basins of the Nile, the Oxus and the Helmund. Sindh was also a land deeply divided and seething with enmity between the Hindus and Buddhists. Qásim exploited this internal weakness and easily cut through the divide, drawing the Buddhist into the Muslim fold as the Buddhist equally weighed the Muslims against the Hindus. With the territories in his control, Qásim ensured that Dáhar's influence was cut down to size and the sea-route trade along the coast of Debal was freed from the Meds, the tribes of the Scythians living in Sindh, who were constantly raiding Arab merchant ships. After securing the maritime interests, Qásim looked towards governance and very astutely did not disturb the administrative machinery, allowing the natives more say in the running of the affairs,

> Those who know the work of building houses and cultivating land, let them carry on their callings freely and diligently. Show kindness and leniency to them in revenue matters.[35]

Qásim maximized revenues through a people-friendly, bottom-to-top approach. However, an unusual incident saw an end to Qásim. Over a misunderstanding, he was instructed by his angered master, Hajjáj Yúsif, the khalifa of Baghdad, to

> . . . put himself in raw leather and come back.[36]

The obedient Qásim immediately did so and died of asphyxiation at the age of twenty. The general who brought down seventy chieftains of Sindh and Hind died

> . . . simply on the slanderous word of a malicious individual.[37]

When the khalifa got to know the truth about Qásim's innocence, in grief, he

> . . . bit the back of his hand.[38]

Most historians do not take Qásim's conquest of Sindh and Multan as a significant event partly because it ended quickly with his quirky death, thus failing to establish any lasting order. However, and interesting to note, is that, in the post-Partition subcontinent, centuries later, the *Jammat-e-Islami* in its Arab-centric conceptualization of Pakistan hailed Qásim as the 'first Pakistani', a true secularist and the '*Yaum Babul Islam*' or the heralder of Islam in India. The Nobel laureate V.S. Naipaul, acclaimed for his novels of 'supressed histories', read the accounts of Qásim as the 'Islamic beginning of the state of Pakistan'.[39] The historian Manan Ahmed Asif notes,

> This beginning, Naipaul argued in his book [*Among the Believers: An Islamic Journey*], was the primary way in which the hegemonic Muslims of Pakistan imagined their separation from India—as conquerors . . .[40]

Qásim laid the foundation of Muslim rule in India, and his tragic death helped briefly in reviving the Hindu power in Sindh. By the middle of the eighth century, the Umayyads were superseded by the Abbasid Caliphate (750–1258). Its capital was moved from Damascus to Baghdad, bringing India closer to the centre of the Muslim Empire. The Arab control in Sindh, which had started to weaken under the Umayyads, regained stability in 831 with the appointment of Musa bin-Yahya Barmaki, the scion of the Barmakis, the great family of *vazirs* and administrators to the Abbasid. Musa's father, the renowned Yahya bin Khalid, a confidante and protector of Haroun-al Rashid, the fifth Abbasid caliph (786–809), was known for building dykes to protect Baghdad from the floods of the Tigris. Haroun, a contemporary of Charlemagne, had presented an extraordinary water-powered clock to the Roman emperor, which became a source of much scientific inquiry. He ruled during what is described as the peak of the Islamic golden age. It was marked by cultural exchanges and the advancement of science and technology, immortalized with great imagination and storytelling in *The Thousand and One Nights* or *Arabian Nights*.

Haroun's successor, Al-Ma'mun, attached great importance to Sindh and established good relations with Musa. With the death of Al-Ma'mun and Musa in quick succession, the new caliph, Al-Mu'tasim Billah, followed the line of succession and conferred the governorship to Musa's son Amran. The latter quickly tackled the rebellious forces, consolidated the region, including Multan, Mansura and Kandabil, and laid the foundation to a permanent military headquarter in a new city, al-Baiza (the White).[41] Amran was ruthless in dealing with the Meds and Jats and with a certain sadistic delight made a *bund* or dyke on the river at Alor after slaying almost 3000 Meds and called it *Sakr-al-Med* or

. . . Dam of the Meds.[42]

Amran's incessant war against the Meds and the Jats led him to exploit various means to harass and massacre the rebels. One such was using water as a weapon for subjugation as he

. . . dug a canal from the sea to their tank, so that their water became salt.[43]

He died not in the encounters with the Meds but as a consequence of the Arab tribe war between the Nazaris and the Yamanis. He was stabbed in the back by the Nazari leader, Umar Abul al-Habbari, who almost a decade later established the Habbari dynasty in 854 with Mansura as the capital. The Habbaris became the hereditary rulers of Sindh. Multan and Mansura broke away from Sindh around 879, and the Hindus re-established themselves in Rohri.

The divided territory and the political space allowed for considerable political stability and the Abbasids respected the semi-independent status by adhering to non-interference with the Habbaris. In times of emergency, for example, after the devastating earthquake that struck Debal in 893, killing almost 1,50,000 people,

the then Abbasid caliph was quick to respond and despatched swift
assistance. The more permanent challenge, however, occurred with
the recurring floods and change in course of the Mihrān. There were,
of course, at that time no flood mitigation efforts but the existing
knowledge systems allowed for the natural inundation of the Mihrān
to minimize the damage. The inundation compensated for the lack
of rainfall and helped irrigate the fields. Sindh on the whole was
notably transformed into a well-irrigated and prosperous region in
the ninth century, with highly developed agriculture and commerce.

As Observed by Foreign Travellers

Sindh's undulating landscape carved by the rapid rivers and stretches
of cultivable lands did not escape the attention of the travellers
coming from the west. One such, Al-Baladhuri of Baghdad, a
chronicler of the history of Mohammedan rule in India, travelled
during 892–3. Roaming the Sindh and Multan, Al-Baladhuri
extensively mentions the existence of an aqueduct by which the
inhabitants of Multan were supplied with water from the Basmad
(Ravi) river. In this context, he gives an interesting account of
Qásim's expedition to Sikkha-Multan. Qásim had sieged the fort
city of Sikkha in a hard-fought battle and after crossing the Basmad
river to Multan, his exhausted troops, with provisions running out,
were reduced to eating ass meat.

> Then a man came to them, asking for protection [*aman*], and
> guided them to the place where the water of which the people
> drank entered. It was water flowing from the Basmad river, and
> was collected in a reservoir like the pool in al-Madinah. They call
> it al-Balah [nalla or talab]. He shut it off, and when they became
> thirsty, they surrendered at discretion.[44]

Al-Baladhuri came to India at a time when Sindh and Baghdad
enjoyed strong cultural interactions with exchange of Hindu and
Muslim scholars. This led to a period of great translation works

from Sanskrit into Arabic on subjects like medicine, astrology, philosophy and many others. He wrote an exclusive chapter 'Futuh Sindh' describing the various Arab campaigns in Sindh and described Debal as '*khawrul*' or an estuary on one of the delta channels similar in description to the Arab mariners who depicted Debal on the junction of the Mihrān at a distance of two *farasangs* or 16 miles to the sea.[45] The travel narratives throw light on the fact that the port-city of Debal was situated far enough inland, beyond the calamities of the tidal waves and cyclonic weather patterns, which allowed for communication further interior into Sindh. In the chapter, Al-Baladhuri observed that the inundation canals in the Sindh region made the land productive and encouraged the Arabs to levy land taxes. Tax structures were differentiated for lands watered by canals from those that were not irrigated; a sectoral outlook, so to speak, to water with administrative rules and principles was rigorously formulated.

Another Arab historian and geographer, El-Masʿūdī, visited India in the tenth century at the height of trade relations between India and the Arab world. Travelling from the coast of Sindh to the mouth of the Mihrān and northwards, El-Masʿūdī reached the Hindu-ruled territory where most of the people

> . . . believe on the metempsychosis or the transmigration of the soul.[46]

He notes the Mihrān being divided into two branches and 'is still now the name of the lower course of the Indus' and like the Oxus in Persia has the same importance

> . . . as frontier as well as in a commercial and agricultural point of view.[47]

El-Masʿūdī makes reference to hunting of the crocodiles or alligators (*susmar*) in the Mihrān, drawing comparison to similar activities on the Nile. But he chides the scholarship of Amr Ben Bahr el-Jahit, the Basra-based Arab prose writer in the Abbasid caliphate in the ninth century who, in his important work, *On the Leading Cities and the Wonders of the Countries*, supposes, just as Alexander of Macedonia had, that the Mihrān in Sindh is the Nile because of the crocodiles in it. El-Mas'ūdī says:

> It is an important work, but he has never made a voyage and few journies and travels through kingdoms and cities, he did not know that the Mihrān of es-Sindh comes from the well-known sources of the highland of es-Sindh from the country belonging to Kinnauj in the kingdom of Budah and of Kahmir, el-Kandahar and et-Takin, the tributaries which rise in these countries run to el-Multan and from thence the united river receives the name Mihrān.[48]

El-Mas'ūdī was by a long shot the first Arab traveller to combine history and scientific geography with first-hand knowledge and observation from the extensive travels he undertook. This is clearly evidenced when he describes Multan in detail with its three hundred thousand villages and estates,

> . . . well cultivated and covered with trees and fields.[49]

The geographical and riverine impression of the Arab traveller, Alberuni, who travelled to India accompanying Mahmud Gazni (999–1030) in one of his numerous campaigns, is remarkable. While Gazni plundered India's wealth and ransacked the temples to fill the treasury with riches, Alberuni spent his 'leisure' time (1017–30) studying and travelling in India. He took particular interest in Hindu philosophy and was impressed with India's knowledge on mathematics and astronomy, although he remained unshakeable in his belief of Islam being superior to all. He also took immense interest in the historic chronology and specific geography of the places he travelled in, recording with details the landscape and the sources and courses of the rivers, and frequently referring dispassionately to the Puranas. It does not seem that Alberuni gave any military advice to

Mahmud Gazni, and certainly did not glorify his military victories, as observed in his book *Kitab-al-Hind*, popularly the *Indica*. Gazni, fearless and fearsome, was his own strategist and tactician who relied on the speed and swiftness of his horsemen, attacking the plains in the heat and dust of summer and retreating before the onset of the monsoon to avoid the rapacious rivers of the Punjab.

Alberuni describes the northern mountains, the snowy *Himavant*, as the boundaries of India,

> . . . whilst the rivers rising on the southern slopes flow through India and fall into the great ocean, some reaching it single, others combined.[50]

He then details the five rivers in Punjab, attributing it through names like *Biyatta* (Jhelum), *Biyah* (Beas) and *Shatladar* (Sutlej),

> . . . united below Multan at a place called *Pancanada*, i.e., the meeting place of the five rivers, they form an enormous watercourse.[51]

Alberuni refers to the Indus as Sindh, but it is the Mihrān in its width and volume that draws his attention:

> The Muslims call the river, after it has passed the Sindhhi city, Aror, as a united stream, the river of Mihrān. This it extends, flowing straight on, becoming broader and broader and gaining in purity of water, enclosing in its course places like islands, until it reaches Almansursa, situated between several of its arms, and flows into the ocean at two places, near the city of Loharani, and more eastward in the province of Kacch at a place called Sindhu Sagar.[52]

After a footfall of Arab travellers and their accounts in the ninth, tenth and eleventh centuries, the learned Ibn Batuta, a Berber Muslim, propelled by the quest for adventure and knowledge, reached India in 1334 during Mohammad bin Tughlak's reign after a phenomenal journey spanning nine years, from Morocco. Ibn Batuta, in the *Rihla* (written in Arabic) of the account of his travels, which took him across the great lands with their great rivers, writes with certain terrain knowledge and cultural sensitivity:

> The Nile which runs through this country [Misr or Cairo], excels all other rivers in the sweetness of its taste, the extent of its progress and the greatness of the benefits it confers. It is one of the five great rivers of the world, which are, itself, the Euphrates, the Tigris, the Sihun, the Jaihun (or Gihon). Five other rivers too may be compared with them, namely the river of Sindhia, which is called the Panjab (or five waters); the river of India which is called the Gung (or Ganges), to which the Indians perform their pilgrimages, and into which they throw the ashes of their dead when burnt: they say it descends from Paradise; also the river Jum (or Jumna); the river Athil (Volga) in the desert of Kifjak, and the river Sarv in Tartary, upon the bank of which is the city of Khan Balik, and which flows from that place to El Khansa, and thence to the city of Zaitun in China.[53]

On his travel to Sindh, Ibn Batuta mentions encountering rhinoceros on the banks of the Indus near Multan.[54] Such observations bring an important understanding to the fauna of the time and how subsequently, as the habitat changed, the pachyderm became extinct.[55] The rhinoceros here that Babur hunted in the sixteenth century,[56] and which later Syedi Ali Reis, the admiral of the Ottoman Empire under Sultan Suleiman, encountered while crossing the Khyber[57] to India, gradually found no mention by the seventeenth century. Centuries later the archaeological excavations undertaken at the Indus Valley sites from 1920 onwards revealed, from the seals found, a profusion of rhinoceros, particularly in Kalibangan.[58]

Continuing his travel, Ibn Batuta, on reaching Delhi, 'a most magnificent city combining at once both beauty and strength', is curiously struck by the existing water and civic system in the city,

. . . Out the city is a reservoir for rain water; and out of this the inhabitants have their water for drinking. It is two miles in length, and one in width.[59]

There is an interesting remark, quite extraordinary, found in the explanatory note of his work, that the waters of the Jumna or Yamuna are

. . . impregnated with natrons as to be unfit for drinking.[60]

For one, it speaks of a scientific understanding of a man (Batuta), who was formally trained in Islamic law or *qadi*, and for another, the quality of drinking water became, probably for the first time, a matter of public health. It took many centuries before a canal for supplying 'purer water' was made in Shah Jahan's reign. Batuta's observation in a very similar way was expressed by Frederick Fitzclarence in the nineteenth century that

. . . the waters of the Jumna, and of the wells, which they [i.e., the inhabitants of Delhi] are now obliged to drinkis so much impregnated with natron, otherwise soda, as to prove at times very injurious.[61]

Fitzclarence, the eldest, though illegitimate, son of King William IV, came to India on a punishment posting and wrote a fascinating journal observing India as the

. . . seat of wisdom and learning.[62]

And since the Brahmins or the learned men found it impossible to cross the Indus, which he describes as Attock or the 'forbidden', it was the travellers from the west that came to visit the

. . . wise men from the east.[63]

Suyya, the Waterman of Kashmir

Trailing the Indus upwards to the mountainous region of
Kashmir, where many small tributaries pour down the Karakoram
range to hurriedly join the Indus, the ninth-century Hindu ruler
Avantivarman (855–83) of the Utpala dynasty, labelled the 'engineer
king', harnessed the bountiful water resources of the kingdom to
bring peace and prosperity. He had inherited a kingdom which
since the glorious days of Lalitaditya (724–81) was in disarray and
disrepute. Kashmir, before that, had come out of a turbulent period
of sectarianism in the sixth century which saw violence between
Buddhism, allowed to spread for centuries in Kashmir by the ruling
elite, and Brahmanical revivalism. With the decline of Buddhism
and the establishment of Brahmanical hegemony, the social order
witnessed exclusivity and orthodoxy, resulting in deprivation and
rampant heresy.

Like the earlier rulers, Avantivarman too had to contend with
the regular floods that ravaged the paddy fields. Attention to flood
management and irrigation was, therefore, of critical importance
to maintaining social order. While some of his predecessors built
stone-lined dykes to protect against inundation, others erected
embankments. Lalitaditya is credited for having introduced the
'water wheel' for lifting water to the higher plateaus, a practice
that continues even today with technical advancement and
modifications. Earlier in the pre-Ashokan age, a channel was dug
called *Suvarnamani* by King Suvarna that helped irrigate the alluvial
plateau to the south of the Rembyar river. The Rembyar was an
important tributary to join the Vitasta (Jhelum) along with the
Vishav to form the great Gambhira Sangam or Sangam at Kakapora
near Avantipore, an important cultural heritage. Given Kashmir's
terrain and heavy dependency on paddy and other kharif and rabi
crops, rulers had to be ever alert and conscious of the food and the
water linkages.

Avantivarman's rule was noted for having brought down the
price of 'one kharwar' (used as a standard weight in Kashmir and

equivalent to eighty kilograms) of paddy from 200 to 36 dinars. This was an extraordinary achievement that could not have come about without the successful irrigation plans by his 'local genius' Suyya, who was way ahead of his time. His

> . . . scheme of diverting the course of the Jhelum was a forerunner to the present-day multi-purpose river valley project.[64]

Suyya, of undisclosed caste, had acutely observed the cause and the solution to the recurrent floods, of which the Brahman courtiers were dismissive, besides often ridiculing his birth. Successful in getting his idea across to the king, Suyya commenced work. He oversaw the demolition of the natural barrier that was preventing the waters of the Jhelum to flow, resulting in floods. Then, in the course of time, he made a network of channels and dug canals throughout the valley, allowing for a sustained flow of water on a permanent basis. Suyya remains a legend in Kashmir and some even regard him as the greatest Kashmiri whose

> . . . signatures are on the riverbed of the Vitasta![65]

The kings and rivers don't go missing in the Kalhana classic *Rajatarangini* (River of Kings) written in Sanskrit. The twelfth-century Kashmiri poet and historian refers to the regulation of the Vitasta river carried out under Avantivarman. The poet also describes with fine observation the physical features of the Indus and the cultural appeal of the Vitasta:

> Our survey of the northern range of mountains has already taken us to the true headwaters of the Sindh near Zoji-la and the Amburnath peak . . . Its ancient name, SINDHU, means simply 'the river', and is hence identical with the original designation of the Indus.[66]

Kalhana accords the Sindhu and the Vitasta the significance of the

. . . largest and holiest rivers of the country with the Yamuna and
the Ganga respectively.[67]

Before Kalhana's historical chronicle of Kashmir, another inveterate
Arab traveller, skilled geographer and seaman, the Persian Buzurg
Ibn Shahriyar (900–50), collected 'travellers' tales' from the Arab
and Persian marines and compiled them into *The Book of the Marvels
of India.* These are, of course, tales interestingly woven but, possibly
in the genre of fantasy, are not completely frivolous. One of the
stories describes a king living in a country

. . . which lies betwixt High and Low Cashmere . . .[68]

who secretly converted to Islam. Another experience describes the
Kashmir landscape:

> Coming down on the Mihran, which runs from Cashmere in as
> large a stream as the Tigris and Euphrates in flood, on bales of
> costus, weighing each of them seven or eight hundreds mens, and
> swathed in skins, smeared with pitch so as to make them waterproof.
> Of these bales, collected and bound together, they make a kind of
> raft, whereon they install themselves and float down the Mihran,
> putting in at the port of Mansura [capital of Sindh], after a journey
> of forty days without the costus coming to any harm by the water.[69]

Rajatarangini is probably the most direct source of information,
factual and objective, inspiring many other critical works on Kashmir
and the Hindu kings. One such is the work of Walter Lawrence in
the late nineteenth century in which he observes the early period of
the Hindu kings:

> About the conditions of the people little is known, but as Hindus
> living under Hindu kings their lot must have been fairly happy,
> and irrigation canals testify that the Rajas did not spend all their
> wealth on temples, but had some thought for the cultivators.[70]

With stresses in the social structure and the decline of the Hindu rule in the fourteenth century, Islam found its way into Kashmir and one of the early Muslims was a Sufi from Turkmenistan known by the name Hazrat Bulbul Shah.

Sufism had attractive appeal wherever it interacted, and it is unlikely that its mystic influence in Kashmir was not influential. In fact, given the rigidity of the Brahmanical order, the society would have been highly receptive to the new philosophy of life and accepted Islam

... voluntarily.[71]

The debate on the 'Islamization of Kashmir' has not completely withered—whether it was forced conversion or voluntary acceptance. Historians, however, are quite united in the fact that Bulbul Shah sowed the seeds of Islam in Kashmir and a testimony of his influence was King Rinchena Shah who embraced Islam by changing his original Buddhist name to Malik Sadr ad-Din and became the first Muslim ruler of Kashmir in 1323. Bulbul Shah found home on the banks of the Vitasta and spent the rest of his life in Kashmir, travelling, preaching and spreading the lessons of Islam.

The Muslim rulers accounted themselves rather poorly in governing Kashmir with religious prosecution, administrative ineffectiveness and little interest or inclination to water development. The only exception was Sultan Zain-ul-Abidin (1420–70) who was popularly known as the *Badshah* and glowingly mentioned by his courtiers Pandit Jonaraja and his pupil Srivara, who wrote the history of Kashmir from where Kalhana left off. The two treatises *Rajatarangini Dvitiya* and *Tritiya*[72] give a good account of the life and times of the rulers and people of Kashmir from 1149–86. Of course, being courtiers to the Sultan, there is exaggeration and prejudice about his rule. However, and as corroborated by other documents and writings, the Sultan inherited a broken administration which he was determined to set right. Agricultural lands and the cultivators were his priority, and he was far-sighted enough to understand that peace could be attained only when people possessed means of sustenance. A critical measure was the construction of canals in the Valley and,

> There was not a piece of land, not a region and not a forest where the king did not excavate a canal.[73]

Zain-ul-Abidin ruled for over forty years and

> . . . left behind him the reputation of a mild, generous and accomplished prince.[74]

Rajatarangini continued to be written until the Valley was conquered by Akbar in 1585. This period of history in Kashmir from the time of King Rinchena is categorized by historians as the 'Kashmir Musalman' or the *Salatini Kashmir*.

Kashmir remarkably possessed an uninterrupted series of written accounts including the period of the Mughals and the Pathans rule, which were chronicled as *Padshahi-i-Chugtai* and *Sahan-i-Durani* respectively. Akbar had little time for Kashmir and its delightful valley unlike his son and successor Jahangir who till his dying breath would want 'only Kashmir'. Jahangir set a fashion of building gardens in Kashmir that was to be followed by his successors and

> though it has been said of the emperors [Mughal] that they were stage kings, so far as Kashmir was concerned, they would be entitled to the gratitude if only for the sake of the beautiful and shady plane-trees.[75]

Much of this and the Mughal connection to the development of water is explained later.

Genghis and the Battle of Indus

Before irrigation and canal construction began to be prioritized in the fourteenth century, the relationship between territory and politics in the Indus basin during the Slave dynasty (1206–90), the first Muslim dynasty to rule India, had significant implications for the region. Shams-ud-Din Iltutmish (1210–36) established the Delhi Sultanate and by shifting the centre of power from Lahore to Delhi, he

> . . . gave the country a capital, an independent state, a monarchical form of government and a governing class.[76]

After consolidating the entire northern India from Bengal to Afghanistan and freeing the Sultanate from the suzerainty of the rulers of Gazni, Iltutmish brought effective administration, built learning institutions and encouraged art and artists from all over the world, turning Delhi into a power centre and a cultural hub. One of the challenges that Iltutmish faced in his newly founded capital was the shortage of water, without which the city life would be unsustainable. As a priority he invested in waterworks by building the *Gandhak ki Baoli* and then in its proximity built probably the first multi-purpose water reservoir, *Hauz-i-Shamsi,* that would supply drinking water, water for irrigation needs and provide storage of rainwater, which, as we learn, was revealed to Iltutmish in a dream by the Prophet. Integrating the dominion as a composite Sultanate was no easy task. Delhi was witnessing an influx of immigrants with diverse ethnic and regional backgrounds from the northwest as a result of Genghis Khan's military campaigns (1218–9) at the junction of Central Asia and Europe. The fear of a possible Mongol invasion and Genghis's legendary brutal nihilism worried Iltutmish and he cautiously hoped that diplomacy and reciprocity would help keep his Sultanate intact.

Genghis was involved in a ferocious battle against the Khwarezmian Empire in Samarkand (1219–21) and the bloodshed that followed would remain unmatched in human history. Muhammad II, the ruler of Khwarezmian, was put into exile, his empire decimated and all his family members hunted down and killed, except his son and heir to the throne, Jalaluddin Mingburnu, who escaped to Afghanistan. With 20,000 of his warriors, Genghis led arguably the largest expeditionary force to capture the prince without a principality. Genghis was determined to destroy any possibility of a Khwarezmian revival. With the help of the local Afghani tribes, Jalaluddin survived and moved to Multan, where he took refuge under Nasiruddin Qabacha, the ambitious governor of the province who had served under Mohammed Ghori, and aspired to usurp power from Iltutmish. For a brief time, Qabacha and Jalaluddin forged a fair-weather alliance and drew clans like the Lahori-Khokhars into their fold to thwart the Mongols and challenge Iltutmish. Genghis eventually caught up with Jalaluddin and with raids in the trans-Indus region positioned his troops on the banks of the Indus, which the Mongol referred to as the Shin or Sin (from Sindh). It brought the Mongols to India for the first time, but not the last. Successive attempts until 1327 to capture India repeatedly failed and the Mongols' ambition, as some historians suggest, ended with Mohammad bin Tughlak defeating the army of Tarmashirin near Meerut. Others contend that Tughlak gave huge wealth and bribed the Mongol ruler to retreat.

The battle of Indus (1221) near Nowshera was not an easy sweep for Genghis despite the ragtag forces gathered by Jalaluddin. Although not insignificant in number, it was surrounded on three sides by a massive Mongol army that included Genghis and his two sons Chagatai and Uktae, and the waters of the Indus behind them. After some initial resistance, the Mongol army eventually annihilated Jalaluddin's soldiers with ruthless efficiency. Genghis was a military genius at par with, if not surpassing, the likes of Alexander, Hannibal, Caesar and Attila, and his military tactics was one of sheer improvisation.[77] There were 'sixteen' such tactics as observed by Giovanni Carpine[78]—the first European traveller to enter the court of Genghis Khan—of which 'encircling tactics' based on the enemy's strengths and formation were commonly deployed:

If the enemy openly exposed his flank and rear, and the city defenders were weak, the Mongols would encircle them from all sides. If the enemy deployed their forces by the rivers, exposing two or three flanks, then the Mongols would encircle them from all sides of the river bank. In 1221, Chinggis destroyed Jalaldin Mangubirdi, who had deployed his soldiers on the west bank of the Indus, by attacking on two or three sides.[79]

Jalaluddin escaped yet again this time by plunging into the Indus with his horse and miraculously crossing the mighty river:

> Rallying seven thousand men around him, Jelal ud din made a desperate charge on the line of his enemy, which gave way for some distance, then he turned quickly, sprang on a fresh horse, threw off his armor and spurring to the Indus leaped from a bank given variously as from twenty to sixty feet higher than the plain of the water. His shield was at his shoulder, and his standard on his hand. Jinghis, who spurred to the river bank swiftly and gazed at his fleeing opponent, cried: How could Shah Mohammed be the father of this man![80]

After the great escape, Jalaluddin found his way to Iltutmish's court in Delhi and pleaded for asylum in the name of Islam. Quick to assess the situation, and aware of possible reprisal from Genghis, Iltutmish, defying the tenets of being a good Muslim, diplomatically made it clear that Jalaluddin was an unwanted guest. As a matter of political expediency it is likely that Iltutmish via his court messengers coaxed Genghis to agree to a 'non-aggression pact' and in reciprocity allowed him to plunder at his will the territories of Uchch and Multan where Iltutmish's sworn enemy, Qabacha, ruled. Historians observe that these astute actions of Iltutmish may have prevented Genghis Khan from invading India. There is, on the other hand, good reason to believe that Genghis, having razed Bukhara, Samarkand, Herat, Tus and Neyshabur before reaching India and having fought what turned out to be an exhausting war against Jalaluddin, would have found crossing the turbulent Indus a challenge for his tired soldiers and the weary legs of the warhorses. The Mongols would thus have decided to halt on the banks and go no further. Genghis passed the winter of 1222–3 by the Indus, and with spring breaking, his homeland beckoned him. It was time, he decided, to return.

Genghis's retrace from the Indus is momentous in the history of India for, had the ruthless warrior crossed the Indus, it is more likely that the Sultanate would have been exterminated with not even the

> . . . cats and dogs . . .[81]

being spared. Genghis Khan, of course, did what he did best, conquering territories. He established the largest land-based empire in the world until his death in 1227. Although India never became part of his conquests, a notable descendant, Timur, by the close of the thirteenth century, rampaged the Sultanate. Later, another of Genghis Khan's lineage, Babur, finished the Sultanate and established the Mughal Empire—the longest uninterrupted empire in the history of India or as described,

> . . . essentially a movement of Mongols and Turks pausing in Afghanistan and then setting up an empire in India.[82]

Jalaluddin continued to be on the run until he died a commoner's death. His leap into the cold blue eddies of the Indus inspired much debate on whether the 'fugitive' prince was a hero or a coward. Some have billed him as a never-say-die, gutsy fighter based on an account of Genghis telling his sons, who were on the battlefield, while pointing to the fleeing Jalaluddin and his jump that

> . . . a father should hope to have a son as courageous as him.[83]

Whether it was said in praise or in disgust it is hard to decipher. Others regard Jalaluddin and his action as desperate and cowardly, having left his troops and family, including his wife and children, to be marauded, while he, on the other side of the river,

... stuck his spear in the ground and hung his wet clothes on it to dry.[84]

After Genghis's return from India, psychologically free of the spectre, Iltutmish, in 1228, launched a series of attacks on the frontier territories or the trans-Indus region, besieging Lahore, Uchch and Multan. Qabacha fled to the island fortress of Bhakkar in the Indus and, according to some versions, drowned in the river while attempting to escape. Another version suggests that he killed himself by drowning in the Indus.[85] It ended a difficult chapter in Iltutmish's reign, and he returned to Delhi much at ease and secure, with the frontier now under his control while his loyal minister, Malik Nasiruddin Aiytim, completed the conquest of Sindh.

Fathering Medieval Canals

Canal construction, with bricks and cement and not just the natural channels of the rivers, dominated the agricultural landscape in the late-medieval period, during which the Tughlak dynasty (1320–1413) had a marked influence. Earlier, the acquaintance with water management and irrigation was localized and small-scale, but under the Tughlaks, it became an expansive system, irrigating larger areas of lands. Ghiyas-ud-din Tughlak (1320–4) laid the foundation of the dynasty and set about addressing administrative problems and improving the finances of the state, which had fallen into disarray because of the unsettled political climate that had prevailed since the time of Alauddin of the Khilji dynasty. Ghiyas-ud-din successfully intervened to increase the arable land and improved the economic condition of cultivators by fixing revenue between one-fifth and one-third of the produce. His son, the learned Mohammad bin Tughlak (1324–51), succeeded him. Described as the 'wise fool' for undertaking wide-ranging administrative reforms that often led to disastrous consequences, he was at least successful in encouraging farmers to build their own wells and water-harvesting systems that led to two harvests of kharif and rabi crops instead of one cultivation.

He established a separate department of agriculture, *Diwan-i-Kohi*, to survey and expand cultivable lands, and from time to time, brought out special schemes and gave loans to farmers to improve cultivation in the Punjab and Ganga-Jamuna doabs. But his administrative measure to enhance land tax, from 5 to 10 per cent at a time when the region was in grip of famine, led to widespread discontent and revolts. He died on the banks of the Indus in Thatta while in pursuit of a rebellious commander of Gujarat and Sindh.

After the death of Mohammad bin Tughlak, his cousin, Feroz Shah Tughlak (1351–88), became the Sultan. In his long reign, notoriously marked by the ascendency of the Muslim orthodoxy and deep-seated aversion towards Hindus, Feroz Shah introduced new perennial canals and waterways leading to the increase in food production.[86] In the almost four decades of his rule, he raised the Delhi Sultanate, which had fallen in disarray in the closing years of his predecessor's reign, to great heights by concentrating on civic amenities and public works. In 1355, he constructed the Western Yamuna Canal followed by another canal from the Sutlej (called *rajwahas* in Persian), principally to quench his love for hunting by taking the waters from the Yamuna and Sutlej to the fauna grounds of Hissar.[87] The network of canals that marked his reign were later upgraded and repaired by rulers to the needs of the time. He constructed four waterways, from Yamuna to the city of Hissar; Sutlej to Ghaggar; Ghaggar to Firuzabad; and waterways from the Mandvi and Sirmour Hills to Hansi in Haryana. Many old riverbeds were turned into irrigation canals, like the Chitrang and the Wah. For the Ghaggar–Firuzabad waterway, the old riverbed of Saraswati was converted as a link canal bringing the water of the Ghaggar to the

> . . . rivulet of Khera (Hakra), upon which he built a city named after him Ferozabad.[88]

Serious attempts were undertaken by Feroz Shah's administration to remedy the arid condition of the land about Sirsa and Hissar by

bringing waters from the Sutlej and Yamuna into the dry riverbeds.
Before this,

> . . . travellers passing that way from Irak and Khorasan had to pay
> as much as four *jitals* for a pitcher of this necessary of life.[89]

Feroz Shah, in his official history, hardly claims any accolade for his
waterworks but rather he wishes to be remembered for his orthodox
Islamic credentials, the destruction of newly built Hindu temples,
the promotion of conversions to Islam, and the foundation of new
mosques and schools.[90] Centuries later, the British, while doing the
assessment of the irrigation system and canals in India in the mid-
nineteenth century, observed:

> The monarch [Feroz Shah Tughlak], of whom it is recorded,
> that he built 'fifty dams across rivers to promote irrigation; forty
> mosques; thirty colleges; one hundred caravan serais; thirty
> reservoirs for irrigation; one hundred hospitals; one hundred
> public baths; one hundred and fifty bridges besides many other
> edifices for pleasure or ornament', is not likely to have constructed
> with great labour the canal that bears his name, solely to supply
> the fountains, or water the gardens, or fill the wells, around his
> favourite hunting palace of Hissar.[91]

In fact, it was Astrabad-born Firishta, the historian of Persian origin
(1560-1620), who credited Feroz with no less than 845 public works,
including canals, dams and reservoirs, but

> curiously not a single road.[92]

Interestingly, Feroz Shah was the son of the Hindu princess of
Dipalpur, a tehsil of the district Okhara (now in Pakistan) on the
banks of the Beas river noted for its potato produce. The site of a
canal in Dipalpur became a critical issue between India and Pakistan
in what came to be known as the 'canal dispute'.

The Tughlak dynasty started weakening towards the close of Feroz Shah's reign. It finally collapsed with the invasion of Timur of Samarkand, who, after his victorious sweep over Persia and Mesopotamia and his sway over the lands of Afghanistan, looked towards Hindustan, the land of 'infidels and polytheists', as the triumph of the faith of Islam. He was cautioned by his nobles that to become the conqueror of the world, the four defences of Hindustan had to be breached, the first of which

> . . . consists of five large rivers which flow from the mountains of Kashmir, after which they unite in their course, pass through the country of Sindh and flow into the Arabian Sea, nor is it possible to cross them without boats and bridges.[93]

After crossing the Indus at Khushalgarh in 1398 and fearlessly tearing through hundreds of miles of forests, Timur, like a whirlwind, ravaged town after town that lay in his march, until he reached the outer walls of Delhi. Here, he faced the army of Nasiruddin Mahmud Shah, the last of the Tughlak rulers. In the ferocious battle that ensued, Timur emerged victorious and what followed was an 'orgy of destruction' upon Delhi that left the city with pestilence, famine and unaccounted deaths. According to Timur,

> The *khutba* of my sovereignty, which is an assurance of safety and protection, had been read in the city. It was therefore my earnest wish that no evil might happen to the people of the place. But it was ordained by God that the city should be ruined.[94]

In the course of his homeward return in 1399, Timur plundered with disdain, leaving behind a history of unfathomable fanaticism and terror. The destruction of standing crops and the burning of grain stores along with the loot of wealth from India had a massive economic impact. On the political front, the tottering Tughlak dynasty collapsed, bringing in a period of weak rule and power tussles—ideal conditions for foreign invasion.

The Sayyid dynasty that followed ruled for thirty-seven years from 1414–51 and when the last of the Sayyid ruler abdicated power to Bahlul Lodi, Delhi was at its weakest. The new Lodi dynasty quickly established its authority over Punjab, and upon his death in 1489, Bahlul left a kingdom almost twice as large as it was in the beginning of his reign. Bahlul's successor, Sikander Lodi, was extraordinarily bigoted, indulging in rampant destruction of Hindu temples, smashing idols and prohibiting Hindus from performing their customs and rites, including preventing them from bathing in the Yamuna. His son and the last of the Lodi ruler, Ibrahim Lodi, followed similar practices.[95] By the end of his reign, the Delhi Sultanate, gripped in incessant and contentious quarrelling, offered a perfect opportunity for Babar (1526–30) to launch his fifth, and the only successful, raid, on the plains of Punjab in April 1526.

Babar won a decisive battle, and with characteristic speed, occupied Delhi three days later. The following month, he majestically strode into Agra, where he built the Ram Bagh on the banks of the Yamuna. Babur had a fine recollection of the lush fields of Fergana Valley, where he grew up, watered by the many rivers meandering through the city Kasan with gardens along the beds, which he eloquently describes in *Baburnamah* (his memoirs) as the 'fine front of the coat'.[96] Conquest and culture became a distinct characteristic of the Mughal rule with gardens or *baghs* as a symbol of aesthetics, enabling a spree of canals and channels watering the beds. But it wasn't always recreational and like in the earlier periods, the Mughals equally developed perennial canals with headworks as an imperative for development. Babar also inherited the five doabs[97] in Punjab and the *Baburnamah* recounts the efforts in improving the existing irrigation system, constructing wells and *baolis* (water tanks). As an all-out expansionist and military campaigner, Babur found little time to consolidate his territorial gains, leaving behind a fragile legacy. Humayun (1530–40 and 1555–6), who ascended the throne, encountered sibling rivalry, court intrigues and bloody plots and, as history notes, was an 'emperor-in-exile'. He eventually returned victorious to Delhi in 1555, only to die a year later descending from the stairs of the Purana Qila, to which a noted orientalist commented,

> He tumbled out of life as he had tumbled through it.[98]

There is little recorded to suggest any noteworthy contribution of Humayun to canal development except that he is associated with the first floating garden built on a wooden structure on the Yamuna on which he would often sail from Ferozabad near Delhi to Agra with his courtiers.[99]

Humayun's reign was mostly about lost and gained territories but his son and descendant to the throne, Akbar (1556–1605), had a remarkable outlook on canals and irrigation. This was far more successful than his *Din-i-Ilahi*, a syncretic philosophy that struggled to be a state religion. Akbar revived the Western Yamuna Canal in 1568, which had become decrepit after the death of Feroz Shah, and his Canal Act of 1568 proclaimed with benevolent outpouring:

> My government is a tree, the roots of which are firm in the earth, and being watered by the waters of God's grace, its branches reach to heaven. In acknowledgement of God's mercy in establishing this great empire, my desire, purer than water, is to supply the wants of the poor; and the water of life in my heart is larger than the sea, with the wish to dispense benefits, and to leave permanent marks of the greatness of my Empire, by digging canals, and founding cities, by which too the revenues of the Empire will be increased.[100]

The revenues were important lest the coffers to finance the reforms run empty. As Akbar expresses,

> God says, sow a grain and reap sevenfold(a). My desire is to reap one-hundredfold, that my crown may become wealthy and that the zamindars may obtain double returns.[101]

Akbar had evolved a system of division of crops based on irrigation in which

> ... land under *charkha* (wheel in Persian) cultivation, one third of produce; on *sailabi* (canal flooding) lands, two-thirds; and in the case of the best lands, yielding cotton, tobacco and sugarcane, as a rule in cash.[102]

The *charkhas* had its limitation and worked well within the flood zones where the water table was high and required less labour. But the flood zones were never stable and notoriously changed location since the pattern of floods in the Indus basin were difficult to ascertain. Resultantly, the practice of flood-based agriculture or settled cultivation was a hazardous proposition as the

> ... river Sind (Indus) inclines every few years alternately to its southern and northern banks and the village cultivation follows its course.[103]

With expanding irrigation in the Indus basin, described by the medieval political-economist historians as 'peasantization', the need for animal power to extract water from deeper depth and in semi-arid conditions led to the inventive *charsa* that used the strength of oxen as 'water lifters'.

Trade and economy with attention to routes was an important policy action of Akbar that included not only land routes and road links for commerce but developing coastal and oceanic routes too. *Akbarnama* records that various *farmans* were issued by Akbar to protect the routes and prohibit transit fees 'variously known as baz, tamgha, zakat, and mir bahri and other various tolls and taxes called rahdari'. Centuries later, in their extensive study of the canals in the Punjab, the British had noted 'Akbar's canal labour' and even chided the historians of Akbar's reign for failing to sufficiently attribute his contribution to canal development. Proby Cautley, a pioneer in perennial canal building in the 1820s,

about whom we will hear more later, observed his appreciation
for Akbar,

> It would therefore appear that, while Feroze constructed in 1351
> the first Indian canal, drawing an intermittent supply from the
> Chetang, it was to Akbar that the country west of the Jumna was
> indebted for a perennial stream drawn from that river.[104]

Jahangir (1605–27) was a striking contrast to Akbar against whom
he openly rebelled, but 'not a fool'. Alert during the day and regaled
by the night, Jahangir took to wine

> . . . until wine from grapes ceased to intoxicate me, and I took to
> drinking arrack.[105]

He may not have fancied, like his father, the Ganges water 'cooled
with saltpetre' but he did, on the lines of the Western Yamuna Canal,
build a perennial one, sound on hydrological knowledge of the time,
from the Ravi to the gardens in Lahore, with the water flowing from
the south and exiting from the north side.[106] He also built with similar
passion and romantic zeal the *Juhi Shahi* Canal from the Lar river
in Sindh to the Nur Bagh (honouring his favourite wife Nur Jahan)
in Srinagar, covering a substantial distance. Jahangir's memoir, in
the tradition of his great-grandfather who had written *Baburnamah*
and his father who wrote *Akbarmana*, brings out a ruler who was
very observant to the surroundings, taking immense delight in the
landscape he encountered. For example, he delightfully describes in
his memoir:

> All the people of Kashmir drink the water of a lake that is near
> the city, and is called Dall. The river Bihat [Jhelum] enters this
> lake and flows through the Panjab by the Baramula Pass, Pakli and
> Dantur . . . In Kashmir there is plenty of water from streams and
> springs. By far the best is of Lar valley, which joins the Bihat in the
> village of Shihabu-d-din-pur. This village is one of the celebrated

places of Kashmir, and is on the Bihat. About a hundred plane-tress (chanar) of graceful form clustered together on one plot of ground, pleasant and green, join each other so as to shade the whole plot, and the whole surface of the ground is grass and trefoil.[107]

Symbols were important for Mughal rulers, and the gardens symbolized the Quranic gardens of the paradise, which Jahangir was noted for.[108] When Jahangir defeated his rebellious son Khusrau in the battle of Bhaironwal, he gave 'extraordinary punishment' to the rebels on account of sedition and rewarded his loyalists by giving them fertile land grants between Jhelum and Chenab.[109]

One of the most interesting impressions of the reign of Jahangir comes from William Finch, a nondescript merchant who came to India courtesy his association with the East India Company. He landed in Surat along with Captain William Hawkins in 1608. Finch had a detail for the topography, and his powerful descriptions of the north Indian cities he visited were, without prejudice, very useful information. He describes Lahore as 'one of the greatest cities of the east', and then notes the

> . . . Ravee [Ravi], a goodly river which falleth into Indus, downe which go many boats, of sixtie tunne or upwards, for Tatta in Sindh, after the fall of the raine, being a journey of some fortie dayes alongst by Multan, Seetpore, Buchur [Bukkur], Raurce [Rohri], etc.[110]

For the first time the Indus served as an important means of commerce, moving merchandise between Lahore and Thatta, though not to the extent as on the Ganges from Bengal to Agra,[111] and bringing new economic opportunities in the landlocked princely states of northern India. Meanwhile, the Portuguese, the early European power, were trading with Surat briskly and Thatta had become an important commercial post. By the late sixteenth century, navigation on the Indus was well established,

... the means of locomotion [to Thatta] is by boats of which there
are many kinds, large and small, to the number of 40,000.[112]

The Mughal economy under Jahangir acquired a global
perspective, trading as they were with the Portuguese, which
was boosted domestically by manufacturing centres that
produced products of great quality and appeal outside. With the
changed economic dynamics, the conditions and techniques of
transportation thus assumed significance. It was an opportune
time for the East India Company to come to India. The
Portuguese, however, were no easy pass over and there were
many failed attempts by the British, including the parleys of
William Hawkins with Jahangir who impressed the monarch
with his fondness for wine and

... acquaintance with the Turkish language,[113]

to get a permit to trade with India. Finally, the skilful and diplomatic
Sir Thomas Roe, representing the English monarch James I, was
granted permission in 1615. As the East India Company merchants
set up factories and negotiated terms of reference with the local
principalities, a number of them documented their travels and these
sources give a good account of the geography and commerce along
with the history and customs. William Fremlen wrote from Surat in
May 1636 about barter trade:

> About the latter end of February (and seldome sooner) very great
> flat bottomd boates, of 100 tonnes burthen and upwards, come
> downe from Lahoare, laden with sugar, sugar-candy, nowshodder,
> ginger dry, and conservd and the like commodities; and those they
> commonly barter away for pepper, tinn, lead, spices, broadcloath,
> dates, cokernutts and the likes ... [114]

Henry Bornford on setting up a factory at Rajapur in March
1639, described Lahore as

. . . the prime citty of traffick in India . . .[115]

where the commodities produced in the adjacent regions were collected and sent down the river by

. . . flatt bottom boates.[116]

He then observed,

. . . from Multan the river is navigable at all times; but from Lahoare in the begining [of] March till the cool tyme enter in October.[117]

Shahjahan's period (1628–58) further improved the canals built by Feroz Shah Tughlak and Akbar, and also from time to time issued farmans that the canal waters should not be harmful to household use and for crops and that adequate waters should be apportioned for agriculture.[118] One such, the *nahr-i-faiz* or *nahr-i-bahist* also known as *Shah Nahar*, drawn from the waters of the Ravi near Shahpur to Lahore, was a hydraulic marvel that ushered in the practice of masonry across streams for not just continuous supply of water for cultivation and for the regal gardens but also had a navigable channel to the Lake Dal; a unique feature not recorded earlier. Ali Mardan Khan,[119] the governor of both Kashmir and the Punjab, had proposed the *Shah Nahar* project. This was later upgraded and modified by Mulla Alual Mulk, one of the first irrigation specialists who adequately understood the links between flow and water level. It was through his expertise that the canal became operational in 1643 with abundant water supply reaching Lahore, which Ali Mardan Khan could not achieve. He, however, amassed immense wealth from his superior talent and it is said that at the time of his death he was worth

. . . 1,895,000l (lakh), which devolved to the emperor, according to the eastern custom of the sovereign being heir to all his subjects.[120]

The details of the making of the *Shah Nahar* give a good understanding of the processes, the structures and the maintenance of the canal and raises

> . . . the issue of relationship between political conditions, nature of state structures, and the making of canals, their remaining functional and getting revived.[121]

At the time of completion, the *Shah Nahar* had a length of 86.2 kilometres (possibly 84) and a width of 20–40 feet with a depth from 1–4 feet.[122] As a lover of aesthetics and creativity, when Shah Jahan commissioned his imperial city Shahjahanabad in 1648 overlooking the Yamuna river, perfumed water canals extended to his palace complex cascading over

> . . . illuminated falls.[123]

Water development continued to be an enduring contribution of the Mughals and each ruler had a certain perspective of water use focusing with varying emphasis on

> . . . paradise symbolism, kingship and social function.[124]

Aurangzeb, the last of the great Mughals, usurped power in the midst of a bloody war of succession. His triumph over his brothers—brutal with guile and guts—is explained as

> . . . a victory of action over supineness, of intrepidity over inertia, and of organization and discipline over confusion and incoherence.[125]

Bestowing himself the title of *Alamgir* (seizer of the world), he reigned, as did his great-grandfather Akbar, for nearly fifty years and like his predecessors, opened canals, constructed tanks and dug wells for irrigation. In his long rule from 1658 to 1707, Aurangzeb constructed inundation canals in the dry Multan area and in the

Sutlej-Chenab doab. In the popular imagination Aurangzeb symbolizes the politico-religious bigotry and the signifier of the oppressive 'Muslim colonialism' of India, but by the end of his rule, and subsequently the decline of the Mughal power, Punjab had 4000 kilometres of inundation canals irrigating 0.4 million hectares (mha) of land.[126]

Indus, the Territorial Marker

Sindh had its encounters of invaders but never really caught the attention of historians, unlike Punjab, where the play of the rivers in the plains and the dramatic accounts of the battles fought with galloping horsemen and rattling sabres fascinated them. Sindh was always the less bloodied and less written about, and its geographical features carved by the braided Indus meeting the sea with the sweeping Baloch hills on its east and the Thar on its west gave it a chary remoteness that could only be reached

> . . . after the dangers of the land and the terrors of the sea, after hardship and mental stress.[127]

However, Sindh became a valuable eastern territory in the golden period of Arab trade, connecting its coast to regions far away to the Atlantic. The water of the Indus was both a life-giver and a wealth-provider, and held Sindh culturally and economically together, a reason possible for it witnessing less violence and bloodshed. Sindh saw rulers coming and going before Akbar—who, coincidentally, was born in Umerkot in Sindh—extended his hold to the mouth of the Indus in 1591 and annexed Sindh to the Mughal Empire.[128] As the Mughal imperial structure began to teeter in the later phase of Aurangzeb's reign, Sindh was handed back to the local Kalhora tribe (1701–83), who claimed their antecedence from Abbas, the uncle of Prophet Mohammad. The Kalhoras were probably the first to represent local aspirations and instilled in the people of Sindh a sense of pride and respect for their culture and social diversity.

Peace and stability in Sindh was to take a turn as Nadir Shah (1736–47) made his entry into India in 1738. After plundering and marauding Delhi, at a scale greater than even Timur's loot and bloodbath, he invaded Sindh and made it a 'tributary state'. It is said that Mian Noor Muhhamad (1719–55), the ruler, fled upon hearing of Nadir Shah's menacing advance. Along with the infamy, the Sindh ruler ended up paying Rs 1 crore and an annual tribute of Rs 20 lakh.[129] In order to ensure the timely payment, Nadir Shah, in keeping with the ruthlessness of his nature, took away Noor Muhhamad's sons, Muradyab Khan and Ghulam Shah, as 'security'.[130] Nadir Shah was notorious for such underhand dealings characterized by holding hostages for ransom. In an irony of history, the brothers who were locked together as hostage by Nadir later fought each other for ascendency and power in Sindh, allowing Nadir's successor, Ahmed Shah Abdali (1747–72), to manipulate the situation. While the Kalhoras were militarily too weak to defend Sindh, they, however, made serious efforts to hold the society together in midst of hunger and hardship with their strong religious beliefs. They equally demonstrated their commitment to development by concentrating on irrigation and agriculture.

Noor Muhhamad built a vast network of inundation canals and, as it turned out, helped to mitigate the Indus floods in 1757. Recurring floods during the period were an outcome of high temperature years followed by low temperature ones,

. . . causing changes in the discharge of water in the Indus . . . and from 1754-1760 AD due to these fluctuations, the river Indus witnessed hydrological changes in its course.[131]

The deltaic region of the Indus (we no longer hear Mihrān) was also experiencing hydro-morphological changes over the last couple of centuries as evidenced by the shifting of ports. Around 1300, the port town of Debal became redundant and a new port at Lahari Bandar was built; similarly, in the mid-seventeenth century, silt accumulation from the Indus led Aurangzeb, who was the governor of Multan and Sindh (1649–52), to build a new port, Aurangabandar, in an estuary of the Indus situated near Thatta, an important trading hub that had established sea-borne commerce with Muscat. With the Indus frequently changing its course, the port moved to a new location, Shahbandar, which like Thatta facilitated trade but lost its relevance by the turn of the eighteenth century to the port town of Karachi.

Sindh had come under the suzerainty of Nadir Shah in 1739, and a similar arrangement was enforced in 1748 with the Afghan Empire under Ahmed Shah Abdali. It was not an easy task to rule Sindh, which required paying tributes to the powerful neighbouring power, which threatened dire consequences in any lapse of payment. Yet, Mian Ghulam Shah (1757–72), who took over the reign after a brief power struggle with his brother, ruled his province with considerable independence. He delivered good administration, building canals (*wah*) to irrigate lands and opening up the province to trade and commerce by permitting the East India Company to secure a saltpetre monopoly and set up a factory in Thatta in 1758. This marked the initial ingress of the English into Sindh, although it was short lived and the factory closed

> . . . when the monopoly was cannibalised by the Dutch in 1777–78.[132]

Around that time, the Indus, with periodic floods, was causing immense disruption to Khudabad, the city from where the Kolhora ruled. Ghulam Shah decided on a new city away from the ravages of the Indus. He chose to rebuild Neroon Kot, renaming it Hyderabad in 1768. This remained the provincial capital of Sindh until the British shifted it to Karachi in 1843. By the time the Kalhora dynasty was overthrown in 1783, Sindh had a robust network of inundation canals that included the 10-mile-long Nurwah, the Begari Canal, the 2-mile-long Shah-ji-Kur and the 20-mile-long Date-ji-Kur.[133] Ghulam Shah's equation with Abdali, as events turned out, was to change the trans-Indus region of Sindh and Balochistan.

After Nadir Shah's assassination in 1747, Abdali, his cavalry commander, quickly took political control and adorned the title *Durr-i-Durrani* (pearl of pearls) to become the irrepressible master from his seat of power in Kandhar. From here, he oversaw territories to his west in Persia and on his east from Kashmir to the Punjab and the Sindh—the territories that were vaguely defined as west of the Indus. One would have hardly imagined this sweep and position of power after Abdali's retreat from India in the battle of Sirhind (1748) against the Mughal forces, in what is described as the 'last hurrah' of a declining Mughal Empire.

Lost but not short of spirit, Abdali came back to India in the latter half of 1748. With the Mughal establishment in Delhi in no position to repel Abdali's forces and offering no troop support, Mir Mannu, the governor of Lahore, sought peace with Abdali. But the terms that were laid down were incredibly harsh—surplus revenue was to be sent to the Afghan emperor and the areas west of the Indus to be ceded on a similar arrangement that was decreed by Nadir Shah with the Mughal durbar. It was the beginning of a boundary determination between the Afghans and India's frontier provinces, and in 1752, the Mughal emperor ceded Lahore and Multan as a

. . . feudatory of the Afghan ruler.[134]

The power shift influenced new frontier assertiveness on the part of the Afghans and other Indian tribal groups, and they began to challenge the imperial authority of the Mughal rule. Some scholarships describe it as 'tribal breakout' or 'hollowing out' that accelerated the

. . . weakening of the old Asian empires, especially Mughal India, permitting the expansion of European power in their wake, not least by the English East India Company.[135]

The political economy of the Afghan invasions meant that

. . . state formation more and more revolved around the frontier between the arid zone and the agrarian cores of the [Indian] subcontinent.[136]

The 'agrarian cores' were the Indus basin region of the Punjab and the adjoining Gangetic belt with a community of settled farmers and the Mughal as the power centre, albeit weak and decaying; while the 'arid zone', which was the first line of contact with the invaders from the west, had

. . . the semi-nomadic highly mobile pastoralists . . .[137]

that relied upon domesticated animals like horses, bulls and camels. The Pashtuns and the Balochis that formed the arid zone's ethnic tapestry

. . . were rooted within the dynamics of campaigning and conquest on the Indian subcontinent, both through their provision of animal power (as pastoralists) and their participation in the military labour market.[138]

As a reaction to the marauding Afghan raids, the Baloch leader, Mir Nasir Khan, also known as Nasir Khan Noori (1749–94), unified the regional tribes of the chieftain states of Makran, Kharan and Lasbela. They put up strong resistance against the invading Abdali, forcing the Afghan leader to negotiate a treaty which came to be known as the Treaty of Kalat (1758). The agreement provided for a military alliance for campaigns in Khurasan (Persia) and the Punjab, and a division of the spoils.[139] The combination of the Baloch and the Afghan forces were unstoppable. In fact, the Baloch assistance in the third battle of Panipat (1761) helped tilt the scale in favour of Abdali, crushing the rising Marathas in north India. The void left by the Marathas was filled by the Sikh forces that had, since the beginning of the eighteenth century and particularly with the end of the Aurangzeb reign, made successive inroads into the Punjab upper-doab.

With the Mughal power under Shah Alam II (1760–1806) virtually in disarray, leading to a saying in Persian that 'the empire of Shah Alam is from Delhi to Palam' (Palam being adjacent to Delhi), the Sikh forces defeated Abdali's representative in Lahore and captured the city in 1761. It was short-lived as Abdali, infuriated by the Sikhs' action, reached Lahore the following year, only to find that the Sikhs had fled the place. The Afghan forces chased them and, at Gujjarwal, 30,000 or so Sikhs were massacred. This is known in Sikh history as *Vada Ghallughara* (major holocaust). No sooner had Abdali left for Kandhar in 1763 than the Sikh horsemen and the guerrilla bands attacked Lahore and defeated the Afghans. By the summer of 1764, whatever little control Abdali's representatives had in Punjab, especially between Chenab and Jhelum in the north-east and the areas around Multan in the south-east and the *deras* (settlers), came to the possession of the Sikhs.

The rise of the Sikh power was seen as so threatening to Islam that the Mughal durbar sought help from Abdali and the Baloch leader, Nasir Khan Noori, to gather forces of the 'brethren-in-faith' and defeat the 'infidel' who were turning the country from 'Ahal-e-Islam to Ahal-e-Harab' or, in other words, proclaiming jihad.[140] On the call of the Mughal ruler, Abdali strode for the seventh time to India, and in the winter of 1764, joined by the Baloch, the Mughal forces, fought the Sikh army. In the many battles and skirmishes that followed along the Bari, Rechna and Sindh Sagar doabs, the Afghan forces were resisted by the Sikh army, and their tactics of avoiding pitched battles and employing surgical strikes continuously pushed the Afghan forces back. In desperation, Abdali decided to set course for Afghanistan and return with more fire power and troop strength, but the Sikhs kept raiding them and looting their material and wealth until Abdali reached the Chenab. The crossing of the river proved disastrous,

. . . as if the Day of Judgement had come,[141]

with Abdali's troops suffering terrible losses of lives and material owing to the strong current prevailing. A leading Sikh historian describes the incident as follows:

> Here [at Chenab] he had a heavy toll to pay. When the Shah sent out his men in search of a ford, somebody came in and said that it was easier to ford the river at the foot of the hill where the river was divided into eight streams. The army moved to that point and crossed six of them. The remaining two were very deep, swift and violent, and were overflowing. When the army and the baggage entered into these streams, the strong currents began their work of destruction and carried away thousands of laden camels and saddled horses and innumerable donkeys, bullocks, buffaloes, tents, treasure and men and women.[142]

The *Jang Namah* records that

> ... so many lives had not been lost in the battles with the Sikhs.[143]

Lahore was once again taken by the Sikhs in 1765, declared as the 'Guru's cradle'—referring to Guru Ram Das's birth in Lahore—and coins were minted in the name of the Sikh gurus.

Standing on the banks of the Jhelum at Rohtas in the early months of 1765, Mir Noori and his Balochi companions bade farewell to Abdali, who was leaving for Kandhar after his seventh invasion to India. Noori remained his brave ally, displaying rare loyalty in the campaigns against the Sikhs. But Abdali was not yet done, and in the winter of 1766, marched into India to settle scores with the Sikhs, now very much a force to reckon with. Crossing the Indus, the Afghan forces were met by the Sikh horsemen at the doab between Jhelum and Indus. Although the Sikhs lost, a massive Sikh presence awaited Abdali in Amritsar. Having assessed the situation, Abdali decided that fighting was not an option; negotiations were. But having failed to convince the Sikhs to acknowledge his suzerainty, war became inevitable. Abdali's frontline commanders met the Sikh *jathedars* in Amritsar and suffered massive casualties. This forced Abdali to take a different route and he encamped at Machchiwara ghat on the Sutlej in the summer of 1767. He directed a number of unsuccessful attacks and skirmishes against the Sikhs and with the fast-approaching monsoon decided to head back, leaving the whole of Punjab in the hands of the Sikhs.

The Sikhs, after their bitter experience earlier in the Sindh Sagar doab and realizing its strategic significance as the entry point of invaders from the west, strengthened this area with the best fighting arm and armoury. Invaders would now think twice before crossing the Indus or, if successful in the crossing, would meet the might of the Sikhs. Abdali launched two more attacks on India in 1768 and 1769, and both proved abortive. With the Mughal power rapidly fading, Abdali kept his attention on India until his death in 1772. The raids that became synonymous with him were audacious in their scale. But most of them had a comical irony to them as the Sikh confederacies or *Misls*, using guerrilla tactics, would 'loot the loot' that Abdali had plundered on his return to Kandhar.

The Afghan struggle for power and dominance over the Sikhs continued with territories regained and relinquished. However, differences amongst the Misls began to unsettle their unity until one by one, although not all, the Misls fell under the absorbing sway of Ranjit Singh who, by 1799, became the absolute master of the Punjab. The Afghan-Sikh saga of rivalry and dominance in a way initiated the settling of a formalized border. The British administrators spent decades trying to determine the boundary until an agreement was signed in 1893 to form what was called the Durand Line, of which roughly 80 per cent of the boundary line followed physical features like the rivers and not ethnic boundaries.

A determined Sikh power kept the Punjab from Abdali's control while, in Sindh, Abdali patronized Ghulam Shah, entrusting him with the task of quelling various rebellions in the deras north of the Sindh. For his loyalty, Abdali bestowed upon Ghulam Shah the title of *Shah Wardi Khan*. The deras to the south of the Punjab, with the Baloch predominating in the hills and the Pakhtuns in the north, had become a commercial hub with the intermingling of Afghan and Hindu traders and was an important link in the trade route between Kandhar and Kabul. It was possibly the same area near Uchch Sharif where Alexander, on his passage back home, laid the foundation of a new city, and as he journeyed southwards to Sind, faced stiff resistance from the locals. In Balochistan, Mir Noori remained Abdali's handy ally and their alliance brought the Afghan and Baloch closer. Helped by the Treaty of Kalat, Noori, by 1794, had stretched the area of his command from Bandar Abbas in Iran to Karachi. Balochistan had its own currency, its national (Balochi) as well as official (Persian) languages and a full-fledged sovereign state. It fell into disarray after Noori's death, with disputes and tribal hostilities creating grounds for foreign intervention.

The Afghan rise brought to attention the frontier states—a loosely defined, undulating territory, part rich plain and part arid, in the Indus Valley, which included the Upper Sindh, Balochistan, Multan and Bahawalpur. By the early nineteenth century, this cross-cultural, cross-religious territory, with geographers and travellers keenly describing it as the trans-Indus region, later as the north-west frontier and then the Khyber Pakhtunkhwa Province, became the 'anvil' on which the future of the British Empire was forged. While Sindh, Balochistan and Multan have been described, Bahawalpur, which in the first half of the twentieth century played a critical role in the various water project disputes in the Indus basin, requires a brief introduction. The princely state of Bahawalpur at the confluence of the Sutlej and Chenab came into existence by the middle of the eighteenth century as the Mughal Empire suffered an attenuation of its power. This was a period of time which witnessed the breakaway of hundreds of semi-autonomous states and fiefdoms across the expansive Mughal Empire of which Bahawalpur was one of the seventy princely states to warrant the title of 'highness' for its rulers. Tracing their lineage to the Daudpotras scion of the Abbasid caliphate, the nawabs of Bahawalpur professed their middle-eastern Arabic identity with an unmistakable Ottoman predisposition and wore the Fez cap with haughtiness, ruling the land until it got merged with Pakistan in 1955.

Along with these four frontier states, Dera Ghazi Khan—between the plains of the Indus and the Sulaiman range in southern Punjab, and founded in 1484 by Ghazi Khan Mirani, a Baloch chief who had declared independence from the Langah dynasty of Multan—formed an important territorial space in the frontier region along with other deras such as Dera Ismail Khan and Dera Fateh Khan. Territorially, the west of the Indus by the end of the eighteenth century was detached from the political authority and legitimacy of the Mughal Empire with the Kalhoras ruling Sindh, the Daudpotras in Bahawalpur, the Afghans in Multan and the successors of the Mirranis in Dera Ghazi Khan. All these rulers ruled with independence and engaged in territorial practices of power.

The frontier assumed its own economic characteristics as a bustling 'mercantile emporia' with the caravans trudging along a line stretching from Balkh to Kabul, Gardiz and Ghazni through the Gomal Pass. The direct consequence of trade and movement of goods was that the frontier states rulers never failed to emphasize the

. . . beneficent rule rooted in irrigation patronage.[144]

They had become masters of canal development on the Indus basin, focusing extensively on farming. The Baloch clan system provided for distribution of water to the communities. Apart from the gravity flow, a more reliable method for irrigation and drinking water was drawing the groundwater by digging tunnels in the slopes. The *karez* irrigation system, as it was locally called, would run underground before sprouting in the open, and the water from the tunnel would then be directed to the lands. The sudden bursts of rainfall with the gush of streams were efficiently captured by *bunds* providing for stored water in dry periods and helped *rod-khoi* (channels in mountains) cultivation. The entire irrigation method and its distribution or what in the modern time is referred to as the last-mile-delivery was a

... community enterprise managed by tribal traditions and run by social control.[145]

Even today in Pakistan these methods of irrigation continue. Distribution of water did create tensions among the Baloch clans, in fact fiercely so between the 'up-irrigators and the low-irrigators' with the former, the first users, utilizing the waters indiscriminately and in unrestrained ways, leading to significant harm for the latter. Many of the bunds built turned out to be *khuni* bunds (bloody dams)[146] as described by the British in their survey of the *derajat* in the latter half of the nineteenth century.

Both Ghulam Shah and Abdali died in quick succession in 1772, ending an interesting phase in the history of Sindh. Mian Sarfraz succeeded his father, Ghulam Shah, with the unanimous consent of the nobility and was conferred the title *Khudayar Khan* by Taimur Shah Durrani, the son of Abdali. Both the successors to their respective fathers' thrones stuck a non-interfering and functional relationship. Mian Sarfraz would rule Sindh only for a brief time and by 1783, the Kalhora dynasty was defeated in the battle of Halani. Sindh came under the sway of the Talpurs, who were ethnically Baloch and Shia by faith, and Mir Fateh Ali Khan, a fourth generation Talpur who had settled in Sindh, became its ruler, declaring himself as the *Rais*. The transition was not entirely smooth. The last of the Kalhora, Abdul Nabi, went to the court of Kabul (the seat of power had shifted from Kandhar, and Peshawar was the winter capital), seeking Taimur Shah's support to restore power to the Kalhora. Concerned over the power struggle that would disrupt the flow of levy to his kingdom, Taimur decreed Sindh to be divided into two parts—one ruled by Mir Fateh and other by Abdul Nabi. He also sent a force to implement the process but backed off upon seeing a massive Baloch army gathered by Mir Fateh at Rohri on the eastern bank of the Indus. The show of strength dispelled any doubts about who would rule Sindh. Mir Fateh consolidated his hold, and to avoid any trouble, continued to pay levy to Kabul. He evolved a system of distribution of power called the *chauyari* or the 'rule of four friends' and divided the territory of Sindh amongst his brothers into three states: Hyderabad, Khairpur and Mirpur. The *ameers*, the title they were bestowed, ruled with even-handedness, showing remarkable religious tolerance and extended their rule over the neighbouring Balochistan, Kutch and Kot Sabzal. By remaining solidly united, the ameers were able to quell the invasion of the Afghan ruler, Shah Suja, in 1832.

Sindh reached a level of prosperity and stability unknown before. The ameers took keen interest in the development of Karachi following the decline of the Thatta and Shahbandar ports.[147] A flourishing land trade route had come about from Jaisalmer to Hyderabad and then down the Indus river to Karachi, a distance of about 150 kilometres,[148] and about 729 canals existed in Sindh from the time of the Kalhora rule to the Talpur period.[149] By the 1830s, each of these states were administered by their respective sons, four ameers in Hyderabad, three in Khairpur and two in Mirpur. In Sindh, more specifically, and as will be explained, politico-strategic interest eventually led to its annexation by the British.

DIPLOMACY *and*
COMMERCE *on*
the INDUS

Minto's Three Wise Men

By the end of the eighteenth century, Britain was the wealthiest and most powerful state in the world and as the economist John K. Galbraith expressed,

> The world in which they lived had no place for maudlin sentimentality.[1]

However, its imperial policy was far from secure in the trans-Indus region or the 'frontier'—a British term that expressed the northern borderlands of India. The frontier's trading route that brought riches also needed to be protected and became a factor in British expansion.

The frontier would prove to be one of the abiding obsessions of the British. To begin with, the British saw Napoleon's attack of Egypt in 1798 and his ambition to invade India, modelled on the likes of Alexander of Macedonia and Nadir Shah, as a potential threat to the empire's stability. Fearing the worst, the British concluded a treaty with the Shah of Persia in 1801. The Shah was a willing partner, worried, in his case, over the Tsarist Russian expansion south towards the Caucasus. The British agreed to protect Persia and supply military equipment in case of an Afghan or French attack. The Shah, reciprocating, agreed to not admit France for any commercial activity into Persia and allow privileges to the East India Company. It was perhaps the most mutually beneficial agreement that could come about and yet the two were unsure of each other. In the next several years, the ever-strategizing British in India lost interest in Iran so to speak, and in fact refused to come to

Persia's assistance in Transcaucasia where Russia was making a deep ingression, compelling Iran to push forward its army.

The Shah of Persia had become increasingly suspicious of the British commitment to the treaty and its recent proximity to Russia to neutralize France. In the circumstances, and with the French and Russian relations under a cloud, the Shah hitched his wagon to Napoleon and signed a treaty in 1807. Even before the ink could dry, Napoleon, the master of continental western Europe at the age of thirty-seven, was luring the even younger thirty-year-old Tsar of Russia, Alexander I. On a raft in the Niemen river at Tilsit in July 1807, he urged a Franco-Russian alliance,

> . . . promising to divide the rule of all Europe with him.[2]

The events stunned both the British and the Shah and prompted Lord Minto, the governor general, to despatch some very skilful envoys to Afghanistan, Persia and Punjab to secure alliances to stymie competition from Napoleonic France. Possibly in desperation, or even paranoia, the British negotiated a treaty with Persia, like they did in 1801. However, never did a right chemistry develop between John Malcolm, the envoy (who had earlier led the delegation in 1800–01), and the Shah of Persia, both of whom found it easier to loathe each other during the negotiations in 1808.

As soon as the British were convinced that the Franco-Russian alliance was merely a chimera, they made a strategic choice between Persia and Afghanistan. They were certain that the former was not a viable barrier, while a powerful ally in Kabul would suit its interest. Minto's chosen envoy to Afghanistan, Mountstuart Elphinstone, who had considerable knowledge of Persian and Hindi, led a diplomatic mission in 1808 to meet Shah Shuja Durrani in the winter capital of Peshawar. The court of Shah Shuja, not accustomed to receiving delegates, let alone an embassy bringing

> . . . elephants with golden howdahs, a palanquin with a high
> parasol, gold-inlaid guns and ingenious pistols with six chambers,

never seen before; expensive clocks, binoculars, fine mirrors
capable . . .[3]

was more than happy to be pampered by the British. It was not the
best of times for the Durrani dynasty with constant successor tussle,
fear of Persia and a shrinking territory. Moreover, the raids into India
to plunder its wealth, in which they had so regularly indulged since
the reign of Ahmed Shah Abdali, had now shrunk considerably,
courtesy the British presence in the north-west frontier region. In
these strained times, Shah Shuja was more than open to an alliance
with the British. He, of course, had his immediate interest to guard
and negotiate, while the British deal was influenced by France's
renewed connection with Persia.

The Franco-Russian alliance was turning sour, and as the prospect
of a French invasion seemed increasingly unlikely, reconfirmed
by a strong British intelligence network, Elphinstone proceeded
to Peshawar in December 1808. In a masterly way, retaining a
considerable upper-hand, he pushed a business-like treaty in 1809 of
'perpetual friendship and non-interference', with Britain agreeing to
pay a subsidy of Rs 30,000 to Afghanistan if it was attacked by Persia
and France. On his part, Shuja would oppose the passage of foreign
troops through his territories. But in an unexpected turn of events,
power was usurped from Shuja, the treaty was rendered null and
void, and the dethroned ruler, a fugitive on the run, accompanied
Elphinstone and the British entourage to Delhi.

Meanwhile, a series of fissures emerged in the Franco-Russian
alliance, and by 1810, the curtains were swiftly drawn as Alexander
I rebuffed Napoleon's proposal to marry one of his sisters. Not
entirely because of the slight, but certainly a strong reason for it,
Napoleon raised one of the largest armies ever to fight the Russians
in 1812. This turned out be one of the biggest follies in the history
of war. The little general with a shrill voice, who had aspired to
cross the Indus and conquer India, had to defend his country from
being conquered. Napoleon's defeat at Waterloo and his subsequent
exile was rejoiced in British India. Napoleon would no longer be the

bugbear. Coincidentally, Arthur Wellesley, the Duke of Wellington who proved to be Napoleon's nemesis at Waterloo and went on to become Britain's prime minister, had an enriching military stint in India. Commanding the colonial forces, he defeated Tipu Sultan, the 'tiger of Mysore', in the siege of Seringapatam. Before leaving for England in 1805, Wellesley won a decisive battle at Assaye against the Maratha Empire that paved the way for British dominance of central India.

The early decade of the nineteenth century was indeed a busy time for British strategists in India, who had to constantly work out strategic adjustments and diplomatic manoeuvring as a direct fallout of the great power rivalry in continental Europe between Russia and France. With the fall of Shah Shuja, who was symbolically hosted by the British in India as a pawn to be used at a convenient time, Britain again opened its diplomatic parleys with Iran with a new treaty in 1814. But when Russia invaded Persia in 1826, the British, in a familiar pattern, acquiesced and a large Persian territory was surrendered. Imperial Russia was now the new enemy of British India. An imminent European threat to British interest always worried the political masters in England and allowed for greater legitimization of the British colonial presence in India.

The frontier, likewise, was convincingly portrayed by the colonial administrators as a fragile region with precarious boundaries requiring special attention. Minto's three wise envoys—John Malcolm, Charles Metcalfe and Mountstuart Elphinstone, in their respective missions to Persia, Punjab and Afghanistan—were convinced that the threat of an external enemy lay in its potential to stir an anti-imperial rebellion inside India, undermining, therefore, the British rule over the colony. Sindh equally required an agreement to check French design, and a commercial mission was sent by Lord Minto in 1809, leading to the treaty of Eternal Friendship in which the ameers of Sindh promised not to

. . . allow the establishment of the tribe of the French in Sind.[4]

The treaty was renewed in 1820 to allow in the Americans, and nothing of great significance happened until the 1830s.

Malcolm and Elphinstone were experienced officers, dealing with the complexities of diplomacy in lands that the British were barely familiar with. Metcalfe, on the other hand, was a twenty-three-year-old assistant to the resident at Delhi when he was sent to the court of Maharaja Ranjit Singh in Lahore in 1809. Ranjit Singh had

> . . . been recently absorbing all the small principalities beyond the Sutlej, and consolidating them into a great empire . . .[5]

and was eager to bring the British side of the Sutlej under the 'common yoke'. Seldom, perhaps, in the annals of Anglo-Indian diplomacy was a delicate task entrusted to one as young as Metcalfe. Ranjit Singh had risen majestically, and only a few years ago he was referred in passing by the British as one of the chieftains of Punjab ruling 'strange people' [the Sikhs]. Lord Warren Hastings noted, before leaving for India in 1784, that they were a sect rather than a nation. The British saw the interaction with Punjab as more than political or economic; it was to be a defensive system arranged as tributary in which the Punjab chiefs would pay for the maintenance of the British force. The dynamics, of course, all changed with Ranjit Singh emerging as the dominant and unchallenged force.

In the changed circumstances, particularly due to their fear of an advance of a European army, the British were forced to reach out to Ranjit Singh as an ally, and a

> . . . Sikh alliance had now become more expedient and more practicable.[6]

In doing so, the British acknowledged the unitary power of the Sikh leader, a radical departure from the plans either to annex the whole of the Sikh territory or to distribute the Punjab between the Sutlej and Yamuna among the four principal Sikh chiefs and define the limits of the territory to each of them, with the British engaging separately with the chiefs. In the given situation, with neither of the options potentially viable, the British thought it better to work upon Ranjit Singh's

> ... hopes and upon his fears, and by demonstrating to him that his own interests would be largely promoted by an alliance with the British, induce him to enter into an engagement for the protection of the frontier of Hindostan.[7]

In June 1809, with the tingling of his young blood, Metcalfe led the mission across the Sutlej to Lahore to dialogue with the Maharaja, or as the British called him, the Rajah of Lahore. Ranjit Singh was no easy customer and remained for the British an unknown quantity with uncertain temper and unscrupulous ambition. To induce him to negotiate a treaty of friendship to counteract the ambitions of Russia and France would require the utmost delicacy of handling. A set of instructions were given to Metcalfe as a guidepost in his mission to Punjab, one of which was

> ... to ascertain the routes through which it is practicable for an army to march from Persia to the Indus and to communicate information respecting the geography of the countries to the westward of that river.[8]

Geopolitically, the west of the Indus was the 'panic zone' for the British, while for Ranjit Singh, the south of Sutlej or the Cis-Sutlej states[9] that included Jind, Kaithal, Jagadhari, Nabha and Patiala, although part of his suzerainty, remained yet to be integrated in his empire. The task, therefore, for Metcalfe was to align two different objectives in the best interest of both the parties and equally ensure to the other Punjab chiefs that their welfare and security would not be compromised.

A series of grandstanding and posturing carefully calibrated by Ranjit Singh was played out and often. When discussion seemed to reach a point of agreement, the Maharaja, without giving any definite answer to the British requisition, would abruptly breakaway to attend to matters more urgent, leaving Metcalfe hopelessly frustrated. This went on for several months with Metcalfe doggedly following him like a man possessed to complete the mission which he was chosen for.[10] All this while, Ranjit Singh was buying time and expanding his territory, hoping to get implied sanction of the British to his conquest on the southern bank of the Sutlej. Meanwhile, the dangers of Napoleon's attack, which was the basis of Metcalfe's mission, having now receded, the balance changed, and it was Ranjit Singh seeking a treaty with the British. For that to be achieved, the restitution of Ambala, Kheir and Faridkote, which Ranjit Singh had acquired since the arrival of the mission, was necessary. With all requisitions complied with, Metcalfe finally concluded a treaty of Mutual Friendship with Ranjit Singh in April 1809 at Amritsar. In no uncertain terms, the treaty divided the territories in the Punjab along the Sutlej river:

> . . . the British Government will have no concern with the territories and subjects of the Rajah to the northward of the river Sutlej . . .

and

> . . . the Rajah will never maintain in the territory which he occupies [occupied by him and his dependents] on the left bank of the river Sutlej more troops than are necessary for the internal duties of that territory, nor commit or suffer any encroachments on the possessions or rights of the chiefs in its vicinity.[11]

After months of displaying forbearance with the Maharaja, Metcalfe, without having realized it, had helped

> . . . build an interethnic bridge to the Lahore court.[12]

The Sikh *quam* (community) was not entirely happy with having to relinquish the territories on the southern side of the Sutlej, but given their superior military strength, the British were successful in avoiding a confrontation. Perhaps to appease his court and make up for the lost territories, the following year, Ranjit Singh campaigned in Kangra and brought it under his kingdom. The Amritsar treaty, as it turned out, was never violated either by the Sikhs or the British and lasted throughout the reign of Ranjit Singh. Word of Metcalfe's conduct at the Sikh court quickly spread, and Lord Minto called him over to Calcutta, desirous to

> . . . know the man who had done such great things for his government.[13]

Metcalfe left the shores of India for Jamaica, being appointed as the governor of the island. Upon his retirement from the colony, of the many tributes that were written by the people of Jamaica, one in particular noted,

> To mean well and to act well is the duty of every governor but few can invoke the experience of forty years of virtuous, brilliant and successful diplomacy.[14]

With its objective of forging alliances, the diplomatic caravan led by Metcalfe travelled the flat plains, deep in mud in the monsoon, and Elphinstone's mission faced the furious blast of the western desert and nearly perished from shortage of water. These were also an exercise in geographic detailing, intelligence gathering and observation of the 'social hierarchy'. The Elphinstone caravan, for example, was a scientific one. He used his mission to Peshawar, which took many months of preparation and about four months of travel across 500 miles from Delhi, to understand and collect information about Afghanistan that was likely to be useful to the British government. On the journey to Peshawar, the mission was systematically tasked to survey stretches of the frontier region, the features of the Indus basin, and observe the history and sociopolitical aspects which Elphinstone scrupulously detailed in his work, *An*

Account of the Kingdom of Caubul.[15] Upon having first sighted the Indus at Oodoo da Kote, Elphinstone with awe pens,

> ... besides its great name, and the interest it excites as the boundary of India, was rendered a noble object by its own extent.[16]

The mission travelled along the Indus until Peshawar, and he describes numerous fascinating accounts of the river and its surroundings, from the mules which were, as observed, of better endurance westwards of the Indus

> ... though they never equal those of England ...[17]

to the Persian wheel being used for raising water from the Indus in Peshawar,

> ... on the banks of which machinery is erected.[18]

In his writing, Elphinstone refers to a certain 'Mr. Durie', a native of Bengal and a son of an Englishman and an Indian mother, who

> ... seized with a great desire to travelling, he crossed the Indus without a farthing in his possession and travelled through the Afghaun country in the character of a Mahomedan, with an intention of proceeding to Baghdad.[19]

Since Durie had spent several months in Kabul and Kandhar in 1811-12 and given that Elphinstone had no personal account of Afghanistan beyond Peshawar, it would only be fitting to incorporate Durie's first-hand knowledge as a

> ... great acquisition.[20]

It is not clear what these pieces of information were or to what extent Elphinstone incorporated them in his work, but he was undoubtedly impressed with Durie's insights and had them written down in his interactions with him in Poona before Durie left by ship to explore Baghdad.

The following years, further surveys of the Indus, its tributaries and the territories it traversed, were undertaken by Lt Henry Pottinger. While traversing Sindh and Balochistan, he noted with rigour the geography of the Indus basin, rectifying the earlier belief that the Indus flowed in a south line from its source to the mouth:

> From these researches we are led to think that the Indus rises between the thirty-fifth and thirty-sixth degrees of north latitude, whence it runs a little to the southward of west, for a distance of seven or eight degrees, forcing its way among the snowy mountains that separate Kashmeer and Little Thibet. About the seventy-second degree of east longitude it suddenly turns more southerly, being denied a further westerly progress by the mountains of Kashkar, and thence it varies its course, between south and south-west, to the fortress of Attock, in north latitude 33°55'. To the northward of that place it is distinguished by the title of Aboo Seen, or Father River, and there it is usually called the Roode Attock, or river of Attock, by which name it is known until joined by the Punjab, or five streams, that water the provinces within the Punjab; there it may be said to enter Sinde, and, accordingly, it seems to be thenceforward exclusively spoken of as the Duryae Sinde, which we must interpret the river of Sinde, though, in reality, it signifies the sea of Sinde. That is, however, used metaphorically to convey an idea of its magnitude.[21]

All the information and observations from Elphinstone's mission and Pottinger's survey were to add to the overall study of the frontier provinces. These become the basis for drawing imperial tactics and strategies during the first half of the nineteenth century and then compiled into a gazetteer.[22] As the missions accomplished their tasks with varying degree of success, the rivers of the Indus basin on its eastern side acted as natural agents to define the territorial demarcations in the Punjab, Sindh and Balochistan. Several more expeditions from Kutch were undertaken

> . . . to the acquisition of full and complete information on the Indus.[23]

The trans-Indus region with its intrigues and local unrest and the fears of foreign invasion remained for the British an

> . . . imperial migraine . . .[24]

yet its control was viewed as critical to Britain's power and prestige. Russia was the new threat and, although seeming incredulous, it did occupy the British mind, and the resultant policies had a big impact in the Indus basin region.[25] The greater the threat perception, the more the desire for an alliance with Afghanistan, with Lahore and with establishing influence in Sindh and Balochistan. These were the true strategic objects for which the British were prepared to take some hazard.

But the question of where the frontier with its incoherent geography should be drawn, continuously worked up the British. Afghanistan, the

> . . . roundabout of empires,[26]

was locked between three empires: the Turkic and later the Russian in the north, Persia to its west and British-India to the south-east, and each had its strategic interest. In this 'roundabout', the British had a number of options to explore, although none easy to implement. Taking the frontier line to the Oxus river in the northern end, far and away from mainland India, would incur difficulties in patrolling. The other was to draw the frontier line closer along the Indus that would, however, render little buffer space and time to respond to the enemies. It also meant the task of governing and policing the fiercely independent Pashtun tribes, scattered from the south of

Afghanistan to the Khurram Valley to Wazirstan. Thus, finding it
difficult to draw the boundary, but certain that they needed as much
land between them and the foreign enemies, the British invaded
Afghanistan in 1839. It took several decades and the unpleasant
outcomes of two Anglo–Afghan wars before in 1893, with the fear
of the Russians moving in, the boundary line was established.

Huff and Puff of Navigation

In the Mughal emperor Jahangir's reign, the Indus was being used in
a limited scale for commerce by employing 'flat bottomed boats' to
send produce down the river from Lahore. The East India Company
merchants, while setting up business, noted with enthusiasm that
some stretches of the Indus, particularly from Multan to the sea,
were navigable throughout the year. Henry Pottinger had equally
observed in his detailed study in 1811 of the flow of the Indus that,

> Notwithstanding the great depth of water . . . the commerce is
> entirely carried on between Sinde and the Punjab and Uffghanistan
> in flat bottomed boats that carry from one to three hundred tons,
> and yet are so constructed, as to draw but a few feet water.[27]

The viability of navigation and commerce remained an exciting
prospect. It was in the 1830s that for the first time, navigation-
highway for sea-going vessels into the heart of the Punjab became
an objective.

The ameers of Sindh were worried rulers, fearing British
annexation of their territory. The British administration in Bombay
under the governorship of John Malcolm, who had taken over from
Elphinstone, was gathering details about Sindh, its rulers, resources,
revenue, trade and navigation. The acquisition of information was
crucial for the British frontier policy, and enhanced, as we shall see,
with the coming of the Burnes brothers from England.

James and Alexander Burnes, aged twenty and sixteen
respectively and great-nephews of the famed Scottish poet Robert

Burns, arrived in Bombay in October 1821, sporting the 'round hat' as instructed by the cadet rule book, after a five-month voyage in the cramped conditions of the *Sarah*. A few years later in 1825, as a regimental adjutant in the 21st Bombay Native Infantry, Alexander distinguished himself in an offensive to drive out the Baloch tribes who had crossed the Indus and raided the army station at Kutch. The Scots' network was remarkable and the Burnes brothers would not have been in India had it not been for the Scottish connection. Alexander's career was given a push by John Malcolm of whom it was said,

> . . . like a true good Scotsman, has a happy knack at discerning the special merits of those born north of the tweed.[28]

The Burnes were brothers in arms, but Alexander got greater attention for having successfully navigated the Indus in 1831, his daring expeditions to Bokhara in Central Asia and then an important diplomatic assignment to Kabul. His brother James was also a man of repute and had become a Freemason in 1828 and later the Grand Master of all Scottish Freemasonry in India.[29] While posted in Sindh as the residency surgeon in 1828 and

> . . . being intimately acquainted with their highness the Ameers . . .[30]

James's personal observations, not part of any official commissioning, on the Indus deserves notice. He observed the Indus as being extremely

> . . . crooked, foul, muddy and full of shoals and shifting sands . . .[31]

in the lower stretches as it entered the sea. It corresponded with Pottinger's survey of 1810–11, which James duly acknowledged. However, while Pottinger saw the Indus collecting all the branches and entering the

. . . Indian Ocean as one vast body . . .[32]

James navigated two large arms of the Indus below Thatta, which
he described as the Meyraum (Mehrān) and the Bugghaur. It clearly
showed the inconstancy of the hydrological dynamics of the Indus
in the lower part of its flow and, therefore, the inconsistency in the
representation of the river from the time of Alexander of Macedonia
and his voyage down the Indus to the sea. James believed that the
ancients, referring to Arrian's account, had a better understanding
of the delta of the Indus than 'the writers of our time' while also
acknowledging,

> . . . Nothing is more perplexing than the diversity of names, so
> common in eastern countries, which is to be attributed to the
> natives themselves, who have many appellations for the same river,
> and who are constantly changing them like a matter of fashion.[33]

Alexander, however, saw opportunities and felt that some of the
challenges of navigation on the Indus could be overcome. During
his posting at Kutch for several years, before navigating the Indus
from the mouth to Lahore in 1831, Alexander (hereon Burnes)
had already visited the eastern mouth of the Indus where he was
informed that the tides rose about 9 feet at full moon. He describes
this part of the Indus basin, where he saw many boats stranded, as
an unforgiving place.

> The tide overflows their banks and recedes to leave a desert dreary
> waste, overgrown with shrubs but without a single tree.[34]

Commerce on the Indus was gaining attention and prompted Burnes
to make some specific notes on the vessels which were invading the
deltaic region. One such category was large boats with sharp build
and 'lofty poop' used for maritime trade from the port of Karachi
to Muscat, Bombay and the Malabar coast. The other set of boats
were the *dingee*, which were used for fishing at the mouth of the

Indus and were an important source of commerce. The third kind were the flat-bottomed twin-masted boats or the *doondees*, large and unwieldy, but which could transport about '100 kurwars' or fifty tonnes of cargo at a rate of 3-miles an hour, needing only 4-feet of water depth.[35]

His overall analysis on transport on the Indus was that boats with keel had little chance to withstand the turbulence, while the doondees had their limitations. Steamboats with specific design and features, according to Burnes, could easily adapt to the navigation and command the waters. Fuels made steamers viable and dependable with the recent discovery of coal along the Indus basin and the existence of wood from before. Since the British were contemplating the annexation of Sindh, Burnes observed:

It would be impracticable to march a force through the Delta, from the number of rivers; and it would be equally impossible to embark it in flat-bottomed boats, for there are not 100 of them below Hyderabad; few are of burthen, and the very largest would not contain a company of infantry.[36]

Laying siege of Karachi, a vulnerable point of Sindh, followed by a land expedition tactically made sense, and as Burnes noted, there was no dearth of food supplies, and in the region camels and diminutive horses were in plenty for transport.

In 1831, as Burnes went up the river against the current to reach Hyderabad from Thatta, the variation in the depth was significant with 5 fathoms in the former and 15 to 20 feet in the latter. Thereon he travelled to Sehwun, Bukkur and Mittun, where the waters of the Punjab united in one stream to fall into the Indus. As he started the expedition from Mittun to Attok, he noted:

The Cabool mission in 1809 came upon that river, at Oodoo da Kote, about 100 miles north of the point in question [Mittun]; and I was desirous of connecting my own surveys with that place,

and thus complete our knowledge of the Indus from the sea to
Attok.[37]

At this point Burnes received a message deputing him to the court
of Lahore to deliver a letter from the King of England. He travelled
through Sindh upstream on the Indus and then sailed up the Ravi

... a foul river ... with dangerous quicksand ... .[38]

to Lahore to present to Maharaja Ranjit Singh

... five great English dray horses and a state carriage.[39]

No explorer since the time of Alexander of Macedonia had fully
navigated the Indus from the mouth to Lahore and mapped the
territories and terrain around it, and Burnes would often with a touch
of haughtiness underline this fact. Traversing the Indus, Burnes
calculated the flow of the mighty river at 2265 cubic metres of water
per second. This, he assumed, exceeded the flow of the Ganges in
the dry season by four times and was almost equivalent to the flow
of the Mississippi in the US.[40] During his stay in the Punjab, Burnes
acutely observed the doabs between the Sutlej and Ravi and noted
that Punjab was a

... poorly peopled country in proportion to its fertility.[41]

This was one of the early pieces of information on the need for
expanding irrigation in the Punjab which, in the second half of the
nineteenth century, became a massive institution of the British.

    After being regaled and showered with presents at the court
of Lahore, Burnes journeyed to Simla to meet Governor General
Lord William Bentinck (1828–35). The economy and commerce
was the first article in Bentinck's programme but he always had,
like many worried British, one eye on the far horizons looking at
a possible Russian threat. Upon carefully hearing the narratives of

Burnes's expedition on the Indus and then later considering all the documents along with the rough sketches of the maps, Bentinck without much ado started the process of laying open the navigation of the Indus to the commerce of Britain. The great expedition that Burnes undertook with the help of an 1810 sketch of the 'Indus from Shikarpoor to the Sea' by Samuel Richards, and then the refined maps that he produced when he went to England in 1834, with the help of his cartographer friend John Arrowsmith, threw new light on the geography of the Indus basin and the territories surrounding it.

Bentinck's letter, through his secretary, formally acknowledged Burnes,

> . . . the map prepared by you forms an addition to the geography of India of the first utility and importance, and cannot fail to procure for your labours a high place in this department of science.[42]

Knowledge and power had a seductive relationship, and Bentinck could clearly see this interface in the tantalizing prospect of the Indus. He instructed Henry Pottinger, now with the rank of colonel and the resident in Cutch, whose study of the region and the Indus though solid, remained much in the shadow of Burnes, to negotiate treaties with the ameers of Sindh to open the navigation of the Indus.[43] There was plenty of speculation over the negotiations, with the *Bombay Courier* reporting:

> We are not aware what the exact state of commerce between the British dominions in India and the countries situated upon the banks of the tributary streams of the Indus at present is but from Burnes' visit to Sinde it would appear that British manufacturers, and cutlery in particular, were scarcely ever known, even at the court of Ameers: it is possible, therefore, that but small quantities, if any, had found their way higher up the river. Under such circumstances, relieving the intercourse with populous countries, like the Punjaub and Cabul, from the fetters which the positions of the Ameers enables them to put on it, would undoubtedly in

a short time increase very considerably the demand for British manufacturers in those countries and add proportionably to the commerce of the place.[44]

Having asked Pottinger to negotiate with the ameers, Bentinck simultaneously encouraged Burnes to undertake journeys beyond the Indus, like Minto's envoys a few decades earlier, in the service of the British government. Since his childhood, Burnes had romanticized the alluring lands of Persia and Kabul where Alexander of Macedonia had roamed. Despite the hazards, in his youthful zest—he was only twenty-six—he promptly agreed to the expedition accompanied by his fellow officer and companion John Leckie, a Muslim native, surveyor Mahommed Ali, and a 'Hindoo lad of Cashmere family', Mohan Lal, who recorded the entire expedition most diligently. By the end of December 1831, the caravan, with Burnes in disguise and using the name Sikander Kahn, was treading through the Punjab plains, taking the left bank of the Sutlej until the river joined the Beas and then passing the solitude of the Indian desert before crossing the Indus and the boundaries of India in March 1832. Burnes's intrepid spirit took him across to the Afghan territory and then to Bukhara (present-day Uzbekistan) where, in the course of his journey, he threw away his English attire, shaved his head and donned the robes of the Afghans with the *cummerbund*. Having met the monarchs of Kabul and Bukhara and many other exalted personages and

. . . gratified to find myself in the court of Persia,[45]

Burnes returned to Bombay through the Persian coast in 1833, and after the prerequisite period of quarantine, went to Calcutta to meet Bentinck.

In the routes Burnes followed, he almost retraced the history of the great travellers and their interaction and experiences with the land and the rivers. His accounts, a series of intrigues, deception, and of maps that were drawn secretly, are extraordinarily engrossing, often imbibing the spirit of Alexander of Macedonia whom he related to. He writes,

> We had beheld the scenes, of Alexander's wars, of the rude and savage inroads of Jengis and Timour, as well as the campaigns and revelries of Baber, as given in the delightful and glowing language of his commentaries.[46]

The accounts were published in three volumes as *Travels into Bukhara* in 1834–5 and made Burnes the toast of England. He had an audience with King William and Princess Victoria, who, in 1838, as the queen, conferred the knighthood on Burnes while he was assigned to Kabul. For his compelling narration, the risk involved and the endurance displayed, Burnes was warmly welcomed to the Royal Asiatic Society and elected a fellow to the prestigious Royal and French geographical societies. His acclaim was undeniable, but sadly undercut other works of significance. One such by Mohan Lal, who travelled with Burnes, deserves attention. A perfect foil to Burnes with a flair for adventure as well as detailing every observation, Mohan Lal's travelogue was first published around 1834 in Calcutta. It had critical statistical information providing the British authorities with military, geographical and commercial knowledge of his

> . . . travels in the Mazari country, and the commercial reports of the different marts on the Indus.[47]

Burnes came back to India as a celebrity in 1835 and was assigned to the Court of Hyderabad under Henry Pottinger who was in negotiations with the ameers to open the Indus for navigation; a task which he realized was neither easy nor pleasant. However, not the best of the equations prevailed between them. Ironically, it was the notes of his elder brother James that Pottinger was reading carefully to understand the behaviour of the ameers. James had observed that the Sindh rulers had great passion for chase or hunting and had turned large tracts of productive land along the banks of Indus into forests. Any treaty thus would mean the inviolability of their *sikhargahs* or hunting grounds. Moreover, the ameers, with no particular fondness for the 'white man' and a fanatical hatred towards Christianity, also felt slighted over the fact that the British had lavished gifts on Ranjit Singh (the dray horses) and were in no mood to give in easily.

The prospects of navigation on the Indus had sent the British government on an overdrive. A company was formed in England and the impatience of the British higher-ups to get the ameers to comply was adding to the pressure on Pottinger, who was at the centre of implementing the process. Having himself investigated the Indus, Pottinger had first-hand awareness of the hydrological difficulties of navigating the waters. But, as the British political representative in Sindh, it was becoming clear that although the region fed by the Indus was fertile, the people of Sindh were largely impoverished and had little or nothing to give in exchange for British goods. The great hoopla over navigation lacked comprehensive economic review, often ignoring the fact that to

> . . . open a profitable market in any country it is necessary that the inhabitants should have, not only a desire for British manufacturers but also the means for paying for them.[48]

Earl Auckland, the new governor general of India (1836–42), thought otherwise. Sensing the need for opening markets up the Indus and beyond for the profitability of navigation, he decided to send Burnes on a

> . . . commercial mission . . .[49]

to the court of Dost Mohammed in Kabul in November 1836 and establish relations that might enable the British to trade with various marts in Afghanistan and Central Asia.

Burnes, this time not in disguise but as an assigned diplomat of the British government, embarked on a commercial exercise that would eventually become one of political character leading to the first Anglo–Afghan War (1839–42). On the route to Kabul, Burnes's sketch of the interplay of the rivers and routes with the socio-economics speaks of his mastery over acquiring geographic information and translating it into maps, and his ability to satisfy both the anxiety and curiosity of the British authorities and the public for information about these regions.[50]An interesting criticism of Auckland's policy was recorded by Charles Masson, the news reporter for the East India Company stationed in Kabul. He wrote:

> The governments of India and of England, as well as the public at large, were never amused and deceived by a greater fallacy than that of opening the Indus, as regarded commercial objects. The results of the policy concealed under this pretext have been the introduction of troops into the countries on and beyond the river, and of some half dozen steamers on the stream itself, employed for warlike objects, not for those of trade.[51]

While Masson himself was controversial—a deserter from the Bengal Artillery who had stumbled upon the ruins of the Harappa in the 1820s and, after receiving a 'royal pardon' in 1834, was posted in Kabul—his criticism was not wholly unfounded. Trade traction with Afghanistan and its surrounding areas was an impression that Lord Auckland wanted to communicate but it was intended

> . . . to watch more closely than has hitherto been attempted the progress and events in Afghanistan and to counteract the progress of Russian influence . . .[52]

Already the British ambassador to Tehran, Henry Ellis, had dropped a bombshell in April 1836 by declaring Afghanistan as the

> . . . border of our Indian empire.[53]

Masson makes no bones about his dislike for Burnes and his disregard for decorum, which also finds familiar tone in Josiah Harlan's memoir and his indictment of British policy that could have

> . . . controlled the movements and the policy of the Avghans by fiscal diplomacy, without incurring the odium of invading and subjugating an unoffending distant free people, whom to subdue to Europeans forms of civilization was impossible.[54]

Harlan was an American Quaker and adventurist who briefly served as a surgeon in the East India Company and then as a paid foreign officer in Ranjit Singh's army before he slipped into Afghan territory. Here, for almost two decades, he played a pivotal role in the bloody Afghan affairs, declaring himself

> . . . in a crowning act of imperial hubris . . .[55]

the Prince of Ghor before being unceremoniously ousted by the British army.

Burnes had established liaison with Dost Mohammed and a healthy personal equation, but typical of his training and character, had built a network of spies constantly feeding him with information on the political development in the country. His ability to extract crucial information made him, according to his detractors, cocky and arrogant, but does not suggest that he wavered from his brief. In one of his letters to William Macnaghten, secretary to Lord Auckland, Burnes writes about his conversation with Dost Mohammed on the prosperous trade route through the Indus. While Dost was agreeable, he expressed his fears,

> . . . I am involved in difficulties which are prejudicial to commerce; my hostilities with the Sikhs narrow my resources, compel me to take up money from merchants and to even increase the duties to support the expenses of war. These are the shifts to which I am driven, for seeking to preserve my honour.[56]

The fact that Dost Mohammed could speak candidly to Burnes about his predicament and honour was useful for the British bosses in India. Burnes notes in his letter that Dost was desperately seeking conciliation with Ranjit Singh, even willing to seek forgiveness from the Maharaja and give horses and

> . . . if Peshawur was given to him he would hold it tributary to Lahore.[57]

In Burnes own assessment of the situation, Dost was an important ally to be nurtured for the commercial viability of the Indus navigation as well as political expediency. Lord Auckland, however, felt no reason to assist Dost in his aspiration to get Peshawar at the cost of British friendship with Ranjit Singh, advising him to

> . . . establish equitable terms of peace with the Maharaja . . .[58]

for which the British would willingly assist. But he also warned that

> . . . should you seek connexion with other powers without my approbation; Captain Burnes and the gentleman accompanying him, will retire from Cabool, where his further stay cannot be advantageous; and I shall have to regret my inability to continue my influence in your favour with the Maharajah.[59]

Peshawar neither belonged to the East India Company nor to Dost Mohammed but to Ranjit Singh wholly and exclusively as part of his territory. In a letter to John Hobhouse, the president of the secret committee of the court of directors, Auckland writes,

> In his pressing need he has courted Persia, he has courted Russia, and he has courted us. But it would be madness in us, though we may wish to see his independence assured, to quarrel with the Sikhs for him.[60]

Lord Auckland knew that Peshawar was becoming an inconvenient conquest for Ranjit Singh and at some point, if the British chose to do so, could either force or cajole the Maharaja to part with it.

The alliances and machinations developing between Persia and Russia had brought the British face to face with the realities in Afghanistan and the region around it. A political and diplomatic confrontation developed between Russia and Britain, almost seeming from time to time to be a final showdown. The Russians had become active in the region ever since the remarks made by Ellis and, by 1837, had increased their diplomatic footprint. Russian diplomats like Count Simonich and Ivan Vitkevich were seen circulating in the power circle of Tehran and Kabul, making their own intrigues and outlining alliances. Simonich, the Russian minister to Persia, was goading the Shah to attack the pro-British Herat with the full support of the Russian empire. Meantime, Vitkevich was spotted by the British travelling purposefully through Persia to Kabul with a personal letter from Czar Nicholas I. It was clear that Russia was trying to establish control over Kabul, Herat and Kandahar, and thereby total dominance of the region. For Dost Mohammed, having lost the goodwill of the British and unwilling to compromise on their terms, the only option left was to seek counsel with Russia. Parleys with Vitkevich helped to get the Barakzai rulers of Kabul and Kandahar together, and facilitated an alliance of the two provinces with Persia, a move that worried Kamran Mirza, the Herat ruler. For the British, the line of the Indus that formed a definite boundary between the kingdoms of Lahore and Kabul seemed increasingly under threat, worse than a

. . . blockade of the Thames estuary by an enemy squadron.[61]

The Persian forces attacked Herat in 1837 and besieged the city for ten months. Eldred Pottinger, the young artillerist and the nephew of Henry Pottinger, was coincidentally in Herat at the time, having crossed over from Peshawar dressed as an Afghan with a sense of adventure and the allure of the land. By offering his services to the ruler of Herat, successfully helping the forces resist the Persians troops and eventually forcing them to withdraw in September 1838, Eldred became the 'Hero of Herat'. Although he was not given the knighthood as was Burnes, he was made a political agent at Herat with a

> . . . salary of one thousand rupees a month, backdated to the opening of the siege.[62]

By then Lord Auckland had sent a flotilla which occupied Kharg island in the Persian Gulf as an effective 'gunboat diplomacy'. And the Whig government in London, with its no-nonsense assertion of national interest championed by its foreign secretary Lord Palmerston, forced Nicholas I of Russia to give in. Both Simonich and Vitkevich who had set up the Iran-Kabul-Kandahar alliance were recalled to St Petersburgh and became personae non gratae.

A few months before Herat was regained, Lord Auckland had decided to exercise the war option instead of diplomacy of engagement with Dost Mohammed. To this effect, he signed a treaty with Ranjit Singh to restore Shah Shuja to the throne of Kabul. In a declaration 'on the assembly of the army of Indus' on 1 October 1838, Lord Auckland stated:

> It is a matter of notoriety, that the treaties entered into by the British government in 1832, with the Ameers of Scinde, the Nawab of Bahawulpore, the Maharaja Runjeet Singh, had for their object, by opening the navigation of the Indus, to facilitate the extension of commerce, and to gain for the British nation, in Central Asia that legitimate influence which an interchange of benefits would naturally produce.[63]

The grand army of the Indus, one of the largest assembled in recent times, was formed by coalescing the Bengal and Bombay armies with one contingent to

. . . march to Shikarpore and Candahar with the Shah [Shuja], and
another to Peshawur with the Shah's son [Shahzada].[64]

The Indus army with strength of over 50,000 men comprised the
Bengal division and the Bombay force under Lt Gen. John Keane.
It included two reserve divisions, the contingents of Shah Shuja
and his son Shahzada, and the Sikh contingent and Sikh army of
observation. Keane assumed the overall command from General
Henry Fane who, while having devolved the final preparation of the
Afghan War,

> . . . never had any enthusiasm and with which he constantly
> disagreed.[65]

To make the Indus army a force to reckon with, several staff
appointments were undertaken that included the best of the British
officers.[66] However, when the time came for the Indus army to launch
an attack on Afghanistan, Ranjit Singh withdrew his support and
refused to let Keane march through his territory. As a result, the British
troops had to find a circuitous route through Sindh and Balochistan
that proved treacherous, and the troops had to eventually retreat. Lord
Auckland had declared war with what would become an oft-repeated
slogan, 'the safety of the Empire was imperilled'. This time it was the
vulnerability along the Indus, and by the spring of 1839, the Indus
army occupied Afghanistan. Shah Shuja, the former monarch, was
restored to the throne in a ceremony in Kandahar where

> . . . under a canopy, sat Shah Shooja; the chief and general staff
> of the British army on his left, and half-a-dozen shabby-looking,
> dirty, ill-dressed Afghan followers on his right.[67]

The commercial diplomacy, spurred by navigation on the Indus
that Burnes was originally assigned by Lord Auckland, transformed
into a geostrategic necessity with the British seeking to establish a
friendly buffer state in Afghanistan.

Less than three years into the British intervention and with a string of tactical blunders and innate resistance of the Afghans to foreign occupation, a revolt erupted in 1841. Burnes met a gruesome end in a country he described as a

> . . . nation of children; in their quarrel they fight and become friends without ceremony.[68]

In the retreat and the subsequent slaughter of the British army, Burnes's decapitated body was left in the street to be gnawed by the dogs of the city. With the House of Commons erupting over the Afghan debacle, the shift of blame was a predictable outcome and in a search for scapegoats, Burnes became the perfect fall guy. John Hobhouse, who till recently had risen in the House to move a vote of thanks to Lord Auckland and praised the military operations and in particular mentioned Burnes as

> . . . one of the most able and intelligent officers that ever served in the Indian or any other army,[69]

was now pointing to Burnes's possible lack of judgement in assessing the Afghan situation. In the retreat of the British army and the annihilation, William Macnaghten, with whom Burnes had corresponded from Kabul and who was assigned to Kabul to guide the government of Shah Shuja after the British occupation, met a similar fate, brutally killed as he tried to negotiate his way out of the city. Some 7500 kilometres away in England, George Fitzclarence with the title Earl of Munster, the first royal blood to have come to India in 1817, possibly depressed over the British defeat and in a 'fit of insanity', shot himself in the head. In the aftermath of this humiliating defeat, the strategic and logistic importance of Sindh and Balochistan along with the derajat increased substantially as Ranjit Singh became increasingly unreliable to the British.

Navigation Steamrolled by Railways

Early interest in steam navigation emerged when a Steam Fund was established in Calcutta in 1823

> . . . to offer prizes for enterprising ventures by the Cape route, the Red Sea route or a river and overland route across the desert from the Gulf to the Mediterranean.[70]

The Bombay government in 1830 launched the steam vessel *Hugh Lindsay* to survey the Red Sea. Encouraged by the event, explorations of new routes for communication between England and India gathered momentum, resulting in a wealth of information and sketch maps on rivers and navigation. It also came against the backdrop of the fear of Russia moving southwards to Asia. This had become an obsession for the British and every Russian move was viewed with alacrity and trepidation. 'They have now steam boats on the Volga and Caspian Sea,' wrote Thomas Love Peacock, the chief examiner of the India House in 1829, known for his close association with the poet Percy Shelley. He further expressed,

> They will soon have them on the Sea of Aral and the Oxus, and in all probability on the Euphrates and the Tigris . . . They will do everything in Asia that is worth the doing, and that we leave undone.[71]

The possibility of steam navigation on the Indus basin was being considerably influenced by the East India Company's search for shorter routes to India through the Tigris-Euphrates Valley in Mesopotamia, where the British retained a good equation with the rulers. A new route, as an alternative to the considerably longer but surer Cape of Good Hope passage, was of critical importance for faster exchange of messages as well as for the transit of troops. Furthermore, it would reduce dependency on the Red Sea route through Egypt, where the French influence held sway.

In 1830, James W. Taylor, an officer in the East India Company, embarked on a journey from Bombay to England, halting at Baghdad where his younger brother Robert Taylor was a political agent. There he received a concession from the Pasha granting the

> . . . exclusive navigation of the Tigris for steam-vessels for the period of ten years.[72]

Taylor was attacked in Mosul and tragically died but the *firman* survived him and soon thereafter surveys were conducted on the lower reaches of the Tigris and Euphrates. One such study in 1831 was undertaken by Capt. Francis Chesney, on the Euphrates from Anah to Basra

> . . . on a raft kept afloat by inflated goat-skin.[73]

The following year, Chesney submitted a report to the government in London and encouraged the directors of the East India Company to consider postal service from London to Bombay by means of steamers on the Euphrates as an alternative route to the Suez Canal. Great hopes ensued, and in 1834, a grant of 20,000 pounds was sanctioned along with two steam vessels to navigate the Euphrates and Tigris. The rivers, however, proved treacherous and the navigation plans were aborted. In spite of Chesney's honest assessment of the unfeasibility of the navigation project, the Board of Control, in the interest of studying further the rivers and its drainage basin, decided to carry out work in Mesopotamia. The larger motive, however, was their desire to maintain their presence in the region which was strategically valuable. The prospects of the Indus being navigable drew exciting visions of steamers bobbing up and down the course of the river. Lt John Wood sailed a small commercial steamer, appropriately named the *Indus*, up the river. Unlike the wreckage on the Tigris, it was successful, and with that navigation on the Indus had flagged off. In less than a decade the British deployed

two steamers on the Indus—the *Planet* and *Satellite*—for military
operations against Sindh.

Sindh assumed strategic significance for the British both since
it commanded the entrance to the Indus and due to its position in
reference to the Punjab and Afghanistan. The primary objective to
obtain free and unrestricted navigation did not go amiss. In 1832,
permission for partial navigation of the Indus was obtained,[74] and in
1834, the ameers made further concessions but, safeguarding their
interests, introduced clauses imposing duties upon boats. With a
view to the Afghan War, as explained earlier, Lord Auckland had
concluded treaties with the ameers in 1839, securing to the East
India Company the right to occupy strategic points on the lower
parts and the mouth of the Indus. The treaty also contained an
important stipulation by which

> ... the Ameers of Scinde pledged themselves to act in subordination
> to the British Government in India, and not to enter into any
> treaty with any other powers without the concurrence of the
> British Government.[75]

Resultantly, the town of Karachi came under the hold of the British
and the city quickly developed as a military cantonment and a port
for exporting goods ferried by the Indus river from the town of Kotri.
With the conclusion of the first Afghan War in 1842, the ameers of
Sindh took advantage of the situation and disregarded the treaty
by levying tolls on the Indus. Not used to such gumption and with
bruised ego, Lord Auckland was unceremoniously recalled to London
and his successor, Edward Law, the Earl of Ellenborough, charged
the ameers with infractions and set new terms of negotiations.

Ellenborough (1842–4) had come to India with the famous
words, 'to restore peace to Asia'. But in his twenty-nine months of
governorship, he found himself occupied by wars. A man of great
presence of mind, Ellenborough was far too haughty to be a good
tenant of office. His arrogance and dismissive attitude towards
civil servants had exasperated the London bosses and with their

patience having run out, he was recalled, marking an end to one of the

> . . . shortest and stormiest . . .[76]

of a governor general's term. His policy was of establishing the British government as the paramount power

> . . . of the peninsula, is concerned in the internal order even of
> independent states, and may justifiably interfere in the interest of
> the general peace, to repress misgovernment and disorder.[77]

It was extraordinarily aggressive but generally accepted by all the successive administrators. By the time Ellenborough left, Sindh was annexed, Gwalior subjugated and with ruthless efficiency the Maratha army disbanded. Ellenborough had a great fascination for the Indus, matched only by his loathing for Russia, and long coveted the complete and unhindered opening of the river. He had recorded his dream of commanding British troops in a battle against the Russians on the banks of the Indus.[78] After the traumatic experience of the British troops and their families in the Afghan War, he firmly decided to make the Indus river his frontier and retain only those strong points on the river which ensured free navigation.

Riled over the ameers' obstinate refusal to concede to the new terms, Ellenborough plunged into war and gave instructions to seize Sindh. The British army from Bombay under Charles Napier with sheer rapine accomplished the task and, in August 1842, the entire territory of Sindh was captured and with it, the flowing Indus. The morally questionable nature of the annexation couldn't have been better expressed, and ironically so, by the man who led it, 'Our object in conquering India, the object of all our cruelties, was money,' Napier wrote and added,

> . . . we shall yet suffer for the crime as sure as there is a God in
> heaven.[79]

Interestingly a story did the round in 1844 courtesy the *Punch*, a recently established weekly magazine of humour and satire, that Napier had sent a despatch to his superiors in London with a one-word message, 'Peccavi', the Latin for 'I have sinned' and a perfect pun for 'I have Sindh'.

The British blamed the ameers for having broken the 1939 treaties which were, in the first place, unjustly forced upon them. It was, as events unfolded, merely a pretext for the British to enforce submission and control the Indus. One of the voices of caution to the annexation plan of Sindh was Major James Outram. As the political agent of both Lower and Upper Sindh from 1839 to 1842, he was engaged in negotiations with the ameers for relief from excessive tolls in the Indus waters, whereby quasi-amicable relations were established. Importantly, Outram advocated the unification of Upper and Lower Sindh and Baluchistan, bringing them under one administrative control. This in effect would strengthen the navigational management of the Indus as one continuous system of waterways, both from the commercial and the military points of view, and for that he had sought advice in his letters to John Colvin who was at the time investigating the Ganges Canal. Outram was one of the very early initiators of the unity of physical landscape that delineates from the political boundaries.

Worried over the takeover of Sindh and the instability and mistrust that it would bring about, Outram wrote with great force to Napier, condemning

> . . . the measures we are carrying out as most tyrannical—positive robbery.[80]

Outram's opposition, to which Napier was never convinced, reflected the contrarian views of some soldiers and a perceptible divide in the British approach to expansionism in the subcontinent. But like a good subordinate, when ordered to act on his duty, Outram heroically defended the residency at Hyderabad against the Baluchis causing Napier, in yet another interesting irony, to describe him as the

. . . Bayard of India.[81]

After his exploits, Napier became Sindh's first chief commissioner and governor (1843–7) and the bloodbath that accompanied the war led to eerie tranquillity and order. The ameers now ousted, Sindh became easily amenable to the British deftness of working with local rulers, setting up rule of law and, when required, using measured force to quell any semblance of resistance. Napier, for all his brutality in war, set up an efficient administration and from amongst the natives set up an effective police force, and in four years turned Sindh into one of the most well-governed provinces. Irrigation and barrages blossomed the fertile fields of the Indus basin into

. . . patchwork quilts of wheat, rice, cotton and fruit orchards.[82]

Navigation on the Indus continued to remain afloat despite the British exploratory disappointment on the Tigris and Euphrates. After the occupation of Sindh, a small flotilla was maintained at Kotri and, in 1859, the Indus Flotilla was established to run cargo from the port of Karachi to the northern Punjab city of Makhad in Attock district. At a time when railway communication in India was at an incipient stage, the Indus as a mode of transport was path-breaking and the reason why sooner or later, Sindh had to be occupied by the British.

Navigation got a beating when the railways made inroads into Sindh and Punjab. Bartle Frere, who was the commissioner of Sindh (1851–9), had a similar exuberance to Napier. Frere's long term in office was predominantly about rail, roads and communication. When he arrived in Sindh he noted dismally,

. . . not a mile of bridged or of metalled road, not a masonry bridge of any kind—in fact not five miles of any cleared road . . .[83]

Taking a cue from John Jacob, who had improved irrigation development when in-charge of Jacobabad district of the North

West Frontier and in Upper Sindh, Frere literally left no stone
unturned in expanding and upgrading the road and irrigation
network. By the time Frere left, almost 6000 miles of road were
constructed in Sindh. Irrigation projects too expanded with the
Bagari Canal, the Ghar Canal and the Eastern Nara Canal all
completed during 1855–9. Frere's point man, superintending
engineer, Lt J.G. Fife, was a driving force in Sindh's canal affairs.
Having observed the existing inundation canals and studied the
periods of paucity and excess of water, both of which hurt the
farmers and their cultivation, Fife developed link canals to bring
assured supply of water to the fields. His vision of a network of
canals in Sindh heralded in water projects like the Sukkur Barrage
and Jamrao Canal and revolutionized civil engineering as never
before.[84] It took many decades though, before his pet projects were
operationalized. Frere, on the other hand, encouraged a cohesive
Sindhi identity to ease administrative functioning and deter any
civil strife. Sindh was after all a strategic outpost from where the
British were observing the happenings in Afghanistan. Political
stability and order within the boundaries of Sindh was, therefore,
a premium.

A large part of Frere's tenure was at a time when Lord Dalhousie
(1848–56) was at the helm of affairs. The 'Maker of Modern India',
as Dalhousie was glowingly described, was certain that British
consolidation would require centralization of power. Known for
his sweeping reforms, Dalhousie created a separate public works
department under which irrigation works were undertaken on an
extensive scale and set about improving inland navigation on the
'silent' Indus. His celebrated Railway Minute of 1853 was a game
changer for communication in India. The detailed assessment that
was despatched to London ended all hesitancy on the suitability of
railway construction. With the first railway successfully, and with
much fanfare, opened between Bombay and Thane, Dalhousie
prepared a blueprint for railways in the Punjab and by the end of
1853, a 173 kilometres railway line was sanctioned between Karachi
and Kotri.

In a notable 'one-for-the-camera' moment, Frere, while inaugurating the work in 1858, grinned from ear-to-ear as he pushed a wheelbarrow at the site in Karachi. At the first sight of the steam engine huffing and puffing, the locals of Sindh thought it to be a *shaitan*. As described by the chief engineer of the project:

> . . . I drove the engine myself of course at a slow speed—the natives thronging all round, I was fearful of some accident. At last I thought I should frighten them away, so I blew the Engine Steam Whistle loudly. Instantly they all rushed back from the 'Demon'—falling over one another, much to our amusement.[85]

It took a few more years before the Karachi-Kotri line was finally opened in 1861. With Multan being connected to Delhi through Lahore and Amritsar in 1865 and later Karachi connected to Lahore in 1878, the Indus Flotilla gradually lost its steam and was reduced to carrying cargo 700 miles upriver between Kotri on the Indus and Multan on the Chenab.

While adverse river conditions, slow movement of cargo and requirement of more effective vessels, increasingly became challenges for inland navigation, the cost of transferring freight from river to railway was becoming unviable. John Brunton, the chief engineer in Sindh who supplied vessels to the Indus Flotilla, records on his journey from Kotri to Multan,

> . . . which took an agonising 34 days [that] I amused myself with my rifle shooting at crocodiles and alligators.[86]

Navigation on the Indus soon became redundant. It is interesting to observe that Chesney testified to a select committee of the House of Commons in 1834 that the Euphrates was not conducive for steam vessels and the hopes with regard to the Indus were far less sanguine than it was earlier.[87] The development of a railway network in north-western India had strategic intent, and by 1878, the railway had bridged the five rivers of the Punjab. The second Afghan War further pushed the necessity for extending the railways up to Peshawar and, by 1879, the line from Rawalpindi had arrived at Attock on the southern bank of the Indus. Bridging the Indus, however, remained a formidable challenge. It was only in 1883 that a bridge at Attock was constructed

> . . . 2 miles below the confluence of the Indus and the Kabul rivers, and 50 miles south-east of Peshawar, and forms the most strategic and commercial connection between the North West Frontier Province and other parts of India.[88]

COLONIZATION, CANALS *and* CONTESTATION

Engineering the Watercourse

With the death of Ranjit Singh in 1839, the Sikh power

> ... exploded, disappearing in fierce but fading flames.[1]

Some resistance continued until, in 1846, on the banks of the Sutlej, the British army under Hugh Gough won a decisive battle. The British annexed the kingdom of Lahore in 1849 and stamped their complete authority, marking an end to the Sikh kingdom. Not too long after, the first war for independence in 1857 led to a Parliament Act that swiftly ended the East India Company. What started as a harmless settlement in Surat in 1608 by some merchant adventurers with nothing more than a streak of European confidence, subsequently became a territorial powerhouse bearing the role of a civil authority. At the height of its dominance, the East India Company controlled nearly half of the world's trade, had a formidable army and built a powerful political network.

From 1858, all of India and its resources came under the control and supervision of the British government—they were unaccustomed to administrating a country on such a scale and vastness. The British undertook detailed topographical surveys to demarcate boundaries between the newly annexed native states and the existing British territories. The Indus basin, by the conquest of the Punjab, came under British control and was minutely surveyed, spurring movement of troops and travellers to many parts of northern India. The Punjab historically witnessed the existence of canals, which were largely inundation except for some which were perennial. But these had become inefficient and a need for extending a large number of perennial canal irrigation schemes was evident. A three-member Punjab Board of Administration was established in 1849 to administer and frame laws in Punjab. In its self-appraisal report (1849–51), the board noted,

> . . . taxation has been fixed, and the Revenue collected, how commerce has been set free, agriculture fostered and the national resources developed . . .[2]

The Lawrence brothers (Henry and John), as members of the board, helped to consolidate British rule in the Punjab. The Lawrences had much in common and their administrative actions in the Punjab were of great significance. Both were good in thought and judgement and inspired affection among the subordinates but differed in their style of functioning.[3] On the issue of revenue and finance towards public works projects, John, a man of facts and details, took a cautious approach. Henry, on the other hand, was far more progressive and wished to move ahead regardless of cost. As fierce sibling rivalry and bickering developed between the brothers, it was apparent that one of them would have to leave the Punjab. John Lawrence stayed on as his temperament suited the strict procedure of British rule, while Henry took a position in Rajputana and later left for England. The board was abolished in 1853, although John continued in much the same vein as the first chief commissioner of Punjab. In 1864, after having spent over three decades in India that included negotiating a treaty with the Afghan ruler, Dost Mohammad Khan, and successfully checking the spread of rebellion in Punjab in the wake of the '1857 Uprising' of the Indian soldiers, John Lawrence became the viceroy of India.

The fertile alluvium plains of great depth with favourable contours that naturally sloped to rivers lending itself

> . . . admirably to the construction of irrigation-works . . .[4]

ushered in a period of canal-cutting and defined the unquestionable quest of the British for constructing and maintaining public works in the Punjab. Irrigation in the Punjab plains was not an unhindered progress. While the probability of returns from such ventures was attractive, the purse string remained tight. It had dawned upon the civil engineers that canals had to generate revenue for them to be viable. Proby Cautley, tasked to examine the Ganges project that John Colvin had conceptualized, quipped,

> To deny the value of irrigation to agriculture in an arid country is like denying the value of manure to a European farmer.[5]

But he clearly observed that construction was only possible after assurance of an increase in the revenue.[6] The Ganges canal project was shelved for almost two decades before digging started in 1842, and by the time water started flowing in 1854, the canal became one of the largest irrigation projects in the world.

The search for revenue and the provision of markets for capital were strong drivers, if not the only reasons, for the British army to enter the Punjab. In 1848, before the Punjab was completely integrated into the British portfolio, a survey of the prospects for canal irrigation was undertaken. Colonel Richard Baird Smith, who served in the Irrigation Department in the North-Western Provinces and took part in the Sikh War and the 1857 siege of Delhi, worked out the details to apply all the waters of Punjab (12,000 cubic feet per second) to irrigate 8 million acres of land with an investment of £6,00,000 or Rs 60,00,000.[7] The cost estimate would have, for sure, put water to the project, except that the returns calculated were an astonishing £3.5 million per annum.[8] It was proposed that a main line of the canal would run through each of the three doabs (Bari, Rechna and Jetch) and from these main lines branches would be carried to the left and right, wherever required, to make Punjab

> ... one of the most profitable acquisitions ever made by the British Government.[9]

The emphasis on irrigation and hydraulic engineering required administrative structuring, and in 1849, the Punjab Public Works Department (PWD) was created under Robert Napier, who had worked with Cautley on the Eastern Yamuna Canal in the early 1830s and, after obtaining a three-year furlough in 1836, travelled the length of Europe studying irrigation works. On his return, he was posted at Sirhind where he was tasked to lay out a new cantonment near Ambala to provide accommodation to the British soldiers returning from Afghanistan. The cantonment was so impressive that it became a model referred to as the 'Napier's System' for all other cantonments to follow. Napier served as Punjab PWD's chief engineer until 1856, overseeing roads and public works, and later became India's commander-in-chief (1870–76).

The Punjab with its vast network of rivers had to be governed differently, and certainly not in the mercantilist ways which the British welcomed in the provinces of Bombay and Calcutta. The British sought to bring social change

. . . with lands changing hands from one social group to another.[10]

With their administrative experiences, the British had come to the conclusion that the basic social unit of Punjab was the 'brotherhood of landowners' in a village. As the British occupied the land, extensive irrigation developments were made available, encouraging large settlements in the western part of the Punjab that came to be known as the

. . . canal colonies.[11]

The virgin lands of the Punjab desert, which the British categorized as Crown-wasteland, also witnessed a large number of canal projects. Water reaching the fields and the yield from agriculture changed the socio-economic dynamic. In an important critique, S.S. Thorburn, a British official of considerable experience in the Punjab, wrote rather controversially:

The gradual transfer of ownership of the soil from its natural lords—the cultivators—to astute but uninfluential Hindu traders and bankers, is directly due to a system of law and administration created by ourselves, which, unless remedied in time, must eventually imperil the stability of our hold on the country.[12]

Criticism like that of Thorburn prevailed but so did the acceptance that the canal irrigation in the Punjab effectively transformed the region

. . . from desert waste, or at best pastoral savanna, to one of the major centres of commercialised agriculture in South Asia.[13]

The construction of the canals with new engineering methods, like a weir to control the flow of the rivers, took a leap forward under the supervision of the Punjab PWD. The Upper Bari Doab Canal (UBDC) from the Ravi was completed in 1860–1 and the Madhopur headwork on the same river soon followed. The Sirhind project was surveyed at Ropar to irrigate areas lying between Sutlej and Ghaggar and was completed in 1882. By then the Sidhnai or the Lower Ravi Canal was proposed, which opened in 1886. A few years later, in 1890, the Lower Swat Canal in the North West Frontier Province (NWFP) was in operation, allowing for a demand-driven irrigation system. Weir methods like the Khanki on the Chenab and Rasul on the Jhelum were built with engineering flourish unmatched before. Despite the challenges, the canals had positive

. . . expansionary forces.[14]

The expansion of canal-based irrigation ushered in a new phase of agricultural colonization in the Punjab, and by the last quarter of the nineteenth century, the total cultivable area was 28.11 million acres[15] and, according to R.D. Buckley, superintendent engineer,

. . . inundation canals of the Punjab aggregate some 2500 miles in length.[16]

Unlike the eastern part of the Punjab, the western side did not benefit from the monsoon rains and resultantly had little settlement. The nine canal colonies that developed as corollaries to the expansion of the canal network were located in the interfluves west of the Beas-Sutlej and east of the Jhelum rivers.[17] The drier West Punjab underwent an agrarian revolution as the five rivers, described by Thorburn as 'capricious tyrants', were harnessed into assets. Technological innovations were introduced in canal development with permanent headworks, head regulators and constructions of distributaries system that rapidly changed semi-arid wastelands into lush green fields. The entire Punjab became a

> . . . hydraulic society . . .[18]

generating revenues and suggesting

> . . . a paradigm which involved fundamentally realigning land and water in new sets of social, political and ecological relationships.[19]

A large recipient of lands in the canal colonies was the military that helped the British build a robust martial institution, thus adding a strategic dimension to it. Punjab steadily saw an impressive growth with expanded cultivated area, increased output, and a flourishing trade that reached not only parts of South Asia but far and away as well. From the 1880s onwards, the Punjab administration undertook vast irrigation works by creating a network of canals in the interfluvial tracts east of the Beas and Sutlej and west of the Jhelum rivers. The idea to create more agriculture rather than to improve it, led to advanced hydraulic engineering in the Punjab. The

> . . . transformation of six million acres of desert into one of the richest agricultural regions in Asia was a stupendous engineering feat that was seen as the colonial state's greatest achievement.[20]

Irrigation Debate

Many nationalists during the nineteenth century questioned the benefits of railway construction in India but few doubted that canal irrigation was an unreserved boon. Romesh Dutt, in his study on the famine of India, noted that the British were making a 'geographical mistake' by not adequately understanding the significance of irrigation and were more familiar with railways than canals.[21] Irrigation works were never short of debate. One such contestable point was on whether irrigation should be solely undertaken by the government or be shared with private companies. Another question related to whether loans were justifiable, and if they were, whether it should be contracted in India or England. Yet another, and which became a recurring theme during the latter half of the nineteenth century, was on the comparative importance of railways and canals. It required the forcefulness of the administrators and their courage of conviction to prioritize irrigation. Proponents like Arthur Cotton— who began his irrigation works in southern India in 1828 and often irritated his superiors by criticizing British apathy towards India— were the torchbearers of irrigation, pointing out that water was

> . . . as precious as gold in India, or rather it was more precious; as it was life.[22]

Likewise, John Lawrence, the viceroy (1864–9) who had little regard for pomp, power or patronage and valued being just and kind to the natives after his stint in Punjab, pledged to improve the life of the people in India. In a letter to the secretary of State for India, he expressed,

> . . . decide whichever way you think best; only give us irrigation, and give it us at once.[23]

In his period of administration in the Punjab, Lawrence had decided—in order to give canal development a push—to economize the privileges of the estates. By the time he demitted office, there was not a province in all of India in which surveys for canals had not been undertaken. New canals were approved, old ones remodelled and the system of canal management reformed. In each of the presidencies a public works department was set up and civil engineers were sent from England to supervise the works in India. Irrigation had now gained wider perspective and fit into the 'steel frame' of British administration not only in terms of financial returns but also as a legitimate means of consolidating British power. On the other hand, the effects of excessive centralization were beginning to weary the British administration, making collection of revenues and monitoring its expenditure none too easy. The recurring famines did not make things any better, but in each famine, there was a lesson to learn. A small famine in 1860 in the NWFP, for example, was actually mitigated by irrigation works and transportation of grains by railway. The famine in Bengal and Orissa in 1866–7 opened the eyes of the British administration towards irrigation-based agricultural advancement which, being capital-intensive, required bringing about equilibrium between revenue and expenditure.

It is a hard task,

Lord Mayo, who succeeded Lawrence, wrote to a friend in 1869, during his grapple with deficit,

> . . . but I am determined to go through with it, though I fear bitter opposition where I least expected it.[24]

His steadfastness and intervention to correct financial shortcomings and decentralize public finances led to separate central and provincial finances in 1870. The provincial governments were granted central revenues to administer services like health, education, policing and roads. In a despatch, Lord Mayo had famously written,

The Government of India is not only a Government but the chief landlord . . . Speaking generally the only Indian landlord who can command the requisite knowledge and capital is the State.[25]

Lord Mayo, regarded as the third most powerful person in the British Empire after the Queen and the prime minister, had laboured to reorganize finances, encourage railways, and promote irrigation. He was, however, murdered in 1872 in Port Blair on the Andaman Islands, a British penal colony, by a prisoner from the NWFP.[26] The incident, while it shook the British establishment, was with deliberate calculations hushed to deny any impression of growing resentment and unrest over the British rule. The process of decentralization that Lord Mayo had undertaken led to an era of legislative thinking and administrative reforms in the public works sector.

In probably one of the first acknowledgements of water as indispensable for development activity and with an aim to utilize and manage the resource, the Northern India Canal and Drainage Act of 1873 was enacted as a statutory guideline for state-led irrigation development in north India. While the act did not directly assert the state's ownership over surface waters, it recognized the right of the government to

. . . use and control for public purposes . . .[27]

and

. . . whereas it is expedient to amend the law relating to irrigation, navigation and drainage in the said territories.[28]

The access and use of waters which were earlier available to the 'native' as a customary system were now proclaimed by the state to be in public interests and were

. . . subjected to the discretion of the state and its officers.[29]

The act dealt with the construction and maintenance of public water works and had an important provision for dispute settlement and a right to appeal if unsatisfied with the sub-divisional canal officer as the arbiter.[30] The act also strengthened state control over surface water and weakened people's rights to engage in traditional practices. It was similarly demonstrated in the Punjab Minor Canals Act, 1905, by empowering the provincial government to acquire private canals

. . . with or without the consent of the owners . . .

to regulate the

. . . flow of water . . .

and to

. . . prohibit their obstruction.[31]

Despite the changed thinking towards irrigation, the railways continued to offer the most vibrant excitement, determined as it was by the capitalist development framework. In contrast, irrigation acquired a welfare-oriented emphasis and was thought to be a divine act. In 1865, the British administrator Richard Strachey,[32] who had served as an engineer officer in the Sutlej campaign (1845–46) also known as the First Anglo-Sikh War, wrote that canal irrigation was one action that the administration was bound to undertake for the people

. . . by all the laws of good government, of civilization, and of humanity . . .[33]

The canals became a symbol of 'moral responsibility' and the British were bent on dispelling the widespread notion of being repressive and inept. Sir Monier-Williams,[34] a Sanskrit scholar at Oxford

University, in a letter to the editor of *The Times* (23 January 1877) wrote that the canals would allow

> . . . even haters of the English rule to admit that no other Raj has conferred such benefits on India.[35]

The irrepressible Arthur Cotton, while addressing a gathering of members of the Indian Association in the newly laid building of the Manchester Corporation in December 1877, expressed that the canals were 'necessary for the development of Indian resources, and for the welfare of the people of that country'.[36] Consistent efforts were made to use canal irrigation to justify their rule in India. A sense of this impression can be gathered in the government's statement in 1889:

> It seemed essential to preserve the tradition of the Punjab as a country of peasant farmers. No other frame of society is at present either possible or desirable in the Province.[37]

To reduce British imperialism to a single cause is never a wise thought. There were other imperial purposes as well—both strategic and economic. On the one hand, the British wanted to secure the Punjab frontier, fearing the advancing Tsarist Empire. The competition and rivalry between the two great empires or the 'Great Game' spanning a good part of the nineteenth century came to an end in 1895, with the demarcation of the boundaries between Afghanistan and Russia—the Pamir Boundary Commission. The economic imperative, on the other hand, was a product of the reverberation felt from thousands of miles away in the American Civil War. Punjab's alluvial soils in its central and western belts turned into cotton fields to meet the 'cotton panic' of the British textile mills resulting from the falling cotton imports from America from 1860–62, described as the 'first raw material crisis' in the economic history.[38] The Punjab became the

> . . . reconstruction of the empire of cotton.[39]

By 1878–9, India's main exports were raw agricultural materials comprising cotton, jute, grains, opium, tea and indigo, whereas manufactured goods constituted only 6.5 per cent of the total exports.[40] The emphasis on agricultural produce became an imperial policy to ensure that India remained predominantly agricultural with its linked industries occupied in sugar refining, leather tanning, manufacture of cotton, silk, tobacco as well as the manufacture of paper, pottery, glass, soap, oils and candles.[41]

By the middle of the nineteenth century, irrigation development was confined to the lowlands of the Chenab, the Sutlej and the Jhelum. These were, however, non-perennial and insecure and required substantial repairs. For over nine decades, until 1940, extensive large-canal systems were constructed for the irrigation of the highlands between the Punjab rivers. Irrigated land expanded with UBDC providing waters to one million acres of land between the Ravi and the Beas which, by the time of Partition in 1947, was irrigating 1.5 million acres in Lahore, Gurdaspur and Amritsar. The Sirhind Canal at its peak commanded an irrigable area of 1.17 million acres.[42] Simultaneously, the old existing canal systems in the lowlands were extended. The pioneer in the great perennial irrigation development was the extensive Lower Chenab Canal taking off from the Khanki headwork on the Chenab, which opened in 1892, to irrigate vast barren tracts in the Rechna doab. D.G. Harris recounts,

> Such was the country . . . which the Lower Chenab Canal has converted from a wild mess into a garden.

Describing the canal, he writes,

> The canal carries the enormous discharge of 10,700 cubic feet a second, six times that of the Thames at Teddington, which is distributed by means of a system comprising 427 miles of main canal and branches and 2,243 miles of distributaries.[43]

In terms of sheer profit, C.H. Buck gleefully wrote,

> A few figures will show what a wonderful success the Chenab canal has proved financially . . . irrigates annually about 2,000,000 acres, while there is a net profit to the State of £450,000, which gives a return of 23 percent on the capital cost.[44]

The Sindh also witnessed upgradation of the existing inundation canals with construction of the flood banks on both sides of the lower Indus river that doubled annual irrigation from 1.5 million acres in 1875 to 3.0 million in 1900.[45] The NWFP (separated from the Punjab in 1901), as part of the larger strategic and economic integration of the British, saw unprecedented water developments on the west side of the Indus, with the Lower Swat Canal completed in 1885 to provide agricultural employment to the tribal areas, followed by the Kabul Canal in 1892. Before the onset of WWI, two more canals, the Paharpur Canal and the Upper Swat Canal, were built. And by the time of Partition, the four canals on the western side of the Indus irrigated 1.5 million acres of land.[46]

The famine crisis remained unabated in the second half of the nineteenth century of which three (1876–8, 1896–7 and 1899–1900) were large, resulting in millions of deaths. Each successive famine reinforced the need for a system of railways and irrigation and yet, ironically, the famine only got aggravated. The reason was more to do with the 'commercialization of agriculture' and its export to England rather than for domestic consumption. In fact, some of the concerned members of Parliament had asked the British government in 1897 to dispose such a sum of money that would enable the Government of India to carry out works to prevent the famines.

The forces of nature were certainly not on the side of Lord Curzon when he became the governor general and viceroy in 1899. India had barely recovered from the famine in 1897 when it was plunged into a far worse visitation affecting over

. . . 400,000 square miles and a population of 60 millions, of whom
25 millions belonged to British India, and the remainder to Native
States.[47]

As a result of the railway development nearing completion,
the irrigation plans received more money and attention. Yet
comparatively, the capital outlay on Indian railways up to March
1901 was £215,668,637 as against only £22,714,721 on irrigation
works.[48] Lord Curzon established a firm grip over the administration
and put his youthful energy in remedying the cumbrous system with
special attention on ensuring

. . . that no sources of water-supply or water-storage are neglected
or ignored in this country.[49]

Punjab had its pockets of famine though not widespread. Except
for the sand-swept *bagar* tract in its eastern parts which witnessed
the Chalisa famine in 1893–4 and the unirrigated areas in Hissar
which was hit by the famines in 1896–7 and 1899–1900, the
Punjab remained largely shielded by the existing irrigation system
which proved to make the land a 'granary or breadbasket' for other
provinces.

In an effort to mitigate famine, Curzon, in 1901, set up the
Indian Irrigation Commission (1901–3) and appointed Colin
C. Scott-Moncrieff to bring out a report on the irrigation of India as
a protection against famine.[50] Scott-Moncrieff had joined the Bengal
Engineers in 1856 and later served on the Eastern and Western
Yamuna Canals as well as the Ganges Canal. His study tour of the
works of irrigation in Italy, southern France and Spain in 1867–68
led to a masterly report that underlined the

. . . value of every drop of water.[51]

And as Scott-Moncrieff gratifyingly wrote about irrigation in India,

. . . how often sound sense and energy are to be met with in the absence of any great professional knowledge.[52]

The Commission highlighted the need for creating more cultivable areas to counter famine. It studied the available flow data of the rivers of the Indus basin, coming to a conclusion that there was great potential for the expansion of irrigation throughout the basin to make the Punjab 'grain surplus' and export the surplus to the famine-prone areas. With the prevailing irrigation facilities in Punjab, it easily concluded that canals should be expanded along with the extension of the railways and roads. Probably for the first time in the history of water development, attention was cast on the volume of surface water that flowed unutilized to the sea. The Commission also noted on Punjab:

> There is no province in which, taken as a whole, the direct profits of irrigation works, as expressed in the returns realized on their capital cost, have been so high, or in which new protective works can be proposed with the same confidence in their remunerativeness as financial investments.[53]

This was an interesting observation as in 1879, during the works of the Famine Commission set by Lord Lytton, the Commission had refuted irrigation works as a

> . . . universal famine preventative . . .[54]

and labelled the proponents of irrigation as 'quacks' seeking significant public expenditure on famine prevention.[55]

The canal systems in the Punjab, built from the mid-1880s, were in their function subjected to a control mechanism in which the locals ceded the release and timing of the water to a non-local distant player or the upstream controller, resulting in an unpredictable water supply. This was particularly witnessed in the winter months when the water levels were low. A dependency-monolith matrix emerged in which the British had command over the physical infrastructure, or, in other words, water became an instrument of control. Indian agriculture from time immemorial had to gamble with the monsoon. In the Punjab, with the advent of widespread canals, it had to also

. . . gamble with the canal.[56]

The irrigation department faced great constraint in delivering adequate and timely water supplies to individual colonies or *chaks*. The engineers had successively tightened the distribution of waters to the colonies by reducing supplies of the distributaries channel.

Tensions started to emerge between the Chenab Colony and the provincial government over the Punjab Land Alienation Act of 1900—the

. . . greatest single piece of social engineering ever attempted in India.[57]

Subsequently, and with no inclination to dialogue or appease, the provincial government introduced the Canal Colonization Bill in 1906, which provided for transfer of property of a person after his death to the government if he had no heirs.[58] The bill entitled the government to sell the land/property to any private or public developer. This went against the prevailing social norms of inheritance and further accentuated discontent among the urban class. With successive years of low farm returns and an increase in water rates, the unrest that started from Chenab Colony, described as the beginning of the freedom movement, became a serious crisis for the British with leaders like Lala Lajpat Rai, who called for 'extreme measures', and Sardar Ajit Singh weighing in behind the protests. The British were, of course, experienced and adroit in dealing with agitation and equally efficient in finding measures to quell the uprisings, as the 1907 Punjab disturbances showed.[59]

What became a mass agitation finally ended with the deportation of Lajpat Rai and Ajit Singh to Mandalay jail in Burma.

Such was the scale of transformation being witnessed that the *Imperial Gazetteer of India* (1909) observed:

> Irrigation has greatly developed lately; and there are green spots about the Indus river and the newly-spread network of the Punjab canals, which are once again slowly but surely altering the character of the landscape, if not of the climate.[60]

A number of projects were placed for evaluation before the Scott-Moncrieff Commission in 1901, one of which was the Triple Canal Project in the Punjab, the most ambitious hydraulic engineering project in the Indus basin. The Commission deliberated on this project in the backdrop of a number of significant interventions that had been proposed and operationalized on the rivers in the Indus basin. Of note was the Marala Barrage in 1887, constructed to supply water to the Upper Chenab Canal (which opened in 1915). On similar principles of the Lower Chenab Canal (which came into operation in 1892), a scheme in 1897 was sanctioned to irrigate the Chaj doab between the Chenab and the Jhelum from a weir at Rasul on the Jhelum river, called the Lower Jhelum Canal. This was opened in 1901.There were, however, critical flow variations that needed to be corrected. One such correction was to supplement the Ravi from the two western rivers—the Jhelum and the Chenab.

The other projects that came up for discussion in the Commission were the Sutlej Valley Project, the Thal Canal and the Haveli Canal. The two link canals to augment the flow of the Ravi were to provide irrigation water to the Crown Lands as well as the two colonies of the Upper Jhelum and Upper Chenab. The Sutlej Valley Project, through a series of channels, was to provide both perennial and seasonal irrigation to Nili Bar Colony and to the princely states of Bahawalpur and Bikaner.[61] Sindh raised concerns over the possibility of the Punjab projects diverting the waters from its rivers. It was probably for the first time that down riparian fears and apprehensions were expressed over upstream extraction and uses of water. Sindh thus proposed the Sukkur Barrage Canal Project to mitigate the province water challenge.

The secretary of the State of India, William St John Brodrick, whose strained relations with Lord Curzon despite a longstanding friendship was quite talked about during the time, sanctioned the Triple Canal Project in 1905. It had an intricate plan to transfer water from one river to another, the first such inter-basin transfer to be taken at such a scale. The objective of the project was to irrigate the vast rural tract of the Lower Bari Doab (LBD) lying between the Sutlej and Ravi rivers. Ideally the waters could have been drawn from the two rivers to the LBD, but the waters of the Ravi were already assigned to the Upper Bari Doab. Initially it was suggested that the waters of the Sutlej be tapped near Harika below the confluence of the Sutlej with Beas, but the owners of the southern Punjab floodplains in Bahawalpur, fearing loss of water benefits, raised fierce objections.

The Punjab farmers' agitation was already on the boil and fearing another front of discontent opening up, two British officials, Sir J. Wilson, the Punjab settlement commissioner, and Colonel S.L. Jacob, chief engineer of the Punjab PWD, decided against tapping the Sutlej and considered shifting the waters of the Jhelum to the LBD. Jacob penned his proposal as thus:

> Make a channel from the Chenab river (at Marala) to the Ravi (at Balloki) to irrigate the LBD. Then to make up the deficiency in the Chenab supply, make a channel from the Jhelum (at Mangla) to the Chenab (at Khanki).[62]

While the Commission eventually agreed to this, it was equally concerned with the fears expressed by Sindh over water being diverted in the Punjab, and put forward the Thal Canal Project to irrigate the Sindh doab. Jacob argued that a better solution would be to consider storage dams, as much of the water in the Sindh flowed into the Arabian Sea unutilized. His view influenced the Commission to prioritize the competing projects and temporarily put aside the Thal Canal Project until the completion of the Triple Canal Project. Likewise, the long years of demand by Sindh for constructing a weir across the Indus at the Sukkur-Rohi site was also shelved, at least temporarily, citing inordinate cost and technical difficulties.

The details of the execution of the Triple Canal Project were handed to John Benton. Having been trained at Coopers Hill, Benton joined the Indian PWD in 1873 and, by 1892, become first grade executive engineer. He had gained considerable knowledge of the Punjab terrain with his involvement in the Bari Doab and the Sirhind canals and later, when posted to Burma, he remodelled the canal at Mandalay. When he came back to India in 1902, he set about executing the Triple Canal Project. Punjab had made great strides in irrigation and in the last three decades the annual irrigated areas had increased from 2.5 million acres to 7.5 million acres and the net revenue returns on the capital expenditure

. . . had risen from nothing to over 15 percent.[63]

However, the principal objective was to bring water to a 1.5 million acre of unutilized land lying east of central Punjab. All the sources of water from the Ravi, Chenab, Beas and Sutlej, near at hand, were either utilized or reserved for other tracts.

What caught Benton's attention was the surplus water of Jhelum but it was 200 miles further north from the Ravi. Unfazed, Benton carefully studied the hydrography, and through complex calculations, he engineered the Triple Canal Project (1905–17) and oversaw its construction. The first two canals, the Upper Chenab Canal and the Upper Jhelum Canal, commenced in 1905 while the third canal, the Lower Bari Doab, started two years later in 1907. Each of these canals was 400 miles in length and had a total of 3000 miles of distributaries and a carrying capacity of 250 cusecs.[64] The entire project was completed in 1917, with an expenditure of £8,000,000. The principal objective of the Triple Canal Project was to expand the cultivable area without compromising on the waters of the

Sutlej–Beas for irrigation in the downstream areas of Bikaner and Bahawalpur. By 1940, the project had exceeded the initial target. Such was the expanse and diversion of the Triple Canal Project that even the landowners of the southern Punjab flood plains and the Bahawalpur state objected to it. In order to find a solution to the emerging upstream and downstream complexities, the Scott-Moncrieff Commission decided, for the first time, to adopt an Indus basin-wide approach.[65]

Spurred by the success of the Triple Canal Project, the Punjab Irrigation Department planned to remodel existing canals and construct new ones in the Sutlej Valley. The banks of the Sutlej on either side had a series of inundation canals that watered 1.5 million acres of land in the states of the Punjab, Bahawalpur and Bikaner. The land on the right bank of the river was in the British-Punjab territory, while that on the left bank was in the states of Bahawalpur and Bikaner. While the Sutlej Valley Projects were being thought through, the grievances of the Sindh state continued to draw inadequate response, more so as the technical experts firmly concluded that the upstream withdrawal would not affect or cause any 'substantial harm'.

Sindh's proposal for a structure on the Indus at Sukkur–Rohi, although debated like earlier times, was put on the backburner. Despite Sindh's objection, the government approved the Sutlej Valley Projects in 1921, and the work commenced a year later and was completed in 1933. With four barrages and eleven canals, this expanded the area of cultivation to a total of 7.581 million acres of which 4.791 was in British Punjab; 2.140 million in Bahawalpur and 0.650 million in Bikaner.[66] The objective of the Sutlej Valley Project was to provide perennial irrigation and thereby expand cultivable areas through a series of weirs or barrages across the river and by introducing regulators at the canal heads. The four barrages were the Ferozepur, the Suliemanki, the Islam and the Panjnad. Each of them had canals 'taken-off', and amongst them, the Ferozepur headworks became an important feature of the post-Partition canal water dispute between India and Pakistan.

Table 1: Chronology of major irrigation works on the Indus basin during British India (1859 to 1947)

Year	Plans/projects	Main aspects
1859	Completion of the Upper Bari Doab Canal	Canal irrigation development began to provide water for kharif (summer) crops and residual soil moisture for rabi (winter) crops.
1872	Completion of the Sirhind Canal	From Rupar Headworks on Sutlej.
1886	Completion of the Sidhnai Canal	From Sidhnai barrage on Ravi.
1892	Completion of the Lower Chenab Canal	From Khanki on Chenab.
1901	Lower Jhelum Canal	From Rasul on Jhelum.
1885–1914	Lower and Upper Swat, Kabul river and Paharpur Canals in Khyber Pakhtunkhwa (Pakistan)	Completed during 1885 to 1914.
1907–1915	Triple Canal Project	Constructed during 1907–15. The project linked the Jhelum, Chenab and Ravi rivers, allowing a transfer of surplus Jhelum and Chenab water to the Ravi.
1933	Sutlej Valley Project	Completed in 1933. Four barrages and two canals, resulting in the development of the unregulated flow resources of the Sutlej river and motivated planning for the Bhakra reservoir.
1930s	Sukkur barrage and its system of seven canals	Considered to be the first modern hydraulic structure on the downstream Indus river.
1939	Completion of Haveli and Rangpur Canal	From Trimmu Headworks on Chenab
1947	Completion of the Thal Canal	From Kalabagh Headworks on Indus

Source: 'Transboundary River Basin Overview—Indus', *Food and Agricultural Organization of the UN Aquastat Report*, Version 2011, p.11.

Disputes and Settlements

The Government of India Act 1858, which transferred power from the East India Company to the Crown, created a position of secretary of State for India with the rank of a British cabinet minister who was vested with complete control over the Indian administration. British India was divided into provinces and princely states, which were allowed a measure of autonomy and had their own laws and courts but were brought under the suzerainty of the Crown on matters of foreign affairs. From 1858 to 1921, issues relating to irrigation in the provinces fell under the purview of the secretary of State.

In 1865, the secretary of State, Charles Wood, in connection with the Sirhind Canal Project, issued a despatch that only those projects should be entertained that

> . . . can be devised irrespective of the territorial boundaries . . .

and

> . . . the benefits of which the native States should be allowed to participate on like terms with our own subjects.[67]

The following year, Richard Strachey was appointed the first inspector general of irrigation to evolve a set of uniform principles in the irrigation sector. The Sirhind Project commenced in 1868, and in 1873 the parties concerned—the government of Patiala, Nabha and Jind—reached an agreement with the British government. Irrigation projects were now a matter of public works. This was in sharp contrast to the general apathy of the company towards public undertakings to which Arthur Cotton had scathingly commented,

> Do nothing, have nothing done . . . let the people die of famine, let hundreds of lakhs be lost in revenue for want of water or roads, rather than do anything.[68]

In an important decision on the irrigation dispute in the Punjab, the secretary of State, George Hamilton, in 1897 directed the Montgomery canal project for the Sutlej river not to be put into effect

> ... without providing for the legitimate claims to irrigation water made by the state of Bahawalpur, a lower riparian.[69]

Hamilton's directive recommended additional studies to determine the claims of existing irrigation in several of the lower riparian provinces on the Indus basin,[70] and subsequently the Montgomery project was postponed. The year was an exceptional one for more than one reason. It was the sixtieth year of Queen Victoria's accession to the throne of England and the fortieth year since the transfer of the Government of India to the Crown. India was in the grip of a severe famine and widespread pestilence, prompting Hamilton to acknowledge in the House of Commons:

> The year will long be notable for the continuous series of misfortune and difficulty which it has presented to India. In no year since [1857] have there been so many troubles packed so closely together in so short a time.[71]

Serious questions were raised on the government's concern for the people in India, and Parliament expressed its disaffection on the administration's callousness and neglect that had left 40 million Indians in a state of semi-starvation. To this, Hamilton resolutely expressed:

> We have established codes of law and procedure far simpler and more expeditious than those in force in this country, and under their influence India is rapidly becoming the most litigious community in the world.[72]

Ironically, as the famine spread and became the severest that India had ever known, the diamond jubilee of Queen Victoria's reign was celebrated with great pomp and show in England and as a 'benevolent' gesture by the Queen, 19,000 prisoners were pardoned in India! The secretary of State for the colonies, Joseph Chamberlain, a leading imperialist and the man behind the lavish commemoration, observed on the Empire's role:

> A sense of possession has given place to a different sentiment—the sense of obligation. We feel now that our rule over these territories can only be justified if we can show that it adds to the happiness and prosperity of the people, and I maintain that our rule does, and has, brought security and peace and comparative prosperity to countries that never knew these blessings before.[73]

Canal irrigation had made great strides, and by 1900–01, the Punjab province had accomplished a total irrigated area of 6,000,551 which was slightly lower than Madras (6,579,284 acres), the highest irrigated province in India then.[74] As the irrigation network expanded with the Triple Canal Project, the Indus basin presented considerable challenge as its physical unity was being constantly intervened by its political boundaries. The states of Bahawalpur and Bikaner and the province of Punjab gathered to discuss the modalities of water distribution of the Sutlej in 1918 with Sir Claude Hill as the representative of the government. Hill served as the finance member of the viceroy's Executive Council and later became the chairman of the Joint War Committee in India. Hill's suggestion, which was accepted by the riparian actors, put forth:

> In considering the method of disposing of the waters made available for irrigation by the Sutlej Valley Project, the general principle is recognised that these waters should be distributed in the best interests of the public at large, irrespective of Provincial or State boundaries, subject always to the provision that established rights are fully safeguarded or compensated for, and that full and prior recognition is given to the claims of riparian owners and that their rights in the existing supplies or in any supplies which may

hereafter be made available in the Sutlej river below the junction of the Beas and Upper Sutlej are fully investigated and are limited only by the economic factor.[75]

The 1918 directive was developed in the context of the British government providing a measure of political unity by having sovereignty over the Indian provinces and handling the foreign affairs of the Indian independent states. Hill had clearly stated that

> . . . as between Bahawalpur State and British Government, the question was really a political one in which the Paramount Power was not only the natural judge of the case but was also the sole owner of the gift solicited.[76]

Paramountcy had no legal basis but was a matter of expediency. Thus, without overemphasizing the principle of law, the 1918 directive, as a policy, urged the province of Punjab and the states of Bahawalpur and Bikaner to settle their disputes by agreement. Upon close examination, the 1918 directive, like the 1865 order by Charles Wood, was political in character. It follows, therefore,

> . . . that the decisions of the Secretary of State for India in 1865 and of Sir Claude Hill in 1918 cannot be equated with any legislative practice or any legal principle.[77]

The 1918 directive later became the guiding principle of the Indus (Anderson) Committee in 1935.

With the constitutional reforms under the Government of India Act 1919, irrigation was made a provincial subject under the purview of the Government of India instead of the secretary of State for India. With the end of WWI, a number of new schemes and projects were put forward for the development of irrigation in different parts of the Indus basin. Despite Hill's directive in 1918, which was, as stated, political in nature, it was hardly surprising that concerns over irrigation withdrawal in the upper reaches of the rivers in Punjab affecting the scope of the projects lower down the system, particularly in Sindh, were raised. Further, the 1919 Report of the Indian Cotton Committee marked a critical intervention on the position of Sindh in the water utilization debate vis-à-vis Punjab. The report noted that the works under the Triple Canal Project, including the planned Sutlej River Projects, were important but also gave a studied observation on the need to construct the Sukkur Barrage as early as possible.[78]

The Act of 1919, seen as a first attempt by the British to introduce self-governance in India, had referred to eventual dominion status in a carefully ambiguous way, and put forth a federal structure with provincial legislatures. Annie Besant had famously described it as

. . . unworthy of England to offer and India to accept,[79]

and the Indian National Congress, not entirely amused, had rejected it. However, it formed the basis for the Government of India Act, 1935, and ultimately the Constitution. In Part II-Provincial Subjects (7), the 1919 Act laid down:

Water supplies, irrigation and canals, drainage and embankments, water storage and water power; subject to legislation by the Indian legislature with regard to matters of inter-provincial concern or affecting the relations of a Province with any other territory.[80]

Under the act, water supplies and development became a provincial subject and the Government of India's responsibility was confined to advice, coordination and settlement of disputes over the right on the water of interprovincial rivers. On the recommendations of the 1919 Act, the Public Works Department was merged with the Department of Industry in 1923 and came to be known as 'Department of Industries and Labour'. Irrigation and power fell under the purview of this department. Later, the Central Board of Irrigation was constituted in 1927.[81]

Lower Riparian Angst

The barren lands of Sindh classified as 'hot desert climate' finally got the go-ahead for the long-awaited Sukkur Barrage Project, first conceived by Fife in 1868. The work started in 1923 and was commissioned to irrigation in 1932 with its system of seven canals serving 2.95 mha in the lower Indus plain.[82] It seems unlikely that the project would have gathered momentum had it not been for the Report of the Indian Cotton Committee and the Act of 1919. One of the reasons that Col Jacob could not agree to the Sukkur Project earlier was the lack of sufficient data on the available supplies of the Indus and its tributaries to ascertain whether the barrage was required. Thomas Ward, the inspector general of irrigation, decided to set up discharge observation stations on the Indus and its tributaries in 1920, and a year later, the Indus Discharge Committee was constituted to observe the daily flow of the rivers at select places. The 'system of gauging' recommended by Ward became an important knowledge source on flow and measurement of rivers to determine whether the sequence of projects proposed by the Punjab—the Thal, the Haveli and the Bhakra—would not impact the necessary supplies for the Sukkur Barrage.[83]

Like Sindh, the state of Bikaner, once a bustling part of the Harappan civilization with famed settlements like Kalibangan and Rangmahal but which unfortunately had turned into vast stretches of desert land, was also venting its grievances against the upstream withdrawals of Punjab. Maharaja Ganga Singh, the ruler who had seen the great famine of 1889–90 wipe out almost one-fifth of Bikaner's population, was determined to bring the waters from the Sutlej in Punjab to make the desert bloom and banish famine. Back in 1885, Col Dyas, who was posted in the irrigation department of Punjab, had mooted the idea of a canal to Bikaner. This was, not surprisingly, shelved due to strong resistance from the Punjab and the state of Bahawalpur, the upper riparians. With great determination Ganga Singh revived the project in 1903, and hired the expertise of Dunlop Smith, the Famine Commissioner of

Rajputana, and A.W.E. Stanley, an engineer, to study the feasibility
of the project. For seventeen years the Maharaja lobbied with the
British government before, in 1920, the Sutlej Valley Tripartite
Agreement between the three provinces (Punjab, Bahawalpur and
Bikaner) was signed which eventually led to the construction of the
Gang Canal (also called the Ganga Canal).

The agreement was historic in many ways and determined a
basic principle,

> ... that these waters should be distributed in the best interests of the
> public at large, irrespective of Provincial or State boundaries . . .[84]

The 1920 Tripartite Agreement concluded a percentage-sharing
formula of water distribution on a daily basis but ran into difficulties
when the flow of the Sutlej became low. This was reworked on a
rotational basis and

> . . . the distribution programme was prepared, published and
> distributed to each village so as to appraise the cultivators about
> the water supplies they were likely to receive for the next six
> months (Rabi crops), during each 10-days period.[85]

The contribution of the Bikaner army in WWI and Ganga Singh's
reputation and prestige as a member of the Imperial War Cabinet
and a signatory to the Treaty of Versailles in 1919 went a long way in
influencing the British in delivering the waters to the parched lands
of Bikaner. Under the Tripartite Agreement, an 84.5-mile-long
concrete canal with 2144 cubic feet of water per second[86] was planned
on the Sutlej from Ferozepur at a cost of Rs 5.5 crore. The canal
with its bed and sides lined up with concrete to conserve water and
prevent waterlogging was unique. Complementing the canal, a 157-
mile railway line was proposed to connect the various canal colonies.
The project commenced in 1925, and two years later, Viceroy Irwin
inaugurated the Ganga Canal, named after the Maharaja, with great
fanfare. Describing the magnificent ceremony, which had Madan

Mohan Malviya, a bitter critique of British economic policy, and a host of luminaries in attendance, the chief minister of Datia State termed it

. . . a miniature of Delhi Durbar.[87]

The Ganga Canal, an 'infinity of skill and labour', transformed the region as never before.

The Punjab, which had historically enjoyed priority in water development, found itself in an unaccustomed situation in which the lower riparian concerns were contesting and impeding its projects. Its effort to establish 'prior claims' to the available water by recalling the Sindh Sagar Doab (older name of the Thal Project) Colonization Act, passed by the Punjab Legislative Assembly in 1902 to irrigate 1.71 million acres of wasteland from the

. . . commencement of work,[88]

failed to get approval by the Government of India in 1919. Undeterred, the Punjab government in 1924 reopened the project as a small experimental canal of 750 cusecs (cubic foot per second) withdrawal, which

. . . they opined, would yield the information necessary for working out the details of the larger scheme.[89]

But with Bombay strongly objecting to it, the Punjab decided to drop the proposal only to, with some technical adjustment, resubmit. Yet again, Bombay, while considering the reworked proposal, emphatically refused to agree to it. In 1929, the Government of India gave their final conclusion in support of Bombay:

That, faced as they are with the unknown effect of the withdrawals which will be necessary for the supply of the Sutlej Valley Canals in the Punjab, the Government of Bombay have the right to object to further withdrawals from the Indus or its tributaries unless and until definite proof can be given that the supplies necessary for the Sukkur Barrage Project will not be endangered thereby.[90]

The Punjab government, while convinced that the Thal Project would not endanger the water schemes in Sindh was, nonetheless, prepared to refer the matter to an impartial committee to which Bombay reluctantly agreed but

. . . reserved the right to appeal.[91]

The Government of India referred the matter to the secretary of State, who while noting that the Sukkur canals had not yet begun to irrigate, stated

. . . that it would be unreasonable to reopen the question.[92]

In 1929, the Indus Discharge Committee (IDC) found out that with the available data, the Thal Project could not be taken up without materially affecting the supplies allocated to the Sukkur Barrage and advised the Punjab that

. . . no further withdrawals should be permitted for ten years by which time the results of the observations at the various discharge stations would be better known and adequate discharge data would have become available.[93]

The Thal Project was put under abeyance and the Haveli Project was shelved.

The Sukkur Barrage was eventually completed in 1932, marked by long years of successful opposition by Bombay to the Punjab's upstream projects. But no sooner had the Sukkur become operationalized than the princely state of Khairpur on the Indus, which enjoyed adequate inundation supply from its own canals, found itself in a situation of being water strained. In the proposal stage of the Sukkur Barrage, perennial supplies were assured to Khairpur but when the barrage was opened, only kharif and early rabi supplies were allowed. Khairpur in disappointment protested against the

> . . . non-provision of a perennial supply to their canals.[94]

This was immediately addressed by the Bombay government as the water was available and Khairpur was allowed

> . . . to withdraw certain *rabi* supplies throughout the full season,
> as a temporary measure, until the question of a perennial supply
> was decided.[95]

As the Thal Project got enmeshed in issues relating to utilization and distribution of water, a proposed storage dam at Bhakra came up for consideration by the Punjab government. The IDC took a favourable decision in 1929 that

> . . . the solution of the problem of further extension of irrigation in
> the Punjab lay primarily in the conservation of the *kharif* supplies
> which were running waste to the sea.[96]

It, however, required investigation on the possible impact of lowering water levels on the inundation canals in Sindh. The investigation submitted in 1930 found that there would be no negative effects downstream. However, the Bhakra Dam was given low priority, and it took almost two decades of planning and assessment before, in 1948, an independent India finalized the project. In the meantime, the government of Punjab concentrated its attention on projects in the predominantly Muslim-dominated western region, such as Sutlej Valley, Haveli and the Thal, to irrigate the vast Crown wastelands.

There were other difficulties experienced by the interested parties in the Indus basin that were dealt with by the IDC in 1932 before the appointment of the Indus Commission in 1935.

For example, the NWFP request to allow additional withdrawal from the Indus for the Paharpur Canal was resolved. However, Bahawalpur and Bikaner, the signatories to the 1920 Tripartite Agreement (along with Punjab), faced some disconcerting challenges related to irrigated land and sufficiency of supplies. On Bahawalpur, the IDC recommended efficiency of water utilization in one of the early thinking, if not the first, on water management, stating,

> Large areas proposed for irrigation should be abandoned, because the soil was such that it could not economically be brought under cultivation.[97]

Punjab as an 'act of grace' was permitted withdrawals at Panjnad owing to the unutilized waters of the shelved Haveli Project, but the concession was allowed only up to 1935. For Bikaner, on the other hand, the insufficiency of water in the Sutlej, particularly during the early kharif time, was far more serious and required the other signatories of the 1920 Tripartite Agreement to share water from their non-perennial canals as a goodwill gesture. Bikaner, as a matter of urgency, strongly claimed for the revision of the agreement and, considering that Bahawalpur, as per the IDC observation, had a reduced area suitable for cultivation than stipulated under the agreement, it sought a redistribution of waters.

By 1935, the issues between upstream and downstream provinces had come to such a pass that the Government of India convened the Indus Committee under the chairmanship of F. Anderson, chief engineer of the United Province. Each of the

> Interested Parties[98]

was invited to nominate one member

> . . . who might bring with him such advisers as he deemed necessary.[99]

The Anderson Committee submitted its recommendations the very year it was set up, which were accepted by the government.[100] The committee extensively dealt with the disputes between the provinces and broadly expressed against any fresh withdrawals of water by the Punjab, which may

> . . . affect not only the existence but also the future rights . . . over the waters of the Indus waters.[101]

It observed that in

> . . . allocating water, the greatest good to the greatest number must be sought, without reference to political boundaries,

emphasized

> . . . economic aspect should be considered . . .

but disallowed

> . . . acquiring of rights in water in perpetuity . . .

and most interestingly called for

> . . . modification to meet the altered conditions.[102]

The Anderson Committee was not a statutory body and did not in any manner enunciate legal principles. The objective was clearly to arrive at a compromise. With no legal emphasis, the committee followed the redistribution formula, giving more water at Ferozepur to Bikaner by reworking the supplies in the Gharra reach of the Sutlej. Likewise, it gave more water to Bahawalpur at Panjnad by waiving the restriction imposed under the 1920 Tripartite Agreement.

Following the Cotton Committee (1919), the Government of India Act (1919) and the Anderson Committee (1935), the

Government of India Act 1935, which came into force in 1937, became another important legislation for down riparian states. Until then, the rivers as they flowed through many administrative units lacked customary law governing them and the policy of equitable distribution only

> . . . could be enforced by the central government, since it had
> executive power to impose its decisions in all inter-provincial and
> interstate disputes.[103]

The subject of water supplies, irrigation canals and water storage was no longer a 'reserved subject' as per the Act of 1919 but a 'provincial subject' as per the Act of 1935. *Inter alia*, the act laid down the principle that no province could be given an entirely free hand in respect of a common source of water and decided that water disputes should be resolved by no less an authority than the governor general.[104] Soon after, in 1937, the Department of Industry and Labour was bifurcated into the Department of Communication and Department of Labour. The latter was assigned the work relating to irrigation and power. Thereafter, on the recommendation of the Secretariat Re-organization Committee, the Department of Works, Mines and Power was created which looked after the subject of 'Irrigation and Power'.

Punjab's eternal passion for water development projects, despite a series of observations from 1919 to 1935 that restricted fresh withdrawals and diversions, remained unabated. However, frequent deadlocks suggested policy incoherence between the need for a centralized authority and the local freedom of action in irrigation works. The proposal of the Bhakra Dam by Punjab that called for storage on the Sutlej compelled Sindh, by now separated from the state of Bombay in 1935, to register its complaint in 1939. The governor general appointed a commission in September 1941 under the chairmanship of B.N. Rau, a judge at the Calcutta High Court, to investigate the complaint. After the first sitting in Shimla of the Indus Commission, as it was referred to, the disputants (Sindh, Punjab, Bahawalpur and Bikaner) asserted their rights to an equitable distribution of waters of the Indus and some of its tributaries.

Rau, an eminent jurist, was never one to be amused by half-baked generalities and had a mind to treat themes with scrupulous accuracy. He familiarized himself with technical details and with untiring thoroughness and resolute impartiality submitted the report in 1942. Some of the principles evolved during the deliberation over distribution of river waters amongst the riparians were ground-breaking and visionary. Two principles in particular stand out for their significance over the debate on the Indus waters in the post-Partition period between India and Pakistan. The first being,

> The most satisfactory settlement of disputes of this kind is by agreement, the parties adopting the same technical solution of each problem, as if they were a single community undivided by political or administrative frontiers.

And the second,

> If there is no such agreement, the rights of the several Provinces and States must be determined by applying the rule of 'equitable apportionment', each unit getting a fair share of the water of the common river.[105]

It also accorded an order of precedence between projects of different kinds: use for domestic and sanitary purpose; use for navigation; and use for power and irrigation.

The Indus (Rau) Commission set up a technical committee to examine the two barrage projects in Sindh and directed the Punjab to not take any action on it until October 1945. It also suggested to both Sindh and Punjab to come to a mutual agreement and noted that

> . . . if the Technical Committee's recommendation was not accepted or if the parties failed to come to an agreement, the

Punjab Government was to be permitted, after the three years period, to proceed with the link and small storage schemes without any conditions.[106]

The Indus Commission's recommendations were neither accepted by the Punjab nor by Sindh. In fact, both approached the Government of India, under Section 131 of the Government of India Act 1935, against the recommendations, which were eventually referred to His Majesty in Council. However, the chief engineers of Sindh and Punjab did start mutual consultations, leading to the Sindh-Punjab Draft Agreement in September 1945, which laid down that in future the Punjab could not construct any dam on river Indus (as opposed to the restriction until October 1945) or on any of its tributaries without the consent of Sindh. It provided a framework for sharing all the waters of the Indus and the five tributaries, which existed in 1945, as well as for all those planned or projected. The agreement never came into full effect owing to Partition in 1947.

As observed, the interprovincial disputes over water from 1920–45 were highly emotive and endangered peace between the provinces on the Indus basin. Some salient points emerge from the period that repeated itself in the post-Partition Indus basin debate between India and Pakistan. First, the lack of storage facilities along the Indus basin. As a result, water flowed unutilized and since water supply was not available throughout the year to meet requirements of irrigation, it increased tension between upstream and downstream provinces. Second, the irrigation network required constant expansion to meet the requirements of the increasing population in the basin. Third, since agricultural land generated revenues, maximizing agricultural production meant increased utilization of water. With the Partition in 1947, the dependency of the irrigated canals to the water supply was inextricably linked and the political implications of this dependency played a crucial role in the relationship of the partitioned independent states—India and Pakistan.

Knowledge-power

The history of canals in the Indus basin offers a fascinating narrative of its interactions with power and knowledge, and how the rivers were negotiated through formal engineering and localized skills. It brought forth, in significant ways, the pioneering role of the civil engineers whose understanding of the hydrology advanced the irrigation system. However, engineers and civil administrators often disagreed on how to run the canal system. While the engineers believed in their surveys, the administrators had their own ideas about the administration of science.[107] Notwithstanding the tussle, many engineers did impress, through constant interactions, the administrators of the overall imperial imperatives of

> . . . control, profit and colonisation.[108]

The overriding economics created a new class of administrators referred to as the 'colonial-official scientist'. This new class formation in a class-conscious England did not go unnoticed. In 1870, the *Spectator* of London described the qualities required of the engineer working in India thus:

> The ideal engineer for India is a man who will take £1000 pounds a year as his average income for life, and insist that all under him shall be content with their wages . . . who will regard an offer of a commission from sub-contractors as a deadly insult; who can keep accounts like a bank clerk . . . [109]

For the engineers, the Indus basin presented a new work culture and a new professional outlook. Some of the colonial civil engineers in the Punjab in the latter half of the nineteenth century were making a scientific mark by writing professional papers on the connection between engineering and management of nature. Prominent among them was Proby Cautley and his works, *Report on the Ganges Canal Works in 3 volumes* (1860) and *A Disquisition on the Heads of the Ganges and Jumna Canals* (1864). Other significant works that become a repository of irrigation knowledge and reference include Captain Haywood's *Practical Gauging of Rivers* (1870) followed in 1879–80 by four papers published in the proceedings for the Institution of Civil Engineering: W.H. Grethed's *Irrigation in Northern India* (1872); Robert Buckley's *Keeping Irrigation Canals Clean of Silt* (1879) and *Movable Dams in Indian Weirs* (1880); and C. Greaves's *Evaporation and Percolation* (1879).[110] All these findings had a deep impact on the irrigation system in the Indus basin. Others engaged in important comparative studies and brought in the best practices from other water development works in Europe. For example, R. Baird Smith's *Italian Irrigation* (1855), Allen Wilson's *Irrigation in India and Spain* (1867) and as earlier mentioned Scott-Moncrieff's *Irrigation in Southern Europe* (1867–68).

At times, the sheer perchance of a natural site inspired impossible engineering as when the governor of Punjab, Louis Dane, an engineer who shifted to administration, floated down the Sutlej in 1908 from his official tour to Bilaspur State and saw with transfixed gaze

> . . . a narrow gauge with high abutments . . .[111]

that made him in wonderment conceptualize a high storage dam which had never been built before in the world. Dane's restless eagerness led to many investigations on the feasibility of the storage dam before, in 1915, the spirited H.W. Nicholson, working in the Punjab Irrigation Department, volunteered to take on the task. In 1919, after extensive study, a detailed proposal was put forward that

> . . . visualised a dam at Bhakra across the Sutlej, 390 ft high impounding 2·50 million acre-ft, of water to extend irrigation in the famine areas of Hissar, Rohtak and all the adjoining states of Patiala, Jind, Faridkot and Bikaner.[112]

And thus was born the idea of Bhakra Dam.

The long history of hydraulic interventions, its designs and operation brought forth accumulated knowledge on structural engineering. Some of the British engineers working on the maintenance and design of the silt- and sand-ridden Punjab irrigation canals undertook studies on

. . . regime channels . . .

and

. . . stable channels.[113]

At different times and through reworking of assessments, R.G. Kennedy's (1895, 1904 and 1907) hydraulic diagrams were used in the Triple Canal Project. Others like F.W. Woods (1917), E.S. Lindley (1919) and Gerald Lacey (1929–30) developed 'silt theory' and empirical equations to understand 'regime characteristics' and its application on prevention of silting and the

. . . need for annual silt clearances in which silting would in theory come to balance scouring over prolonged periods of operation.[114]

With the new knowledge gathered, a critical phase of dam designs and its operation dawned in India.

An Indian engineer employed in the provincial service, with colonial condescension to deal with, was far removed from the quintessential British engineer who was a 'man of character and resource'. It was inordinately challenging, to say the least, and very occasionally Indians achieved prominence in the public works departments but rarely attained the highest positions.[115] Amongst the early notable Indian engineers was M. Visvesvaraya, whose stint at the water supply project at Sukkur in the Sindh Province in 1893–5, marked a high point in engineering innovation when he devised a method of 'collector wells'[116] to filter the muddy waters of the Indus on the riverbed and created a passage to bring drinking water to the pumping station. Visvesvaraya continued to make breakthroughs in dam engineering. He foresaw multi-purpose utility of dams for not only irrigation and power generation but also flood control, and the 'automatic flood gates for dams'[117] that he created allowed passage of flood without the water in the reservoir reaching its maximum level. His extensive knowledge and expertise was later used in post-Independence India to build the Hirakud Dam to reduce flood ravages in Orissa and thereon to mitigate floods in Hyderabad and Secunderabad.

A.N. Khosla, unlike Visvesvaraya, graduated from the Thomason Engineering College in 1916, after already having finished a degree in arts, and joined the Punjab PWD. His first assignment was as a surveyor of the Bhakra Dam Project (1916–21), and he continued to be relentlessly engaged with its design until it was finally decided in 1948 to proceed with the project. Very early in his career, Khosla was sent on deputation to the Mesopotamia as a commissioned officer in the Indian Expeditionary Force, where he developed the 'Khosla Disc' for precision levelling across rivers and wide valleys. On his return, he was involved with the Suleimanke Barrage in the mid-1920s and soon after was sent to the US to study some of the advanced technologies in dam construction. With the experience he gathered while working on the Panjnad headworks and the Sutlej Valley Project, he co-authored the *Design of Weirs on Permeable Foundation*,[118] the findings of which went a long way in revolutionizing dam structures in India. Another Thomason Engineering College graduate was Kanwar Sain who, as the chief engineer of the state of Bikaner, conceptualized the Rajasthan Canal and successfully implemented the Ganga Canal Project. He had accompanied Khosla to Denver (US) to study the dams on the Colorado river. They not only developed a convivial bonding but also a professional rapport that eventually saw them work together on the Bhakra Dam, the genesis of which had begun in 1919.

Often missed in the story of the evolution of the Bhakra Dam is the prominent role of the Punjab leader Chowdhry Chhotu Ram, who had no formal technical training but as member in the Punjab

Legislative Assembly relentlessly asked questions for the taking up of the Bhakra Dam. Chhotu Ram co-founded the Unionist Party in 1923 to empower peasants. In the 1937 provincial elections, the party won decisively against the Muslim League and the Congress and dominated the Punjab political landscape until 1945.[119] Chhotu Ram led the Unionist challenge against Muhammad Ali Jinnah's call for partition of India on communal lines in 1940 and

. . . stood like the rock of Gibraltar . . .[120]

against Jinnah's verbal onslaught on him. Like Maharaja Ganga Singh who endeavoured for the prosperity of Bikaner, Chottu Ram was devoted to the agriculturists whom he represented and changed the face of rural Punjab. Upon their return from the US, Sain was posted to the Thal Project while Khosla in 1942 was made chief engineer in the Punjab government by Sir Chhotu Ram (now knighted and the revenue minister). With the likes of Khosla at the helm of affairs, Sir Chottu approved of the Bhakra Dam and got an agreement signed between the Maharaja of Bilaspur, on whose territory the waters of the Sutlej were to be impounded, and the Punjab government in December 1944, a few weeks before he died. Thereon, Khosla and Sain worked in tandem on the project and it took another decade and a year before the concrete placement ceremony was performed by India's first prime minister, Jawaharlal Nehru, in November 1955. Such was the magnitude and breathtaking scope of the project that Nehru said,

Bhakra-Nangal project is something tremendous, something stupendous, something that shakes you up when you see it. Bhakra the new temple of resurgent India, is the symbol of India's progress.[121]

With significant constitutional reforms and changes in British industrial policies in the interwar years, the acceptance of Indian engineers in the institutional bodies grew steadily. In 1901, there were thirty 'natives' representing 538 India resident members in the Institution of Civil Engineers. In 1940, the natives comprised 33 per cent or 213 of the 613 Indian members. A similar trend was witnessed in the Institution of Mechanical Engineers, where the representation rose from 5.65 per cent in 1901 to about 31 per cent in 1940. Membership in the Institution of Electrical Engineers rose sharply from 13 per cent in 1902 to 68 per cent in 1939.[122] A number of native Indian engineers joined the PWD of Punjab, the biggest employer of engineers in the country. In 1912, a total number of ninety engineers were employed in the Punjab PWD of which sixteen were of Indian origin.[123] With their numbers on the rise, a desire arose amongst the employees to form, like the British institutions, a professional body and soon the Punjab PWD Congress, which later, in 1916, became the Punjab Engineering Congress, was established. E.S. Lindley, executive engineer in the Punjab Irrigation Branch, published in 1919 an important paper, *Regime Channels,* under the Punjab Engineering Congress. He mentions in the discussion section of his paper, without any elaboration, a person by the name Bihari Lal Upall, in all probability a member of the Congress. Lindley records his observations:

> He said that the author [Lindley] had tried to fix the law of variation of width and depths, from the data of which he had access, not by any rationale method, as he said, but entirely by empirical rule.[124]

A reference to this only goes to suggest that Indian engineers were making their mark and were confident enough to challenge assumptions.

A.N. Khosla, Kanwar Sain and the peerless M. Visvesvaraya in their

> ... integrity, unselfishness, coverage and consistency ...

were true practitioners of what can be described as

. . . nationalist engineering.[125]

As the newly independent India, after almost 200 years of British rule,[126] put itself on the road to development and well-being of the entire society, water projects became an integral part of the ideas of progress. The engineering understanding of the topography and on-site knowledge of the projects on many occasions secured India the advantages of the Radcliffe Award and later in the Indus waters negotiations. Niranjan Gulhati, another prominent civil engineer and a product of the Thomason College, as the leader of the Indian delegation in the Indus waters negotiations (1954–60) had fought 'consistently and stoutly' to get the best possible deal. Having worked on the canals in the Punjab from 1926 to 1945, his knowledge and experience served India well in the long and hard negotiations on the Indus waters.

PARTITION *of* LAND *and* RIVERS

Drawing a Line in a Maelstrom

The growing nationalist feelings and anti-imperialism had led British Prime Minister Clement Attlee, on 20 February 1947, to announce the decision to

> . . . transfer power to responsible Indian hands by a date not later than June 30, 1948.[1]

The decision of the Labour government had sent ripples across the opposition Conservative party, none more so than its leader Winston Churchill who angrily commented and in a very communal tone,

> The government by their 14 months' time limit have put an end to all prospects of Indian unity . . . How can we walk out of India and leave behind a war between 90 million Muslims and 200 million caste Hindus, and all the other tribulations which will fall upon the helpless population of 400 million?[2]

The self-effacing Attlee, unlike Churchill, was wise to bend Britain's politics to new circumstances and read the writing on the wall that Britain as a 'moral enterprise' no longer appealed to the educated Indian middle class. Concerned, therefore, with maintaining the Empire's reputation over the disintegration of the administration, Attlee further announced 'a boundary commission' on 3 June 1947, referred to as the

> . . . June 3 Plan.[3]

As a matter of urgency, the Bengal and Punjab Boundary Commission was set up in July 1947. Muhammad Ali Jinnah had initially supported the suggestion of the United Nations or the International Court of Justice (ICJ) to be tasked with demarcating the boundaries but eventually relented to Jawaharlal Nehru's refusal on grounds that the international bodies' involvement would lead to

> ... undue delay.[4]

Time was of the essence, particularly with the Congress leaders who had long struggled for independence and

> ... were now ageing men and they were not prepared to delay independence further.[5]

Time was also a deficient resource for Lord Mountbatten, the viceroy, who foresaw a subcontinent spiralling into unstoppable chaos. With the Congress and the Muslim League in bitter discord and his own position of power increasingly tenuous, the last thing Mountbatten wanted was the transfer of power to be delayed as

> ... there would be none left to be transfer, none to inherit effectively.[6]

The speed at which things were hurriedly implemented had its grave consequences but that still, according to Mountbatten, was better than arriving at no decision. He thus seized upon the situation to nominate Cyril Radcliffe, a personal friend, as the Chairman of the Boundary Commission on 27 June 1947. Mountbatten was more than convinced that Radcliffe, with a well-established legal reputation, was the right man for the job and both the Congress and the Muslim League had no option but to accept the nomination.

While the leaders had prepared themselves for Partition, no one had braced themselves for the maelstrom that followed. History, it is said, has no closure and historians have argued that the chaos and bloodshed could have been prevented had the Partition not been rushed. They thus denigrate Mountbatten for pushing back the date from June 1948 to August 1947. Others argue that history has not been kind to Mountbatten as the decision could not have been entirely of his own doing. But it was entirely on his insistence that Attlee was obliged to fix a terminal date for Partition before Mountbatten accepted the viceroyalty.[7] Mountbatten would certainly not have desired his upcoming position in India to be construed as a perpetuation of the Empire. In his tumultuous time in India, he pretended to have more clout and influence than he actually did; he was

> . . . an important interlocutor, and a good one, but no more than that.[8]

Mountbatten erred on many counts during the process of the Partition, as history reveals, but to suggest that he was predetermined to sever India is rather far-fetched. In fact, in Attlee's Cabinet Mission Plan, the directive to

> . . . keep India united . . .[9]

was at the behest of Mountbatten. Much after the Partition, Mountbatten reflected,

> Looking at the problem, the first thing that stuck me (and an opinion that I have not changed) was that the right answer would have been to have kept a united India.[10]

Jinnah was a constant thorn for Mountbatten, a

> . . . clot . . .

and an

> . . . evil genius in the whole thing . . .'[11]

as Mountbatten recounted of him years after the Partition. So
divisive and exhaustive was the Partition process that Mountbatten
admitted,

> . . . I've at last made a mess of things through overconfidence and
> over-tiredness. I'm just whacked and worn out and would really
> like to go.[12]

If anything else, the Partition only brought the two dominions
to a stand-off and the canal disputes that soon arose added to the
distrust. A deeply divided political landscape emerged in which the
partitioned Punjab made future cooperation uncertain and Kashmir
made it completely difficult.

The Indus basin,

> . . . one of the most homogenous physiographic regions on
> earth . . .[13]

with the western rivers (Indus, Jhelum and Chenab) flowing
unhindered into Pakistan while the eastern rivers (Sutlej, Beas and
Ravi) ceaselessly crossing into Pakistan from India, was politically
divided, as never before in its history, to meet a political compromise.
By the time of Partition, the Indus system of rivers irrigated more
land than any other river system in the world. The irrigation system
consisted of 37 million acres of irrigated land of which 31 million
acres, larger than the total irrigated area of the US, were now in
West Pakistan. The entire basin still had a potential to irrigate an
additional 46 million acres.[14] Those associated with it regard the
efforts that went into the developments of the Indus basin

> . . . as one of the proudest achievements of human endeavour.[15]

Yet there remained vast fertile lands to be irrigated for more
food. Before Partition, the basin was divided amongst a number
of provinces and princely states[16] with a set of quasi-international

law that governed the distribution of water and despite the various principles that were framed, the competition for water remained unabated.

The intricate irrigation canals, fed by the Indus river system, which had made a difference in the productivity of the Punjab had strangely escaped the attention of Jinnah. One reason could be that Jinnah looked at both Punjab and Bengal as an undivided unit and desired for a federated India that allowed for power sharing and autonomy to Muslim majority provinces. But the larger desire for power and an arrogant dependence on his tactical skills possibly constrained Jinnah's perspectives to the hydrological disadvantage that Pakistan would encounter. He at best viewed it as administrative chaos. Jinnah's vision of Pakistan embraced the entire Punjab along with the NWFP, Sindh, Baluchistan, Bengal and Assam, which implied, though not stated, the cohesive hydrological unity. Conscious of the dangers of partition of the Punjab and Bengal, he expressed in a letter dated 4 May 1947,

> If such a process were to be adopted it will strike at the root of the administrative, economic and political life of the Provinces which have for nearly a century developed and built up on that basis and have grown as functioning under present constitution as autonomous provinces.[17]

By then it was too late. Jinnah's reputation invariably preceded him. Referring to Jinnah's remark that the Partition would be disruptive, Rajendra Prasad, the president of the Constituent Assembly, said,

> He forgets he is responsible for disrupting these and many more valuable ties which have been forged in the course of centuries, by seeking to divide India.[18]

This, of course, does not absolve the Indian National Congress, which, having championed national unity with gusto, succumbed to communal pressures so easily and accepted the Partition plan. When the India Independence Act was passed by the British Parliament on 18 July 1947, the boundary line that was to divide the Punjab and Bengal into two dominions was not even determined.

A month earlier, on 3 June 1947, in the magnificent Viceroy House, Mountbatten in a 'dramatic fashion' presented the thirty foolscap pages of the 'The Administrative Consequences of Partition' to the startled leaders of the Congress and the Muslim League by raising it above his head and banging it on the table.[19] The paper, masterly in its language, exposed the enormous material implications and the associated complexity of dividing the country of all its assets and liabilities right down to the 'typewriters'. Mountbatten, humouring himself, remarked,

> The severe shock that this gave to everyone present would have been amusing if it was not rather tragic.[20]

As the Partition moved towards a decisive conclusion, and fearing imminent disputes over dividing 'men and material', an Arbitral Tribunal was formed. The earlier Partition Council resolved most of the matters in a congenial manner and those that were left unresolved,

> . . . were not referred to the Arbitral Tribunal as the representatives of India and Pakistan were able to sort them out by December, 1947.[21]

The Canal dispute in 1948 changed the situation, and it was no longer cordial but one of intense bitterness.

Jinnah died on 11 September 1948, a little over a year after he became Pakistan's first governor general and president of its Constituent Assembly. An enigmatic figure, although not infallible, like all the iconic personalities of the Partition time, he too had his complexities. Having altered the destiny of Muslims in the subcontinent

> . . . more than any other man,[22]

through the tumultuous times since he proposed the Partition of India in the Lahore meeting of the Muslim League in 1940, Jinnah eventually realized his dream of an independent state of Pakistan. Yet the homeland he begot, in his own words, was

> . . . truncated or mutilated moth-eaten.[23]

Pakistan, partitioned from India, was predominantly agricultural, with as many Muslims outside its territory as there were Muslims within. It inherited problematic borders and a measly share, about 10 per cent, of the industry. All the large cities remained in India, including Delhi, Bombay and Calcutta. Even Lahore, with Hindus and Sikhs in majority, at one point, recalled Radcliffe in a conversation with Kuldip Nayar, was almost given to India,

> . . . but then I realized that Pakistan would not have any large city. I had already earmarked Calcutta for India.[24]

Furthermore, Pakistan got a poor share of the colonial government's financial reserves—it inherited only 17.5 per cent of the financial assets.[25] Its coffers were almost empty and virtually nothing was left for economic development. However, Jinnah, crestfallen and desolate at the outcome, continued to resolutely say, 'better a moth-eaten Pakistan than no Pakistan at all.'

And that was not all. The new international boundary cut across the basin, giving the upper reaches of the main Indus and its eastern tributaries to India while the lower reaches came to lie in Pakistan. The new frontier set forth new political conditions. The constitutional provisions hitherto available for lower basin provinces to seek remedies against the upper provinces' overuse of river waters, ceased to exist. Its vulnerability, as a lower riparian country, to what it considered a hostile India, quickly dawned upon Pakistan. Thus, probably one of the first questions that the new government of Pakistan faced was riparian in nature: What would not a hostile India do? Jinnah's thirst for Partition overlooked the hydrological

disadvantage. There is no evidence to suggest whether Jinnah
factored the waters except for an interesting fact that his paternal
grandfather came from a

> . . . decidedly well-watered province . . . [26]

of Kathiawad in Gujarat and was a native of Paneli not far from
Porbandar, where Gandhi was born. Almost a decade after Partition,
Wilfred Cantwell-Smith asked about Jinnah:

> Is it not perhaps time to bring into question his statesmanship,
> his political sagacity, in view of his apparent failure to foresee—
> apparently even to try to foresee—the concrete outworking of
> his proposals? One is left with the impression that he had never
> studied a map of the Punjab or Bengal; let alone envisaged the
> former's canal system.[27]

Nehru, much younger and healthier than Jinnah, lived to administer
India through its formative stages until his death in 1964 and would
oft say that India and Pakistan

> . . . could not be enemies forever.[28]

During the torrid Partition process, Nehru and the Congress leaders
were decidedly more alert to the significance of the canals and the
headworks than Jinnah and the Muslim League hierarchy were. The
perspectives of civil engineers like Sarup Singh and A.N. Khosla in
the Punjab Irrigation Department, and Kanwar Sain in the Bikaner
Irrigation Department, who had worked tirelessly to develop
the canal system, also played an instrumental role in sensitizing the
Congress political leadership to the criticality of utilization of the
waters of the eastern rivers. They thereby regained the headworks,
which would have gone to West Punjab had the Radcliffe Award
not been intervened upon. The details of the Partition had its
intrigue, manipulation and back-channel influence, but through tact

and persuasion, the Congress leadership ensured that the Award maximized India's position.

The entanglement and the disentanglement of the Partition

> . . . required not only the delimitation of the physical boundaries, but the settlement of many other matters . . .[29]

The business of literally drawing the line on the map was assigned to Cyril Radcliffe. The authorized pencil could not have been more historic than the one which Radcliffe wielded. With little time on his hand, merely five weeks since he arrived in India on 8 July, he had to draw what turned out to be the most tumultuous and tragic line. Radcliffe left India the day after he submitted the awards with a bitter taste in his mouth, possibly unconcerned but certainly helpless and frustrated and, as revealed later, burnt all the papers, and even refused to take his fees of a handsome 3000 pounds. In a famous interview with Kuldip Nayar many years later, Radcliffe responding to a question said,

> I had no alternative; the time at my disposal was so short that I could not do a better job . . . However, if I had two to three years, I might have improved on what I did.[30]

It was the Punjab and Bengal provinces, with neither of the two having either Hindu or Muslim absolute majority, that had to face the brunt of an arbitrary map done in haste and without field surveys. But it was done and thus came about an inglorious end to

> . . . what many Britons considered their finest achievement in Asia—the political unity of the sub-continent.[31]

Years later in 1966, W.H. Auden, the acclaimed Anglo–American poet, whose works had a major influence on the poetry of the twentieth century, in an unsparing poem on Radcliffe wrote:

The next day he sailed for England, where he quickly forgot
The case, as a good lawyer must. Return he would not,
Afraid, as he told his club, that he may get shot.[32]

A four-member Punjab Boundary Commission with Radcliffe as
the chairman was announced by Mountbatten on 30 June 1947, and
the following month, the Commission met in Lahore and for ten
days (21–31 July), excluding a Sunday, deliberations were conducted
on behalf of the Indian National Congress, the Muslim League and
the Sikh members of the Legislative Assembly.[33] A number of other
interested parties from the states of Bahawalpur and Bikaner also
argued before the Commission. Observing the deliberation although
not participating in it, Radcliffe writes on the Punjab boundary,

> It became evident in the course of our discussions that the
> divergence of opinion between my colleagues was so wide that an
> agreed solution of the boundary problem was not to be obtained.[34]

The Boundary Commission principally kept the division/demarcation
of the borders on the basis of religious demography—Muslim versus
non-Muslim majority districts—and settlement maps but had to
contend with 'other factors', especially in the Punjab.

The interpretation of the 'other factors' saw heated exchanges
between M.L. Setalvad[35] and Zafrullah Khan, who were the legal
counsels in the boundary commission. The former argued that
while the demography was undoubtedly the principal factor for
demarcating the boundary, 'other factors' such as the administrative,
economic and physical features were

> . . . not subsidiary but equally important.[36]

Setalvad thus argued for the boundary to be pushed as far west
along the course of the Chenab river starting from east and moving
south-westwards to include Lahore and Sheikhupura and the canal
colonies of Lyallpur and Montgomery districts. Zafrullah, on the

other hand, attached little importance to the 'other factors' and emphasized on ascertaining the Hindu and Muslim contiguous majority areas and argued for the numerical majority of the Muslims in the tehsils. Zafrullah demanded for West Punjab the boundary extending up to the Chenab. Harman Singh pleaded for a Sikh homeland between the Beas and the Chenab, including the canal colonies that the Sikh had toiled hard to make prosperous, while the Bikaner and Bahawalpur states made claims for the retention of the Ferozepur headworks in East and West Punjab respectively. All the three dominant communities, Muslims, Hindus and Sikhs, had their own concerns and demands, with rivers as a reference point. In the circumstances it was, therefore, not an easy task for Radcliffe to follow the majority principle or to take into consideration the 'other factors'. Moreover, while advocating the division along existing tehsil/thana lines, Radcliffe had to rely on an outdated 1941 population census of India, which as he noted was 'very unreliable'.

The rivers and the fertile lands it watered made the Muslim majority districts of Gurdaspur, Lahore and Montgomery and the Muslim minority district of Amritsar in the Bari Doab extremely contentious.[37] But while the Muslims were in majority in some of the districts, the economy was in the hands of the non-Muslims. The case of Gujranwala was interesting. The Hindus and Sikhs formed little more than one-third of the city's population but contributed 55 per cent of its taxes and revenues and owned more than two-third of the city's property and business activity.[38] The high economic stake led the Sikh representatives to argue strongly during the deliberations of the Punjab Boundary Commission for Gujranwala and its surrounding areas to be awarded to India. Radcliffe, however, drew his eventual line based on population. Resultantly, Gujranwala went to Pakistan and during the days and months after the Partition almost the entire city's non-Muslim population, as throughout West Punjab, migrated to India. This added further to the growing resentment among Sikhs that had already reached a dangerous situation on 5 August 1947, with widespread protests led by Master Tara Singh. Jinnah had demanded strong action and even called for the arrest of Master Tara Singh, while Sardar Patel exercised caution lest the situation aggravated. Incidents like this only went to prove the volatility of the situation. The failure to arrest the Sikh leaders became

> ... one of the chief Pakistani grievances against Lord Mountbatten, ranking along with his alleged pro-Indian leaning in the application of partition . . .[39]

Radcliffe clearly could not grasp the complex hydrology that the river presented and perplexed over it, showed no particular inclination to using natural boundaries like rivers and watercourses as 'other factors'. Although every now and then, much to his discomfort, the rivers would inescapably present their vagaries, making them difficult to ignore. While Radcliffe admits that the boundary line based on the notoriously erratic rivers in Bengal was far more challenging than in demarcating the Punjab Boundary, yet when the Bengal Award was presented,

> The District boundaries, and not the actual course of the River Ganges, shall constitute the boundary between East and West Bengal.[40]

When he did apply the river as the boundary it was unfortunately administered without rigour, as when he designated Mathabhanga as the border for Nadia. The wayward river had already changed its course and was not marked on the official map of Bengal, which Radcliffe used. A wrong reference resulted in almost 500 square miles of territory going to East Bengal, which should have been in West Bengal.[41] Another riverine feature, very common to the Bengal landscape, which Radcliffe missed accounting for was the *chars*—strips of sandy land formed as rivers changed their course. The rivers Ichhamati, which defined the boundary between Khulna and the 24 Parganas, and the Padma which divided Murshidabad and Rajshahi, were dotted with chars, some of which, given their size, attracted settlements leading to claims of the land.[42]

Pressured for time, uncertain and confused but yet trying to find impartial settlement, Radcliffe eventually applied both the communal composition of the area and the river course. The Punjab Boundary Award, for instance, stated:

> The boundary between the East and West Punjab shall commence on the north at the point where the west branch of the Ujh river enters the Punjab Province from the State of Kashmir. The boundary shall follow the line of that river down the western boundary of the Pathankot tahsil to the point where the Pathankot, Shakargarh and Gurdaspur tahsils meet. The tahsil boundary and not the actual course of the Ujh river shall constitute the boundary between the East and West Punjab.[43]

It was a curious decision; after following the Ujh river as the cut-off point for the border, the tehsil suddenly became the boundary. Resultantly and probably the most controversial aspect of the boundary award was that three of the four tehsils of Gurdaspur district on the eastern bank of the Ujh river (tehsils of Gurdaspur, Batala and Pathankot) were awarded to India and only one, Shakargarh, was assigned to Pakistan. While in Bengal, the Muslim majority district of Murshidabad was given to India in order to keep the water route from Calcutta to the Ganga in India. In return, the Hindu majority district of Khulna was included in East Pakistan, later Bangladesh.[44] The Chittagong Hill Tract with 85.5 per cent Buddhist and 10 per cent Hindu population was given to Pakistan, leading to a virtual uproar with Sardar Patel expressing his indignation in an angry letter he wrote to Mountbatten.

Radcliffe remained conscious of the 'pressures' in delimiting the boundary in the Punjab but did not fathom

> ... why Nehru and Mountbatten's greatest concern over the new Punjab border line was to make sure that neither of the Muslim-minority *tehsils* of Ferozepur and Zira nor the Muslim majority district of Gurdaspur should go to Pakistan, since that would have deprived India of direct road access to Kashmir.[45]

Radcliffe

> . . . with little knowledge and less appreciation of its
> complexities . . .[46]

changed his mind about Ferozepur when Nehru and V.P. Menon
threatened that the attachment of Ferozepur with Pakistan would
become a reason for a dreadful war. In Gurdaspur, Radcliffe followed
the natural boundary line of the Ravi but ignored the Muslim
population in majority and gave it to India.[47] Road access to Kashmir
was critical for the Congress. The attachment of Gurdaspur with
India was to provide mobility to the Indian troops into the Kashmir
valley. A popular belief about the Radcliffe Award was that the
'other factor' was in favour of India but not to Pakistan. Radcliffe's
own assessment expressed in the Boundary Commission report was:

> In my judgment the truly debatable ground in the end proved to
> lie in and around the area between the Beas and Sutlej rivers on
> the one hand, and the river Ravi on the other. The fixing of a
> boundary in this area was further complicated by the existence of
> canal systems, so vital to the life of the Punjab but developed only
> under the conception of a single administration, and of systems
> of road and rail communication, which have been planned in the
> same way.[48]

This area between the rivers broadly covered the districts of Gurdaspur,
Amritsar, Lahore and Ferozepur in Lahore Division. He also tried
his best not to cut or sever transportation and communication setups
that would have economic impact. Probably playing the part of a
lawyer more than a cartographer, which he was not but had to be,
Radcliffe considered assets like the formidable irrigation system in
the Punjab under the 'joint control' of both sides. He notes:

> But I must call attention to the fact that the Dipalpur Canal, which
> serves areas in the West Punjab, takes off from the Ferozepore

headworks and I find it difficult to envisage a satisfactory demarcation of boundary at this point that is not accompanied by some arrangement for joint control of the intake of the different canals dependent on these headworks.[49]

In all possibility, Radcliffe's joint control may have been influenced by the principle of equitable apportionment based on the concept of community of interests that had gained legal prominence since the pioneering Madrid Resolution in 1911 on 'International Regulations Regarding the Use of International Watercourses for Purposes other than Navigation'. In its 'statement of reasons', the Resolution stated:

> It is recommended that the interested States appoint permanent joint commissions, which shall render decisions, or at least shall give their opinion, when, from the building of new establishments or the making of alterations in existing establishments, serious consequences might result in that part of the street situated in the territory of the other States.[50]

When Radcliffe suggested to Nehru and Jinnah that the Punjab water system should be a joint venture run by both countries, the latter retorted, 'He would rather have Pakistan deserts than fertile fields watered by courtesy of Hindus,' and told Radcliffe 'to get on with his job'. Nehru, equally displeased by the idea of joint management of the canals, at a time when the atmosphere was vexed, responded to Radcliff,

> What India did with India's rivers was India's affair.[51]

Having not taken too kindly to Radcliffe's cooperative plans on the canal system initially, Nehru later became one of the prime movers of the Indus Waters Treaty which was eventually signed in 1960. While hosting a lunch at the United Service Club in Simla in the first week of August in what was to be the last meeting of the Boundary Commission, Radcliffe said,

Gentleman, you have disagreed and therefore the duty falls on me to give the Award which I will do later on.[52]

The Award was to be binding.

Radcliffe tried to 'balance' dissatisfaction in one area by offsetting it with concessions in another. It remarkably had no consistencies and the principle of balance in itself was left to various interpretations. Many observers have noted that there was nothing radically new in Radcliffe's Award. It was a replication of the 'breakdown plan' worked out by Viceroy Wavell in 1946 in which any plan for a division of India would affect at least two divisions (Ambala and Jullundur) of the Punjab and almost the whole of Western Bengal, including Calcutta, which could only be joined with the Indian Union. Thus 'only the husk would remain' and would diminish the attractiveness of Pakistan to Jinnah. Wavell had wanted the unity of India as his objective while Radcliffe was tasked as an employee on a fee to create the boundary of a divided India.

The Partition led to an uneasy atmosphere, and resulted in claims and counterclaims. Arguments were made that all 'movable government property' and 'every kind of fixed asset', after being valued by the Arbitral Tribunal, was divisible and

. . . financial adjustments made in accordance with the general or some special ratio.[53]

The types of fixed assets that were listed included, specifically in the Punjab,

. . . Crown lands, Canal Colonies, irrigated forest plantations.[54]

Canals also existed in Bengal while in Assam, apart from the buildings, roads and bridges, irrigation embankments were listed. With the boundary commission report, a greater proportion of the assets of the old undivided province went to one than the other.

West Bengal was apportioned more government buildings, roads
and canals than East Bengal. West Punjab got far more

> . . . Crown lands, Canal Colonies and irrigated forest plantations
> than East Punjab.[55]

Clearly, satisfaction between the concerned parties over the division
was nigh impossible. With no easy solution, the Tribunal decided
that

> . . . all fixed Government assets which were man-made required
> a basis of valuation to be determined and applied to irrigated and
> developed Crown lands, including Canal colony lands, forests,
> canals, roads, bridges and buildings.[56]

Critical supply issues, like the canal waters with the headworks in
East Punjab, became an existential concern for West Punjab, the
resolution of which was not easy.

The Partition affected the irrigation systems in the Punjab with
inevitable friction. There were nineteen headworks and thirteen
canals in the Indus basin system. Four of the nineteen headworks
and two of the thirteen canals came to East Punjab (India) and
the remaining fifteen headworks and ten canals went to West
Punjab (Pakistan). The Upper Bari Doab Canal (UBDC), one of
the thirteen canals, was divided between East and West Punjab.[57]
The UBDC had two canal systems, namely the Central Bari Doab
Canal (CBDC) and the Dipalpur Canal. With the Partition, the
headworks of the CBDC at Madhopur and the Dipalpur Canal
at Ferozepur came to India. The distributaries of the CBDC and
the Dipalpur were wholly or partly in Pakistan but were dependent
entirely on the headworks in India. For West Punjab, having got
the large share of the irrigated fields, the immediate problem was to
assure the continuity of water supplies to the UBDC.[58]

The Partition also gave the control of the headworks of Ropar
and Hussainiwala on Sutlej to East Punjab. The significance of the

Ferozepur headworks, constructed under the Sutlej Valley Project in 1927, lay in the fact that it had three canals 'taking off' from its location: the Dipalpur Canal on the right, irrigating Lahore and Montgomery districts (in Pakistan); Eastern Canal on the left, irrigating part of the Ferozepur district; and the Bikaner Canal irrigating the northern part of the Bikaner State. Importantly, the Ferozepur headworks, the last point on the Sutlej under India's jurisdiction, acts as an important defence barrier. Downstream to the headworks, the river meanders to form a common border. Pakistan's angst over the Ferozepur headworks being allocated to India remains central to its interpretation of the history of Partition—of the cunningness and connivance of the British and Indian leaders.

An Engineer Named Kanwar Sain

How did the Ferozepur headworks come to India? While much of the Partition history is about the role of the great leaders, their differences, actions and miscalculations, the foresightedness of the Indian civil engineers in understanding the seriousness of the asset distribution, in this case the headworks, and their fear of India being at a disadvantage by the boundary has received inadequate attention. Kanwar Sain's account in his memoir is riveting. He writes:

> The Award was to be declared on August 15, 1947. Sarup Singh, Chief Engineer, Irrigation, Punjab, left Lahore on August 8, 1947. On reaching Ferozepur, in the evening he learnt from the Deputy Commissioner, Ferozepur, that the latter had received instructions from the Governor of Punjab to select his headquarters outside the three *tehsils* of Ferozepur district, namely Ferozepur, Zira and Fazilka, as these were likely to be allocated to Pakistan. This meant the transfer of Ferozepur Headworks and the reach of the Gang Canal to Pakistan. He realised the seriousness of this proposal both to east Punjab and to Bikaner. He immediately sent a special messenger to me with a secret, sealed letter written in his own hand, informing me of the situation.[59]

Perturbed by the possibility of the three tehsils being awarded to Pakistan and that the Ferozepur headworks along with the Ganga Canal would be 'lost to India', Sain hurriedly went to Sardar Pannikar and apprised him of the situation. Pannikar, who did not hesitate to play tough with the Maharaja of Bikaner, was the prime minister of the princely state since 1944 and had received the Rajput title of 'Sardar' for his illustrious service. Sain explains the urgency:

> At first, Sardar Pannikar argued that even if the Ferozepur Headworks went to Pakistan, Bikaner state would receive its share according to the 1921 Tri-partite Agreement for sharing the waters of the Sutlej river. I expressed my doubt and anxiety and requested that the matter be brought to the notice of His Highness [of Bikaner], who was contacted immediately. Within an hour, Sardar Pannikar and myself were called to Lalbagh Palace. Explaining to His Highness, I expressed my strong fear that if the Ferozepur Headworks and the Gang Canal went to Pakistan, the Gang Canal Colony, which had been established by his Highness' illustrious father, would be ruined, as on one pretext or the other, it would not receive its fair share of water. This caused anxiety to His Highness. He asked what could be done. I explained that whatever could be done at my level, I had already done in submitting a strong representation to the Radcliffe Commission.[60]

Sain was not too sanguine about Bikaner's concerns on the Ganga Canal being addressed by the Punjab Boundary Commission. It prompted him to search for another route—to influence Mountbatten and impress upon him Bikaner's situation. Mountbatten had known the Maharaja Sadul Singh as they had served together in the trenches of WWI. The Maharaja had hosted Mountbatten when he visited Bikaner in July 1947 along with his wife and daughter with great pomp and show, accompanied by a smart march-past, splendid uniforms and magnificent bearings of all military units. In the investiture ceremony that followed at the

Lalbagh Palace, Mountbatten invested the Maharaja as a Knight Grand Commander of the Star of India, an exalted honour.[61] Sain suggested that the Maharaja 'take advantage' of the friendship he had developed with Mountbatten and drafted a telegram on behalf of him. After some amendment by Sardar Pannikar, this was dispatched to Mountbatten. It read:

> It is strongly rumoured that Boundary Commission is likely to award Ferozepur Tehsil to Western Punjab. This Tehsil contains headworks of Bikaner Gang Canal and under existing agreement State is entitled to receive for its perennial canal specified amount of water. Fear greatly that administration and regulation of this water exclusively to western Punjab may gravely prejudice interest of Bikaner State as its economic life is to very large extent dependent on water supply from Gang Canal. Have every confidence that your Excellency in finally arriving at decision on award of Boundary Commission will be good enough to safeguard interests of Bikaner State especially as we as one of the parties to the Agreement were not consulted in arrangements that are being made. Request your Excellency to very kindly give an opportunity to my Prime Minister and Chief Engineer Irrigation, to place facts before Your Excellency prior to final decision being arrived at. They are reaching Delhi on morning Monday eleventh.[62]

Maharaja Sadul Singh, whose father Ganga Singh had successfully parleyed with the British administration to build the Ganga Canal and change the destiny of Bikaner, was presented with a desperate situation. News that Ferozepur districts and the headworks, which supplied the waters of the Sutlej to the Ganga Canal, were to be awarded to West Punjab was disappointing. A momentous decision beckoned for Sadul Singh. In the interest of Bikaner, he would, as told to Mountbatten by Kanwar Sain, have

. . . no option left but to opt for Pakistan.[63]

Despite his idiosyncrasy and

> . . . a number of bees in his bonnet,[64]

Sadul Singh played a notable role in the entry of the Princely states, some of whom were hesitant, into the Indian Union for which Sardar Patel acknowledged his contribution.[65] But it was his reply to Liaquat Ali Khan's provocative statement (22 April 1947) that states had succumbed to the pressure of the Congress that raised his stature. The Maharaja had replied,

> We decide to do so certainly not due to any pressure from anyone, much less the Congress, but because we consider it to be in our own interests as well as in the greater interests of India.[66]

Nehru was equally impressed and wrote to the Maharaja (29 April 1947),

> Your statement, however, was as good a reply as any that could have been given.[67]

Upon hearing of the Maharaja's decision to opt for Pakistan, Mountbatten's face, as Sain relates, 'changed colour.' He remained silent and said nothing and

> . . . we left his Excellency's room.[68]

Initially, in the meeting at the Viceregal House on 11 August 1947, when Sardar Panikkar presented the aide-memoire regarding the Ferozepur headworks and quickly briefed Mountbatten about the difficulties that Bikaner would face over the headworks being allotted to Pakistan, Mountbatten had furiously retorted,

> The Viceroy had nothing to do with the Radcliffe Commission. That Commission has been appointed by His Majesty's Government. Radcliffe is not to report to me.[69]

The evening before the meeting with Mountbatten, Pannikar and Sain explained the situation to Nehru, Sardar Patel, as well as to V.P. Menon, who was the secretary general of the State Department. How much this meeting influenced the Congress leaders is not established, but Nehru did send an urgent message to Mountbatten that

> . . . both from the strategic and irrigation point of view it will be most dangerous to let Ferozepur go to Pakistan. Whatever may be the decision about area west of Sutlej, no area east of the Sutlej must on any account be accepted, even as a recommendation of the Boundary Commission . . . Similarly no joint control of electricity must be accepted.[70]

On the evening of 11 August, it was announced that the Radcliffe Award would be delayed for a few days. On no account, as Larry Collins and Dominique Lapierre reveal,

> did Mountbatten want the details revealed before the Independence ceremonies could be held.[71]

And finally when the Award was announced on 17 August, the Ferozepur headworks and the

> . . . entire area on the left bank of the river in which Gang Canal was located, were left with India.[72]

It was a remarkable turn of events, pointing, if not with complete certainty, to the successful collective pressure of Sadul Singh and his officials Sardar Pannikar and Kanwar Sain, and Nehru's very own influence on Mountbatten. This is also corroborated by Barney White-Spunner,

> Radcliffe had, Beaumont [secretary to the Boundary Commission] said, sent Mountbatten a note with a draft map explaining what

he was recommending so that he could give Jenkins [governor general of Punjab] early warning. This had allegedly been shown to the Chairman of the Central Waterways Commission Lala Adjudhia, who promptly told Patel.

White-Spunner further recounts:

> . . . the evening before the report was due to be submitted, V.P. Menon appeared at Radcliffe's residence seeking an audience. The meeting did not transpire, but the next day, Radcliffe was summoned to lunch with just Mountbatten and Ismay. When he came back he allegedly changed the line so that Ferozepur and Zira went to India. The allegation is that the Maharaja of Bikaner, an important ally in the princely camp, put pressure on Mountbatten alongside Nehru, threatening to accede to Pakistan if Ferozepur went.[73]

It was in such a critical situation that the Nehru–Mountbatten rapport worked to the Congress's advantage. Mountbatten had always regarded Nehru as a suave and highly intelligent man and immediately took to him when they first met in Singapore in 1946. Their friendship further intensified when Mountbatten came to India in March 1947. They both relied on each other. However, as Mountbatten later remarked,

> I had a sort of funny feeling that Nehru actually required my presence in order to be able to function, and after Gandhi it was me. He used to go back to Gandhi, and Gandhi was less and less use to him.[74]

It thus seems that Radcliffe was no more than a lawyer to his client Mountbatten, and Nehru had greater influence on Mountbatten than Jinnah. But there was another important influence on Mountbatten on the Partition process: V.P. Menon. As the secretary of States, his intelligence, presence of mind and ability to understand the complexity of the Partition made him an indispensable adviser to Mountbatten, who in return

> ... invariably accepted Menon's advice.[75]

Mountbatten had his own skilful ways of building networks and connections that went beyond his friendship with Nehru. He built a close and almost confidential association with Menon because the latter was a trusted man of Sardar Patel. Kuldip Nayar writes,

> Indeed, it was Patel through Menon who helped Mountbatten evolve the partition plan.[76]

Radcliffe gave the awards for Bengal and Punjab on 12 August and for Sylhet on 13 August and sailed for England the next day. The awards were announced by Mountbatten on 17 August 1947. Jinnah's comment,

> We have been squeezed in as much as it was possible . . .[77]

captured the disappointment over the tehsils of Ferozepur and Zira in Ferozepur district, Nakodar and Jalandhar in Jalandhar district, Ajnala in Amritsar district and Gurdaspur and Batala in Gurdaspur district, which had Muslim majority and were almost contiguous to West Punjab, being given to East Punjab. For Pakistan, the boundary commission awards were

> ... territorial injustice . . .[78]

but for India it was a strategic imperative to establish for itself a land corridor to Kashmir and to not allow Pakistan any corridor through India to link its eastern and western territories. The situation for Pakistan became further debilitating as the Madhopur headworks upon which 6,61,000 acres in West Punjab depended for irrigation through the CBDC, and the Ferozepur headworks upon which 10,41,000 acres in Pakistan depended for water through the Dipalpur Canal and the Bahawalpur State Distributary, came to East Punjab.[79]

While grudgingly accepting the award and in no position to reject it,[80] the Pakistani leaders considered unilateral actions. One such was the covert construction of a

> . . . cut from a loop of the Sutlej which entered Pakistan territory before the Ferozepur headworks.[81]

The Indian intelligence office viewed it as an anti-gun trench, but the Bikaner irrigation department assessed it as an action to nullify the Radcliffe Award. Fearing that West Punjab would continue with such plans, the latter considered measures to

> . . . increase the supply through a creek which was located entirely in the East Punjab territory.[82]

As the lower riparian province, Bikaner had always feared consequences of upstream actions in the Punjab and despite the award of Ferozepur headworks to East Punjab, its water dependency still remained. In its effort to be water secure, a new set of dynamics developed with the Dominion of India. In June 1948, Bikaner planned to construct headworks at Harike to reduce its dependency on the Ferozepur headworks. In fact, the idea of Harike goes back to the Sutlej Valley Project negotiations in the 1920s, when Bikaner had proposed to construct the headworks at Harike-Pattan just below the junction of the Sutlej and Beas rivers on similar technical lines of the Ferozepur headworks. Sain writes,

> Harike headworks once constructed would provide a permanent and important control to the Dominion of India over the supplies of the Beas River. Harike is about 20 miles from the Pakistan border and is not so easily vulnerable by enemy action as Ferozepur Headworks is at present.[83]

The princely states in Rajasthan led by Bikaner, having acceded to the Indian Union, set ambitious irrigation targets to make fertile seven million acres of land in the Bikaner and Jaisalmer provinces. In 1948, the Maharaja of Bikaner met Nehru to discuss various issues, including the supply of water from East Punjab. Briefing Sardar Patel on the meeting, Nehru wrote (11 April 1948):

> The Maharaja of Bikaner came to see me today with Mehr Chand Mahajan, his new adviser. He spoke to me chiefly about the Bhakra Dam project. This was originally intended to supply water to a part of Bikaner state also, but it appears that the East Punjab Government now intends to absorb all the water and not to give any to Bikaner. Prima facie this seems to me unreasonable. We must look at it from the all-India point of view and as far as I can make out, food production should be much greater if some of this water went to the good land in Bikaner State which lacks water.[84]

Kanwar Sain's role could not have been less significant. He had made great impressions during his stint as the chief engineer in Bikaner with his technical insights, timely interventions and ability to convince his 'masters', which proved extremely beneficial in the Punjab Boundary Award. Surprisingly, Sain in his memoir does not mention Lala Adjudhia, the chairman of the central waterways commission, while White-Spunner, citing the notes of Beaumont, writes of Adjudhia's knowledge on the Ferozepur headworks award.[85]

Punjab Canal Water Dispute

On 12 August 1947, with the boundary award nearing its dramatic conclusion and with Partition and Independence arriving together, a Stand-still Agreement, the draft of which was formulated on 3 June 1947, was put in place. It provided that all the administrative arrangements then existing between the British Crown and the state would remain unaltered between the signatory dominion and the princely state until new arrangements were made. While Nehru and Jinnah had differing views over the Stand-still Agreement, eventually Radcliffe was assured that the arrangements would be respected. The Arbitral Tribunal then handed down decisions premised on the continuance of irrigation supplies.[86] But because it did not specifically 'order' the continuance of irrigation supplies, since the party concerned did not request so, it became subject to interpretations. As soon as the monsoon flows receded and with the sowing season arriving, Sarup Singh and Mohammed Abdul Hamid, the chief engineers of East Punjab and West Punjab respectively, met on 20 December 1947 and signed ad hoc agreements referred to as Stand-still Agreement,

> providing, *inter alia*, that until the end of the current rabi crop, on March 31, 1948, the *status quo* would be maintained with regard to water allocation in the Indus Basin irrigation system.[87]

The agreements provided that 'the parties to the agreement may during the currency thereof execute a further agreement for any period subsequent to the aforesaid date.' Within these limitations, the agreement further stated that

> . . . in the distribution of supplies to the channels that are now situated within the territories of the East Punjab and West Punjab, the *status quo*, i.e., the system in vogue prior to the partition of the Punjab shall be maintained.[88]

February 1948 was a month of bickering, with talks on the matter of supplies of raw cotton to India and of cloth and yarn to Pakistan remaining inconclusive. Pakistan had complained about India not honouring the agreement on the allocation of cloth for August–September 1947, which India repudiated. By the end of the month, India had declared Pakistan as foreign territory with customs to be levied from the following month.[89] In end March, the Arbitral Tribunal was dissolved and the following day (1 April 1948), East Punjab discontinued the delivery of water from the Ferozepur headworks to Dipalpur Canal and to the main branches of the Upper Bari Doab Canal. West and East Punjab assessed the situation in different ways. The latter was significantly alert to the expiry date of the Stand-still Agreements (December 1947) and with the Tribunal also coming to an end on 31 March, it immediately sought to assert a right and refused to restore the flow of water in the canals. Several motives could be attributed for this action, for example to pressurize Pakistan to withdraw the 'volunteers' who had infiltrated Kashmir or as a retaliation against a Pakistani levy of export duty on raw jute from East Pakistan.[90] But the most credible motive seems to be East Punjab's legalistic assertion of an upper riparian establishing its sovereign water rights. Moreover, East Punjab claimed that West Punjab's agreement to pay water dues in the Stand-still Agreement of December 1947 was

> . . . tantamount to recognition by Pakistan of India's proprietary rights.[91]

Pakistan, on the other hand, insisted on the right of prior allocation and that the payments made were exclusively for the costs of maintaining and operating the irrigation works.

Many years later, when the International Law Association met in 1954 to inquire into the law governing the uses of international rivers, East Punjab's action aroused considerable interest. S.M. Sikri, the Advocate General of Punjab, was one of the members of the committee and he expressed his view that

> . . . co-riparians on international rivers have no legal right to share in the waters, their claims being those only of comity based on good neighbourliness.[92]

Sikri had cited the case of the US in 1895 to substantiate his claim. Indeed, US Attorney General Judson Harmon, defending his country's withdrawal of water that led to reduction of the flow of the Rio Grande at the Mexican border, concluded that

. . . a country is absolutely sovereign over the portion of an international watercourse within its border . . .[93]

His conclusion was based on the premise of the absolute sovereignty of every nation within its own territory. In his arguments, Sikri was asserting, at least by implication, India's 'proprietary rights' as an upstream country based on the fact that Partition had created a new political boundary and gave it *a priori* basis.

> It could, on one hand, maintain that it had succeeded to the rights of British India as a sovereign state. On the other hand, India could assert that because there was no sovereign Pakistan before 1947, there could be no responsibilities of a successor state toward Pakistan.[94]

After Partition, West Punjab inherited a weak bureaucracy that lent to lack of policy process and planning and until the expiry date of the agreements had not taken any initiative to negotiate any further agreement with East Punjab. On 17 March 1948, the Arbitral Tribunal had upheld India's argument that the canal system in West Punjab was worth more than what Pakistan was claiming. In its wisdom, the Tribunal assumed the existing water supply would thus be maintained.[95] A feeling of assuredness could have possibly made West Punjab complacent to the outcome. Be that as it may, on 1 April, in the absence of an agreement and with no initiatives by West Punjab to enter into negotiations, India, now an independent country in its interest established legal right to the waters flowing from its territory. The Pakistan government

> . . . stopped operation of lockers and removal of household effects in retaliation.[96]

The 1 April 'stoppage of water' was a rude awakening to the reality of its lower riparian position. War was not an option for Pakistan although there were irascible voices which called for such a drastic action. It would have been fatal for Pakistan as India had all the strategic advantages, including the critical headworks which supplied waters for about 5.5 per cent of Pakistan's cropland. Negotiation was thus the only option for Pakistan. History had seen many bloody wars on the Punjab plains, but 1 April 1948 will be marked as the first dispute on the Indus basin between two sovereign countries. The world often looks at East Punjab's discontinuation of waters to the canals in West Punjab as Machiavellian duplicity or as a costless strategy

> . . . since Pakistan, as the lower riparian, could not prevent India from any of a set of schemes to divert the natural flow of water from the Himalaya-Karakorum mountain belt into the Indus Valley.[97]

This could not be further from the truth as the sequences of wireless messages exchanged between East and West Punjab indicate that the latter was informed about the expiry of Stand-still Agreement *via* a message on 29 March 1948 from the irrigation secretary of East Punjab. In response to the urgent situation, although rather late, on 2 April, the chief engineer, West Punjab, sent a message to his counterpart Sarup Singh,

> Hear you have stopped supplies Central Bari Doab Canal and Sutlej Valley Canals. Kindly extend period of Stand-still Agreement pending next joint meeting.[98]

In response East Punjab stated,

> We are prepared to consider the matter on terms to be mutually agreed upon. Chief Engineers, Irrigation Branch, East Punjab, would be glad to meet your Chief Engineers at Simla on fifteenth April. Please make this convenient. It is understood that the question of modification of the boundary at Ferozepore and Suleimanki would also be considered.[99]

West Punjab, while agreeing to meet in Simla though not to discuss the boundary question, continued to insist on water supply having been 'stopped' without 'good cause' and to

... restore water supply immediately . . .[100]

This was further supplemented by the West Punjab governor who wrote to his counterpart in East Punjab,

> Shall be grateful if you will pass orders for the immediate resumption of supplies pending extension of the stand-still agreements in view of the fact that we have agreed to pay 43 per cent of the cost of the entire canal system for the Upper Bari Doab and 69 per cent of the cost of Headworks in the case of Dipalpur.[101]

While the messages travelled to and fro, the larger 'nationalist' argument wedded in both the political and strategic defined India's right or the rationale, as an upper riparian country, to establish claim of the waters in its territory before

... downstream utilisation became a perspective right.[102]

Niranjan Gulhati writes:

> The East Punjab Government felt that if, in the absence of a formal agreement, it did not discontinue, at least temporarily, the use of UBDC for the benefit of West Punjab, the latter might acquire some sort of legal right to UBDC . . . namely its continued use for the benefit of CBDC.[103]

These were undoubtedly the first signs of upstream–downstream tensions that would engulf the two dominions until finally, after long years of hard and often bitter negotiations, the Indus Waters Treaty would, seemingly, settle the matter. Gulhati further writes,

> There is no question but that, under the conditions then prevailing, the action then taken by East Punjab could not but be regarded by West Punjab and Pakistan as provocative.[104]

Jagat Mehta interestingly notes that the decision was entirely that of East Punjab without the knowledge of the Central government, thereby reducing it to a more localized administrative action of the East Punjab, which irked Nehru.[105]

Urgent negotiations followed between the two provincial governments for the restoration of flows to West Punjab. Important to note is the fact that it was at the invitation of East Punjab government that officials from the irrigation department of West Punjab met their counterparts at Simla in April 1948. Two Stand-still Agreements were signed on 18 April 1948, referred to as the Simla Agreements, to take effect upon ratification by India and Pakistan. The first of the Simla Agreements dealt with the CBDC and restored status quo until 30 September 1948. The second related to the non-perennial Dipalpur Canal's supplies from the Ferozepur headworks, including other such canals 'offtaking' from the Sutlej, which was to expire on 15 October 1948. The Simla Agreements broadly provided for the continued supply of water to the Pakistan canals for a limited period, but also recognized India's claims to the UBDC system and Ferozepur headworks. Pakistan, however, declined to ratify these, and so the water from East Punjab was not restored.

In Pakistan, information regarding the Simla Agreements was being twisted by its leaders, with the *Dawn* newspaper merrily leading a tirade against India for deliberately stopping the water and imposing severe terms,

> . . . as no self respecting nation could accept.[106]

Pakistan Prime Minister Liaquat Ali Khan kept the pressure on Nehru with numerous communications suggesting water as the 'new front' of tension. Liaquat was well respected by Jinnah and while the latter founded Pakistan, it was Liaquat who truly established it. In his telegram to Nehru (28 April 1948) Liaquat 'requested' him

> . . . to order the opening of supplies pending settlement of the entire question.[107]

Liaquat was persistent with his correspondence to Nehru on the canal water. Earlier on 15 April, he wrote to Nehru:

> I regret that before we have had time enough to settle our existing problems, the Government of East Punjab has thought it fit to create new ones . . .[108]

The situation with Pakistan was getting vexed. On 21 April 1948, the United Nations Security Council Resolution 47 was adopted, concerning the Kashmir conflict with a three-step process,[109] and a five-member commission, including the US, was authorized to go to the subcontinent and restore peace and order. After having initially resisted the idea of taking Kashmir to the UN, Nehru had decided to approach it in January 1948. The international body was now beginning to play on his mind. The negative India diatribe in Pakistan and fear that the UN, with suitable encouragement from Pakistan, might meddle in other matters beyond Kashmir conditioned Nehru to seek early resolution to the water dispute. The mood in East Punjab, however, was far more provincial, rooted in the ground reality of water requirement that did not reflect the lofty reconciliatory goals of Nehru. In a letter to Premier of East Punjab Gopichand Bhargava (28 April 1948) Nehru writes:

> . . . I am greatly worried at the stoppage of canal water which used to flow to Lahore district. Whatever, the legal and technical merit may be, there is little doubt that this act will injure us greatly in the world eyes, and more specially when food production is so urgently needed everywhere.

He also explained to Bhargava the inputs from the military that

> . . . owing to the stoppage of water there is too much water
> roundabout Pathankot and this is coming in the way of our
> building a bridge which is so urgently needed. I have little doubt
> that water will have to be allowed in future because such stoppages
> cannot occur normally unless there is actual war. To stop water
> for the fields is supposed to be rather an inhuman act. I suggest
> to you, therefore, to consider this matter afresh. If we act with
> grace now (although it is getting rather late for it), we might get
> the benefit of it. Otherwise there will be no grace left and no
> benefit.[110]

For Nehru, an idealist and socialist as he presented himself,
pragmatism, respect for rule of law and realism were equally
relevant, more so as he was at the helm of affairs. He was anxious
that the canal water dispute be resolved at the earliest and feared
getting bogged down with it with the result that it would draw
his attention from other serious issues. Nehru was conscious and
sensitive to the international implications partly also because of the
Kashmir situation which had flared up, and the UN involvement in
the subcontinent. He visualized a working arrangement between the
two dominions on certain vital matters affecting both the countries
for mutual benefit. As he would say months later,

> . . . India has no intention of invading Pakistan. In the world of
> today, problems are not solved by means of war.[111]

Water supply was restored by East Punjab on 30 April 1948, creating
the condition for the Inter-Dominion Conference, which Liaquat
Ali had put forward in a letter to Nehru on 24 April, saying:

> . . . the terms of the Shimla Agreements [the 18 April Agreements
> in Shimla] have far-reaching consequences and it will be necessary
> to hold Inter-Dominion Confidence [sic, should be 'conference']

to discuss them. Will you kindly suggest a suitable place and date for such conference as early as possible.[112]

Nehru, keen to get the monkey off his back, suggested 3–4 May in Delhi.

In a conversation with Pakistan's finance minister Ghulam Mohammad on the evening of 3 May, Nehru notes that Mohammad expressed

> . . . regret that the Inter-Dominion conference had suddenly broken up. The conference, he said, was proceeding calmly and cooperatively and an attempt was being made to find a way out of the difficulties. Mr Gadgil was helpful. At a later stage, however, Dr Ambedkar intervened and laid down the law rather harshly and brusquely. Dr Ambedkar would consider no interim arrangement and insisted that the legal position as maintained by the East Punjab Government must be accepted or else there could not even be a temporary agreement.[113]

As Nehru tried to explain to Ghulam Mohammad that the legal position of East Punjab was justified, the latter kept underlining Ambedkar's hard-line position on the canal water,

> . . . Mr Gadgil had appeared to favour some such solution [West Punjab to make alternate arrangements] when Dr Ambedkar put an end to such discussion.[114]

The next day on 4 May, Nehru along with N.V. Gadgil, minister of works, mines and power, and Swaran Singh, minister of irrigation in East Punjab, sat with Ghulam Mohammad and the ministers from West Punjab, Shaukat Hyat Khan and Mumtaz Daultana, to resolve the issue which had reached an impasse. An agreement was finally worked out. A marked temperamental difference was seen in how Nehru dealt with Pakistan through negotiations and mediation as a preferred approach rather than disengagement with which Ambedkar proceeded the previous evening. The inter-dominion agreement was crucial for the fledgling state of Pakistan. As a matter of survival, it was essential that Pakistan secured an agreement on access to water resources that originated in India. The option of war that Pakistan had contemplated turned out to be foolhardy as India successfully pushed back the Pakistani invaders in Kashmir. The only option thus for Pakistan was to push for negotiations for the restoration of water. Eventually, New Delhi got Islamabad's recognition of its rights on the eastern rivers (Sutlej, Beas and Ravi) and secured from Pakistan its commitment to pay for any water supplied by India until Pakistan could find replacement from the other western rivers (Indus, Jhelum and Chenab).

The Inter-Dominion Agreement of 4 May 1948 or the Delhi Agreement, while recognizing that a water supply dispute had arisen, stated that the 'proprietary rights' (determined by the Partition Order, 1947 and the Arbitral Award) did not allow West Punjab to claim any share of the East Punjab waters

. . . as a right.[115]

This, the agreement further stated, is disputed by the West Punjab Government,

. . . its view being that the point has conclusively been decided in its favour by implication by the Arbitral Award and that in accordance with international law and equity, West Punjab has a right to the waters of the East Punjab rivers.[116]

The agreement importantly noted,

The East Punjab Government has revived the flow of water into these canals on certain conditions of which two are disputed by West Punjab. One, is the right to the levy of seigniorage charges for water and the other is the question of the capital cost of the Madhopur Head Works and carrier channels to be taken into account.[117]

The agreement concluded that the water issues in the future should be settled in a 'spirit of goodwill and friendship' and to

> . . . approach the problem in a practical spirit on the basis of the East Punjab Government progressively diminishing its supply to these canals in order to give reasonable time to enable the West Punjab Government to tap alternative sources.[118]

The agreement finally ended on a note that West Punjab was willing to deposit

> . . . such *ad hoc* sum as may be specified by the Prime Minister of India. Out of this sum, that Government agrees to the immediate transfer to East Punjab Government of sum over which there is no dispute.[119]

The details of the agreement aside, it was based on 'assurance' of East Punjab to West Punjab to not withhold water and give the latter time for tapping alternative sources; and for West Punjab to 'recognize' the need of East Punjab to develop areas where it is underdeveloped. The Inter-Dominion Agreement, without conferring great advantage to India, gave all the water to Pakistan as a matter of urgency in return for the deposit of a small sum of Rs 1.2 million a year in escrow with the Reserve Bank of India.[120]

The Inter-Dominion Agreement had no terminal date unlike the Simla Agreements and for the first time gave practical shape to the 'principle of replacement.' India could withhold water from Pakistan canals but

> . . . not suddenly . . .[121]

so as to give Pakistan time to develop its alternative sources available in West Punjab. All the arrangements in the agreement were between East and West Punjab but ended with the two Dominions expressing

. . . the hope that a friendly solution will be reached.[122]

The essence of the Inter-Dominion Agreement was to, in the best of bilateral spirit, consider long-term settlement in respect to the Indus basin. What remained an issue between East and West Punjab since the Partition was now a political matter between the two dominions and subsequently the Partition Committee relinquished all responsibilities on the canal waters. Undala Alam, with a down-stream perspective, explains,

> . . . It became clear almost immediately, that the Delhi Agreement of May 4, 1948 had not been successful in allaying Pakistani fears about its upstream neighbour, nor had it determined an avenue that could resolve the dispute on the River Sutlej.[123]

The West Punjab government found the wording of the Inter-Dominion Agreement unsatisfactory. The text implied accepting East Punjab's

> . . . right of pre-emption over supplies from the headworks located on the latter's territory.[124]

Avatar Singh Bhasin, a Partition historian who headed the historical division of the Ministry of External Affairs, writes,

> After initial working of this agreement, Pakistan wanted to renege from it, on the pretext that it was signed by Pakistan under duress, which hurt Nehru to no end, since he had personally negotiated and signed the agreement to ensure full justice to Pakistan.[125]

Despite the goodwill that the Inter-Dominion Agreement created and despite the fact that the canal waters was now an India–Pakistan issue beyond the provincial confinement, Pakistan in its impetuosity started 'digging' a new water supply route on the right bank of the Sutlej in West Punjab to 'connect to the Sutlej river above Ferozepur, directly to the Dipalpur Canal, by-passing the Ferozepur headworks in India.' The matter of the digging was first taken up by the East Punjab Irrigation Department with the West Punjab Irrigation Department on 15 May 1948.[126] Despite Nehru's writing to Liaquat (18 May),

> . . . I must ask that the matter be taken up immediately,[127]

reports confirmed that

> . . . excavation of the canals, one near Wagah and the other a few miles up Ferozepore, is being proceeded with by the Muslim volunteers and National Guards unremittingly.[128]

While to Pakistan the 'digging' was a precautionary measure against a 'possible' future action of India to tap the Sutlej, according to the engineers, it could structurally endanger the Ferozepur headworks, which for India was a serious concern. It was the first body blow to the spirit of the Inter-Dominion Agreement.

The negotiations of the Simla Agreements in April 1948 and the Inter-Dominion Agreement in May were also conducted in the backdrop of the Kashmir issue. India's decision on Kashmir, irrespective of the UN, was firm and clear

> . . . till the last of the Kashmir raiders was driven out of Kashmir, India's forces will not leave its borders.[129]

It would seem impossible for the canal waters not to be politicized or to be divorced from the divisive atmosphere that India and Pakistan were gripped with. Nehru's repeated assurances of no harm and non-interference and even a

No-War Declaration[130]

had little resonance in Pakistan which unrelentingly baited India and its intention to undo the Partition. As with the Kashmir issue, the canal waters were becoming a prelude to a third-party arbitration without which Pakistan would not accept any Indian proposal.

Flurry of Correspondence

If Nehru took himself far too seriously on resolving issues with Pakistan, it is because, as a prime minister, he felt that he had an outstanding role to play and

> . . . positioned the office of the prime minister as the one having precedence.[131]

It is not that Nehru was not aware of the intransigence of Pakistan, nor was he not conscious to the digging of the channels. In a letter to Sri Prakasa, India's High Commissioner to Pakistan, on 16 June 1948, Nehru writes: 'This digging is most dangerous from our point of view as it will lead to the breach of an embankment and thus to the Ferozepur headworks being made rather useless.' In the same letter he says,

> We do not propose to weaken in Kashmir and we shall fight on, Pakistan or no Pakistan.[132]

While indeed he was disillusioned and even angry, yet, more often than not, he failed to see Pakistan in black and white. N.V. Gadgil, member of independent India's first cabinet, had said,

> Nehru used to say that politics should always be flexible. I used to tell him that if he did not take a firm stand somewhere, he would get no time even to admit his mistakes.[133]

The Pakistani media, a product of a virulent Partition, caught on the visible differences of opinion between Nehru and some of the leaders in India, particularly Sardar Patel. Nehru was no darling in Pakistan. The *Dawn* had eloquently penned,

Mr Nehru again and again imagines Pakistan as an unfortunate petitioner knocking at the portals of his palace seeking permission to join the thrice holy Union of India and seeks sadistic pleasure in driving away the beggar with a flourish of his royal sceptre.[134]

But the media would also often describe him as someone trying to undo the damage done by the 'bluster of his deputy' Sardar Patel, who was seen as being nasty and a

. . . patron saint of the RSS.[135]

The conflict in Kashmir built a strong resentment in India against Pakistan and vice versa which spilled into the canal dispute, so much so that, at the bilateral level, the two became inseparable. The interlinkage of the issues suited Pakistan well; in fact, expanding the canal dispute to bring in other parties was a clever and convenient exercise that Zafrullah Khan, the foreign minister of Pakistan, well understood. He was an important member of the Muslim League brain trust and his note on the Two Nation theory in 1940 had impressed Jinnah, who always held him in high regard. By making Zafrullah, a non-Muslim Ahmadiyya, his valued minister, Jinnah resolutely stood against the conservatives reminding them of his famous statement in 1944,

Who am I to call a person non-Muslim who calls himself a Muslim.[136]

As the canal dispute percolated through bilateral relations, Zafrullah, seizing the moment, expanded the parties (East and West Punjab) to the canal dispute by bringing in the state of Bahawalpur. Briefed by the Punjab irrigation department, Nehru in his letter (5 June 1948) called his bluff:

Bahawalpur State distributor of Eastern Grey Canal is a non-perennial channel and does not run during rabi season . . . in the discussions at Delhi which preceded the Inter-Dominion Agreement of May 4, 1948, no mention was made of any requirements of water for this distributary, although Khan Bahadur Abdul Aziz, Chief Engineer, Bahawalpur, was actually present at these meetings.[137]

Yet, in the same letter, Nehru strangely concedes to allow Bahawalpur to join the discussion,

> We shall gladly discuss this matter either on a Dominion level or as between East Punjab Government on the one hand and the West Punjab and Bahawalpur State on the other . . . The Bahawalpur matter to which you have referred could be included in such discussions.[138]

India eventually conceded on the Bahawalpur supply through the Eastern Canal on terms similar to those mentioned in the Inter-Dominion Agreement, although it was under no obligation to supply water to Bahawalpur.

Following on his communication on 4 June and Nehru's response to it the following day, Zafrullah sent another telegram to Nehru (19 June 1948), crafted as a helpless victim to the situation, saying,

> Fortunately the restoration of water supplied although delayed and on terms inconsistent with our rights removed immediate danger, it however in no way restored confidence.[139]

In the same letter, Zafrullah notes on the new link channel,

> Unless water is actually drawn through new channel (and there is no possibility of this so long as normal supplies continue).[140]

Responding to Zafrullah's telegram with a copy to Gopichand Bhargava, the Premier of East Punjab government, Nehru writes, pointing to the digging of a 'new channel',

. . . the very digging of new channel is preventing this restoration of confidence because it is a constant threat to East Punjab and would even threaten supply to Bahawalpur. It was for this reason that I laid great emphasis on the cessation of work in digging this channel which would, to some extent, restore confidence and enable all of us to face problem dispassionately and in the interests of all concerned. I earnestly hope, therefore, that West Punjab Government will immediately stop this digging of the canal.[141]

While the tone in the letter to Zafrullah is uncompromising and factual, the letter which Nehru writes to Bhargava (20 June) is quite different:

I think we should ourselves while remaining firm in our main contentions be conciliatory as far as possible as continuing conflict on this issue will be injurious to all parties concerned. I would suggest our laying stress again on main contentions and at the same time agree to water being supplied to Bahawalpur pending our next Inter-Dominion meeting. It should be made clear, however, that we adhere to our position. It is important that the inter-dominion meeting be held as early as possible.[142]

In response (21 June) Bhargava referred to the channel being dug by the West Punjab government to which Nehru replied (23 June):

You know, I suppose, the messages I have sent to the Pakistan Government on this subject and their answers. In one of them they said that they would try their utmost to stop the West Punjab Government from proceeding with their channel. But I do not expect anything out of this. I do not know what more I can do. Our relation with Pakistan is deteriorating in many ways.[143]

Zafrullah saw Nehru as approachable unlike Sardar Patel, who felt that India should be left alone and not be deluded by the rhetoric of peace.[144] Nehru seemed to dislike Zafrullah but characteristically, he would often keep his personal feelings aside while dealing with these issues. There are eleven recorded communications between Zafrullah and Nehru on the canal water dispute between May and July 1948 that explains the challenges that Pakistan faced as a downstream country and Nehru's response and understanding, which gradually evolved into a 'basin-management' approach leading to the making of the Indus Waters Treaty.

On 6 July 1948, Pakistan informed India that the digging of the new channel had been stopped, thereby creating a conducive atmosphere for a meeting to find solutions to the canal dispute.[145] This was held in Lahore on 21 July and it was possibly the first time that an Indian delegation, led by N. Gopalswammi Ayyangar, went across the border to discuss the issue, albeit with no concrete outcomes. Both India and Pakistan stuck to their respective positions. The Indian delegation insisted that the 'propriety rights' of the rivers vest wholly in East Punjab. It now became a starting point of all negotiations on the canal waters. This position was unacceptable to Pakistan which, in the 'Statement' handed over to India said:

> Pakistan would be entitled to have recourse to such means and procedure as may be open to it by agreement between the two Dominions or without such agreement to obtain an adjudication of these rights which should be binding upon both Dominions.[146]

The two positions stifled any forward movement on the canal water dispute. Pakistan sought refuge in the Inter-Dominion Agreement of May 4. The agreement, to recall, would have not come about without Nehru's intervention.

Accepting the Inter-Dominion Agreement meant accepting the Simla Agreements of April 1948, which were to terminate on 30 September (supplies to CBDC) and on 15 October 1948 (water releases below Ferozepur). Pakistan was desperate for an assurance that the supply of waters would not be stopped and drew attention to the Inter-Dominion Agreement that provided for water supplies not to be 'withheld suddenly'. This was expressed in the telegram of 15 September 1948,

> At conference held September 1st–September 3rd at WAGHA between East and West Punjab engineers it transpired that interpretation placed by East Punjab on Delhi Agreement of May 4th was that Agreement only modified Simla draft agreements in certain respects and therefore its life was same as that of Simla draft agreements that is up to 30th September.[147]

It also underlined,

> We consider Delhi Agreement clearly provides for continual supplies to West Punjab till final Agreement is arrived at between two Dominions and at the same time accepts Simla Agreements excepting 2 disputed points.[148]

By now communication between Nehru and Zafrullah had stopped and the Ministry of External Affairs was directly dealing with Pakistan Ministry of Foreign Affairs. In a letter on 18 October 1948, the ministry informed Pakistan:

> We do not accept your interpretation of the Delhi Agreement of 4th May, 1948. We consider that Delhi Agreement imports by implication only some of the terms of the Simla Agreements in so far as they related to the supply of water to Dipalpur and Central Bari Doab Canals. We deny that the Delhi Agreement provides for continual supplies to West Punjab till a final agreement is arrived at between the two Dominions.[149]

Pakistan Strides towards a 'Third Party'

The Inter-Dominion Agreement, consistent with the conflicting positions of the two countries, did not settle permanently the canal water dispute but the framework provided the modus vivendi for a possible settlement in the future. Under the mechanism, India was 'compensated' by Pakistan for the share of water released. The final concession that East Punjab undertook under the Agreement was to restore supplies to Central Bari Doab and Dipalpur Canals for its 1949 kharif harvesting.[150] This came about after Pakistan, on 18 March 1949, formally requested Nehru to 'fix amounts' for the water supplies to West Punjab for the quarter beginning from 1 April 1949.[151]

The Inter-Dominion Agreement was clearly wearing down Pakistan and it was only a matter of time before it would denounce the agreement. The first indication of this came on 13 June 1949 when Pakistan communicated,

> Present *modus vivendi* is onerous and unsatisfactory to PAKISTAN and final solution should NO longer be postponed. In a separate note we are proposing procedure for resolving our differences in a manner that will safeguard our respective rights, comply with our respective duties as members of United Nations and fulfil our desire to promote good-neighbourly relations. Pending such a solution we urge that status quo at partition be respected and that neither side assume to itself right (to) be arbiter of differences that have arisen over our common waters.[152]

Another note (16 June) from Pakistan followed, stating:

> An interruption such as occurred over a year ago [1 April 1948] in the flow upon which essential food-growing areas of Pakistan depend or a diminution in that flow, or even a threat of interruption or diminution, creates a situation likely to endanger the maintenance of international peace and security and is inconsistent with the obligations of membership in the United Nations.[153]

It further noted in the same communication,

> The legal contentions of India and Pakistan may be such that they can be resolved only by adjudication; but it does not follow

that a fair, practical solution cannot be found, leaving the legal contentions to one side. If it develops that legal differences stand in the way of a friendly and peaceful settlement between the two countries, it then becomes their duty as members of the United Nations to submit their dispute for adjudication.[154]

By stating that a 'practical solution can be found', Pakistan left space for possible negotiations and proposed a conference before 16 July 1949. The purpose was to discuss

> . . . equitable apportionment of the flow of all waters common to Pakistan and India and of resolving by agreement all disputes incidental to the use of these waters.[155]

India suggested that the conference be held on 4 August 1949 in Delhi. The second Inter-Dominion Conference on canal water dispute made a few critical observations that would subsequently determine the fate of the Indus basin. Appendix-I noted,

> . . . that there is likely to be enough water in the Indus Basin to satisfy the irrigation needs of cultivable areas situated in India and Pakistan, within the physical limits of command.

Appendix-II had far more significant approaches,

> c) Pakistan shall be supplied with daily gauge-discharge data and periodical water accounts of the rivers and canals concerned and full facilities shall be afforded to Pakistan engineers to inspect and check gauge discharge sites, equipment and data concerned.
>
> d) A joint committee shall be set up to supervise the effective working of these arrangements including the proper allocation of waters and the supply of data.
>
> 5) Every effort shall be made to conclude the joint investigation within a period of six months from the date on which the joint commission which is to carry out the investigation is set up.[156]

In Appendix-III, Gopalaswami Ayyangar, minister of transport, who led the first delegation to Lahore, in a letter to Zafrullah noted,

> It was entirely with an idea of being helpful to both sides that I accepted the suggestion made by the Government of Pakistan to treat the Indus basin as one unit for the purposes of an overall investigation.[157]

Pakistan's clarification stated,

> If the joint investigation does not disclose the existence of surplus resources of water or results in disagreement . . . or in case of the affirmation of the existence of surplus resources an agreement cannot be reached . . . the parties shall jointly submit the dispute to the International Court of Justice whose opinion shall be binding on the two Governments and shall be given full effect to by them.[158]

Responding to Pakistan's eagerness to knock at the doors of the ICJ, Nehru, with no particular objection, explains in a note (28 September 1949),

> I do not myself see how the International Court can deal with an issue largely of fact and partly of law, unless it appoints a Commission to examine the position on the spot.

He then elaborates,

> We cannot ultimately avoid the International Court, unless we accept some form of arbitration. At the most we can choose between the two . . . To refuse both the International Court of justice and arbitration is to place oneself in an impossible position.[159]

On 5 October, the Indian High Commissioner to Pakistan, in a communiqué to the Pakistan foreign office, made a few clarifications in reference to the note by Pakistan that was handed to the leader of the Indian delegation B.K. Gokhale at the second Inter-Dominion Conference. It observed:

> There can be no question of altering, in any way, the terms of the Inter-Dominion Agreement of the 4th May 1948 until a fresh agreement on the subject has been negotiated after the Report of the Joint Technical Commission is available or until, after a consideration of this Report, it unfortunately becomes apparent that no agreement is possible.[160]

For Pakistan, the Inter-Dominion Agreement had become an albatross around its neck, while for India it was the fundamental starting point for any forward movement on the Indus basin. By mid-December 1949, India took the lead in setting up a Joint Technical Commission and nominated B.K. Gokhale, A.N. Khosla and M.R. Sachdev as its three negotiators, and urged Pakistan to similarly do so.[161] The following month, Pakistan nominated Mohammad Ali, H.A. Majid and Pir Mohammad Ibrahim as its negotiators and suggested that the first meeting be held in Karachi on 27 February 1950. Nehru had expressed his trust on the factual investigations carried out by the Joint Technical Commission to arrive at a settlement. He equally felt that if after the investigation a settlement was not reached, then

> . . . we are quite prepared to refer the matter to arbitration or some tribunal approved of by both Governments.[162]

Pakistan, however, remained consistent in its diatribes and recriminations even as the negotiators got their heads together to reach an amicable solution. It accused India of an

> . . . 'international wrong' of 'using or threatening to use force contrary to the obligations of membership of the United Nations',

and

> . . . 'of continuing to use their physical power as a means of inducing acquiescence in India's position'.[163]

The Technical Commission's meeting from 29–31 May 1950 observed that the disagreement had little to do with technical questions but rather with the question of the fundamental rights of the riparians of international rivers. The factual data collected neither appealed to Pakistan, as it would not agree to a reduction of its share of supplies from the Sutlej river, or to India, to suspend the projects which would not respect the water allocated to Pakistan. Liaquat wrote to Nehru

> . . . I believe we are both agreed that there should be arbitration if negotiation fails. It seems clear now that negotiation has failed.[164]

He further wrote,

> Since our differences are juridicial, the International Court of Justice appears from every point of view to be the most suitable forum.[165]

This was followed by a communiqué from the Pakistan Ministry of Foreign Affairs stating:

> The decision of the Government of India, disclosed at the meeting of the negotiators held on the 29th to the 31st of May, 1950, to continue the present interferences with the flow of water allocated to areas in Pakistan and to appropriate additional supplies of water vital to Pakistan, has created a situation so serious as to endanger international peace and security and justice unless other peaceful means of settling of the dispute are promptly agreed upon in compliance with the United Nations Charter.[166]

Pakistan's obduracy to an interim arrangement that preserved the status quo at Partition until the time the ICJ adjudicated its decision was now well beyond Nehru's capacity to resolve. Pakistan had shifted the disagreement from the bilateral to the international arena by evoking Article 2(3) of the UN Charter 10 to

> . . . settle their international disputes by peaceful means in such a manner that international peace and security, and justice, are not endangered.[167]

Nehru had been confident that the technical commission would be able to resolve the differences on the Indus basin but with no headway made, he was uncertain how the involvement of the ICJ, which seemed inevitable to Nehru, would work out for India. Nehru's letter to Liaquat on 18 January 1950

> If it is not found possible to reach a settlement, we are quite prepared to refer the matter to arbitration or some tribunal approved of by both Governments . . .

was coming to haunt him. Nehru wrote to the governor of Punjab, C.M. Trivedi, seeking his suggestions and expressing his dilemma,

> If we leave out war, we come back to some form of arbitration or a reference to a judicial tribunal.[168]

Although not expressing regret, Nehru candidly informed Trivedi about his letter of 18 January and further wrote,

> We have thus entered into a commitment about a reference to arbitration or to some tribunal approved of by both Governments. We need not stress again on a technical or other commission to find out the facts. But, in any event, we arrive at the same conclusion.[169]

There is no doubt that Nehru was more than anxious to solve the canal water dispute as well as other issues with Pakistan irrespective of the fact that East Punjab and the Ministry of Water, Mines and Power were unrelenting in their approach. Nehru firmly concluded in the letter,

> Your Government as well as our W.M.P. (Ministry of Water, Mines and Power) have been reluctant to accept arbitration. I do not see how they can avoid it. Personally I think it is the proper course and we should not be afraid of it.[170]

To come to a final conclusion Nehru invited the East Punjab administration for a conference on the canal dispute in Delhi on 11 September 1950.

Not confident about Nehru's position on arbitration, if not totally in disagreement, Trivedi in his response wrote,

> I myself feel that it will be very difficult for arbitration to proceed until there are technical data, and one of the terms of reference will probably have to be the appointment of a joint technical commission.

His second suggestion was,

> The Pakistan Government should, at the same time, agree to the reference of the evacuee property dispute to arbitration. Here also the terms of reference must be defined by agreement.[171]

Importantly, Trivedi pointed out to Nehru,

> Pakistan proposes that during the pendency of arbitration no further works should be constructed . . . I think that there can be no question whatever of stopping the works at Bhakra or Nangal, but it may be possible to arrive at some satisfactory arrangement about Harike, provided Pakistan is really earnest to reach a satisfactory

interim settlement. Our engineering representative will suggest a
way out, and this may be considered, if deemed suitable.[172]

Interestingly, a few days later, Trivedi wrote to Sardar Patel of his
desire to meet him in Delhi, enclosing the copy of his letter to Nehru.
    Sensing the gravity of the water dispute and the likelihood of
arbitration, Nehru for the first time took Sardar Patel into confidence.

> We do not propose to deal argumentatively with many of the points
> that have been raised in the Pakistan letter. That is to say, we do
> not deal with the merits of the case. We shall, of course, deal with
> certain important aspects such as the agreement of 4 May 1948 and
> their assertion that it was under coercion. We shall also deal with
> our repeated attempts to have a technical survey which we consider
> quite essential in any event, whatever further steps might be taken.[173]

But in a typical way, having already firmed his mind on arbitration,
Nehru put forward two options to Sardar Patel,

> The argument has revolved round two points: One, whether we
> should in the final analysis agree to the Hague Court or arbitration
> tribunal, and, secondly, which of these two is preferable.[174]

Ignoring the two options that Nehru presented and waiting for
the final draft of the conference in Delhi on 11 September, Patel
responded,

> I am glad about the manner in which you have linked the two
> questions of canal water dispute and evacuee property. I am also
> glad to know that Gopalaswami has written to Liaquat Ali Khan
> formally suggesting arbitration about evacuee property.[175]

The evacuee property referred to the properties left behind by the
displaced Hindu, Sikh and Muslim people after the Partition. The
estimated value of property of the Hindus and Sikhs was Rs 300 crore,

while for the Muslims it was calculated to be Rs 100 crore. Besides, the Hindus and Sikhs had left behind 90 lakh acres of irrigated land in West Punjab, whereas the Muslim evacuees left about 60 lakh acres in East Punjab

> . . . comparatively of much inferior quality.[176]

It was clear to the Indian establishment that Pakistan would not agree to any payment of difference and its impractical insistence to allow the displaced person to visit their properties and sell or exchange them was a ploy to keep the negotiations going without seeking closure. The end objective of Pakistan was, as in the canal water dispute, to frustrate India to agree to an international arbitration. The Liaquat–Nehru Pact of 8 April 1950 had only lofty ideals to

> . . . create an atmosphere in which the two countries could resolve their other differences . . .[177]

without any resolution to the vexed issues.

A conference was called by Nehru on 11 September 1950 to firm up a response to Pakistan's communication of 23 August that challenged the Inter-Dominion Agreement of 4 May 1948 and noted,

> It has been the view of the Government of Pakistan that agreement by negotiation would be facilitated if each side bound itself in advance to accept, on any issue where negotiation failed, the arbitrament of the International Court of Justice.[178]

The Indian draft that was prepared after discussion with the Punjab authorities and the Ministry of Waters, Mines and Power under the chairmanship of Nehru noted the following on the arbitration:

> The Government of Pakistan have always expressed a preference for reference of the dispute over canal waters to the International

Court of Justice. The Government of India do not question the high authority of that judicial body. There are two reasons, however, why they feel that this matter should be dealt with by an *ad hoc* tribunal. The first is that, for a correct and prompt settlement of the dispute, it will be necessary for those to whom adjudication of the dispute may be entrusted to appraise the relevant factual data in the light of first-hand knowledge of the geographical and engineering elements of the problem. This can be done more conveniently and effectively by a small group of persons working in India than by a court which has its seat at The Hague.

It continued:

The other, and even more important, reason is the great urgency to settle the question of evacuee property. The continued failure to do so merely prolongs the sufferings of millions of refugees on both sides of the border, and the passions engendered by a sustained sense of frustration and grievance inevitably have an adverse effect on the relations between India and Pakistan. In order to ensure a prompt solution of this problem, the Government of India consider it desirable that it be referred immediately for decision to an *ad hoc* body. For obvious reasons, this task cannot be entrusted to the International Court of Justice. An *ad hoc* tribunal, working in the sub-continent, could apply itself at once to the solution of both the problems, namely, the problem of evacuee property and the dispute over canal waters.[179]

For Nehru, having committed to resolving the canal dispute, the draft response agreed upon could not have been better balanced or come at a better time. While proposing that India and Pakistan form a judicial standing committee comprising two judges from each country to resolve the differences, the draft kept alive Nehru's proposal to seek arbitration but without third-party involvement, and simultaneously heeded to Punjab and the MWMP's insistence on data that would be essential for understanding the Indus basin.

Importantly, for the first time the Indian leadership was able to de-emphasize the canal dispute by bringing in evacuee property settlement. In essence, it was a re-emphasis on bilateralism dressed in judicial competence, impartiality and technical know-how. The draft ended by stating,

> They see no reason why a body so constituted should not be able to arrive at agreed conclusions on the issues refereed to it.[180]

A wiser Nehru, in a letter to Liaquat, soon after the draft response and before it was officially communicated to Pakistan on 15 September 1950, writes,

> This proposal may be adapted subsequently to the settlement of other disputes between the two Governments of a nature which can be dealt with in this way. Thus, this procedure would fit in with the proposal we have been considering for the adjustment of present and future disputes between the two Governments in connection with a 'No-War Declaration'.[181]

If India felt that its response would adequately draw Pakistan into investigating the canal dispute in more practical ways such as the non-third-party tribunal suggested, it was woefully mistaken. The sheer adamancy with which Pakistan communicated its favour of international conformity is striking and a lesson in persuasiveness. Nehru went at length to explain, often at times even lecture, Liaquat on the demerits of a third-party role. In a letter dated 8 October 1950, Nehru reprovingly writes,

> I am not aware of any instance where two independent nations have bound themselves down to refer every dispute, whatever its nature, to a particular authority, much less to an external authority.[182]

He cites the example of the US and Canada having set up an international commission to resolve their differences without the involvement of any 'outside members' and educates Liaquat by telling him,

> You seem to think that such disagreement is almost certain to occur and that only outsiders can decide for us. I confess that I am unable to appreciate the force of this argument . . .[183]

While India continued its insistence on the merits of a bilateral tribunal, it never seriously defined its modalities, except for its composition. This turned out to be to Pakistan's advantage as it would juxtaposition the already established and functioning ICJ. Creating discomfort, Liaquat in his letter to Nehru asks him,

> It would add to the reassurance given by the Government communication [15 September] and your note [12 September] if the proposed commission were authorized to make joint measurements of current flows and withdrawals on both sides of the border to verify that the pre-partition allocations are being respected.[184]

Not one to be seen as ignorant, Liaquat responds to Nehru's reference to US–Canada arrangements,

> I believe this arrangement was made at a time when the International Court of Justice was not in existence. I am inclined to the view that the creation of the International Court of Justice and the voluntary acceptance of its jurisdiction by various countries marks a much bigger step forward towards peace and progress.[185]

It is now Liaquat's turn to educate Nehru,

> Only recently Afghanistan and Iran agreed to refer the dispute over the apportionment of the water of the Helmond river to an independent tribunal of three nations. For the matter of that both of us appointed Justice Bagge of Sweden as the Chairman of the

Tribunal in our boundary dispute and agreed to abide by his award.
I do not, therefore, think that the appointment of an independent
tribunal for arbitration is in any way inconsistent with national
honour, prestige or independence.[186]

Liaquat even becomes patronizing,

By submitting our water dispute to that Court and abiding by its
decision we again demonstrate that the highest act of sovereignty
is to act in conformity with International Law. The International
Court stands for the very same high principles of international
conduct with which you have always identified yourself.[187]

Between 1949–52, India and Pakistan locked horns in the UN on
the validity of the Inter-Dominion Agreement of 4 May 1948.
Pakistan's mission in the UN was continuously raising its objection
to the agreement as being 'without present effect', citing India as
'withholding water' and committing an 'international wrong' that
ran contrary to the obligations of membership in the UN, and thus
as an 'offender', it could not confer any enforceable rights.[188] As a
pre-emptive action (22 September 1949), India forwarded to the
UN various agreements on the canal water dispute, including the
Inter-Dominion Agreement, for registration with the Secretariat.
This was eventually done on 10 May 1950.[189] On 6 April 1951,
Pakistan transmitted a statement certifying that the Inter-Dominion
Agreement was effectively terminated by a formal notice (23 August
1950) given to India. Taking strong objection, India, in a note to the
UN (7 November 1951), contended that

. . . a simple unilateral notice of termination of an international
treaty cannot, by itself, render such termination valid unless the
treaty itself provides for such termination.[190]

The Inter-Dominion Agreement had no provision for unilateral
termination, nor did India accept any notice of termination from

Pakistan. India registered its complaint to the UN on 1 May 1952 that Pakistan's statement of termination should be cancelled.

On the framing of rules of decision and procedure of the Tribunal, Nehru writes (27 October) to Liaquat more as an afterthought,

> As regards the tribunal's powers, I think we should lay it down that it should have final authority to deal with the matters referred to it. The judges can decide unanimously or by majority. They will have all the powers of superior courts in regard to summoning of witnesses, etc. They will settle their procedure and method of working, as such tribunals do. We must invest the tribunal with the highest authority and not make it feel that it is just a stepping stone to something else. We must agree to abide by its decision in all matters referred to it.[191]

From its unshakeable position of international arbitration on the Indus basin, Pakistan framed a counter-narrative to the Inter-Dominion Agreement and the Evacuee Property by questioning the legal nature involved and arguing that, like the water dispute, Evacuee Property too could not be resolved by mutual accommodation. Nehru appeared frustrated with the continuous distortion and denouncement by Pakistan, yet he never tired of underlining India's position or let pass any charges. On the other hand, Liaquat, considerably irked at Nehru's seemingly unflinching integrity, writes,

> If you would permit me to say so, you are so convinced of the rightness of your stand on every issue that I seem to have utterly failed to persuade you that there may be another side to any issue pending between us.[192]

For all practical purposes, Liaquat's letter to Nehru (27 November) stated that the 1948 Inter-Dominion Agreement was made under compulsion. He also made it clear that Pakistan could no longer seriously regard the proposal of 15 September 1950 as an attempt to implement the agreement to adjudicate the dispute.

It was Liaquat's last letter to Nehru on the water dispute, and he signed it off with utmost rigidness and an uncompromising posture. In the numerous letters exchanged between the two prime ministers, between Zafrullah and Nehru and between the concerned ministries and high commissions, a common pattern emerged of Pakistan raising objections and India perpetually responding to them in defence. An examination of the conduct of East Punjab, which established territorial sovereignty over the canal water dispute with West Punjab on 1 April 1948, and the subsequent events thereon, demonstrates that it never actually followed the doctrine in its practice. On the contrary, questions of downstream right to object to the water uses of upstream country predominantly shaped the discourse.

With the deadlock continuing over the issue of adjudication, both the countries as members of the British Commonwealth were bound to resolve their bilateral disputes within the Commonwealth comity. This suited India well as it was the first of a number of countries which decided to remain within the Commonwealth despite becoming a republic. But for Pakistan, it was sheer frustration. It had approached the Commonwealth members to play the role of a mediator and even called for a roundtable discussion, but it found no sympathy. There was a growing opinion in Pakistan that since it had gained nothing from its membership of the Commonwealth, it would stand to lose nothing if it withdrew. Jinnah too had lost faith in the Commonwealth and questioned its purpose,

What is the value of membership of the Commonwealth, if no family gesture is made to help members in distress.[193]

Pakistan leant ever more so towards the UN which it felt was the only forum that could protect the weaker country from the wrongs of the powerful nations. Simultaneously it changed the expressions on the canal dispute dramatically from 1951, referring to the canals as 'international canals' and describing India's water uses as 'interference'. From time to time it also took a unilateral position to delay the final settlement of the evacuee property. However, it continued to pay its share of the actual maintenance cost of the canals. The propaganda machine in Pakistan started working overtime, accusing India of deliberately withholding canal waters, and with a belligerent media calling for drastic action the situation seemed intractable.[194] Despite the unwillingness to compromise, both nations were anxious to find a way forward, fully aware that the water issues could lead to unmanageable hostilities if unresolved. In fact, Nehru realized the gravity of the escalation over the waters very early. The concern is evident in his letters to Gopichand Bhargava, in one of which he writes,

> Our stopping water supply to West Punjab will not lead to a settlement but rather to desperate measures and possibly it may lead to war.[195]

TVA-inspired Water Projects

Soon after Independence, one of the most crucial challenges facing India was to develop new infrastructures for economic development. Irrigation and electric power, the basis of agriculture and industry, received high priority in the Reconstruction and Economic Development Plan. India's external financial position (1948–9) was burdened with food imports, leading to an adverse balance of payments and disequilibrium in the economy. During the preceding years, India was paying more than Rs 100 crore a year for importing food at exorbitant prices. Undivided India had 33 million acres of land, but the Partition resulted in more than half (20 million acres) of the total irrigated land going to Pakistan. Of the total of 4 lakh cubic feet of water conveyed through canals per second, half of that also went to Pakistan.[196] The way forward, and the only way out, was to increase the domestic production of food.[197] Irrigation, therefore, was of utmost necessity, a national purpose and not merely for bringing commercial benefits to the particular province or provinces where the projects were to be located.

Ambedkar had, a few years ago, placed his faith in the strength of scientific and technological progress for social upliftment. He had played a stellar role in overseeing the planning process for the optimal development of water and power resources by virtue of his position as a member, Labour Irrigation and Power in the Executive Council of Viceroy from 1942–6.[198] One is relatively unaware of his pioneering contribution to water management in the country and his specific role in planning the Damodar Valley Corporation (DVC) in Bengal and Bihar, the first river valley project in India. In fact, when the DVC was first taken up for formulation under Lord Wavell, the viceroy of India, Ambedkar, as a member of the Viceroy's Executive Council, had sharply contested with the viceroy over the appointment of the chief engineer who would plan and execute the DVC. Wavell's prejudiced choice was a British expert who had worked on the Aswan Dam in Egypt, while Ambedkar favoured expertise from the Tennessee Valley Authority (TVA) and argued that the British lacked knowledge in building big dams and flood control. The fact that Ambedkar could challenge the Viceroy's authority,

> . . . tantamount to indelible audacity . . .[199]

spoke volumes of his courage to take a position on an issue of national interest. He prevailed in the end, and W.L. Voorduin, a senior engineer of the TVA, was appointed to study the Damodar and made his recommendations in August 1944. A national discourse evolved on multipurpose river valley projects and a policy statement was prepared by the Labour Department in consultation with the provincial governments that focused on the development of

> irrigation, waterways and drainage; development of electric power, and inland water transport . . .[200]

Ambedkar continued his involvement in the planning of water development and considered that the water resources would best be governed by the Centre. This led to the establishment of two premier technical organizations: the Central Technical Power Board and the Central Waterways, Irrigation and Navigation Commission, to study and plan how best to utilize the water resources. This was in contrast to the Government of India Act, 1935, which virtually debarred the Central government from assuming executive authority over provincial subjects and from intervening in interprovincial matters. Ambedkar had interestingly observed:

> There is only one thing, which the Government of India expects from the Provinces to do. It expects the Provinces to bear in mind the absolute necessity of ensuring that the benefits of the project get ultimately right down to the grassroots, i.e., everyone living in the Valley and some of those in the vicinity, all have their share in the prosperity which the project should bring. This, in my view, is essential, and it is for this reason that we want the establishment of some agency early enough so that that agency can set about planning at once in which its essential and ultimate object can be secured.[201]

The DVC, which was established by an Act of Parliament in July 1948, ushered in other projects like the Bhakra-Nangal Dam (highest gravity dam), Hirakud Dam (longest major earthen dam) and Sone river valley project. As irony would have it, a man whose untouchability had once denied him water in school became the principal architect of India's multipurpose approach for water resources and water policy.

In a debate on the DVC Bill in the Constituent Assembly of India on 11 March 1948, M. Ananthasayanam Ayyangar from Madras led the early part of the discussion. He stated,

> So far as money is concerned we are prepared to vote it, even though there may be deficit budget.

But then he went on to raise questions on the experience of the engineers in dam construction.

That is the difficulty,

he said, noting,

> No dams have been constructed in the Punjab till now or anywhere
> in the North. Dams were only constructed in the South.[202]

There was a wide belief of professional rivalry between the engineers
of the south and north India on matters relating to construction
of dams and when asked if 'southern' expertise could be involved,
Ayyangar doubted whether the engineers from southern India would
be willing to serve under those who had not had such experience. He
instead suggested to N.V. Gadgil, the minister of Works, Mines
and Power, to be careful in selecting the right people for the DVC
and other big projects that were planned.[203] Earlier, the American
engineer John Savage, involved with the TVA, had been invited
to India to survey a dam site at Bhakra in 1944 but returned to
Colorado finding 'money and manpower' hard to get. Ayyangar had
sharply observed,

> Instead of wasting Rs. 10,000 a month over such a person [John
> Savage demanded this amount to stay on] let us have a pool of
> officers, give them attractive salary, even Rs. 5000 a month for a
> short term contract—small organisation of all the engineers who
> had anything to do with dam construction—and let the work be
> entrusted to them.[204]

Another notable bottleneck that was raised in the debate over the
bill was the clause over the sharing of loss between the Centre and
Bengal. Upendra Nath Barman from Bengal had observed, with
no intended provincialism, that the Centre was ready to share the
profits but not any loss. Led by Barman, a number of members in
the Constituent Assembly proposed that this proviso be omitted.
Barman's proposition was that

. . . if Government will be prepared to accept the removal of that
proviso from the clause of the Bill, I am ready to accept that
position and share equally with the Centre either in the profit or
loss that arises out of that flood control project. If, however, the
Centre is determined that it shall not share any loss arising out of
the flood control project, in that case my proposition is that the
Centre should let alone the province of West Bengal so far as its
operations regarding the flood control project is concerned.[205]

The DVC Bill was intended to give a direction to similar multipurpose projects in the near future. It was widely felt that its success
would help reduce India's food deficit of 5 million tonnes and by
doing so conserve India's foreign exchange. Interestingly the debate
also cautioned in a certain sense that the utility of the project should
not be seen as a stunt for vote bank politics as was witnessed in
Punjab, during the British rule, when the Unionist Party used the
Bhakra Dam slogan to win elections for over a decade without the
project making any headway. The emphasis was on timely completion
of the project. But more often than not the TVA experience was
brought up in the debate from various perspectives, especially in
matters relating to the DVC paying central taxes and the question
of allocation of expenditure on the three different aspects of the
project, namely irrigation, power and flood control. Referring to the
allocation of expenditure on the floor of the house, Gadgil stated,

> In the case of the Tennessee Valley this question was considered for years
> together and what is ultimately known as the principle of 'alternative-
> justifiable expenditure' was accepted to be the most equitable.[206]

A few months later when the DVC became an Act, on matters
relating to taxes, the Act laid down that the

> . . . Corporation shall be liable to pay any taxes on income levied
> by the Central Government in the same manner and to the same
> extent as a company . . .

and

> . . . the Provincial Governments shall not be entitled to any refund
> of any such taxes paid by the Corporation.[207]

Despite the fears of nationalization and socialization on the one
hand and scepticism over the corporation becoming an autocracy on
the other, the DVC brought in a new thinking in the economics and
social development of India and the TVA, as a model of structural
and social engineering, largely captured the imagination of the
legislatures. With an aim towards higher agricultural productivity
that required infrastructural inputs like electricity and fertilizers, the
involvement of scientists and civil engineers became a necessity and
their coordination was of utmost significance for the multipurpose
projects to be sustainable. The engineers could not

> . . . with their fat salaries go on making maps sitting comfortably
> in their chairs . . .[208]

without not making the connection between applied science to
production and development.

Like Ambedkar's consequential interventions in the DVC,
Subhas Chandra Bose's address to the Indian Science News
Association in 1938,

> What is wanted is a far-reaching cooperation between science and
> politics . . .[209]

awakened the Indian scientific community to science as a task for
national purpose. Leading the thinking to disseminate science
amongst the public, India's foremost scientist, Meghnad Saha,
acclaimed for his theory of thermal ionization, had set up the Indian
Science News Association in 1935. The journal that it brought
out, *Science and Culture*, became an important medium to express
scientific economic planning for India, and had impressed Subhas

Bose. But more importantly, Saha persuaded Bose, as the president of the Indian National Congress (1938), to set up a National Planning Commission. In its initial period, M. Visvesvaraya became the chairman of the Committee. However, Saha always felt that to gain rightful traction, such a platform required stewardship of an eminent political figure, probably none better than Jawaharlal Nehru. Together, the two worked closely on the Planning Commission, trying to translate ideas into realities but, unfortunately, their understanding became estranged especially on the creation of the Atomic Energy Commission to which Saha was not a great votary. Saha's abiding interest in astrophysics was, of course, well known, but he was also deeply concerned with the recurring floods and the devastation that it caused. Without proper scientific assessment of the rivers, Saha felt flood policies would be weak and ineffective. The floods in Bengal in 1943 made Saha devote his time to finding responses to the calamity, first by sensitizing the issue through writings and speeches, and then by working with Ambedkar on the planning of the DVC. It is in this context that Saha went to Denver, US, as member of the Indian Scientific Mission that was instituted to promote scientific cooperation between India and the advanced countries.[210] Saha travelled the Tennessee state extensively, soaking in knowledge on the functioning of the dams built there under the guidance of Savage. Back in Calcutta he was more than convinced about the TVA model of planning and hydrology for the DVC.[211]

The sweeping vision of the TVA, with its technical and scientific application to social development, was hard to brush aside even as concerns on issues of displacement were expressed in the Constituent Assembly debate. Gadgil wanted the best of minds to be involved in the project and had already instructed Sudhir Sen, the economic adviser in Moscow, to visit the TVA and study its management. On his return, Sen became the chief executive officer of the DVC.[212] Likewise, Kanwar Sain was called to duty from Bikaner to the Centre for national needs and in April 1949, he joined the Central Water and Power Commission. Civil engineers like Sain saw the transition from the colonial aspirations of making engineering advantageous for society to the national takeovers of the projects as a natural progression for the advancement of the modern state.[213]

After Partition, East Punjab and the adjacent princely states were important areas for agricultural development. In order to maximize the flow of the Sutlej, the Beas and the Ravi for substantial expansion of irrigation, a large number of multipurpose projects were planned that could store water. Simultaneously, constructing additional canals for the delivery of water and remodelling the existing ones were also undertaken in the Punjab and in Rajasthan.

Table 2: Details of canal infrastructure after Independence

Sr. No.	Project Name	Year	River	Location
1.	Bhakra Dam	1963	Satlej	Bhakra (HP)
2.	Nangal Dam	1948	Satlej	Downstream of Bhakra Dam
3.	Nangal Hydel Channel	1954	Satlej	Nangal Dam
4.	Bhakra Main Line Canal	1950–54	Satlej	Ext. Nangal Hydel Channel
5.	Old Sirhind Canal System	1952–54	Satlej	Ropar Headworks
6.	Harike Headwork	1954–55	Satlej-Beas	Harike
7.	Madhopur Beas link	1955–57	Beas-Satlej	Madhopur
8.	Rajasthan canal	1958–61	Satlej-Beas	Harike Headworks
9.	Ferozepur Feeder	1952–53	Ravi-Beas	Harike Headwork
10.	Pong Dam	1974	Beas	Pong
11.	Beas Sutlej Link	1977	Beas-Satlej	Pandoh (HP)

Sr. No.	Project Name	Year	River	Location
12.	Shanehar Headwork	1983	Beas	Downstream of Pong Dam
13.	Mukerian Hydel Channel	1982	Beas	Shanehar Headwork
14	Ranjit Sagar Dam	2000	Ravi	Upstream Madhopur Headwork
15	Shahpur Kandi Dam	2006–07	Ravi	Downstream of Ranjit Sagar

Source: Government of Punjab, Punjab Irrigation Department

On the other side of the boundary, with the Ferozepur headworks given to East Punjab, Iftikar Hussain Khan Mamdot, the chief minister of West Punjab, acted with urgency to find an alternative supply that would reduce his province's vulnerability. He was a popular figure and had worked hard to oust the Unionist Party and ensure the success of the Muslim League in the Punjab provincial elections in 1946. Jinnah had personally congratulated him on the success of expanding and strengthening the Muslim League in the province. He was in true spirit, like his father Sir Shah Nawaz Khan, a Muslim Leaguer and sincerely believed that the aspirations of the Muslims in India could only be safeguarded by the Muslim League. One of Iftikar Hussain's important contributions as chief minister of West Punjab was to oversee the construction in 1948 of the 100-mile-long Bombanwala–Ravi–Bedian–Dipalpur (BRBD) Link Canal for the diversion of Ravi flows to the Sutlej in anticipation of future stoppages by East Punjab. In quick time, surveys were done, the feasibility assessed and the work on the link canal began at a feverish pace to divert the flow of the Chenab and the Ravi to compensate for the loss of the Sutlej–Beas waters to India.[214] The project entailed the upgradation of the old Raiya branch to a full-fledged canal with a bed width of 63.41 m. The link canals were built across the doabs of West Punjab, bringing water from the Indus to the Jhelum, from the Jhelum to the Chenab, and from the Chenab to the eastern rivers. Iftikar Hussain had rallied the people of Lahore in building the canal as an important line of defence against aggression from India and received whole-hearted support with a large number of men and even schoolchildren turning out to work on the canal.

The BRBD Link Canal was completed in 1950, and with its water supply Pakistan was no longer dependent on the Ferozepur headworks to keep the Lahore branch and the Dipalpur Canal from running dry. No project in Pakistan has ever since been completed in such a short span of time. Soon after the BBRD Link Canal was completed and in order to 'tap alternative sources', Pakistan started the construction of the Balloki–Sullemanki (BS) Link Canal in 1951 to transfer 15,000 cusecs of water from Balloki on the Ravi to Sullemanki barrage on the Sutlej to improve water supplies of the Sutlej Valley Project Canals.[215] The canal was opened in 1954. This was immediately followed by the Marala–Ravi Link Canal to transfer 22,000 cusecs of water from the Chenab to the Ravi and thereon from the Ravi via the BS Link Canal to supply additional waters to the Sutlej Valley Project canals.[216] The above-mentioned canals were undertaken as a reactive measure and with a sense of urgency fearing India appropriating the West Punjab water shares by building the Bhakra and the Rajasthan canals. India had realized in 1948 that by closing the CBDC system and the Dipalpur Canal the surplus water accumulated without necessary infrastructure to utilize it would only mean that the waters would eventually have to be allowed to flow downwards to Pakistan.

MAKING *of*
the INDUS
WATERS TREATY

US Knocks at Kashmir's Door

The destiny of India–Pakistan riparian relations was not to be shaped in the subcontinent's dangerous allure of politics but some 12,000 kilometres away in Washington, D.C. Here the Truman administration was still getting the hang of the epic developments unfolding in the partitioned region and how the future peace and stability would be determined by the tumultuous event. By the middle of December 1947, the Kashmir situation had become grave, and Mountbatten's mediatory efforts to bring a reconciliation between Nehru and Liaquat reached an impasse with an angry, frustrated and belligerent Nehru speaking of striking at invaders' camps inside Pakistan.[1] Disturbed by the outburst and not doubting Nehru's intention, Mountbatten

> . . . intervened to suggest a reference to the UN, as mentioned in Chapter 12.[2]

Mountbatten had often given the impression that India had a solid case in the UN, but behind that was the more serious task of restraining India. An outbreak of war would have meant the withdrawal of all British military personnel from the subcontinent, rendering Pakistan weak and vulnerable. It was clear that the British government was rattled by Nehru's

> . . . Brahmin logic . . .[3]

of Kashmir being a part of India, and it was left to Mountbatten to influence and even shrewdly manipulate Nehru to discard the notion of war. While firm on India's right to self-defence and appropriate military actions across the border, Nehru, however, agreed to refer the Kashmir matter to the UN. Narendra Sarila, who was the aide-de-camp to Mountbatten and later joined the Indian Foreign Service in 1948, writes,

> When the Indian Cabinet members agreed to complain about Pakistan's aggression to the United Nations, they did so under the impression that it was a prelude to India marching towards the invaders bases if they did not withdraw within a short time. However, the fact remains that though the complaint to the UN was lodged on 1 January 1948, no military preparations were made by the Indian C-in-C for carrying out any operations.[4]

It marked possibly the beginning of many of Nehru's vacillating decisions on Pakistan. At one level, Nehru was unapologetic and determined to deal with raiders from Pakistan as firmly as he could, but at another, he was quick to question his own rationale. In a letter to Sardar Patel on 29 December 1947, Nehru explains,

> Among the consequences to consider are the possible effect on the British officers in the Army and also the reaction of the Governor-General (i.e., that he may decide to leave India).[5]

This was, on the one hand, quite baffling to say the least as Nehru was more than aware of the British duplicity in recognizing Pakistani raiders in Kashmir and of Indian troops withdrawing to Jammu.[6] On the other hand, it was equally true that Mountbatten's continued presence was seen as a stabilizing influence in the difficult post-Partition times, and the fear that Mountbatten would leave India must have weighed heavily on Nehru. A paper reasoning why Mountbatten should stay on in India had outlined,

> Field Marshal Auchinleck has clearly stated that, if Lord Mountbatten left, he himself would resign. The Commander-

in-Chief of the other services and Army Commanders have expressed similar intentions. . . . Opinion is unanimous among all, including the Indian political leaders, who have any knowledge of the problem, that this would lead to disastrous results. The one stable element in India, namely the Indian Army, might well disintegrate and riot and bloodshed on an appalling scale would result.[7]

Be that as it may, it cannot escape attention that the ideals of Nehru (argued earlier as well) had from time to time begun to irk some of the Indian leaders. In a conversation with Mountbatten in October 1947, Sardar Patel had frustratingly said,

I regret our leader [Nehru] has followed his lofty ideas into the skies and has no contact left with the earth or reality.[8]

The seriousness of the situation in the subcontinent prompted the British government to seek the influence of the US to open lines of communication with India, hoping that Washington's counselling would encourage New Delhi to accept the Security Council's recommendations of a three-step process for the resolution of the 'Kashmir dispute'. The US, however, had its own calculations and maintained cautious neutrality by suggesting to Pakistan that it rein in 'irresponsible elements' and to India to maintain peace and tranquillity. Thus began the US's early interest in the post-Partition subcontinent courtesy the British lobbying in Washington with key officials like secretary of State, George Marshall, and under-secretary of State, Robert Lovett, and in New York with Warren Austin, the US ambassador to the UN.[9] As Kashmir was being extensively debated in the Security Council in the early months of 1948, the US gradually developed an understanding on the issue. The British were successful in influencing Austin and the American delegates in the UN to support Pakistan on the grounds that Jammu and Kashmir had 77 per cent Muslim population and to adequately pressure India to concede. However, Washington had a different view and unlike the British who treated Kashmir as a 'territory in dispute', the secretary of State office reasoned that

> ... Kashmir was a state about which a dispute had arisen between India and Pakistan

and that it

> ... found it difficult to deny the legal validity of Kashmir's accession to India.[10]

Dean Rusk, who later became the US secretary of State, officially consulted with the British in Washington and was not sufficiently impressed with the British proposal of Pakistani troops policing the process of plebiscite in Kashmir, saying,

> ... the furthest we could go would be to envisage the use of Pakistani troops as a result of an agreement between the Governments of Kashmir and the Governments of India and Pakistan.[11]

It was becoming increasingly clear that a gradual strategic orientation was being shaped in Washington towards the subcontinent in which the US would become the key influencer. This was a role the British were accustomed to but in the changed circumstances, found themselves materially, emotionally and financially incapacitated. In a letter on 4 March 1948 Marshall wrote to Austin,

> ... the SC [Security Council] cannot impose settlement under Chapter 6 of the UN Charter but can only make recommendations to parties. Such recommendations must necessarily be made in the light of India's present legal jurisdiction over Kashmir.[12]

The bitter mood prevalent in India over Austin's collaborative biases and the British delegates' unfair stand on the Kashmir issue in the Security Council may have allowed for such an expression. However, in the US's larger global strategy, with one eye on the Soviet Union, the anti-communist position of Pakistan steadily found favour in the US policy circle.

The Kashmir issue thus became less about the technicalities and merits and more a chessboard of power rivalries. For India, it was

> . . . a very rapid education in the field of international relations.[13]

Despite the US sympathy towards Pakistan, the attitude of the British delegation at the UN which was clearly stacked against India, and the lack of interest of the Soviet Union, the Security Council Resolution (47) that was finally adopted on 21 April 1948[14] was not, given the circumstances, unfavourable to India. The resolution called for a plebiscite, which India wanted and rather quickly so, for a settlement to the Kashmir issue. The plebiscite on Kashmir was, according to the UN resolution, subject to two conditions being sequentially fulfilled, which was critical as the British had earlier pushed for plebiscite to be the

> . . . first issue.[15]

First, Pakistan was to

> . . . secure the withdrawal from the State of Jammu and Kashmir of tribesmen and Pakistani nationals . . . and to prevent any intrusion into the State of such elements and any furnishing of material aid to those fighting in the State.[16]

and second,

> . . . when it is established to the satisfaction of the Commission, set up in accordance with the Council's resolution 39 (1948) that the tribesmen are withdrawing and that arrangements for the cessation of the fighting have become effective.[17]

India, in response, was to withdraw its own forces

> . . . from Jammu and Kashmir and reducing them progressively to
> the minimum strength required for the support of the civil power
> in the maintenance of law and order.[18]

For Pakistan, the UN Resolution was a let-down as it had hoped
that the world body would recognize the presence of its troops
in the Muslim-majority Kashmir, and as a result it continued
fighting and holding on to the portion of Kashmir under its
control, thereby never fulfilling the first necessary condition for
the plebiscite. In May 1948, the Pakistan Army had reportedly
dispatched its regular troops to Kashmir to resist the Indian
Army's all-out offensive to clear out the 'raiders' once and for
all.[19] What was alarming for Pakistan was the fear that the
Indian military offensive could result in the Mangla headworks,
which controlled and supplied water from river Jhelum through
the upper Jhelum canal, falling into the control of India and the
Marala headworks, which was within a mile or so of the border,
coming under threat.[20] It was a disastrous scenario for Pakistan as
its irrigation system and hydroelectricity projects were dependent
on the Kashmir rivers and the

> . . . occupation of these rivers and their dams by the Indian army
> and the eventual diversion of their waters through canals would
> have meant Pakistan's quick economic death.[21]

Adding further to Pakistan's fear was the fact that India had already
established upper riparian rights on the headworks on Sutlej and Ravi
in East Punjab. By November 1948, Indian troops had crossed the
Zojila and were determined to recapture Mirpur and Muzaffarabad
situated on the Pakistan frontier. The Indian soldiers' high morale
and determination to launch a decisive offensive sent shivers down
Pakistan's spine and had equally worried Attlee, who saw Pakistan
as a 'valuable ally' to be protected at any cost.

With the US, at this stage, taking a hands-off approach and playing wait-and-watch to the unfolding situation in Kashmir, which it felt was pro-Pakistan, Attlee was left to rely on his military officers and diplomats to influence Nehru to seek a political solution rather than a military one. Even Mountbatten, who had left India in June 1948 and continued to maintain correspondence, 'counselled' Nehru to strongly consider a ceasefire. Had the Indian offensive to recapture Muzaffarabad and Mirpur in November gone ahead, India could have reclaimed most of Pakistan-occupied areas and the territorial context of Kashmir would have significantly changed. British high commissioner, Archibald Nye, and commander-in-chief, Roy Bucher, were successful in convincing Nehru to the folly of the offensive and eventually Nehru conceded. On 1 January 1949, the Karachi Agreement's ceasefire order made a de facto partition of Kashmir, resulting in 65 per cent of the territory being under Indian control and the remainder with Pakistan. The British realpolitik and its 'Pakistan strategy', along with the somewhat crystallization of the Cold War and the actions of the nascent UN, all contributed in different ways to the fortunes of Kashmir in 1948. Kashmir, the pivot of geopolitical dynamics, marked high points in India's military capabilities and the admission of the Pakistan Army's involvement but none more significant than its 'internationalization', leading to the involvement of major powers.

With the Truman Doctrine taking firm root by 1948 to provide assistance to democratic nations and contain threats from Soviet totalitarianism, global affairs began to distinctly change. In the backdrop of Britain's imperial decline, the Marshall Plan,[22] providing economic aid for Greece, Turkey and Western Europe, became an important instrument of the Truman administration to preserve the political integrity of democratic nations against Soviet aggression. It went a long way in establishing the US's dominant role in the coming decades. Asia, however, presented a radically different set of challenges. Securing strategic and economic interest in areas geographically far and away from the US was inordinately difficult. China, which the US had hoped to befriend, had turned to communism in 1949, leaving the

> . . . Indian subcontinent, as the place where democracy might make a stand—perhaps its last—in Asia.[23]

India joined on its own terms the Commonwealth in 1949, much to the relief of Britain and also the US. The Commonwealth, the US hoped, would provide the required platform for it to champion its world view without being directly involved in the Indian subcontinent.[24] In what appeared to be straightforward, the US policy was to 'encourage cooperation' between India and Pakistan lest the region become 'Balkanized'. Its view on Kashmir was one of concerned approach and intermittent advice through the period of 1948–9 despite British encouragement to play a decisive role. Kashmir was a Commonwealth problem and the American officials strongly felt that

> . . . if any third party had to be caught in the Kashmir grinder, better Britain than the United States.[25]

The US approach of non-interference in the Indian subcontinent, however, was short lived and a number of US planners came to believe that an alliance with Pakistan would help strengthen its policy towards the Middle East, which was facing daunting challenges as a result of

> . . . endemic political and economic instability, the bitter Arab-Israeli dispute, tensions among the Arabs, and lingering resentment over Western colonialism.[26]

The US alignment with Pakistan aroused considerable criticism for bringing in the Cold War to the doorsteps of South Asia and which

. . . deeply alienated India and Afghanistan to foster their ties with the Soviet Union.[27]

Despite the US's growing preference for Pakistan in its larger global strategy and India's substantial tilt towards the Soviet Union, the relationship between Washington and New Delhi was not an open-and-shut case. India's regional significance and its preference for democratic values encouraged a section of policy thinkers in Washington to consider India as the bulwark against the spread of communism in Asia. Such impressions quickly wilted when Nehru visited the US in October 1949 and delivered his 'Voyage of Discovery' speech at the US Congress, saying,

> Yet, though we may know the history and something of the culture of our respective countries, what is required is a true understanding and appreciation of each other even where we differ.[28]

It was more than clear, as the American officials discovered, that India would not in any circumstances shift from its independent nonaligned position. Nehru's maiden visit to the US had created enormous excitement and much expectation of a possible alignment, but ended with deep divide on key global issues, including the Soviet Union. The Indian prime minister's diffidence was too stark to go unnoticed. In contrast, Liaquat's visit to the US in May 1950 was one of bravura and an open embrace of American policy.

The following month, when the war broke out in the Korean peninsula along the 38th parallel, with the Soviet-backed North Korea aggressively moving south to Seoul, the US committed itself to a combined UN military effort to defend South Korea. By the end of September, South Korea was regained and a few days later, the UN forces were moving into North Korea, inspiring country singer Jimmie Osborne to record the song 'Thank God for Victory in Korea'. The objective was accomplished but at a heavy cost as the Chinese entered the war, as they had threatened to do, in far greater numbers and military capacity than the US intelligence had predicted.

The war would continue for thirty months, heightening tensions between the Soviets and the US. The Truman administration, with widespread domestic anti-communism sentiments, could no longer be seen as being 'soft' on communism abroad. This undoubtedly had a reverberation in South Asia, and Pakistan became for sure a better bet than India.

Who's There? The World Bank

Soon after his tenure as the chairman of the Atomic Energy Commission (AEC), David E. Lilienthal, planned a personal visit to the subcontinent in January 1951. Before undertaking the journey, he had consulted Dean Acheson who, as secretary of State, was more than happy to facilitate a visit that would be

> . . . very helpful, very useful in a number of ways.[29]

The Americans had sympathized with nationalist movements in Africa and Asia, recounting their own experiences of the American revolution and the US administration was eager to anchor relationships in a brave new world with new nations, particularly India. The US, however, had very little knowledge and understanding of India's history, culture, religion or politics except for the fact that American diplomatic historians had been attentive to the Indian National Congress's struggle for Independence and viewed in admiration the Congress leaders' efforts.[30] In this context Lilienthal's visit could not have been more significant. Walter Lipmann, the political commentator noted for his persuasive critique of democracy,[31] suggested that Lilienthal should also visit Pakistan since the core of the Kashmir problem stemmed from the

> . . . struggle over rivers, rivers with their headworks in Kashmir, flowing through Pakistan.[32]

Lilienthal met Nehru, spending almost a week at the sprawling Teen Murti complex and was impressed by his outlook, describing him as a

. . . predominantly modern man.[33]

He also met Liaquat who, when asked about the issue of water between India and Pakistan, 'snapped this answer' in a tone of anger and frustration,

> Unless the Kashmir issue is settled it is unreal to try to settle the issues about water or about evacuees.[34]

Lilienthal returned to the US, having made copious notes of his observations that included his long discussion with Sheikh Abdullah about Kashmir and interactions with engineers with whom he visited the works on the Indus, the Damodar Valley Corporation, the Hirakud project and even the proposed dam site on the Kosi river. But what probably most impressed him was the relief map of the Indus basin that he saw in Delhi's North Block.[35] Lilienthal always believed that

> . . . he had something to say, and something that needed saying badly.[36]

In October 1943, as the chairman of the TVA, he had recorded his relief over completing the manuscript for *TVA: Democracy on the March*, which was eventually published in March 1944.[37] It would have been a shame if Lilienthal had not published an account of his visit to the subcontinent and, as things transpired, *Collier's* commissioned him for a set of articles. In the first of the articles, 'Are We Losing India?', Lilienthal wrote,

> We [Americans] are witnessing today what may be the beginning of the end of friendly relations with India.

But he concluded by expressing,

> Nehru represents democracy's last hope (though not insurance) against another major reversal for democracy in Asia.[38]

In times of deep McCarthyism and 'red scare', which aimed to enforce an ideological conformity against the Soviet Union, Lilienthal had greater insight and optimism over India and its leaders, in particular Nehru than, for example, the acerbic William Bullitt, who, as the former ambassador to Soviet Union and a foreign policy adviser to Roosevelt, continued to retain influence in the Capitol Hill with his militant anti-communism diatribes. Nehru's own idea of the 'balance' in the Cold War between the US and Soviet Union, interpreted as a tilt towards Moscow, had riled Bullitt to such an extent that in his two-part article in *Life* magazine, he castigated Nehru for all the trouble in the subcontinent, characterizing him as

. . . an elegant and exquisitely Anglicized aesthete,

a

. . . Marxian socialist of the Harold Laski school

and a

. . . political Peter Pan.[39]

In 1951, Eugene Black, who became the president of the World Bank a few years earlier and subsequently transformed the institution into a

. . . powerful and indispensable agent of economic growth throughout the world,[40]

had picked up a copy of *Collier's* magazine and while turning the pages, discovered an article by Lilienthal with an appealing title,

Another 'Korea' in the Making?[41]

Collier's was a well-established, weekly magazine particularly noted for its investigative journalism and for raising social issues but fell into financial disarray and eventually folded in 1957. Lilienthal was well known across half the world as the chairman of the TVA, but the wide admiration and even adulation that he commanded in no way suggested that the TVA had an unchallenged appeal.[42] His article instantly attracted Black's vision of a post-colonial world in which technology and planning would act as a catalyst for economic development. Black recalls in an interview,

> I read this article. I bought the magazine. I don't usually buy magazines, but I bought this one. I picked up a telephone and called Lilienthal and told him I read this article, and that I thought I would take steps about it. So he said he thought that was a fine idea.[43]

Lilienthal responded to Black, whom he in a friendly manner always addressed as 'Gene', in a letter dated 20 June 1951,

> I was greatly pleased and reassured by your approving remarks about the article on India; I shall remember to send you a copy of my analysis of what might be done to ease the Pakistan-India relations. This will also appear as an article in *Collier's* late in July...[44]

Once it did, Lilienthal quickly sent a mail on 24 July alerting Black to the piece,

> In this week's *Collier's* I have a companion piece to the one on India about which you were so generous in your appraisal. This one makes a specific proposal for an eventually peaceful resolution of the Kashmir controversy. The proposal, as you will see, involves the World Bank. While I would hardly expect you to comment upon it, at this stage, naturally I hope the line of thought appeals to your judgment as being a move in the right direction, in an obviously difficult situation.[45]

It was Lilienthal's firm belief of extending a helping hand to India in its quest to be a modern nation that made Black sit up as he read through Lilienthal's intriguing account. Lilienthal writes ('Another "Korea" in the Making?') that while Kashmir is 'pure dynamite', it need not necessarily be so and explains,

> The real issue is not the plebiscite, but how best to prevent war between Pakistan and India; how best to promote and insure peace and a sense of community in the Indo-Pakistan subcontinent; how best to avoid a UN situation that will create another, though different, Korea.[46]

More than just a casual onlooker, he perceptively observes,

> Kashmir, in short, is Communism's northern gateway to the great strategic materials and man power of the Indo-Pakistan subcontinent, and to the Indian Ocean.[47]

This was a moot point as there was genuine concern in the US administration over the spread of communism in the 'Third World' and, in Asia, it was widely perceived that the Soviets were stealing a march over the US as the technological leaders. The Soviet Union and its 'great experiment' to transform itself into a modern, industrial society in a relatively short time seemed attractive to the newly liberated countries. As one political analyst observed decades later,

> And whether we like it or not, the problem of the developing nations will remain one of the major irritants (not tranquilizers) in Soviet-American relations, for the development of emergent nations is taking place in the context of an intense confrontation of the two world social systems.[48]

For Black the situation in the subcontinent, grim as it may have looked, presented an opportunity for the World Bank to offer its good offices and extend technical assistance to resolve water issues in the Indus basin. Wasting no time and after having been suitably informed by Lilienthal that the dispute could be resolved and that the division of water resources in the Indus basin was amenable to a technical solution, Black wrote to the prime ministers of India and Pakistan on 6 September 1951,

> I should be most happy to recommend that the Bank lend its good offices in such directions as might be considered appropriate by the two governments.[49]

Before Nehru responded to Black, he sent a letter to his cousin B.K. Nehru (Birju as Nehru affectionately called him) on 22 September 1951. Nehru observed that while Lilienthal's article in the *Collier's* was 'full of mistakes and factual errors' there was nonetheless 'something in the proposal' that he found attractive and that was, as he writes, a 'joint technical survey' of the entire Indus basin. Nehru also categorically mentions in the same letter that the

> Canal waters dispute has nothing to do with the Kashmir issue. . . any engineer or intelligent layman can see that we cannot stop the Kashmir waters running into Pakistan. If there is the slightest doubt about it, there can be a guarantee which may be affirmed by the UN. Thus the canal waters issue must be considered apart from the Kashmir issue.[50]

Both Nehru and Liaquat formally accepted the initiative in their letters of 23 and 25 September respectively. Nehru concurred with Black that it was,

> an engineering matter and should be dealt as such.[51]

Encouraged, Black again contacted the two prime ministers and took particular care to highlight the fact that the negotiations that he was suggesting had been inspired by Lilienthal and that

. . . it would not adjudicate the conflict, but, instead, work as a conduit for agreement.[52]

Thus began the World Bank's involvement, which subsequently became intensive, on the transboundary water affairs between India and Pakistan. For eight years the World Bank's resoluteness and inventiveness kept the negotiations buoyant until finally the Indus Waters Treaty was signed in 1960.

It is quite remarkable that the World Bank, with no political or ideological appeal and scorned as a capitalist and prejudiced agent by the Indian system, became deeply involved in what was, after all, an internal and sensitive matter for India. The national leaders, having struggled long and hard for Independence and indignant over the flight of capital out of India, regarded the World Bank as anything but suitable for the country's development. To Nehru, capitalism appeared to have failed and he found in the Soviet style of progress, with its central planning and public sector investment, a model to be considered, with an added anti-colonialism and socialism appeal. On the other hand, the Indian civil engineers looked beyond the frame of ideology and saw the US as a 'child of modern engineering', successfully integrating science and technology to the needs of society by harnessing the rivers for cheap and renewable energy. Lilienthal's meeting with Nehru must have created a lasting impression as the TVA became a beacon for India's extensive water development starting with the DVC, which was modelled directly on the TVA and inspired numerous other such projects.

One of Black's first signing as the president of the World Bank was a $34 million loan to India in August 1949.[53] This came about after a World Bank mission visited India earlier in the year to assess the financial and economic conditions and survey some of the development projects that India put forward to the World Bank for consideration. In the backdrop of deteriorating India and Pakistan relations, another World Bank mission visited India in February 1950 to evaluate India's capacity to service further dollar loans. The outcome of this was a loan agreement of $18.5 million to finance the development of the DVC. With a set of loans sanctioned, Black was hopeful that he could turn around the not-so-favourable Indian views on the World Bank to becoming a

... partner in their struggle for economic progress.[54]

Black had a nuanced understanding of world politics but with a sort of conservative, problem-solving and pragmatic approach. Food was critically important for India in the immediate post-Independence period. President Truman had promised $190 million worth of food assistance to India until June 1951, but it kept getting delayed because of a divided US Congress and uncharitable diplomatic calculations. The Soviet Union was quick to respond and shipped food grains to partly take care of India's needs. The US's apathy had not registered well with the Indian establishment, creating a deep wound of suspicion and mistrust.

Black seized the moment despite the bitterness that had developed between the US and India and put the weight of the World Bank behind the Indus basin.

We know . . .

as Black would emphasize,

that the problems economic development creates. . . can only be made manageable with more economic development.[55]

Black writes,

I wrote a letter to Nehru, a personal letter. I wrote a letter to Liaquat Ali Khan, who was then Prime Minister of Pakistan. I told him I'd read this article, and I wanted to offer the services of our Bank in trying to work out a program like this.[56]

Black was not sure how his proposal would be viewed by the political masters but was sanguine that if the engineers got together, a new narrative might develop on the Indus basin.

> I felt that engineers were different from other people, that they were interested in combating nature, that they were above politics, they didn't care much about politics. I thought if he'd [referring to Liaquat] get all of them together, we could do it. But I was naive in that because I didn't realize the feeling between the two countries and the historical difficulties involved.[57]

Nehru had outlined the difficulties of the proposal while being appreciative of treating the Indus system as a 'single unit' but on the condition that the Bhakra-Nangal project,

> . . . will have to continue.[58]

Pakistan's response, equally supportive of the World Bank proposal, had sent feelers through its counsel about the legal right of Pakistan to its existing use of water resources that was being denied by India. Pakistan had already objected to the World Bank examining the possibility of a loan to India for the construction of the Bhakra on the Sutlej in 1949.[59] The issues of legality, Lilienthal felt, would 'torpedo' any chance of success of the Word Bank proposal. It was an important intervention, as Lilienthal convinced the Pakistan counsel that

> . . . Pakistan had nothing to gain by that.[60]

Liaquat was assassinated on 16 October 1951, an unfortunate event that would upset both Lilienthal and Black, who had together laboured to develop a good equation with the prime minister. Liaquat strongly believed in internationalism and had famously said,

> The world's future lies not in establishing blocs but in international relations.[61]

On his death, Khwaja Nazimuddin took over as the prime minster. Undeterred by the change, Black wrote a second letter to the two prime ministers on 8 November 1951, indicating,

> The Indus basin water resources are sufficient to continue all existing uses and to meet the further needs of both countries for water from that source. The water resources of the Indus basin should be cooperatively developed and used in such a manner as most effectively to promote the economic development of the Indus basin viewed as a unit.[62]

The letter had four specificities: a) to look at the development on the Indus basin without its relation to past negotiations and claims; b) the two countries would each designate a qualified engineer to study and prepare a long-range plan on the Indus basin; c) the World Bank would likewise select an engineer to work with the two countries' designated engineers and; d) the working party thus formed would determine the procedures.

The letter outlined the 'essential principles' of Lilienthal's proposal. Lilienthal by then had retired from the AEC and had decided to enter into consultancy. On the advice of his friend, Joseph Davies, he joined Lazard Freres, a well-known investment banking firm based in New York. The firm's managing partner Andre Meyer happily offered Lilienthal a starting retainer of $25,000

> . . . with the understanding that even though he did not have any specific duties defined, Lilienthal would bring his knowledge of economic development and his network of political contacts (at home and abroad) to Lazard.[63]

Excited that his ideas were taking shape on the Indus basin but equally aware of his consultancy interest of development and finance, Lilienthal was keen that Black meet the senior partners at Lazard Freres, especially over the Indus basin. Whatever the intention might have been, a few years later in 1955, Lilienthal along with

Gordon Clapp, his successor at TVA, formed the Development and Resources Corporation (D&R) with Lazard that would provide regional economic development services, like the TVA, with a focus on water resources and the construction of dams. The company worked frequently in many river basins around the world but not on the Indus.[64]

Black undertook his first visit to Pakistan and India in January 1952 and met Nehru and the Indian director of the World Bank, B.K. Nehru, on 11 February, followed by a meeting with Nazimuddin in Karachi. He was genuinely satisfied with the outcome and observed:

> I have found common understanding as to the bases on which we can go forward under the Lilienthal proposal . . . except, as the two sides may hereafter agree, legal rights will not be affected and each side will be free to withdraw at any time . . . while the cooperative work continues with the participation of the Bank neither side will take any action to diminish the supplies available to the other side for existing uses.[65]

Gulhati's observation to Black's proposal is significant:

> Since no Indian canal received any water from Pakistan, this provision placed a restriction only on India. It estopped India from 'progressively diminishing its supplies to these canals' (CBDC and Dipalpur) which India was entitled to under, and in accordance with, the terms of the Agreement of May 1948. This provision also put an embargo on India's freedom, under the 1948 Agreement to increase her withdrawals any further from the Sutlej as that would have reduced Pakistan's 'existing uses'.

Gulhati then makes another striking observation:

> It would thus be seen that Pakistan, though she did not get what she wanted, viz., a confirmation by India of her existing uses, secured a positive gain from the new arrangement: estoppel of any

reduction by India in Pakistan's 'existing uses' during the currency of the co-operative work. Apparently India did not at that time appreciate the full significance of this concession to Pakistan; naively perhaps, she felt like the Bank, that a final solution would be reached in about 'six months'.[66]

By making the engineers come together, the World Bank found a way to break years of logjam by making both India and Pakistan formally agree to the proposal of 'jointly developing and jointly operating the Indus Basin river system' with the World Bank as the 'good officer'. The World Bank's plan to substantially increase the use of the waters of the Indus basin was attractive to India given its planned water development projects on the eastern rivers. A few months later in May, a meeting between engineers from India and Pakistan together with World Bank engineers began to study the

> . . . technical measures to increase the supplies of water available from the Indus system of rivers for purpose of economic development.[67]

In the pre-Partition period, as earlier observed, attempts were made at settling disputes which arose because of different projects. But no 'master plan' of development for the entire Indus basin was considered. Despite there not being a single storage reservoir, the basin was able to irrigate almost 26 million acres through a network of canals that depended on the

> . . . ever-varying river flow and on such natural storage such as was provided by the snows and glaciers in the Himalaya.[68]

The World Bank, therefore, was confident that, through technical interventions, it could maximize the available waters of the basin, which, otherwise, went unused into the sea.

As the engineers spread the Indus relief map on the drawing board for a thorough examination of technical measures to enhance the supplies of water available from the Indus system of rivers, the India–Pakistan political relations continued its characteristic struggle of two diametrically opposed philosophies. Nehru visualized a working arrangement for mutual benefit on certain matters affecting both the countries, but talk of partnership hardly translated into action and channels of communication were choked by virulent anti-India propaganda. Kashmir left very little room for India to vary its position while, on the canal waters and evacuee property, India was willing to explore possibilities, including some kind of arbitration and reference to an international court.

The World Bank had taken a giant leap into an area of water sharing that was politically charged and highly emotive. This involved eight years of difficult negotiations, which eventually resulted in the signing of the Indus Waters Treaty. The World Bank would never ever venture towards settling a water dispute anywhere else.

Unequal Music on the Indus

The Working Party was set up on 12 March 1952 and Black informed the two prime ministers the following day,

> I am happy to say that I have found common understanding as to the basis on which we can go forward under the Lilienthal proposal.[69]

The ultimate objective, as the letter confidently expressed, was to increase supplies through engineering measures

> . . . beyond what they have ever been.[70]

This was a quintessential Lilienthal vision and it had come to be known by then as his preference of an 'Asiatic TVA'. There was no mention of the word 'negotiations' in the letter but 'cooperative work', with neither of the two parties taking any such action to reduce the supply of water for existing uses. Before the letter was sent, Lilienthal had reached an understanding with A.N. Khosla, the head of India's team, and India's ambassador to the US, Binay Sen, that India would not 'suddenly' diminish the water supply. Pakistan typically had employed the services of two lawyers, John O'Brian and John Laylin, to safeguard its interest on the water deliveries to the Sutlej Valley Canals and CBDC, clearly signalling that it had little trust in India. Lilienthal's principle that the source of water would not remain the same, but the quantity

. . . would not diminish . . .[71]

formed the basis of carrying out the engineering approach.

It became established early that the World Bank had to ensure adequate management and having collated the twenty-five years of flow discharge from the measuring points, it got the two sides to study it. Lt Gen. Raymond Wheeler, the World Bank's engineer adviser who had earlier worked on the flood protection project on the Tigris in Iraq, was not only able to establish a professional relationship with the two countries' engineers but also a working understanding between the Indian and the Pakistani designees. The hydrology data was essential and as Wheeler noted in an interview, the

. . . Bank is a solution of the problem.[72]

The working party meetings in Karachi in December 1952 and in Delhi in January 1953 entailed site visits and project inspections on either side covering

. . . more than 9,000 miles of road, rail and air . . .[73]

and more

. . . studies and statistics were exchanged . . .[74]

in preparation for the next meeting in September in Washington to determine the cost estimates and time schedule of the new projects.

In the background of what had been achieved by the engineers, Nehru in his address at the fifty-eighth session of the Congress in Nanal Nagar, Hyderabad, on 17 January 1953, spoke of India's international engagement as 'positive neutrality' and of pursuing a policy of 'friendliness and firmness' towards Pakistan. He explained to the gathering the four major points of dispute: Kashmir; treatment of minorities in Pakistan resulting in a large number of refugees coming to India; the evacuee property; and the canal waters. While acknowledging that these issues had no easy approaches, he, however, appreciated the role of the World Bank in finding a way forward to resolve the dispute over the canal waters. Coincidentally, a day later, Yusuf Haroon, the vice president of Muslim League, called upon the

... peace loving nations of the world . . .[75]

to intervene for solutions on the canal waters, emotionally expressing that the vast food grain areas of Pakistan would be virtually turned into desert lands

... if India is allowed to get away with its design.[76]

Internally, Pakistan was in the throes of a constitutional crisis and political turmoil with the anti-Ahmadiyya riots and food shortage that created extraordinary challenges for Prime Minster Nazimuddin, who was eventually dismissed by Ghulam Mohammed, the governor general, a victim of a bureaucratic–military coup. Nehru, amused over the events, described it as 'Gilbertian' but equally concerned, noted,

A number of unscrupulous persons control the destiny of this unfortunate country (that is, Pakistan) and I do not quite know where they will take it . . .[77]

Jinnah's imposing authority and respect that held the system together had become weak with intrigues and dogfighting between powerful leaders with political ambitions.[78] The interior ministry cultivated connections with powerful newspapers to pitch a belligerent anti-India line, with a flurry of news items complaining about India cutting off, or reducing, canal waters, and connecting it with the Kashmir issue.[79] The extremist forces in Pakistan were from time to time not only baying for India's blood but had started to cause irreparable damage to the foundations of its fragile democratic structure. A politically fragmented Pakistan with strong anti-India sentiments hardly boded well for the progress of bilateral issues. In India, some members of Parliament were losing patience with Pakistan, accusing Nehru of appeasement and not being stern. In a response, on the floor of the Lok Sabha, Nehru said,

> Whenever we have asked as to how we can show strength, some suggestions have been made, which appeared to me then, and which appear to me now, as totally impracticable and undesirable as this suggestion about breaking off diplomatic relations.[80]

In fact, Nehru got greatly exercised, which he himself acknowledged, over the endless concerns over the canal waters in Pakistan. On 18 March 1953, he wrote to the chief minister of East Punjab, Bhimsen Sachar,

> The International Bank has come into the picture and generally an impression has been created that we have not kept to our word and our assurance in this matter. This was bad enough at any time. It is much worse when a third party like the International Bank is concerned. What has troubled me greatly is the difficulty in getting at the facts.[81]

Nehru's worldview from Delhi did not necessarily match the Punjab province's outlook of reward and punishment to West Punjab. There is little doubt that the authorities in Punjab were not abiding with the directives from Delhi and were reducing the water supplies to Pakistan canals from the Ferozepore headworks.[82]

If the engineers thought the Indus basin would be immune to the politics of India and Pakistan, they were seriously mistaken. The relationship between the two countries was sliding into uncertainty. The two prime ministers met in London in June 1953 and towards the end of July, Nehru visited Karachi in a further attempt to improve relations. The following month, in Kashmir, Sheikh Abdullah, after his dismissal and arrest, went from agreeing to full accession to India to openly espousing independence and plebiscite, much to the embarrassment of the government. The implosion within Kashmir led to bitter reaction in the press and the political circles in Pakistan. Soon after Abdullah's unceremonious exit, the two prime ministers met again in New Delhi and issued a communique deprecating any propaganda in the press. Diplomatic intent aside, negative campaigns had already gathered steam in Pakistan on the use of the waters of the Indus river. Resolutions were passed by the Punjab Provincial Muslim League (November 1952) and the Punjab Legislative Assembly (December 1952) on the 'grave situation' owing to the headworks being built at Harike and the dam at Bhakra by the Indian government.

Punjab Chief Minister Mumtaz Daultana, responding to the anti-India sentiments and having made an alliance with Jamaat-e-Islami, warned that the canal waters dispute

. . . may develop into a first-class international crisis.[83]

The domestic outcry on the waters was uncomfortably seeping into the working party arrangements, with the World Bank none too happy about the outcome that made

. . . professional principles secondary to politics and emotion.[84]

Not only did Pakistan frame water as a 'politico-religious instrument' but, as reported by the *New York Times*,

. . . referred to the secretariat of the United Nations . . .[85]

complaining that India was diverting waters. Many years after the signing of the Indus treaty, Gulhati notes that he was

> . . . unable to find in the UN secretariat any record of the complaint or of action taken on it.[86]

Using its lower riparian fears, raising bogies and pressurizing the World Bank to act tough on India, Pakistan had worked out its strategy impeccably. How else could one explain Black deputing B.K. Nehru, the nephew of Nehru and India's executive director with the World Bank in Washington, to Delhi to convince the government to allow the World Bank engineers to be posted at various points on the Sutlej and Ravi to monitor the supply of water to Pakistan? Incredibly, the Indian foreign office had no serious objection to the proposal and required the strong reactions of the irrigation officials to shoot down

> . . . such imposition.[87]

Nehru too disagreed with having any foreign observers monitoring the canals. In the midst of the charged political atmosphere between India and Pakistan, that made technocratic solutions seem only good on paper, and despite the resoluteness of the engineers to overlook political considerations and concentrate on a comprehensive plan, the international community unnervingly looked at the Indus basin as a 'flash point'. The situation prompted the US, having 'dodged' the British attempt to involve it in the subcontinent, to have an active approach even if it meant

> . . . without—indeed in spite of—India.[88]

The external factors thus began to, in varied ways, influence the Indus basin.

As the working party engineers commenced a series of meetings in Washington starting September 1953, the embassy of Pakistan in the country issued a pamphlet stating with directness that 'India closes the canals', and

> ... Kashmir is a symbol of danger for the whole world.[89]

Kashmir, like a

> ... cap on the head of Pakistan ...[90]

continued to stymie any progress. Pakistan was playing the victim card to invite international attention to the water issues. The new set of interpretations that Pakistan put for the existing use of water, threatened to undermine the 'unified system' of an engineering solution. Sensing a possible deadlock to its efforts of joint development/common approach to the basin, the World Bank suggested to the two countries to develop their own water use and allocation plans. Engineers from both the sides, together with the engineers of World Bank,

> ... resumed their discussions of technical measures for increasing the supplies of water from the Indus River system.[91]

Each, not surprisingly, differed from the other. According to the Indian plan, of the 119 million acre-feet (MAF) of total usable water of the Indus basin, 29 MAF would be allocated to India and 90 MAF to Pakistan. But according to the Pakistan plan, which estimated 118 MAF of total usable water, 15.5 MAF would be allocated to India and 102.5 MAF to Pakistan.[92] Pakistan's proposal in effect meant

> ... 30 percent of the waters of the Eastern Rivers and none of the Western Rivers to India, and 70 percent of the Eastern Rivers and all of the Western Rivers to Pakistan.[93]

It did not require rocket science to understand that the two proposals were as different as chalk and cheese. On the face of it, the figures were heavily in favour of Pakistan even in the Indian proposal. Was India too generous in its proposal? Did the generosity have a calculated gain? These are questions that continue to intrigue. On instructions from the World Bank, the US was to enter into a contract to deliver to India 1.5 million tonnes of wheat in each of the years 1954, 1955 and 1956 at a value of $450 million.

The World Bank was convinced that waiting for the right political equation between India and Pakistan would be a futile exercise, much like Samuel Beckett's tragicomedy *Waiting for Godot* (1952), in which the two characters, Vladimir and Estragon, wait endlessly for the mysterious Godot for hope and direction, but he never arrives. Black had earlier envisaged that the Indus dispute could most realistically be resolved if the functional aspects of disagreement were negotiated. Finally, in February 1954, after nearly two years of negotiations, the World Bank stepped beyond the limited role it had defined for itself and Black forwarded the World Bank's own proposal to the two prime ministers. The proposal offered India the three eastern tributaries of the basin and Pakistan the three western tributaries. In broad terms, the proposal, based on 'fairness' and 'equitable apportionment' stated that

> ...with flow supplies Pakistan was to meet her historic withdrawals, bring most of the Sutlej Valley Canals up to allocation and meet the requirements of projects in progress. Supplies from the Western rivers not required for these uses were to be transferred to meet to the extent practicable Pakistan's existing uses on the Eastern rivers. India was to have the full use of the supplies thus released and all surplus supplies on the Eastern rivers.[94]

While India was amenable to this arrangement, Pakistan found it difficult to accept and threatened to pull out, noting that the proposals

. . . impose great sacrifices on Pakistan.[95]

According to Pakistan, the new distribution viewed did not account for the historical usage of the Indus basin and repudiated its negotiating position. Pakistan would often seek consultancy from engineering firms bypassing the 'good office' of the World Bank. It had earlier used the expertise of O'Brian and Laylin and in the case of the World Bank's current proposal, sought the help of the US's leading irrigation consultant, Royce Tipton, who concluded that the flow supplies of the western rivers

> . . . demonstrably are not adequate to meet Pakistan's historic and pre-Partition planned uses.[96]

This completely challenged the objective of the World Bank's study, leading to a series of discussions with the Pakistan side. It was eventually agreed that Pakistan would

> . . . accept the Bank's proposal in principle as the basis for agreement on the assumption that a workable plan can be prepared on that basis which will provide, from the flow of the Western Rivers, all the uses envisaged . . . including supplies adequate to meet the planned requirements of Gudu and Sukkur.[97]

Both sides returned to the table but the departure from the spirit of Lilienthal's proposal of the 'unity' of the Indus basin

> . . . could not have been more dramatic.[98]

The World Bank proposal was transformed from a 'basis of settlement' to a 'basis for negotiation' and for the next four years, the engineers were literally locked in arguments and interpretations. Pakistan had carefully cultivated an unspoken theory of 'balancing' India on the Indus basin and the sum of all its settlement was that its share of waters should be based on pre-Partition distribution. In retrospect, Pakistan overinvested in consultants to make a case for its water settlement and now it had to negotiate the World Bank proposal. As Nehru categorically insisted in his letter to the World Bank, there would have to be negotiations before the end of August 1954 and

> . . . an agreement for a new phase of the cooperative work on the basis of the Bank proposal.[99]

The ground had considerably slipped from beneath Pakistan's feet and it shifted its attention on compensation for its water rights.[100] By December 1954, each side had replaced its primary representative, with Niranjan Gulhati for India, G. Mueenuddin for Pakistan, and W.A.B. Iliff for the World Bank. It hoped to usher in a new approach to conciliation based on scientific knowledge and realistic appreciation.

It is to the resilience of the World Bank that it never forewent its objective of working patiently towards 'water for peace' on the Indus basin despite the sheer frustration of getting the negotiations on track. The World Bank was aware of the lack of water regimes and the underdeveloped legal dimensions on consumptive uses to guide it, but was prepared to take the risk. It carefully studied the politico-legal, technical and emotive aspects of the water sharing and disputes that included the provincial water disputes on the Indus basin between the Punjab, Sindh, Bahawalpur and Bikaner in the pre-Partition times.

The issue of absolute or limited sovereignty on the Indus basin that the World Bank had to grapple with had its explanatory root in the 1812 judgment in which John Marshall, the fourth chief justice of the US and one of the greatest jurists, observed:

> A nation would justly be considered as violating its faith, although that faith might not be expressly plighted, which should suddenly and without previous notice, exercise its territorial powers in a manner not consonant to the usages and received obligations of the civilized world.[101]

In 1895, much inspired by the 'American First' objective and
selectively using the Marshall judgment, the US attorney general,
Hudson Harmon, embraced the principle of absolute territorial
sovereignty to conclude that the US did not have any legal obligation
to Mexico to curtail US diversion on the mainstream of the Rio
Grande, which flows from the US to the border with Mexico. In a
nutshell, Harmon emphatically proclaimed that upstream actions,
legally, have no liability or obligation and only as a matter of policy
it could not insist upon 'absolute and complete jurisdiction'. The
Harmon decision since then has been much debated the world over,
particularly as the non-navigable utility of water increased with the
diversion of water for irrigation.

In an effort to formulate rules concerning systems of international
waters, the International Law Association (ILA) in its thirty-ninth
conference in Edinburgh in 1954, established a committee on rivers
headed by Clyde Eagleton of the US to draw a blueprint. The report
that was prepared, as mentioned earlier, had a dissenting note from
S.M. Sikri, member of the committee who later became the chief
justice of India. Sikri adopted the view that

> . . . a riparian of a system of international waters is under no legal
> obligation to its co-riparians with respect to waters of the system
> while in its territory.[102]

When the report was put for consent at the conference in Dubrovnik
(Yugoslavia) in 1956, Sikri's view was rejected by unanimous vote.
The conference called for the enlargement of the committee on
rivers and the continuation of the study to be deliberated at the
next meeting. Sikri was born and educated in Lahore and had seen
the horrors of Partition. For a short time he was the legal adviser to
the Ministry of Works, Mines and Power in 1949 and dealt with the
irrigation plans of the Indus basin. Although his point of view failed
to impress the international jurists, it had a strong resonance amongst
the administrators and civil engineers in the Punjab. Interestingly,
the resolution on the Uses of the Waters of International Rivers

that was moved at the Dubrovnik conference was seconded by three jurists, including M.C. Setalvad, the attorney general of India, along with Manzur Qadir, a senior advocate of the Supreme Court of Pakistan.

The East Punjab upper riparian claims had often frustrated Nehru as he searched for a practical solution to the canal dispute. The World Bank, too, had to encounter East Punjab's claim to use the waters flowing from its territory into Pakistan as it saw fit. The World Bank realized that the 'absolute sovereignty principle' of using waters within its territory, as the Harmon Doctrine suggested and as Sikri commented, was problematic as it would give undue advantage to India and defeat the purpose of common interest of other parties. On the other hand, the 'absolute integrity of the river basin' which was diametrically opposite to the 'absolute sovereignty' was limited in its scope, allowing for only 'in-basin' uses of waters of a natural catchment. 'Out-of-basin' transfers of water were prohibited. Later, a third principle emerged, of 'equitable utilization' and avoidance of 'appreciable harm'. The World Bank worked around this principle and envisioned the basin as a 'necessity of life' governed by 'rules of common riparian law'. The 1931 New Jersey v. New York et al. case was an important guidepost. The state of New York proposed to divert a large amount of water from the tributaries of the Delaware to the Hudson river in order to increase supply of water to the city of New York. Concerned over such an action, New Jersey insisted on strict application of the rules of common law governing riparian proprietors. The other actor, the state of Pennsylvania, also intervened to protect its future needs. Oliver Wendall Holmes, the US justice of the Supreme Court, on delivering the opinion in the case observed:

> A river is more than an amenity, it is a treasure. It offers a necessity of life that must be rationed among those who have power over it . . . The different traditions and practices in different parts of the country may lead to varying results, but the effort always is to secure an equitable apportionment without quibbling over formulas.[103]

Negotiations continued and venues changed from Washington to Rome to London and back to Washington but there seemed to be no light at the end of the tunnel and by the end of 1958, a treaty outcome seemed a remote possibility. Pakistan remained resolute in not accepting any Indian plan that gave it 'control' over part of Chenab waters in Kashmir and allow its diversion. At this point, the World Bank, having received assurance of financial support from the US on the water development projects, effectively intervened and split its negotiations two ways: one with India and the other with Pakistan. The shape of the final solution came to rest on, as Gulhati observes:

> . . . the Bank negotiating with India, broadly on the light of the Indian plan, the amount she would pay towards the cost of replacement; and the Bank negotiating with Pakistan outlines of a realistic plan of replacement-cum-development works, such as would be put on the ground and the cost of which could be met from such aid as the Bank would raise from the United States and other friendly countries and the Indian financial contribution.[104]

From almost breaking down, the time had now come to draft the treaty which began in August 1959. What started on the principles of 'equitable' and 'fairness' became a financial deal. The World Bank, having extracted a solution, was to put an initial price of $250 million as India's contribution towards the cost of water projects to be built in Pakistan, but India had set its limit to the range of $158 million. Eventually India agreed to contribute about $174 million or 62,000,000 in sterling in ten equal annual instalments. Pakistan, on the other hand, to loosely use the phrase, 'laughed all the way to the bank'. The World Bank was now its financial guarantor, undertaking to underwrite the entire cost of her water development works from assistance by friendly countries. To that effect an Indus Basin Development Fund Agreement was simultaneously worked out along with the treaty.[105] The total cost of the entire development programme on the Indus basin was to the tune of $1.07 billion of which $870 million was to be spent on works in Pakistan and $200 million in India.[106] The US had the largest contribution (as loan) to the fund (about $3 million more than India's contribution) and, not surprisingly, a number of US engineering firms eyed the prospect of works on the Indus basin. Congressman Otto Passman, who chaired the House Appropriations Subcommittee on Foreign Aid, observing in a rather amused manner the rush to Indus said,

This is a pretty good kettle of stew here.[107]

For India, its financial contribution and the 'period of transition' was sobering and was hotly debated in Parliament, as shall be observed.

Clamour for Water and Peace

In 1953, Dwight Eisenhower, the five-star general who led the victorious forces in Europe during WWII, became the president of the US. Riding on the irresistible slogan 'I like Ike', the seasoned warhorse won a sweeping victory and immediately set about signing a truce that brought peace along the border of South Korea. With the demise of Stalin, the Eisenhower administration committed itself to easing tensions of the Cold War and maintaining world peace. The Middle East and South Asia, however, remained a strategic concern with no easy approach.

The dilemma had equally gripped the Truman administration. It often contemplated providing necessary inducement to Pakistan in its Middle East defence efforts but feared alienating India. Pakistan, on the other hand, made no bones about joining the US-proposed Allied Middle East Command but was keen to extract a political price in the form of an early settlement to the Kashmir dispute. The Truman administration was not fully certain as to how meaningful Pakistan's troops would be in countering Soviet threats in the Middle East. Moreover, as assessments revealed,

Currently, the danger in this area to the security of the free world arises not so much from the threat of direct Soviet military attack

as from acute instability, anti-western nationalism and Arab-
Israeli antagonism that could lead to disorder and eventually to
a situation in which regimes oriented toward the Soviet Union
could come to power.[108]

Notwithstanding the indecisiveness in the US policy circle towards
Pakistan, Islamabad remained relentless in its endeavour and actively
played its Islamic card as the most suitable candidate to the defence
of the Middle East and continuously raised its strategic relevance as
a bulwark against communism. It almost paid off as the joint chiefs
of staff on 5 November 1952,[109] recommended military assistance
to the Middle East countries, including Pakistan, for its strategic
objectives. The following weeks, however, saw expected uproar in
India and an infuriated Nehru informed the US ambassador Chester
Bowles, in no uncertain terms, that arms to Pakistan would only
embolden the latter to seek a military solution to Kashmir and
that India would be left with no choice but to increase its military
expenditure.[110] Bowles, an ardent advocate of India, strongly
expressed his views to Washington against any moves to undermine
Indo–US relations. The November 1952 electoral outcomes, with
the Republicans coming to power and the lame-duck period of
the Truman administration, ensured that the arms deal did not
immediately fructify.

Despite Eisenhower's differences with Truman, during the
presidential campaign in 1952—of note was his visit to Korea to seek
an end to the war which Truman denounced as 'demagoguery'—there
was nothing remarkably different between the two administrations'
Middle East policy or opinion on Pakistan's strategic value, except
that Eisenhower took calculated risks and eventually stuck his neck
out for Pakistan. A format of a defence plan for the Middle East had
brought differences in the Anglo–American understanding. The
British had, for various reasons, insisted on a Middle East Defence
Organization (MEDO) modelled loosely on the North Atlantic
Treaty Organization, instead of the Allied Middle East Command.
The former, the British argued, would not require the participating

countries to contribute military forces but only participate in joint planning, thereby reducing possible domestic outcry.

For all the British urgency to the proposed MEDO, their own relationship with Egypt was fast deteriorating and negotiations over the future disposition of the British base at Suez had reached a deadlock. The British were also getting restless over Iran's leader, the ever-popular Mohammad Mossadegh, who had nationalized the Iranian oil industry and swiftly ended any further involvement of the British in Iran's oil. Red-faced over the outcome in Iran, Britain with the help of the US and the CIA orchestrated the overthrow of Mossadegh and reinstalled Mohammad Reza Pahlavi, the last Shah of Iran.[111] The change of regime in Iran in August 1953 clearly indicated that Eisenhower was willing to take clinical action to determine the world order unlike the many perceived critical 'inactions' of Truman. With political instability in Iran, the wariness of the Arab states to align with Western powers and widespread fervour of nationalism in the Middle East region, Pakistan's strategic value continued to impress the US policymakers. Unlike Truman, who had never visited Asia or the Middle East during his presidency and often lamented on the difficulty of obtaining facts,[112] Eisenhower was more hands-on and relied on factual information to assess the world.

In May 1953, John Foster Dulles, the secretary of state, embarked on an extensive visit to the Middle East and South Asia to get a feel of the ground and to evaluate the viability of the MEDO proposal. His impression was that, Egypt, as a nucleus of MEDO, was untenable and suggested instead a northern-tier formation of Turkey, Iraq, Iran and Pakistan to bolster a US-led defence alliance. Turkey was more than willing to consider its participation in the alliance, fearing the threat of the Soviet Union, as was Pakistan. A few months later, as explained earlier, a compliant regime was established in Iran. All this boosted the prospect of the formation of the alliance and for Pakistan a revisit of military aid from the US. Throughout the years (1953–4), the Eisenhower administration, like that of its predecessor, debated the efficacy and the quality

of military aid to Pakistan. India still remained a factor and the
Kashmir issue could easily drift into a flash point. In Pakistan, both
the military and political leadership were already proclaiming the
military aid as a done deal, much to the embarrassment of the US
and the consternation of India. Gen. Ayub Khan, governor general,
Ghulam Mohammed, and foreign minister, Zafrullah Khan, made
a procession to Washington in a concerted effort to push the US
for military assistance. With Vice President Richard Nixon, who
unabashedly favoured Pakistan, visiting Karachi in December 1953,
the pro-US Prime Minister Mohammed Ali could not have been
happier with the prospect of the deal coming through. The breathless
Pakistani diplomacy proved extraordinarily effective as Eisenhower
approved of the Pakistani aid programme in January 1954.

What Truman could not accomplish, Eisenhower eventually did.
In return, Pakistan became the US's military ally against the Soviet
Union, providing manpower and airbase to the US. It eventually
became a founding member of the US-supported Baghdad Pact of
1955.[113] Eisenhower's decision was not without its critics. Bowles
had expressed:

> I believe we will isolate Pakistan, draw the Soviet Union certainly
> into Afghanistan and probably into India, eliminate the possibility
> of Pakistan-Indian or Pakistan-Afghan rapprochement, further
> jeopardize the outlook for the Indian Five Year Plan, increase the
> dangerous wave of anti-Americanism throughout India and other
> South Asian countries, open up explosive new opportunities for
> the Soviet Union, gravely weaken the hopes for stable democratic
> government in India, and add nothing whatsoever to our military
> strength in this area.[114]

It was a strategic choice the US made, determined principally for
containing Soviet expansion in the region. While it can be debated
whether the 'choice' made was well assessed or not, or whether
Pakistan could in effect actually thwart any Soviet design, it can be
reasonably concluded that Pakistan's diplomacy won the day and

the arms that it most desperately sought restored confidence in its military leadership to deal with its principal rival, India.

With Pakistan now an undisputed military ally of the American global strategy and India's democratic model as a pièce de résistance to the spread of communism in the region, an ironic situation emerged. On the one hand, a hostile India was detrimental to the US and on the other, India's hostility came about because of the US arms sale to Pakistan. The US hereon, as a policy priority, invested considerable attention to resolving growing India–Pakistan tensions. The World Bank had already got the two sides to the negotiating table on the Indus basin. For Washington, water would be the perfect catalyst for achieving a larger settlement between India and Pakistan and, therefore, it gave its political blessings to the ongoing negotiations. The prospect of 'water for peace' and the World Bank as a 'third party' in the Indian subcontinent may have encouraged the US administration, as a notable reference, to use water as a means to foster cooperation and search for avenues with Israel and the Arab states on the development of the Jordan river. In October 1953, Eisenhower appointed Eric Johnston as his special representative who would

> . . . undertake discussions with certain of the Arab States and Israel, looking to the mutual development of the water resources of the Jordan River Valley on a regional basis for the benefit of all the people of the area.[115]

Eisenhower's statement further elaborated,

> He [Johnston] will indicate the importance which the United States Government attaches to a regional approach to the development of natural resources.[116]

Parallels can be drawn to the initiatives undertaken on the Indus basin and the Jordan river. In both the cases, an emotive history and the accompanied emotional trauma of the division of land was

. . . like an open wound . . .[117]

and impacted the negotiating process. The plan for the utilization
of the waters of the basins was greatly influenced by the TVA. In
the case of the Indus basin, Lilienthal's experience as the chairman
of the TVA inspired the World Bank to undertake the task, while
in the case of the Jordan basin, the US consulting firm Chas T.
Main, under contract with the TVA, prepared the water plan.
Like Lilienthal and Black in the case of the Indus basin, Johnston
had to conduct 'shuttle diplomacy' with technical and political
representatives of the Jordan basin countries. The prevailing political
developments in the respective regions made their task cut out and,
therefore, the effort was to keep the negotiating process low key and
away from the gaze of the media. And finally, a 'unified plan' for the
development of the basin became the foundation for the agreement.
The ongoing development on the Indus and Jordan basins formed
the basis of extensive studies on understanding the pattern of water
and conflict. As the events unfolded in these two basins, some of
the assumptions that water itself was the cause of conflict were
challenged. On the contrary, it was argued that water could be an
enabler to cooperation and that identity formation creating the
'other' impeded dialogue on water. The two basins also brought to
the fore analyses on competitive behaviour amongst the riparians and
as the events revealed, the fear of impending harm in the absence of
water cooperation drove concerned actors to reach out for solutions.
The presence of a third party was an important feature. The US and
the World Bank became deeply embedded in the water dialogue
on the Jordan and Indus basins respectively and later, in 1957, the
Mekong Committee on the Mekong river in South-east Asia was set
up under a statute endorsed by the UN.

The US stake in the outcomes of the water negotiations on the
Jordan and the World Bank-initiated discussions on the Indus basin
was high. Given the political condition in the two regions, water could
serve as a starting point for collective economic development and
prevent any possible escalation of conflict, so the US administration

felt. There, however, was no quick resolution either on the Indus or
the Jordan basin. Much to the dismay of the World Bank, neither
India nor Pakistan seemed willing to compromise on their positions
on the allocation of waters. On the Jordan basin, the Arabs viewed
Johnston's mission as

. . . yet another manifestation of pro-Israel policy . . .[118]

and a manipulative attempt to coax the Arabs to recognize the Jewish
state.

That the Indus and the Jordan basins required political management
to achieve technical details of water sharing was adequately clear.
However, it was also felt that by easing water tensions through third-
party involvement, constructive space could be created for dealing
with complex political and historical difficulties. Johnston worked
tirelessly for two years from 1953 to 1955 to bring out a negotiated
water-sharing agreement between Jordan and Israel. The technical
representatives from both the countries secretly engaged in 'Picnic
Table Talks' at the site of the confluence of the Yarmuk and the Jordan
rivers on issues of water allocations, but these parleys did not have
political sanctity.[119] As an adversary and as a principled position it was
not possible for Jordan to enter into a formal diplomatic agreement
without first Israel and the Palestine Liberation Organization (PLO)
having come to a political understanding.

The water talks, though, proved fruitful in reducing minor
tensions and building trust and confidence. Jordan adroitly used the
covert water dialogues with Israel and the US to offset threats from
Syria and the PLO. The US, on the other hand, along with Britain,
secretly drafted a comprehensive solution to the Arab–Israeli and
Palestinian–Israeli conflicts in 1955, known as Operation Alpha. In
fact, both the countries, while attempting to work out the terms of
the settlement, observed that the

. . . success of the Johnston Mission would be most helpful in
creating a favorable atmosphere for Alpha . . .[120]

The plan, however, was categorically rejected by both Egypt and Israel and it took almost four decades before, in 1993, Israel and Palestine reached an agreement, thus paving the way for the Israel–Jordan Peace Treaty in 1994. On the Indus basin, once the treaty was signed, the US Congress was informed of its participation in the Indus Basin Development Program and a legislation was embodied in the Mutual Security Act of 1960.[121]

Heated Debate in the Lok Sabha

The Indian National Congress, which had functioned as an umbrella organization during the struggle for India's Independence, had then permitted members of other groups, in particular the socialists, to work within the party. However, it had now became a competitive political party eager to continue with power and not share it. In the post-Independence period, intense contestation between the 'ministerial', or the men who made policies, and the 'organizational' leaders, led to breakaways from the Congress Party. The Congress Socialist Party, for example, decided to abandon the word Congress and find a new political space as a responsible opposition and an effective political alternative to the Congress. Leaders like Acharya Kripalani, who was the Indian National Congress president at the time of Independence, quit the party and formed the *Kisan Mazdur Praja Party* in 1951. The following year, it merged with the Socialist Party and became the *Praja Socialist Party* (PSP). A few years later, a section led by Ram Manohar Lohia broke from the party to re-establish the Socialist Party.

The decade saw the consolidation of the socialist principles with non-communist leaders like Jayaprakash Narayan, Acharya Narendra Deva, Ram Manohar Lohia, Ashok Mehta and many others articulating strongly India's social and economic transformation and advocating self-help in building a 'socialist state'. Such thinking was not exclusive to these leaders and there was always the 'left' of the Congress that championed socialist ideas. These leaders and the parties they represented were what one can describe as the

. . . opposition socialists.[122]

This, however, did not translate into any notable political gains in the 1957 general elections and the grand old party, the Congress with a Nehruvian brand of socialism, won more seats than it had in 1951–2 and increased its vote share substantially. Nehru emerged, once again, as the undisputed leader wielding extraordinary political power. By 1958, with over a decade as prime minister, a reflective Nehru often thought about individuals

. . . to rise above petty self and thus think in terms of the good of all.[123]

But he had to equally contend with the growing ideational influence of the socialists who could not be easily shunned. They were, though not in numerical strength a 'strong' opposition group in Parliament, found upholding democratic norms, raising questions fearlessly, and forcing the government to clarify issues, which otherwise, with its absolute majority, would have passed without debate. The Indus Waters Treaty was subject to such political treatment in Parliament.

Parliament was in session until 9 September 1960 and the Indus Waters Treaty was signed on 19 September 1960. The Lok Sabha, the lower house, was not in full knowledge of the provisions of the treaty or whether it was ratified. It was not clear whether the government had consulted the leaders of the recognized all-India parties as to how the treaty would affect India.[124] The opposition felt strongly that India had yielded to Pakistan's terms at the cost of its own interests. In a motion for adjournment in the Lok Sabha on 16 November 1960, Narayan Gore, the leader of the PSP, questioned Nehru's statement a couple of days previously that the IWT had been ratified. Correspondingly, a young parliamentarian, representing Balrampur constituency, Atal Bihari Vajpayee, sought clarification on the issue and raised a 'question of privilege'. Making his submission without entering into an argument, Nehru responded:

This was ratified, I think, on the 24th of September. On the 8th October, the Pakistan Government was informed that we have ratified it. It is one thing to ratify a thing; and it is another thing to have the formalities of it, the exchange of what are called the 'Instruments of Ratification'. That is a technicality.[125]

Vajpayee, whom Nehru had predicted would one day become the country's prime minister, responded with pointed urgency,

May I submit that the ratification of the treaty is not complete until the exchange of Instruments takes place.[126]

Peeved, but not disregarding parliamentary methods, Nehru replied,

. . . the exchange of instruments is a technicality to which the honourable member, perhaps, has not paid attention.[127]

Sitting in the House and perturbed over the lack of meaningful debate, the renowned Odia writer Surendra Mahanty of the Ganatantra Parishad sharply observed that the treaty

. . . is agitating the minds of the people and the government must come forward with this motion.[128]

What began as a procedural issue opened up to a long debate a few weeks later on 30 November 1960 that not only sought various clarifications of the details of the treaty but also prised open old wounds and revisited the history of the India–Pakistan water dispute.

The pulse-beat on the treaty signed by Nehru was not healthy.[129] Several mainstream newspapers had castigated the government for giving in to Pakistan, making

. . . concessions after concessions . . .[130]

as the negotiations progressed and even

. . . yielding to Pakistan's wishes . . .[131]

Bhagirath, published by the Ministry of Irrigation and Power, in its editorial captioned 'A memorable agreement', noted with no triumph,

> This attitude of steady negotiations have lasted over more than a decade and called for considerable patience and sacrifice on the part of India and involved a heavy gift of money and water supply from our rivers for a further period of 10 years with both of which India could well do for herself in this crucial period of the growth of our economy.[132]

In Rajasthan, a strong Congress belt, the mood of the state over the treaty, which it always viewed with trepidation, was hardly encouraging. Harish Mathur, a Congressman representing Pali, unflinchingly said on the floor of the House,

> The progress and the developmental programmes will be retarded and it is all to the advantage of Pakistan.[133]

A number of parliamentarians were of the view that, had India conceded to the needs of Pakistan in 1948 as a 'human consideration', the treaty would have possibly not been required and would have also saved tonnes of paperwork and notes, and many a blush. Was then the treaty a sheer giveaway? Would it have been better for India to have conceded in 1948, when Pakistan's demand was limited, rather than to have become so generous in the negotiations leading up to the treaty? As things developed, Pakistan's demand became bigger and bolder. 'I wish,' said Mathur,

> Our Government takes note of the feeling in this country. It is not that our over-generousness should be at the cost of our own people and at the cost of the development of this country.[134]

Nehru's government had a lot of explaining to do on a treaty that seemed to backtrack from its earlier position. In preparation for a meeting between the Indus negotiators in Rome in 1958, Nehru had expressed,

> I am not at all happy about the way our discussions with the Bank are proceeding in regard to this matter. Step by step, we are dragged in a direction unfavourable to us.[135]

A few months earlier, the newly appointed irrigation and power minister, S.K. Patil, an undisputed leader of Mumbai who was regarded as Sardar Patel's man in Maharashtra, had stated firmly over the prolonged Indus negotiations that

> . . . India will not wait indefinitely for a settlement, ignoring the needs of her people . . .[136]

and that not a drop of water will be given to Pakistan beyond 1962. This had worried Eugene Black, who wrote to Nehru (14 May 1958) about Patil's outburst, to which Nehru replied,

> I agree with it and do not see anything in it which is contrary to our policy and to which the Bank or anyone else can take reasonable objection.[137]

A feeling had emerged that India had agreed to terms that were acting against its own advice and at the cost of its own people. It was calculated that India would lose about 5 million acre-feet of water from the Chenab, resulting in a perpetual loss to the country to the extent of about Rs 70–80 crore per year. The Lok Sabha was keen to understand the advantage or, as many felt, the disadvantage of the treaty.

Ashok Mehta, who liked to challenge Nehru on issues of decentralization and nationalism and was later invited by Nehru to assume the deputy chairmanship of the planning commission for which he (Mehta) was expelled from the PSP, summed up India's position,

> This is a peculiar arrangement wherein the other side's obligations are not brought into the focus at all and unilaterally we come forward to make significant concessions.[138]

Right from the time of the Nehru–Liaquat Agreement in 1950, India, it was felt, often undermined its interest for the larger cause of peace with Pakistan. The Nehru–Noon Agreement of 1958 to end disputes along the Indo-East Pakistan border areas, resulted in an exchange of enclaves and a part of Berubari went to Pakistan, apparently without the West Bengal assembly being consulted. West Bengal was up in arms and the Supreme Court, in a unanimous judgment, held that Article 253 was not sufficient when it came to the question of cessation of national territory.[139] While it was the privilege of the executive to come to international agreements which Nehru exercised, within the democratic framework, it was equally incumbent to consider the opinion and the sentiments of the country and the House. Nehru was chastised repeatedly for placating Pakistan. The issue prompted Arun Guha, a Congress representative from West Bengal, to ask,

> . . . Has Pakistan responded in any friendly manner?[140]

Nehru was not averse to participating in the discussions on foreign policy or economic planning. In fact, he was more than up to it, viewing it as a test and a demonstration of his ability and power unlike his unequivocal stand on social reforms which he candidly confessed to not being knowledgeable about. Nehru had faced the heat of the Parliament over the Tibetan crisis in 1959 with many opposition leaders, including those of the PSP and Jan Sangh, except the Communist Party of India, demanding that the government review its policies of India–China friendship. The spate of adjournment motions on Chinese aggression on Tibet had rattled Nehru as he defended his government's decision to accept Chinese suzerainty over Tibet as a rational choice. The debate on the Indus treaty offered similar intensity and presented some very uncomfortable facts for the government to respond to.

These facts can be categorized into three sections: first, the unfairness of the treaty; second, the cost of the replacement of canal works; and third, the overall context of India–Pakistan relations. Repeatedly the House highlighted India's disadvantage over the partition of the Indus basin. The division resulted in three-fifths of the Indus basin in Pakistan and two-fifths in India. Of the irrigated land in India, only 19 per cent had irrigation facilities while in Pakistan it was 54 per cent. Fundamentally, therefore, India was left with lesser irrigated land and even lesser irrigation facilities. This could hardly be justified as being 'fair' to India. The House strongly voiced its dismay over India being pushed continuously to disadvantage during the course of the negotiations.

> It is a kind of second partition which we are experiencing. . . this is being done again with the signature of our honourable prime minister,[141]

argued Ashok Mehta. While the treaty gave the western rivers to Pakistan and the eastern rivers to India, in terms of volume, 80 per cent of water went to Pakistan and only 20 per cent to India. The ratio of 4:1 heavily favoured Pakistan, and India's initial demand for 25 per cent of the water was gravely noted by the House as a failure in negotiations. In fact, one argument insisted that India should have been given 40 per cent of the volume of water.

From the time of the canal dispute in 1948 until the signing of the treaty, Pakistan gained substantial advantages over India and, by 1960, the per capita use of irrigation infrastructures in Pakistan was three and half times that in India. From the western rivers, India was stipulated to use a small amount, and from the eastern rivers, which in principle were assigned to India, a vast amount of water was flowing unaccounted into Pakistan. In each case it was argued that India had become water deficient while Pakistan, water surplus. With more waters flowing into Pakistan, the House wanted the prime minister to explain how the treaty would help India to increase its irrigation. A linked question to this was whether in actuality Pakistan required 80 per cent of the water and whether Pakistan had the capacity to utilize it. From every point of view, noted Guha,

> . . . this deal has been quite unfair to India and has been over-generous to Pakistan. The more regrettable thing is that waters which India would need badly would be allowed to flow into the sea unutilised and yet we shall be denied the opportunity of developing our own land with that water.[142]

Since Pakistan was now to have surplus water, emphasis on the infrastructure development and the large amount of money being spent towards it was reasoned as being misplaced. Ashok Mehta noted,

> If huge financial payments are to be made, surely one should take into consideration the obligation that the other side owes to us.[143]

The money allocated was indeed a vexed issue and on every count it seemed to disadvantage India. Pakistan was to get grants and not loans to the tune of about Rs 400 crore of the Rs 450 crore required to build their link canals, while India would get Rs 27 crore of the overall requirements of Rs 100 crore to build her link canals. The money was to be given as loans and not grants—Rs 15 crore from the US and Rs 12 crore from the World Bank. But this was not all. India's commitment to make a payment of Rs 83 crore to Pakistan in pound sterling without settling the earlier financial dues with the country was something the House could not comprehend. The payment was to be made in ten annual instalments starting from 1960. The House observed that considering the very desperate foreign exchange position of India, this was foolish. In a scathing attack, Guha said,

The interests of Indian citizens and the Indian nation have not been properly protected by the negotiating party on behalf of India.[144]

In terms of adjustment of debts that Pakistan owed India, only a small sum of Rs 6 crore as dues by Pakistan for the waters that India spared over the years was adjusted, while all other debts remained unsettled.

Nehru would often say, in light of his foreign policy approach, to not miss the larger picture. Having signed the treaty, he emphasized,

It is the context that we have to consider, not a particular bit.[145]

In the political environment of the 1950s, India and its leaders were not averse to reaching out for peace and tranquillity. These were requisites for the stability and development that India desired. Not surprisingly, in 1959 when Ayub Khan advocated a 'common defence' in which

. . . in case of external aggression both India and Pakistan should come together to defend the subcontinent,[146]

Indian leaders like Jayaprakash Narayan and C. Rajagopalachari welcomed the idea. Even the military commander, Gen. K.S. Thimayya, was not entirely opposed to it, although it was cold-shouldered by Nehru, who had acerbically asked,

Who is the joint defence aimed at?[147]

Nehru deeply believed in the idea that India's relations with China could be sustained and considered any formal alliance with Pakistan as

. . . hobnobbing with a junior partner in the Cold War.[148]

The House, when debating the treaty, was not against any reconciliation or confidence-building efforts towards Pakistan.

It may be a price worth paying if the healing process is created.[149]

India may have hoped to usher in goodwill and friendship with Pakistan with its generosity and sacrifice. However, soon after signing the treaty, Pakistan President Ayub Khan talked about the physical possession of the upper reaches of Indus basin rivers and refused to talk about the Kashmir problem. Only a year ago, in September 1959, when the treaty was being negotiated, Ayub Khan, on the request of the Indian government, had happily stopped at Palam airport during one of his routine visits to Dacca and met Nehru. He was affable and gung-ho about the Indus treaty and India–Pakistan relations. But, after having signed the treaty in which Pakistan had successfully extended the transition period from ten to thirteen years and got for itself a substantial amount of $870 million (of a total of $1070 million) to undertake a system of replacement works of the canals, Ayub was singing a different tune. It was even snuggling up to China by

> ... handing over to it sizeable chunks of the territory in the northern part of Kashmir in return for China's support of Pakistan's claim for the annexation of Jammu and Kashmir.[150]

It dawned upon the members of the House that the 'context' that Nehru talked about required two to be working together in cooperation and harmony. For Pakistan it only meant calculated claims and once achieved, it became a pretext for making a new set of claims.

Every concession becomes a thin end of the wedge,[151]

noted Ashok Mehta. This was reinforced by Guha,

Why should we make all these sacrifices when Pakistan is not in a mood to be on friendly terms with India.[152]

In the midst of the criticism of the treaty, it required the intervention of an independent representative, A. Krishnaswami from Chingleput constituency (which no longer exists today because of delimitation), to present the positives without in any way suggesting that the treaty was foolproof. Putting it in proper perspective, Krishnaswami said,

We have reached an agreement on terms which only a far-seeing Government could have accepted.[153]

There can be little doubt that India desired an equitable settlement, but the challenge was to separate the water agreement from the political issues. Krishnaswami focused on the gains on the eastern rivers, which in 1947 irrigated about 4 million acres in Pakistan and 5 million acres in India. He explained that, as a result of the treaty, the eastern rivers gave India the opportunity of irrigating 15 million acres in the future. In order to protect its interest India agreed to financially assist Pakistan to the tune of Rs 83.3 crore for the replacement works to be built in Pakistan. He agreed that India was frustrated with Pakistan's obduracy and its constant threat to withdraw from the negotiations. Nehru was equally conscious of this, at times sanguine and at times disillusioned over the progress. On the question of India's financial payment to Pakistan, Krishnaswami stated,

The cost was determined entirely by Indian engineers, and it was their estimate that was really accepted ultimately by the World Bank and the Government of Pakistan.[154]

At no point in the debate was the World Bank looked at with suspicion, given the fact that it was a bête noir for certain political parties. There was a broad consensus, despite some misgivings, that had it not been for the efforts of the World Bank, the treaty would eventually not have been signed. As Krishnaswami underlined,

. . . historically, this is the biggest international cooperative effort, and unlike the Marshall Plan the impetus has come not from one country, but an internationally constituted organisation and through the dedicated efforts of a single person, the vice-president of the World Bank.[155]

The World Bank's interest in settling the water dispute did require greater scrutiny for a better understanding of the treaty. In a studied observation bringing the past canal dispute and the present treaty into play, Mahanty, who had earlier expressed that the treaty was a surrender which India could well have resisted, said:

At that point of time [the canal dispute in 1948], Pakistan insisted that the two issues [seniorage charges and capital cost of Madhopur headworks] be referred to the World Bank [actually it was a world court] for interpretation; whether India was entitled to seniorage charges and whether she should pay the cost of the Madhopur headworks. At that point of time the Government of India boldly resisted this suggestion. The Government of India insisted that there was no case for interpretation of the agreement. Here what was necessary was implementation of but not interpretation. At this distance of time, I think, the World Court would have been the more appropriate body, it would have been the most judicial body and it could have gone into this dispute between India and Pakistan. I wonder why the World Bank was entrusted with this job. It pains me to say . . . that never in the history of two sovereign nations were a group of commercial bankers entrusted with arbitrating upon such issues of great moment. Why was not this left to the World Court to determine? They could determine whether India was entitled to seniorage charges, whether India should be called upon to pay the construction cost of the Madhopur headworks and carrier channels. Today we are made to pay Rs 83 crores in Sterling, when our foreign exchange position is bad. I hope the hon. Prime Minister will tell us why it was in Sterling and not in Rupees.[156]

Earlier in the debate, Guha had expressed,

> Considering the very desperate foreign exchange position of India,
> it was the height of folly to agree that Rs 83 crores would be given
> to Pakistan in sterling at the rate of Rs 8.3 crores every year.[157]

Mahanty's observation overturned the treaty. First, the scope of
the water dispute, which was limited during the canal dispute,
was widened with the Indus treaty. Second, the seniorage charges,
which was the principal contestation of India in the canal dispute,
was surrendered as the negotiations on the Indus treaty proceeded.
Third, when Pakistan had suggested for a 'third party' to settle
the seniorage charges and the issue of payment for the Madhopur
headworks, India boldly resisted it on the grounds that there was no
case for interpretation of the 1948 agreement. The irony of it was
stark. In 1948, India, it was felt, should have conceded to a third
party but decided to resist. With the Indus treaty, it should have
resisted the third party but eventually conceded. Undoubtedly for
Pakistan, the World Bank was its lifeline and it never fell short of
heaping praise. Months before the signing of the treaty, Ayub Khan
had confidently expressed,

> The English-speaking world ought to feel a special responsibility
> to assist Pakistan. It is not a claim. It is in fact the dictate of
> history.[158]

Nehru, in contrast, while responding to the World Bank proposal on
the cost of the replacement works and the transition period in May
1959, dourly noted,

> Financially very big, and rather overwhelming to our thinking,
> and the period is rather long.[159]

Did the canal dispute of 1948 come to haunt him? Was he
contemplating India's losses in terms of water, time and money? Was

all this generosity worthwhile? Some of his statements, as mentioned earlier, did suggest India's huge burden towards fulfilling the treaty and his own frustration over Pakistan's recalcitrant behaviour and fissiparous demands. However, in the end, with all the trials and tribulations Nehru may have had, he went to Karachi hoping for a better future with Pakistan.

> The welcome at Karachi was formal and correct but not enthusiastic . . . a lot of the local populace had gathered along the streets to have a glimpse of Panditji. But they did not cheer him. It was evident that the military authorities had ordained it that way . . .[160]

wrote K.V. Padmanabhan, the acting high commissioner to Pakistan. On the evening of 19 September 1960 at the

> . . . brightly illuminated . . .[161]

President's House, with a host of dignitaries having gathered for the occasion, Nehru signed the Indus Waters Treaty with Ayub Khan and William Iliff, the vice president of the World Bank. This proved to be Nehru's last visit to Pakistan and the treaty has now lasted for sixty years.

Nehru Convincingly Unconvincing

Nehru had witnessed it all. The bloody Partition, the canal disputes, the exchange of letters with Lilienthal and Black, the droughts of 1957–8 that saw agriculture losses in India as high as 50 per cent, the long years of water negotiations and the uncomfortable task of having to deal with the seven prime ministers in Pakistan who were sacked from 1947 to 1958. As fate presented, Nehru, a model of democratic leadership, had to sign the Indus treaty with Ayub Khan, Pakistan's first military dictator. There could not be a greater irony. But now, in front of the House, Nehru had to respond to the sentiments of the Opposition as well as some of his party members in what probably was one of his biggest defences, on an issue which had bedevilled him for long. Some of his cabinet members had expressed strong reservations over the financial and strategic implications of the treaty. These included the incorruptible and the very austere finance minister Morarji Desai and Krishna Menon, the defence minister, who was being disparagingly referred to as

. . . India's Rasputin.[162]

After having patiently listened for almost two hours to the speeches of the members, Nehru rose to speak on the fateful day on 30 November 1960. As the leader of the House, exhilarated as he always was on such occasions, Nehru began a shade aggressively by expressing his disappointment over the members' view on the issue, saying

. . . so lightly and casually and in such a narrow minded spirit.[163]

A host of critical questions had been put forward by the House broadly signifying India's foolhardy generosity, its unnecessary commitments and inability to settle the Partition debts. Concerns over the Kashmir issue, dispute regarding the Rann of Kutch, status of Azad Kashmir where the Mangla Dam was being constructed by Pakistan while India's proposal to build a dam over Chenab was put on hold owing to Pakistan's insidious pressure, were ventilated by the members with a full sense of their responsibility. Nehru had his plate full, had made notes while carefully listening to the speakers and with

. . . passion but not with malice . . .[164]

set about answering it.

The treaty had to be considered in the context of India–Pakistan relations. Nehru said,

If the hon. Member asks me why Rs 80 crores and odd, well, I cannot give an answer about Rs 80 crores and odd except to relate it to the whole context and say whether in that context it was right for us to agree to that sum or not. If the hon. Member asks me why we have agreed to give more water here or there, for this period or that period, again, I say, it has to be considered in the context of things.[165]

He agreed that the events since the canal dispute of 1948 had not been a pleasant period and one of great frustration, but in the same breath humbly submitted that

> . . . it is a good treaty for India and I have no doubt about it in my mind.[166]

While assuring the House that close attention was paid to each detail, he tactfully praised the engineers

> . . . who fought for India's interest strenuously.[167]

As the prime minister, 'I got only the broad facts,' noted Nehru and the engineers were the

> . . . experts in this matter.[168]

He came back to the canal dispute explaining that the time and circumstances then were radically different,

> It was not a detailed examination; it was a broad approach. I regret to say that that approach was not followed later by the other side, as it often happens.[169]

The role of the World Bank was a less controversial issue to respond to, given that the House was not categorically vehement about the World Bank's role except for some pointed observations by Mahanty.

For Nehru, the World Bank's engagement in the negotiations was an 'ordinary thing to happen', least of all alarming,

> They were not becoming arbitrators or anything.[170]

Recalling his conversations with Lilienthal and Black on the active support of the World Bank, Nehru said,

> It was only a question of an attempt, if you like, at the most, to help in our coming to an agreement between ourselves. They could not impose anything.[171]

From his disappointment on what he felt was the 'narrow mindedness' of the House on the treaty to his explanation of the circumstances of history and the complexities of the issue, Nehru enlightened the House on the question of consulting the Parliament.

> Are we to come at every step and ask Parliament?[172]

Allowing the rhetorical question to seep in, he then elaborated,

> . . . very wisely, the Constitution and convention lay down that in such agreements, Government has to stake its own judgment, its future, on it. There is no other way. One takes a risk; maybe that Government may go wrong. But there is no [o]ther way to deal with it.[173]

However skilfully Nehru tried to separate himself as the carrier of a 'broad perspective' from the nitty-gritty of the negotiations that the engineers engaged in, there was an undeniable Nehruvian internationalist mindset to the entire water issue with Pakistan. Nehru's interest in international problems was well known. His ideals of oneness, though, clashed with the realities of power politics and interest-oriented relations which he understood but adamantly refused to accept. More than a decade ago, he had hoped for an emergence of Asia as an influence on world peace, which soon fell apart. Later, his famous enunciation at the Bandung Conference in 1955 that laid the foundation for the nonaligned movement,

... let us not align ourselves ... but have a line of our own,[174]

was immediately contradicted by the creation of two military pacts, the SEATO and the Baghdad Pact (later CENTO). On the Indus treaty, having heard the diatribes, he asked the House,

Is that the way to approach an international question?[175]

And in a pedantic tone expressed,

Something is done because it is considered, in the balance, that is desirable ... In such matters there has to be give and take.[176]

Nehru did regret the fact that the negotiations were long-drawn and that he had anticipated a year at best to reach a settlement. But there was no remorse in stating,

... we purchased a settlement, if you like; we purchased peace and it is good for both countries.[177]

Nehru excused himself from the House as he had to accompany the crown prince and crown princess of Japan who were on a visit to India, but not before he clarified the issue of consultation with the state governments on the negotiations,

Whenever any proposals were put before me, I asked the Commonwealth Secretary [M.J. Desai] ... Only when he said 'Yes', did I look into it ... It may be that what the Commonwealth Secretary reported to me was due to some misunderstanding. He thought that they agreed when they had not.[178]

It is a pity that Nehru did not stay on for the entire length of the debate as Vajpayee, not convinced with his defence and in his rhythmic Hindi which became a trademark, raised an important question on the Indus Commission, which hitherto had not been inquired into. He cited Ayub, who soon after the treaty was signed had said,

> By accepting the procedure for joint inspection of the river courses, India has, by implication, conceded the principle of joint control extending to the upper region of Chenab and Jhelum, and joint control comprehends joint possession.[179]

Vajpayee expressed his deep concern over the possibility of the UN Security Council intervening in the issue. He was also puzzled over Ayub Khan's statement that, had it not been for the intervention of Nehru, the treaty would not have been signed. '*Kaun si baat thi*?' Vajpayee, raising his eyebrow, wanted to know. Nehru had already left and one will never know what Ayub Khan's statement meant or whether it was anything other than being deliberately conspiratorial.

The permanent Indus Commission was incorporated by India in the first draft of the treaty in the London meeting on 9 December 1959 along with the acceptance of Pakistan to the principle of storage by India on the western rivers, which was to be detailed in the annexures of the treaty. Like a watchdog, the purpose of the Indus Commission was to maintain the implementation of the treaty and oversee the arrangement for the supply of water to the Pakistan canals from the eastern rivers during the transition period. Any doubt or question of a 'technical nature' was first to be referred to the Permanent Commission and, if unresolved, would become a matter of difference to be settled by a 'neutral expert' appointed for the purpose. Any other difference not in the ambit of being defined as 'technical' would be regarded as a dispute to be resolved by negotiations between the two governments. If yet unsettled, it was to be referred to a court of arbitration. Pakistan had wanted a permanent neutral chairman of the Indus Commission and was adamant to the extent of wrecking the negotiations, which had reached a draft stage. Vajpayee's concerns during the debate, if not prophetic, had substance, and as noted by India's chief negotiator during the course of the negotiations,

> It seemed, sometimes, that Pakistan wanted to secure a springboard for numerous further disputes.[180]

The Indian negotiators had scored an important victory over Pakistan by not agreeing to a neutral chairman and simultaneously acquiring storage rights over the western rivers. The sweet success, one can argue in the sixty years of the functioning of the treaty, has now left a bitter taste, with Pakistan knocking at the door of the International Court of Arbitration for every hydro project that India plans to execute in Kashmir.

There is good reason to suspect that the framework for arbitration which is increasingly pinching India today would not have come about had it not been for the masterly influence of Zulfikar Bhutto, the Oxford-educated lawyer who had joined Ayub Khan's cabinet as the minister of water, power, communication and industry. Bhutto played an active role in the final phase of the Indus negotiations but more significantly, his statement in the UN, as a member of the Pakistan delegation, draws a crucial link to arbitration. A Soviet draft resolution on the question of defining aggression was put forward in the UN General Assembly in October 1957, and Bhutto had said:

> . . . If we are to adopt a definition then this definition must contain an article . . . stating clearly and unambiguously that economic aggression or indirect aggression is perpetrated if lower riparian are deprived of natural rights in use of rivers which flow through two or more countries . . . If there is any interference in the normal and assured supply of irrigation waters, my country would face the threat of total annihilation.[181]

Bhutto's discerning mind had endeared Ayub Khan until the war with India in 1965 changed the equation and Bhutto was 'given a notice'.

In Pakistan, there was no public opinion on the Indus treaty, only the diktat of Ayub Khan prevailed. It is a matter of conjecture whether a civilian government in Pakistan would have signed the treaty. Ayub's right had none to dispute and the very few that did, like Fatima Jinnah and Masud Khaddarposh, were promptly labelled as 'traitors' and forced to 'shut up'. Fatima—the younger sister of Jinnah who later contested Ayub in the 1965 presidential indirect elections and made the Indus treaty the point of attack against the government, arousing considerable public sentiment—had dared to question the rationale of the treaty, to which Ayub had replied that he got Rs 900 crore for it.[182] Not one to be silenced, she responded,

> Is that adequate price for losing permanently the water for all times? Is it not frittering away our permanent water rights?[183]

Khaddarposh, an outspoken senior bureaucrat in the Ministry of Food and Agriculture, had derided Ayub for having sold off the rivers to India and sought explanations on the rationale for the treaty. He never got a reply to his criticism and upon meeting Ayub, was threatened dire consequences.[184]

A Few Lines to Conclude

For all the intelligence, energy and the mountain of paperwork that the two countries spent in the negotiations, the Indus Waters Treaty was strangely viewed by both the parties as a 'giveaway' of their respective water interests. That for the World Bank, which had seriously thought the Indus basin to be a tinderbox, was a success in itself, for it meant each getting something and peace, however fragile, prevailing. India came through the years of torrid negotiations democratically stronger, learning in some way about a greater need for domestic consensus-building, while for Ayub Khan, what eventually mattered was to soak in the historic moment of the signing ceremony when the gaze of the dignitaries gathered at the President's House in Karachi turned to the shining teak table at which he sat, flanked by Nehru on his right and William Iliff on his left. The treaty may have prevented 'another Korea' and achieved a mutually agreed 'divorce settlement', but it did not fundamentally change Pakistan's lower riparian angst nor its perception of the upper riparian dominance of India.

The entire history of the Indus basin has had its dramatic encounters, institutional achievements and misreading, disputes and tales of men shaping their destiny through the vagaries of the rivers. In the long history of the Indus basin, the treaty of 1960 will be remembered as a hydro-diplomatic moment—a pause in a potentially conflict-ridden situation.

Postscript

Ah! well a-day! what evil looks
Had I from old and young!
Instead of the cross, the Albatross
About my neck was hung.

—Samuel Taylor Coleridge, *Rime of the Ancient Mariner*, 1798

It is sixty years of the Indus Waters Treaty. Negotiated at a moment of political opportunity, it has remarkably survived the kerfuffle of India–Pakistan relations, including wars and numerous military stand-offs. Suspending or terminating a treaty during armed conflicts is not an uncommon practice. However, India and Pakistan have so far chosen not to do so. Even during the course of the wars in 1965, 1971 and the Kargil conflict in 1999, there were no recorded strategic decisions by either of the countries to attack the other's hydraulic installations or make them unusable. The rationality of the treaty that 'envisaged the most complete utilization of the Indus system of rivers'[1] was of greater benefit than actions that would have contravened it.

For Pakistan, as a lower riparian 'having got the best that was possible',[2] the treaty remains an insurance of all the material benefits it has accrued. Had it not been so, Pakistan would have been constrained to build grand hydraulic works at considerable cost to transfer water from the western rivers to meet its irrigation uses and become independent of the eastern rivers. And without the eastern rivers being given exclusively to India, the latter would have struggled to operationalize the Bhakra and Nangal Dams. The Rajasthan canal would not have made much progress and in all probability, the Ravi–Beas link canal would have failed to take off. Had the Indus Waters Treaty not been signed in 1960, it is unlikely that these dams and canals would have ever come about. The Indo-Sino conflict in 1962, followed by the 1965 India–Pakistan War altered the geo-political dynamics of the region and would have, in all likelihood, rendered it entirely unconducive for any negotiations on the Indus basin.

History, it seems, has its eyes on the Indus treaty. For all its demonstrable 'robustness'—a noun now commonly associated with the treaty—it has to increasingly interface with a strong nationalistic exuberance in India that looks at correcting perceived historical errors. At the other end, the treaty has become, for a certain section of Pakistan's political-military leadership, a convenient scapegoat to cover up its poor water management policies, which in successive years has seen inefficiency in its irrigation system and excessive water waste in the agricultural sector. Interestingly, Pakistan has never advocated either abrogation or revision of the treaty but has not shied away from blaming India for its water woes. Officially, while the Pakistani Indus commissioner meets regularly with the Indian counterpart to discuss issues and concerns over the provisions and restrictions of water use and water projects in the most meaningful way, in the public space the feeling largely runs contrary. Water, as a 'lifeline' issue, is not forgotten history in Pakistan and the sharing of the waters with India still remains an unfinished business. What also remains unfinished is linking the waters to Kashmir and issues of territoriality. The raison d'être of the IWT was precisely to delink the water issue from territorial disputes.[3]

To put things further into perspective, the IWT neither had an overriding political objective nor was it intended to be an exercise in peacemaking. It was, at best, a classical lesson in international mediation. There is no mention of 'politics' or 'security' in the text of the treaty. The principal objective was to deal with the problems of geography and irrigation development in the Indus basin as a result of Partition and the competing sovereignty that followed. The framers negotiated the differences by balancing the water rights of Pakistan without compromising on India's needs and won the day through concessions and unprecedented statesmanship. The drafters were audacious in reasoning that once the division of the Indus basin was agreed upon, water-sharing determined and compensation calculated, India and Pakistan, to use a popular South Asian expression, would be 'locked into each other's intestines', unable to detach. It can be argued that the division of the river system into two segments—eastern rivers and western rivers—was not the most ingenious of solutions, and that a formula for sharing all the rivers of the Indus basin or a joint integrated planning and management, as Cyril Radcliffe had first brooked, would have been better. All this is an academic exercise now since the treaty is done and dusted.

As a product of civil engineering and quantitative thinking, the treaty provided in its carefully worded twelve articles and technically explained eight annexures (A–H) a range of 'provisions and restrictions' on water development and utilization. It had no 'exit clause'; in other words, there was no provision for abrogation. It, however, mentioned 'modification of the provisions' (Article X) by another duly ratified treaty concluded for that purpose between the two countries. Given the fractious politics, the drafters realized the nigh impossibility of achieving another treaty. Despite the treaty's limited objective, it was masterly craftsmanship involving checks and balances and a give-and-take formula. India's 'exclusive right' over the eastern rivers (Article II) was balanced by 'unrestricted use of waters' of the western rivers (Article III) by Pakistan. But since India had to make fixed compensation towards the cost of replacement works for the canal systems of Pakistan to draw supplies from the western rivers instead of the eastern rivers, which were entirely for

India's use, the treaty gave certain provisions for India to use the waters of the western rivers.

On the western rivers, India was under obligation to let flow and not to permit any interference, except for 'domestic use, non-consumptive use, specified agricultural use and generation of hydro-electricity subject to certain restrictions or criteria'.[4] Provisions also exist for India to construct reservoirs on the western rivers with aggregate storage capacity limited to 3.6 MAF (1.60 MAF for hydropower, 0.75 MAF for flood moderation and 1.25 MAF for general storage for non-consumptive uses, including power generation) and entitlement for agriculture use of 7.01 lakh acres over and above the area irrigated as on 1 April 1960. India had to also supply specified data of hydroelectric plants and storage works at specified periods in advance of their construction. Pakistan was entitled to raise objections, if any, within specified periods thereafter. On matters of transparency, exchange of data of flow and utilization of water and irrigated cropped area were to be shared (Article VI). A notable feature was the establishment of Permanent Indus Commission (Article VIII) with one commissioner from each country to implement the treaty as well as settlement of differences and disputes by agreement, neutral expert, court of arbitration or any other manner as agreed.

There was an unwritten 'spirit' of the treaty implying, in a nuanced way, upstream responsibility in sharing the waters. This is widely scoffed at today both in India's water relations with Pakistan as well as its wider regional diplomacy, in which it is seen as conciliatory. An animated constituency in India feels the treaty has imposed an enormous cost on India; this is similar to the tenor of the Parliament debate in November 1960 when questions of India's 'generosity' and the 'fairness' of the treaty were raised. Time and again, a clamour for abrogating the treaty as a response to cross-border terrorism puts pressure on the political leadership to exact a hard price on Pakistan. Inevitably, the discourse shifts away from the rationality of the treaty to using the shared rivers as an instrument of coercion and a tool of punishment—war by other means.

Jingoism aside, the fact remains that the provisions of the treaty entitled for India on the western rivers remain woefully unutilized. In not utilizing the provisions to good effect, particularly by enhancing storage capacity on the western rivers, especially in times when water scarcity is becoming a critical challenge, is nothing short of being reckless and callous. In the past five years though, India has woken from its slumber and, as a national priority, fast-tracked a number of multipurpose projects both on the eastern and western rivers. Projects like the Ujh and Shahpurkandi with storage capacity of 0.82 and 0.012 MAF respectively along with the second Ravi Beas Link Project, will stop the free flow (not entitled) of waters into Pakistan from the eastern rivers.

On the western rivers in Jammu and Kashmir, India has barely developed one-sixth of hydropower generation in the last fifty years. Projects have been identified for storage purposes and hydroelectricity. The Bursar multipurpose project will store about 1 MAF and produce 800 MW of electricity and the Gyspa, with a storage capacity of 0.74 MAF, will generate 300 MW. Other projects that have won techno-economic approvals are Sawalkote (1856 MW), Kwar (540 MW), Pakal Dul (1000 MW), and Kirthai II (930 MW). All these projects are on the Chenab and are run-of-the-river as per the treaty. It is estimated that hydropower on the Chenab will triple in the coming years.

With the waters of the Indus basin being abstracted as never before, both in terms of irrigation and hydroelectricity, the entire sustainability of the river system comes into question. There are 300 million people living on the Indus basin and the total water withdrawal in the basin is estimated at 299 cubic km, of which irrigation accounts for 93 per cent.[5] Issues such as food and energy will increasingly have intricate linkages to water while demographic pressures on water availability will critically impact water management. Climate trends, glaciology and run-offs, though still far from conclusive, are showing signs of impacting flow variation in the Indus basin. The Indus and the Sutlej originate from the Tibetan plateau, a part of China. The plateau described as the 'roof of the world' with its surrounding mountains that contain the largest mass of snow, ice and permafrost outside the polar region has 14 per cent of the total catchment area of the Indus basin and provides an annual flow of 181.62 cubic km to India. It will at some point become necessary for India to have technical cooperation with China, like on the Brahmaputra, on data exchange on the flows, especially with trends suggesting the melting of permafrost in Tibet.[6] A new ordering of the Indus basin might be in order under changing climatic and socio-economic conditions. In the immediate term, however, the sustainability of water resources in the Indus basin seems to be strained more by the socio-economic.

Climate concerns and its impact on water resources were not foreseen in 1960. Remarkably, the means to overcome some of the projected water challenges are in the IWT itself. The question, therefore, of replacing the treaty with another or even abrogating it does not stand to logic. Article VII opens up a range of possibilities for future cooperation through 'common interest in optimum development of the rivers' and 'undertaking engineering works on the rivers'. This will require proper survey of the Indus basin along with the employment of a new set of technologies for dam construction and de-siltation that integrate with ecosystem dynamics. The Indus basin is under the same pressures that most international river basins endure. A new riparian equation between India and Pakistan would need to be worked out, beyond the treaty, to ensure that the waters of the Indus basin remain 'uninterrupted and uninterruptible'.

Acknowledgements

After one has gone through the surreal experience of writing a book comes the most difficult part of penning acknowledgements. There are a number of people—family members, friends, and well-wishers—who have supported me in this exercise for which I am forever grateful. Fearing the risk of inadvertently missing some I will refrain from mentioning each name and thereby save the blushes. I do apologize, however, for this uncharacteristic departure.

This apart, there are a few mentions that I cannot ignore.

First and foremost, I would like to thank Penguin Random House with its 'wonky hand-drawn bird' for having agreed to publish the work and in particular Elizabeth Kuruvilla for taking charge of the manuscript. Her editorial wisdom along with Saloni Mital's attention to detail has gone a long way in strengthening the book.

The book project has been a result of my fellowship at the Nehru Memorial Museum and Library (NMML) housed in the sprawling Teen Murti campus in the heart of Delhi where the winter sun seeps past thick tree branches and the unforgiving summer heat is shielded by the sylvan surroundings. With its archival materials, private papers of distinguished individuals, resource materials on microfilm and microfiche along with a varied collection of books, periodicals and photographs, the NMML is a researcher's paradise, more likely to fire the imagination than not. And nothing can be pleasanter than the pleasant staff at the NMML and I would like to thank each one of them for their cooperation. It is well said that good libraries build services and great libraries build communities. Likewise, the library staff at the Manohar Parrikar Institute for Defence Studies and Analyses have been equally helpful and unflinching in their support. I owe them all my gratitude.

Above all, I want to thank Swati, my wife, for keeping the faith and my son Divakar for constantly making me hum the Liverpool football anthem, 'you'll never walk alone'.

Uttam Kumar Sinha

Notes

Preface

1. Edward Gibbon, *The History of the Decline and Fall of the Roman Empire*, Vol.6, chapter LXXI, Fred de Pau and Company: New York, 1788, pp. 1083–84. Gibbon's work was published in six volumes between 1776 and 1788.
2. Baron de Montesquieu, *The Spirit of the Laws*, tr. by Thomas Nugent, Hafner Publishing: New York, 1949, p. 289.

Part I: Settlers, Invaders *and* Successions

1. John Marshall (ed.), *Mohenjo-daro and the Indus Civilization*, Being an official account of Archaeological Excavations at Mohenjo-daro carried out by the Government of India between the years 1922 and 1927, Volume I, Arthur Probsthain: London, 1931, p. v.
2. Nayanjot Lahiri, *Finding Forgotten Cities: How the Indus Civilization Was Discovered*, Seagull Book: New York, 2006, p. 3.
3. Neha Gupta, 'Why the Social Context of Archaeology Matters in the Study of the Indus Valley Civilization: Insight on Banerji's "Pre-Buddhist" Period at Mohenjodaro', *Heritage: Journal of Multidisciplinary Studies in Archaeology*, Vol. 1, 2013, p. 38.
4. S.P. Gupta, *The 'Lost' Sarasvati and the Indus Civilization*, Kusumanjali Prakashan: Jodhpur, 1995. Also, R. Bernbeck and S. Pollock, 'Ayodhya, Archaeology, and Identity', *Current Anthropology*, Vol. 37(1), 1996, pp. S138–S42. The *Rigveda*, Book 6, mentions the Sarasvati as 'surpassing in majesty and might of all other rivers'. By the time Book 10 of the *Rigveda* is written the Indus is the prominent river.

5.   Rita P. Wright, *The Ancient Indus: Urbanism, Economy and Society*, Cambridge University Press: New York, 2009, pp. 1–16; J.M. Kenoyer, *Ancient Cities of the Indus Valley Civilization*, Oxford University Press: Karachi, 1998, pp. 6–9.

6.   Silky Agarwal, et. al., 'Archaeological studies at Dholavira using GPR', *Current Science*, 114(4), 25 February 2018, pp. 879–87.

7.   Liuvu Giosan, et al, 'Fluvial landscapes of the Harappan civilization, '*Proceedings of the National Academy of Sciences*, 29 May 2012, p. E1688–94.

8.   'Notes on the Lost River of the Indian Desert', *The Calcutta Review*, Vol. LIX(CXVII), Thomas S. Smith: Calcutta, 1874, p. 21.

9.   Ibid., p. 15.

10. Harish Jain, *The Making of Punjab*, Unistar Books: Chandigarh, 2003, p. 29.

11. Ibid., p. 32.

12. Edward Gibbon, *The History of the Decline and Fall of the Roman Empire, Vol. I*, Fred de Pau and Company: New York, 1776, p. 35.

13. James R. Penn, *Rivers of the World: A Social, Geographical and Environmental Sourcebook*, ABCE CLIO: Santa Barbara, LA, 2001, p. 114.

14. T.T. Jones, 'The Genesis of Military River Operations: Alexander the Great at the Hydaspes River', *The Military Engineer*, Vol. 56(374), November–December 1964, p. 426.

15. K.C. Sagar, *Foreign Influence on Ancient India*, Northern Book Centre: New Delhi, 1992, p. 64.

16. This section relies on the translated work of Arrian. See, *Arrian's History of Alexander's Expedition*, Vol. II, tr. from Greek by John Rooke, Allen and Co. and J. Walker and Co.: London, 1814, pp. 52–3.

17. Ibid., p. 59.

18. Ibid., p. 62.

19. Ibid., pp. 63–4.

20. K.C. Sagar, *Foreign Influence on Ancient India*, Northern Book Centre: New Delhi, 1992, p. 62.

21. Accounts suggest that Alexander when he arrived at Pattala took the right route of the Indus venturing into the sea and came back to Pattala before making his westward journey by land.

22. Arrian, *The Anabasis of Alexander*, Book VI Chapter XX, tr. by E.J. Chinnock, Hodder and Stoughton: London, 1884, p. 349.

23. *The Calcutta Review*, 1874, p. 4.

24. Nearchus, 'A Lost River of the Indian Desert: A Comment', *The Calcutta Review*, Vol. LX(CXX), Thomas S. Smith: Calcutta, 1875, p. 323.

25. Richard A. Gabriel, *The Madness of Alexander the Great: The Myth of Military Genius*, Pen and Sword: Barnsley, Yorkshire, 2015, p. 96.

26. Rooke (tr.), 1814, p. 42.

27. Plutarch, *The Parallel Lives* cited in *Complete Works of Plutarch*, Delphi Classics: East Sussex, 2013, p.345.

28. Cited in H.C. Verma, *Harvesting Water and Rationalization of Agriculture in North Medieval India*, Anamika Publishers: New Delhi, 2001, p. 27.

29. Raja Chach who ruled Sindh towards the end of the seventh century was a Brahman and in his reign the Buddhists were marginalized. His successor and brother, Chandra, was a Buddhist and the Hindus in his rule became restless until he was overthrown by Dáhar, the son of Raja Chach.

30. *The Chachnamah, an Ancient History of Sindh*, tr. from Persian by Mirza Kalichbeg Fredunbeg, Sindh Commissioners Press: Karachi, 1900, p. 74. Mirza Kalichbeg is celebrated as the first Sindhi novelist. *The Chachnamah* was written in Persian by Ali Kufi in the thirteenth century, who claimed his work was a translation of an eight-century work in Arabic. It remains one of the most referred historical sources of Sindh in the seventh and eighth centuries and the principal source of information on the Muslim conquest in Sindh. Henry M. Elliot translated major portions of *The Chachnamah* in *The History of India, as Told by Its Own Historians*. Elliot's work in eight volumes was edited by John Dowson between 1867–77. Both the sources (Kalichbeg and Elliot) are referred. Manan Ahmed Asif notes, 'The earliest comment on *Chachnama* by a Company official [East India Company] is from Captain James McMurdo, who traveled the Indus River in 1812. Later, Lt Thomas Postans and his colleague Richard F. Burton translated parts of *Chachnama* in their respective travelogues and histories. This material was then used by Company historian Mountstuart Elphinstone in his 1841 *History of India: The Hindu and Mohametan Periods*. Then Henry Miers Elliot, in his *The History of India, as Told by Its Own Historians*, translated major portions of the text, which were used by subsequent historians such as Vincent A. Smith and Stanley Lane-Poole to compose universal histories of India by the early twentieth century.' See Manan Ahmed Asif, *A Book of Conquest: The Chachnama and Muslim Origins in South Asia*, Harvard University Press: Boston, 2016, p. 163.

31. Kalichbeg, 1900, p. 77.

32. Ibid., p. 83.

33. Ibid.

34. Henry M. Elliot, *The History of India, as Told by Its Own Historians: The Muhammadan Period*, Vol. I, Trubner and Co.: London, 1867, p. 203.

35. Ibid., p. 111.

36. Ibid., p. 123.

37. Súrijdew, the elder daughter of Raja Dáhar, along with her younger sister, were brought to the court of the khalifa in Baghdad. The khalifa Hajjáj Yúsif was taken by her beauty and began to take liberties with her. To save herself and showing remarkable presence of mind, Súrijdew said, 'May the king live long: I, a humble slave, am not fit for your Majesty's bed-room, because the just amír, Imáduddín Muhammad Kásim, kept us both with him for 3 days, and then sent us to the Khalífah. Perhaps your custom is such, or else this

kind of disgrace should not be permitted by kings.' The Khalifa blinded by his passion for the girl was driven into a rage. Without making any inquiry, he wrote a letter directing Qásim to 'put himself in raw leather and come back to the chief seat of the Khalífah'. See, Kalichbeg, 1900, p. 124.

38. Ibid.
39. V.S. Naipaul, *Among the Believers: An Islamic Journey*, Andre Deutsch Limited: London, 1981, p. 133.
40. Asif, 2016, p. 6.
41. Henry M. Elliot, *The History of India as Told by Its Own Historians: The Muhammadan Period*, Vol. V, Trubner and Co.: London, 1872, p. 5.
42. Ibid., p. 22.
43. Ibid.
44. Al Baladhuri, *Kitab Futūh al-Buldān*, Part II, tr. from Arabic by Francis Clark Murgotten, Columbia University Press: Columbia, 1924, p. 222. Part I was translated by Philip Khuri Hitti in 1916. Also see reference to the aqueduct in Elliot, 1867, p. 123.
45. Elliot, 1867, p. 15.
46. El-Mas'ūdī's, *Historical Encyclopaedia Entitled 'Meadows of Gold and Mines of Gems'*, Vol. I, tr. by Aloys Sprenger, W.H. Allen and Co.: London, 1841, p. 177.
47. Ibid., p. 243.
48. Ibid., pp. 233–4.
49. Ibid., p. 386.
50. Edward C. Sachau, *Alberuni's India*, Vol. I, Kegan Paul, Trench, Trubner and Co. Ltd.: London, 1910, p. 258.
51. Ibid., p. 260.
52. Ibid.
53. *Travels of Ibn Batuta*, tr. from the Abridged Arabic Manuscript Copies by the Rev. Samuel Lee, the Oriental Translation Committee: London, 1829, p. 13. The full title of his book in Arabic is *Tuhfat al-anzar fi gharaaib al-amsar wa ajaaib al-asfar* (A Gift to Those who Contemplate the Wonders of Cities and the Marvels of Travelling).
54. *Ibn Battuta Travels in Asia and Africa, Book III*, tr. by H.A.R. Gibb, Routledge and Kegan Paul: London, 1929, pp. 596 and 727.
55. Irfan Habib, *Economic History of Medieval India 1200–1500*, Pearson and Longman: New Delhi, 2011, p. 34. The word used by Habib on the rhinos becoming extinct is 'eliminated'.
56. John Marshall, when finding the rhinoceros appearing on the Mohenjo-daro seals, writes, 'This animal also rarely appears on the seals, Nos. 341–7 being the only examples that we have as yet. In every case it is the single-horned animal that is represented, probably the great Indian rhinoceros which was formerly found along the base of the Himalayas as far as Peshawar where it was hunted by the Emperor Babar.' John Marshall (ed.), 1931, Volume II,

p. 387. Babar's memoir mentions the rhinos roaming the forest near the Ghaggar river.

57. *The Travels and Adventures of the Turkish Admiral Sidi Ali Reis: In India, Afghanistan, Central Asia and Persia during the Years 1553–1556*, tr. from Turkish by A. Vambery, London, 1899. Also George W. Briggs, 'The Indian Rhinoceros as a Sacred Animal', *Journal of the American Oriental Society*, Vol. 51(3), September 1931, pp. 276–82.

58. Divyabhanusinh, et.al., *The Story of India's Unicorn*, Marg Foundation: Mumbai, 2018, p. 121.

59. *Travels of Ibn Batuta*,1829, p. 111.

60. Ibid.

61. Lt. Col. George Frederick Fitzclarence, *Journal of a Route Across India, Through Egypt, to England, in the Latter End of the Year 1817, and the Beginning of 1818*, John Murray: London, 1819, p. 236.

62. Ibid., p. 394.

63. Ibid.

64. Jagmohan, *My Frozen Turbulence in Kashmir*, Allied Publishers: New Delhi, 1991, p. 44.

65. Ghulam Rasool Nahami, 'Suyya: The Brain Behind the Idea to Counter Kashmir Floods, Part V', *Kashmir Watch*, 5 October 2014.

66. *Kalhana's Rajatarangini: A Chronicle of the Kings of Kashmir*, Vol. II, tr. by M.A. Stein, Motilal Banarsidass Publication: New Delhi, 1900, p. 418.

67. Ibid., p. 419.

68. Buzurg Ibn Shahriyar, *The Book of the Marvels of India: Arabian Travellers' Tales*, tr. from Arabic by L. Marcel Devic, George Routledge & Sons, Ltd.: London, 1928, p. 2.

69. Ibid., p. 89.

70. Walter R. Lawrence, *The Valley of Kashmir*, Henry Frowde: London, 1895, p. 196.

71. For arguments that Islam was not forced into the society see, Yoginder Sikand, 'Hazrat Bulbul Shah: The First Known Muslim Missionary in Kashmir', *The Journal of Muslim Minority Affairs*, Vol. 20(2), 2000, pp. 361–7.

72. The tradition of writing the history of Kashmir under the title *Rajatarangani* continued after Kalhana with Jonaraja (*Dvitiya*). The tradition continued after Jonaraja as well with Srivara (*Tritiya*) and then Prajyabhatta and Suka (*Chaturtha*).

73. Srivara, *Jaina-Rajatarangini*, tr. by Jogesh Chunder Dutt, Calcutta, 1879, p. 141.

74. Lawrence, 1895, p. 192.

75. Ibid., p. 195.

76. P.N. Chopra, et. al. (eds.), *A Comprehensive History of Medieval India*, Sterling Publishers: New Delhi, 2003, p. 25.

77. Owen Lattimore, 'The Geography of Chingis Khan', *The Geographical Journal*, Vol. 129(1), March 1963, p. 3.

78. Giovanni Carpine after his return recorded his observation in two works from 1245–7, *Historia Mongalorum quos nos Tartaros appellamus* (History of the Mongols Whom We Call the Tartars) and *Liber Tartarorum* (Book of the Tartars).

79. Urgunge Onon, *The Secret History of the Mongols: The Life and Times of Chinggis Khan*, Routledge Curzon: London, 2001, p. 287.

80. Jeremiah Curtin, *The Mongols: A History*, Little Brown and Company: Boston, 1908, pp. 127–8.

81. Ibid., p. 125.

82. Bijan Omrani, 'The Durand Line: History and Problems of the Afghan-Pakistan Border', *Asian Affairs*, Vol. XL (II), July 2009, p. 178.

83. Curtin, 1908, p. 127. The author observes that Jalaluddin, despite the daunting army of Genghis Khan, as remaining 'unterrified'. Muhammad Juwayni also known as Ata Malik, the thirteenth-century Persian historian, gave a detailed account of the Mongols in his work titled *Tarikh-i Jahan-gushay* in three volumes. Nasim Hizazi, (Sharif Hussain), a popular Pakistani Urdu novelist in the post-Partition period, used Islamic history as a background to his novels. His novel *Akhri Chataan* was based on Genghis Khan and Jalaluddin and the Khwarizm dynasty. Hizazi describes Jalaluddin as a valiant warrior glorifying an Islamic character against the Mongol, whereas Juwayni's is a more dispassionate account of an historian.

84. Salman Rashid, 'Jalaluddin Khwarazm', *The Express Tribune*, Karachi, 27 January 2012.

85. Abd al-Malik Isami, *Futuh's Salatin*, tr. by Agha Mahdi Husain, Asia Publishing House: New York, 1967, p. 225. Also see S.A.A. Rizvi, *The Wonder That Was India*, Vol. II, Picador India: New Delhi, 2005, p. 25.

86. See the works of Lallanji Gopal, Harbans Mukhia and Ranabir Chakravarti on agricultural technology and economic life in Medieval India.

87. Iqtidar Hussain Siddiqui, *Authority and Kingship under the Sultans of Delhi: Thirteenth–Fourteenth Centuries*, Manohar: New Delhi, 2006, pp. 260–5.

88. *The Calcutta Review*, 1874, p. 8.

89. Ibid., p. 3. *Jitals* were metal coins used during the Sultanate period.

90. Feroz Shah Tughlak official history, *Futuhat-e-Firozshahi* (Gifts of Firoz Shah) gives us an account of his reign, which was longest of the Tughlak dynasty.

91. *The Calcutta Review*, Vol. XII, 1849, p. 80.

92. Stanley Lane-Poole, *Medieval India Under Mohammedan Rule, 712–1764*, G.P. Putnam's Sons: London, 1903, pp. 144–5. Also see Tarikh-i-Firishta, *Rise of Mahomedan Power in India*, tr. by John Briggs, London, 1829.

93. As recounted by Elliot, 1872, pp. 176–7.

94. Cited in Meenakshi Jain (ed.), *The India They Saw: Foreign Accounts, 8th–15th Centuries*, Ocean Books: New Delhi, 2011, p. 255.

95. Abdulla, *Tarikh-i-Daudi*, Vol. IV, Kitab Mahal: Allahabad, 1964, p. 447. Also see John F. Richards, 'The Economic History of the Lodi Period: 1451–1526', *Journal of the Economic and Social History of the Orient*, Vol. 8(1), Aug. 1965, p. 52.

96. *Babur-Nama*, (Memoirs of Babur), translated from the original Turkish text of Zahiru'd-din Muhammad Babar Padshah Ghazi by Annette Susannah Beveridge. Two Volumes Bound in One, Low Price Publications: Delhi, 1921, p. 10.

97. The five doabs were: Bai Jallandhar Doab (between the Sutlej and the Beas); the Bari Doab (between the Beas and the Ravi); the Rachna Doab (between the Ravi and the Chenab); Chaj Doab (between the Chenab and the Jhelum); and Sindh Sagar Doab (between the Indus and the Jhelum).

98. Lane-Poole, 1903, p. 237.

99. S.M. Jaffar, *The Mughal Empire from Babur to Aurangzeb*, reprint, S. Muhammad Sadiq Khan: Peshawar, 1936, p. 42. Under the instruction of Humayun, carpenters (*najjars*) made four boats for him to float on the Jamuna. There were shops, bazaars and gardens on those boats. It is said that the moving garden was made on the surface of the water of the Jamuna especially for the emperor.

100. A translation from Persian. Cited in Lieut. Yule, 'Canal Act of Emperor Akbar with some notes and remarks on the History of the Western Jumna Canals', *The Journal of the Asiatic Society*, Vol. XV, 1846, pp. 213–4. (a) is explained through Koran as, 'The similitude of those who lay out their substance, for advancing the religion of God, is as a grain of corn which produceth seven ears and in each ear a hundred grains.' The author writes in the beginning: 'For the following translation of a decree of the Emperor Akbar, forming an interesting Appendix to the History of the Canals, given by Col. Colvin in the 2nd volume of the A.S.' Also see Sunil Amrith, *Unruly Waters: How Mountain Rivers and Monsoon Have Shaped South Asia's History*, Basic Books: New York, 2018, pp. 42–3 and p. 45.

101. *The Journal of the Asiatic Society*, Vol. XV, 1846, p. 215.

102. Abdul Fazal Allami, *Ain I Akbari*, tr. by Col. H.S. Jarrett, Vol. II, Asiatic Society of Bengal: Calcutta, 1891, p. 362.

103. Ibid., p. 331.

104. Proby T. Cautley, 'Canals of Irrigation in the North Western Provinces', *The Calcutta Review*, Vol. XII, 1849, p. 81. Cautley had done reports on the Grand Ganges Canal; on the Eastern Jamuna or Doab Canal; on the Watercourses of the Deyra Dhoon. Major Baker did reports on the Western Jamuna or Delhi Canals and on Projected Canals in Delhi Territory.

105. *The Tuzuk-i-Jahangiri or Memoirs of Jahangir*, tr. by Alexander Rogers, Royal Asiatic Society: London, 1909, p. 308.

106. See Muhammad Hadi, *Tuzuk-i-Jahangiri*. The memoirs in two volumes written in Persian and commonly known as *Jahangirnama* were completed by Muhammad Hadi, the eighteenth-century historian. It was first translated by Sayyid Ahmad in 1864 and then refined further by Alexander Rogers and published in 1909. More recently, *The Jahangirnama: Memoirs of Jahangir, Emperor of India*, tr. by Wheeler Thackston, Oxford University Press: Oxford, 1999.
107. Rogers (tr.), 1909, pp. 93–4.
108. Elizabeth Moynihan, 'The Lotus Garden Palace of Zahir al-Din Muhammad Babur', in *Muqarnas*, 5, 1988, p. 100.
109. Ibid., p. 69.
110. William Foster (ed.), *Early Travels in India: 1583–1619*, Oxford University Press: London, 1921, p. 161.
111. Nazer Aziz Anjum, *Economy of Transport in Mughal India*, Unpublished thesis, Aligarh Muslim University: Aligarh, 2010, p. 9.
112. Jarrett (tr.), 1891, p. 337.
113. William Hawkins, described as a 'bluff sea-captain' was the nephew of the famous Sir John Hawkins and the first to display the English flag at the mouth of the Tapti river in Surat on 24 August 1607. Foster (ed.), 1921, p. 61 and p. 64.
114. William Foster, *The English Factories in India, 1634–1636: A Calendar of Documents in the India Office, British Museum and Public Record Office*, The Clarendon Press: Oxford, 1911, p. 244.
115. William Foster, *The English Factories in India, 1637-1641: A Calendar of Documents in the India Office, British Museum and Public Record Office*, The Clarendon Press: Oxford, 1912, p. 135.
116. Ibid., p. 137.
117. Ibid.
118. Pir Ghulam Hussain Koyahami, *Tarikh-i-Hasan*, Urdu tr. by Shams-ud-din, Shams-ut-Tawarikh, Srinagar: 2003, pp. 292–197.
119. Muhammad Afzal Khan, 'Ali Mardan Khan: The Great Iranian Noble of Shah Jahan', *Proceedings of the Indian History Congress*, 44, 1983, p. 198. The author writes, 'Ali Mardan Khan came along with his family and a large retinue of officers and companions in 1638, having made over Qandahar to Shahjahan . . . became the highest Iranian noble of Shahjahan.'
120. Fitzclarence, 1819, p. 237.
121. Tripta Wahi, 'Shah Nahar: Its History, Technology and Socio-Political Implications', *Proceedings of the Indian National Congress*, 74, 2013, p. 285.
122. Major R. Napier 'Report on the Shah Nahr or Hasli', Foreign/Secret, 28 April 1848, nos. 57–66, p. 39, National Archives of India, New Delhi.
123. Michael H. Fisher, *A Short History of the Mughal Empire*, I.B. Tauris: London, 2016, p. 176.

124. James Wescoat, 'Early water systems in Mughal India', *Environmental Design*, Vol. 2, January 1985, p. 51.

125. Jaffar, 1936, p. 271.

126. Chandrakant Thatte, 'Indus Waters and the 1960 Treaty between India and Pakistan' in Olli Varis, Cecilia Tortajada and Asit Biswas (eds.), *Management of Transboundary Rivers and Lakes*, Springer-Verlag: Berlin, 2008, p. 176.

127. Cited in Finbarr B. Flood, *Objects of Translation: Material, Culture and Medieval 'Hindu-Muslim' Encounter*, Princeton University Press; Princeton, 2009, p. 15.

128. Actually, Akbar displaying political sagacity made Sindh part of Multan without giving Sindh the *suba* status but moved Mirza Baig the defeated ruler of Sindh as subedar to Multan thereby lessening his influence and undermining his power. See Amita Paliwal, *Sindh in the Mughal Empire (1591–1740): A Study of its Administration, Society Economy and Culture*, thesis submitted to Aligarh Muslim University: Aligarh, 2010, p. 38.

129. Hazrat Syed Yaqoob Bazmi, *Muqaddama-E-Sirajul Absar, Vol. Two*, tr. by Syed Sharief Khundmiri, Trafford Publishing: Victoria, Canada, 2013, p. 1141.

130. Ibid.

131. Ibid., p. 1132.

132. Jagjeet Lally, 'Beyond Tribal Breakout: Afghan in the History of Empire, CA. 1747–1818', *Journal of World History*, Vol. 29(3), September 2018, p. 374.

133. Irrigation Department Lahore, Report no. C-12, 1998, p. 13.

134. Kaushik Roy, 'British-India and Afghanistan: 1707–1842' in Kaushik Roy and Peter Lodge (eds.), *Chinese and Indian Warfare—From the Classic Age to 1870*, Routledge: London, 2015, p. 96.

135. Lally, 2018, p. 370. For 'hollowing out', see C.A. Bayly, *Imperial Meridian. The British Empire and the World, 1780-1830*, Longman: London, 1989, p. 35.

136. Jos Gommans, *The Indian Frontier. Horse and Warband in the Making of Empires*, Manohar: Delhi, 2018, p. 69.

137. Ibid., p. 72.

138. Ibid., p. 75.

139. Treaty of Kalat provided the following: Mir Naseer Khan Baloch will not pay any tribute to Shah-e-Afghan in the future and will not supply military assistance. But provided that he is at war against external enemies, the Khan would supply a military contingent as a token of help, on the condition that the Afghan King provided annually Rs 1,00,000 and military weapons and provided for the expenditure of the army as rewards. Shah-e-Afghan in future was to never interfere in the internal affairs, disputes and matters of Balochistan.

140. Teja Singh and Ganda Singh, *Short History of the Sikhs*, Vol. One (1469–1765), Publication Bureau Punjabi University: Patiala, 2006, p. 171.

141. Qazi Nur Mohammadin, *Jang Namah*, tr. and summarized by Ganda Singh, Sikh Historical Research Foundation: Amritsar, 1939, p. 165.
142. Ganda Singh, *Ahmad Shah Durrani: Father of Modern Afghanistan*, Asia Publishing House: London, 1959, p. 306.
143. Ganda Singh (tr.), 1939, p. 168.
144. David Gilmartin, *Blood and Water: The Indus River Basin in Modern History*, University of California Press: California, 2015, p. 4.
145. Muhammad Fazle Karim Khan and Muhammad Nawaz, 'Karez Irrigation in Punjab', *GeoJournal*, Vol. 37(1), 1995, p. 91.
146. F. & C. Grey (eds.), *Tales of Our Grandfather or India Since 1856*, Smith, Elder and Co.: London, 1912, p. 97. Also cited in Gilmartin, 2015, p. 30.
147. Amar Farooqui, *Smuggling as Subversion: Colonialism, Indian Merchants and the Politics of Opium 1790–1843*, Lexington Books: Lanham, 2005, p. 149.
148. Ibid.
149. Khundmiri (tr.), 2013, p. 1134.

Part II: Diplomacy *and* Commerce *on* the Indus

1. John K. Galbraith, '"The Turbulent Frontier." As a Factor in British Expansion', *Comparative Studies in Society and History*, Vol. 2(2), Jan, 1960, p. 150.
2. Kelcie Daniels, Hannah Michael-Schwartz and Nick Spring, 'The Grand Manifesto of Alexander I', Napoleon Translations, *The Institutional Repository at DePaul University*, Chicago, 2011, p. 2.
3. Cited from William Dalrymple, *Return of a King: The Battle of Afghanistan, 1839–42*, 2014, Bloomsbury: London, 2014, p. 4. Originally from Sultan Muhammad Khan bin Musa Khan Durrani, *Tarikh e Sultani* (in Farsi).
4. Edward Thompson, *The Making of the Indian Princes*, Oxford University Press: London, 1943, p. 156.
5. John William Kaye, *The Life and Correspondence of Charles, Lord Metcalfe, Vol. I*, Smith, Elder and Co.: London, 1858, p. 167.
6. Ibid., pp. 170–71.
7. Ibid., p. 171.
8. Ibid., p. 175.
9. The Cis-(Latin for this side of) Sutlej States were on the British or southern side of the Sutlej.
10. Charles Metcalfe's mission to Lahore was to ascertain the disposition of the Maharaja towards the British government and accordingly structure the negotiations with him. As Metcalfe advanced into the Punjab, it became increasingly clear that Ranjit Singh had little intention in receiving the British embassy, much less to negotiate a treaty. On many occasions Ranjit Singh would communicate his intentions not to meet the envoy, dragging

the British emissary 'hither and thither'. For details of the diplomacy between Ranjit Singh and Metcalfe see Kaye, 1858, pp. 254–84.

11. Ibid., pp. 220–1.

12. Shah Mahmoud Hanifi (ed.), *Mountstuart Elphinstone in South Asia: Pioneer of British Colonial Rule*, Oxford University Press: New York, 2019, p. 159.

13. Kaye, 1858, p. 315.

14. *The Farewell Addresses of the Inhabitants of Jamaica, To the Right Honourable Sir Charles Theophilus Metcalfe, Governor of the Island*, Jordan, and Osborn: Kingston, 1842, p. 27.

15. Mountstuart Elphinstone, *An Account of the Kingdom of Caubul, and Its Dependencies in Persia, Tartary, and India: Comprising a View of the Afghaun Nation, and a History of the Dooraunee Monarchy*, Vol. 1, Longman, Hurst, Rees, Orme and Brown, and J. Murray: London, 1819, pp. iii–iv.

16. Ibid., p. 41.

17. Ibid., p. 230.

18. Ibid., p. 483.

19. Ibid., p. 324.

20. Ibid., p. 325.

21. Lt. Henry Pottinger, *Travels in Beloochistan and Sinde*, Accompanied By a Geographical and Historical Account of Those Countries, With a Map, Longman, Hurst, Rees, Orme, and Brown: London, 1816, pp. 356–57.

22. Edward Thornton, *A Gazetteer of the Countries Adjacent to India on the North-West; Including Sinde, Afghanistan, Baloochistan, Punjab and the Neighbouring States, In Two Volumes*, W.H. Allen: London, 1844, p. 226.

23. Sir John Malcolm the envoy to Persia who later became the governor of Bombay minuted in the records of government in August 1830. See Alexander Burnes, *Travels Into Bokhara; Being The Account Of The Journey From India To Cabool, Tartary, and Persia; Also, Narrative Of A Voyage On The Indus, From The Sea To Lahore, With Presents From The King Of Great Britain; Performed Under The Orders Of The Supreme Government Of India, In The Years 1831, 1832, And 1933. In Three Volumes*, Vol. III, John Murray: London, 1834, p. 2. Burnes's memoir was a popular read and continues to be so. His other important account was *Cabool: A Personal Narrative Of A Journey To, And Residence In That City In The Years 1836, 7, and 8*, John Murray: London, 1843.

24. The expression used by Charles Miller. See *Khyber, British India North-West Frontier: The Story of an Imperial Migraine*, Macmillan: New York, 1977.

25. M.A. Yapp, 'British Perceptions of the Russian Threat to India', *Modern Asian Studies*, Vol. 24(1), October 1987, p. 647.

26. Arnold Toynbee, *East to West: A Journey Around the World*, Oxford University Press: New York, 1958, p. 2. Toynbee developed roundabout theory to explain 'regions on which routes converge from all quarters of the compass and from which routes radiate out to all quarters of the compass again'. He

distinguishes it from culs-de-sac 'which are regions on the fringe that have received successive influences from the centre but have not been able to pass these influences on to regions farther afield'.

27. Pottinger, 1816, pp. 360–61.
28. Cited in Craig Murray, *Sikunder Burnes: Master of the Great Game*, Birlinn Ltd.: Edinburgh, 2016, p. 15. Murray ranked Alexander Burnes along with Richard Burton and David Livingstone as the three great nineteenth-century explorers.
29. Freemasonry is a secret society spread by the advance of the British Empire and came about with declining cathedral buildings. Lodges were set up to protect the masons. James Burnes wrote, *The Sketch of the History of the Knight Templars*, W.M. Blackwood and Sons: Edinburgh, 1840.
30. Writing to the Political Resident in Cutch on 10 June 1828. James Burnes, *Narrative of a Visit to the Court of Sinde at Hyderabad on the Indus; Illustrated with Plates and a Map; With a Sketch of the History of Cutch and an Appendix*, Longman and Co.: London, 1839, p. iv.
31. W. Ainsworth, 'A Narrative of the Visit to the Court of Sinde by James Burnes', *The Journal of the Royal Geographical Society of London, Vol. I*, John Murray: London, 1832, p. 230.
32. Ibid.
33. James Burnes, 1839, p. 138.
34. Alexander Burnes, Vol. III, 1834, p. 241.
35. Ibid., p. 243.
36. Ibid., p. 246.
37. Ibid., p. 281.
38. Andrew Goudie, *Great Desert Explorers*, Silphium Press: London 2016, p. 184.
39. Ibid., p.182. One of the horses died on the way.
40. Ibid., p.184.
41. The letter dated 6 December 1831. Alexander Burnes, Vol. III, 1834, p. 299.
42. Alexander Burnes, Vol. I, 1834, p. 131.
43. Alexander Burnes made his work public and better known than Pottinger. Burnes published his work on Cutch in the *Transactions of the Royal Geographical Society for 1834.*
44. *Bombay Courier*, 15 November 1832. Cited from Asiatic Intelligence, *The Asiatic Journal and Monthly Register for British, Foreign India, China, and Australasia*, Vol. VIII, 1832, p. 24.
45. Alexander Burnes, Vol. I, 1834, p. 115.
46. Ibid., p. 242.
47. Mohan Lal, *Travels in the Panjab, Afghanistan and Turkistan to Balk, Bukhara, and Herat; and a Visit to Great Britain and Germany*, Allen and Co.: London, 1846, p. vi.
48. *The Athenaeum*, No. 823, London, 5 August 1843, p. 709.

49. Letter from Secretary to the Governor General of India to Alexander
    Burnes, 5 September 1836, *Indian Papers, No. 5: Correspondence Relating to
    Affghanistan, No.3*, The House of Commons, 27 March 1839, p. 4.

50. Alexander Burnes, 'On the Trade of the Upper Indus or Derajat', *Reports
    and Papers, Political, Geographical and Commercial Submitted to Government
    Employed on Missions in the Years 1835–36–37 in Scinde and Afghanistan,
    and Adjacent Countries*, G.H. Huttmann, Bengal Military Orphan Press:
    Calcutta, 1839, pp. 99–100. Lt R. Leech from the Bombay Engineers
    and assistant to the Kabul mission, describes in more detail the route
    from Dera Ghazee Khan to Candahar through the Sakee Sarwar pass and
    another route through the Boree pass in, 'Description of the Passes over
    the Hindoo Coosh Range of Mountains from the Koh Daman of Cabool',
    *Reports and Papers, Political, Geographical and Commercial Submitted to
    Government Employed on Missions in the Years 1835–36–37 in Scinde and
    Afghanistan, and Adjacent Countries*, G.H. Huttmann, Bengal Military
    Orphan Press: Calcutta, 1839, pp. 38–40. Also see Alexander Burnes,
    1843, pp. 102–10.

51. Charles Masson, *Narrative of Various Journeys in Balochistan, Afghanistan,
    Punjab, and Kalat, Vol. III*, Richard Bentley: London, 1844, p. 432.

52. Secret Committee of the East India Company to Lord Auckland on 25 June
    1837, cited in M. Edwardes, *Asia in the European Age*, Praeger: New York,
    1963, p. 61.

53. Mikhail Volodarsky, *Soviet Union and Its Southern Neighbours: Iran and
    Afghanistan, 1917–1933*, Routledge: London, 1994, p. 8.

54. Josiah Harlan, *Memoir of India and Avghanistaun*, J. Dobson: Philadelphia,
    1842, p. 11.

55. Ben Macintyre, *The Man Who Would Be King: First American in Afghanistan*,
    Farrar Straus Giroux: New York, 2004, p. iii. Harlan inspired Rudyard
    Kipling to write a short story, *The Man Who Would Be King*, in 1888 while
    living in Allahabad in British India.

56. Letter from Alexander Burnes to W.H. Macnaghten, 4 October 1837, *Indian
    Papers, No. 5: Correspondence Relating to Affghanistan, No. 7*, The House of
    Commons, 27 March 1839, p. 10.

57. Ibid., p. 12.

58. Letter from Lord Auckland to Dost Mahomed Khan, 20 January 1838,
    Indian Papers, No. 5, Correspondence Relating to Affghanistan, No. 18, The
    House of Commons, 27 March 1839, p. 25.

59. Ibid., p. 25.

60. Letter from Lord Auckland to John Hobhouse cited in Percy Sykes, *A History
    of Afghanistan, Vol. 1*, Macmillan and Co. Ltd.: London, 1940, p. 406.

61. Volodarsky, 1994, p. 8.

62. J.A. Norris, *The First Afghan War 1838–1842*, Cambridge University Press:
    Cambridge, 1967, p.238.

63. Declaration of the Governor General of India, on the Assembly of the Army of the Indus, 1 October 1838. Cited in *Dublin Review*, C. Dolman: London, 1841, p. 400.

64. Letter from Alexander Burnes to William Macnaghten, 28 August 1838, Indian Papers No. 5, *Correspondence Relating to Affghanistan, No. 18*, The House of Commons, 27 March 1839, p. 24.

65. J.A. Norris, 1967, p. 236.

66. Cited in *Dublin Review*, 1841, p. 412.

67. Ibid., p. 416.

68. Alexander Burnes, Vol. I, 1834, p. 144.

69. Sir John Hobhouse, *Thanks to the Indian Army*, House of Commons Debate, 6 February 1840, Vol. 51, column. 1324. Also see Alicia Albinia, *Empires of the Indus: The Story of a River*, John Murray: London, 2008, p. 43.

70. J.P. Parry, 'Steam Power and British Influence in Baghdad', *The Historical Journal*, Vol. 56(1), March 2013, p. 150.

71. Quoted in Halford L. Hoskins, *British Routes to India*, Longmans, Green and Co.: London, 1928, p. 148.

72. *Asiatic Journal and Monthly Register*, New Series Vol. V, part II, May-August 1831, p. 46. Cited in Winifred Bamforth, *British Interest in the Tigris–Euphrates Valley: 1856–1888*, M.A. thesis May 1948, ProQuest: An Arbor, MI, 2016, p. 34.

73. Ibid., p. 35. Francis Chesney (1789–1872) was an engineer and a gunner. After a brief stint in Egypt and Syria he was posted in Mesopotamia, commanding the expedition for the survey of the Euphrates in 1834–37. He later became Lt General and played an active role in finding an alternative route to India from Mesopotamia. Chesney visited India where he remained for five months.

74. Article 3 of the 1932 Treaty laid down: That the British Government has requested a passage for the merchants and traders of Hindostan by the river and roads of Scinde, by which they may transport their goods and merchandize from one country to another; and the said government of Hyderabad hereby acquiesces in the same request, on the three following conditions: 1, that no person shall bring any description of military stores by the above river or roads; 2, that no armed vessels or boats shall come by the said river; 3, that on [sic] English merchants shall be allowed to settle in Scinde, but shall come as occasion requires, and having stopped to transact their business, shall return to India. See, *The Ameers of Scinde*, House of Commons Debate, 8 February 1844, Vol. 72, column. 366.

75. The British prime minister, Sir Robert Peel, explained the treaty in the House of Commons, HC Debate, 13 February 1843, Vol. 66, cc. 418–9.

76. H. Donaldson Jordan, Review of Albert H. Imlah book Lord Ellenborough: A Biography of Edward Law, Earl of Ellenborough, Governor General of India, *The American Historical Review*, 46(3), April 1941, p. 637.

77. John Andrew Hamilton, 'Edward Law, Earl of Ellenborough (1790-1871)' in Sidney Lee (ed.), *Dictionary of National Biography*, Vol. XXXI, Macmillan and Co.: New York, 1892, p. 225.

78. Craig Murray, 2016, p. 56.

79. Sir Charles Napier, *Lights and Shades of Military Life, Vol. I*, Henry Colburn: London, 1840, p. 323.

80. James Outram, *The Conquest of Scinde: A Commentary, Part II*, William Blackwood and Sons: Edinburgh and London, 1846, p. 555. Also cited in R.E Holmes, *Sir Charles Napier*, reproduced by Sani H. Panhwar, California, 2009, p. 31.

81. Napier drew comparisons of Outram's actions to Pierre seigneur de Bayard (1473–1524), the French soldier known as *le chevalier sans peur et sans reproche* (the knight without fear and without reproach).

82. Bina Shah, *A Season of Martyrs*, Speaking Tiger Books: New Delhi, 2014, p. 3.

83. Frere's observation in a minute written at Calcutta, ten years later on 23 September 1861. See John Martineau, *Life and Correspondence of Sir Bartle Frere*, Vol. 1, Cambridge University Press: Cambridge, 1895, p. 92.

84. Timothy D. Haines, 'Building the Empire, Building the Nation: Water, land and the politics of river development in Sind, 1898–1969', thesis submitted to the Royal Holloway College, University of London, 2011, p. 39.

85. John Brunton was the chief engineer of the Karachi-Kotri railway project. John Brunton, *John Brunton 1812–1899, Memoirs of An Engineer*, Cambridge University Press: Cambridge, 1939, p. 105.

86. Ibid., p. 108.

87. For the 'Inquiry into the best means of promoting communication with India by steam' see, Hansard House of Commons Debate, 3 June 1834, Vol. 24, column. 142. Also see Steam Navigation to India House of Commons, 23 July 1834, *The Asiatic Journal*, Vol. XVII, New Series, May–August 1835, p. 276.

88. William T. Everall, 'The Reconstruction of the Attock Bridge across the River Indus on the North Western Railway, India', *Minutes of the Proceedings of the Institution of Civil Engineers*, Vol. 230(1930), 1930, p. 234.

Part III: Colonization, Canals *and* Contestation

1. John James Hood Gordon, *The Sikhs*, William Blackwood and Sons: London, 1904, p. 150. Also quoted in V.P. Menon, *The Story of the Integration of the Indian States*, Orient Longmans Ltd.: Calcutta, 1956, p. 391.

2. Report of the Administration of the Punjab. For the years 1849–50 and 1850–5, T. Jones: Calcutta Gazette Office, 1853, p. 175. Also known as the First Punjab Administration Report (1849–51).See Edwin Arnold, *The Marquis of Dalhousie's Administration of British India*, Vol. I, Saunders Otley & Co.: London, 1862, pp. 404–5.

3.   Herbert Edwardes and Herman Merivale, *Life of Sir Henry Lawrence*, Macmillan: New York, 1873, p. 20.

4.   Sir John Benton, 'The Punjab Triple Canal System', Paper No. 4137, Minutes of Proceedings, 16 November 1915, University of Sussex, p. 24.

5.   Quoted in Herbert M. Wilson, *Irrigation in India (Second Edition)*, US Geological Survey: Washington, 1903, p. 90. Also see Proby T. Cautley, *Reports on the Ganges Canal Works, from their commencement until the opening of the canal in 1854*, Smith, Elder and Co.: London, 1860.

6.   Proby T. Cautley, 'Canals of Irrigation in the North Western Provinces', *The Calcutta Review*, XII, 1849, p. 80.

7.   Colonel H.M. Vibart, R.E., *Richard Baird Smith. Leader of The Delhi Heroes In 1857. Private Correspondence of the Commanding Engineer During the Siege, and Other Interesting Letters Hitherto Unpublished*, Archibald Constable and Co.: Westminster, 1897, p. vi.

8.   Cautley, 1849, pp. 141–2.

9.   Ibid., p. 141.

10.   Latika Chaudhary and Anand V. Swamy, 'A Policy of Credit Disruption: The Punjab Land Alienation Act 1900', *Semantic Scholar*, October 2008, p. 6.

11.   The canal colonies were: Sidhnai Colony (1886–8); Sohag Para Colony (1886–8); Chenab Colony (1892–1905 and 1926–30); Chunian Colony (1896–8 and 1904–5); Jhelum Colony (1902–6); Lower Bari Doab Colony (1914–24); Upper Chenab (1915–9); Upper Jhelum Colony (1916–21) and Nil Bari Colony (1916–40).

12.   S.S. Thorburn, *Musalmans and Money-lenders in the Punjab*, William Blackwood and Sons: London and Edinburgh, 1886, p. 1.

13.   Imran Ali, *The Punjab under Imperialism, 1885–1947*, Princeton University Press: New York, 1988, p. 3.

14.   Ian Stone, *Canal Irrigation in British India: Perspectives on a Technological Change in a Peasant Economy*, Cambridge University Press: Cambridge, 1984. Stone, in his positivity of the canal irrigation, is a counter to the argument of Whitcombe's negative externality.

15.   Report on the Census of Punjab, 1868, p. 16. Cited in Sukhwant Singh, 'Agricultural Science and Technology in the Punjab in the Nineteenth Century', *Indian Journal of History of Science*, 17(2), 1982, p. 192.

16.   R.B. Buckley, *Irrigation Works in India and Egypt*, E. & F.N. Spon: London, 1893, p. 20. He also wrote, 'Keeping Irrigation Canals Clear of Silt', *Proceedings Institution Civil Engineers*, 58, 1879.

17.   The doabs were named with the coupling of the rivers: the Bari (Beas-Sutlej and Ravi), Rechna (Ravi and Chenab), and Jech (Jhelum and Chenab), the Sindh Sagar (Sindh and Jhelum) and Bist (Beas-Sutlej).

18.   See Karl Wittfogel, *Oriental Despotism: A Comparative Study of Total Power*, Yale University Press: New Haven, 1957. Wittfogel's central argument was

that hydraulic civilizations in the Orient were different from those of the Western world.

19. Rohan D'Souza, 'Water in British India: The Making of a Colonial Hydrology', *History Compass*, 4(4), 2006, p. 622. D'Souza argues a case for the term 'colonial hydrology' that impacted the Punjab region's fluvial endowments in specific and unprecedented ways.

20. Ian Talbot, 'The Punjab under Colonialism: Order and Transformation in British India', *Journal of Punjab Studies*, 14(1), 2007, p. 7. Also see Mridula Mukherjee, *Colonizing Agriculture: The Myth of Punjabi Exceptionalism*, Sage: New Delhi, 2005.

21. Romesh C. Dutt formulated what is now recognized as the classic diagnosis of the history of the Indian economic problem under colonial rule. See R.C. Dutt, *Famines and Land Assessments in India*, Kegan Paul: London, 1900.

22. Cited in R. Bosworth Smith, *The Life of Lord Lawrence, Vol. 2*, Smith, Elder & Co.: London, 1885, p. 364.

23. Ibid., p. 365.

24. Cited in W.W. Hunter, *A Life of the Earl of Mayo: Fourth Viceroy of India*, Vol. II, Smith, Elder and Co: London, 1876, p. 4.

25. Ibid., p. 322.

26. The stabbing of Lord Mayo by the prisoner, Sher Ali, a Pathan from the NWFP who pleaded 'not guilty' for the murder he was convicted of, is regarded as an act of Jihad which started with the assassination of Judge Norman, the acting Chief Justice of the Calcutta High Court in 1871. See Helen James, 'The Assassination of Lord Mayo: The "First Jihad"?', *International Journal of Asia Pacific Studies*, 5(2), July 2009, pp. 1–19.

27. See text of the *Northern India Canal and Drainage Act, 1873. Act No.8 of 1873: An Act to Regulate Irrigation, Navigation and Drainage in Northern India.* This tendency was progressively strengthened with the Bengal Drainage Act, 1880, The Punjab Minor Canal Act, 1905 and the Madhya Pradesh Irrigation Act, 1931.

28. Ibid., Act VIII of 1873.

29. Iqbal Ahmed Siddiqui, 'History of Water Laws in India' in C. Singh (ed.), *Water Law in India*, Indian Law Institute: New Delhi, p. 300.

30. Clause 68 (1) and (4) of the Canal and Drainage Act, 1873.

31. See text of the Punjab Minor Canal Act, 1905.

32. Richard Strachey headed the Strachey Commission (1878) under the Viceroy of Robert Lytton that looked into the recurring famines of the nineteenth century in India. One of the recommendations was to develop irrigation facilities as also setting up the famine fund of one million pounds.

33. Government of India 1867, p. 49. Cited in Patrick McGinn, *Capital, Development and Canal Irrigation in Colonial India*, Institute for Social and Economic Change, Working Paper 209, 2009, p. 1.

34. Monier Monier-Williams was born in Bombay and taught Sanskrit at the college there. After the East India Company came to an end in 1858, he contested along with Max Mueller for the Boden Chair of Sanskrit in Oxford University in 1860. After his appointment to the chair he declared that the conversion of India to the Christian religion should be one of the aims of orientalist scholarship.

35. McGinn, 2009, p. 1.

36. Ibid., p. 1. John Bright, a liberal statesman and an advocate of a free trade policies and a brilliant orator, was also invited to speak in Manchester on 11 December 1877. Impassionedly he said that, 'India is essentially a country at this moment of great and abject poverty, and that the reputation of its wealth has only been founded upon the fact that it is a country which marauders have always found it easy to plunder.' John Bright, Selected Speeches of Rt. Hon. John Bright M.P on Public Questions, J.M. Dent & Co.: London, 1853, p. 39.

37. Cited in Imran Ali, 1988, p. 20.

38. Allen F. Isaacman and Richard L. Roberts (eds.), *Cotton, Colonialism, and Social History in Sub-Saharan Africa*, Heinemann: Portsmouth, N.H., 1995. p. 255.

39. Ibid., p. 279.

40. See Government of India, 1880, pp. 96–8. Cited in McGinn, 2009, p. 5.

41. Ibid., pp. 175–6.

42. Herbert M. Wilson, *Irrigation in India (Second Edition)*, U.S. Geological Survey: Washington, 1903, pp. 98–9.

43. D.G. Harris, *Irrigation in India*, Humphrey Milford, Oxford University Press: London, 1923, p. 55.

44. C.H. Buck, 'Canal Irrigation in the Punjab', *The Geographical Journal*, 27 January 1906, p. 65.

45. Niranjan D. Gulhati, Indus Waters Treaty: An Exercise in International Mediation, Allied Publishers: Bombay, 1973, p. 33.

46. Ibid.

47. H. Caldwell Lipsett, *Lord Curzon in India, 1898–1901*, Messrs Everett & Co.: London, 1903, p. 55.

48. Ibid., p. 71.

49. Ibid., p. 80.

50. The arrival of Lord Lytton to India as the Viceroy (1876–80) coincided with the great famines (1876–1878). In 1878, Lytton created a Famine Commission. In 1880, the Famine Commission was codified. One million pounds a year Famine Insurance Fund was created. A budget of 500 thousand pounds was set for railway construction and 250 thousand pounds was allocated for irrigational projects. Despite his apparent concern over the famine, Lytton was more concerned about the money allocated for famine that could be useful for British expansion in Afghanistan. In a famous

reaction to pleas for relief, Lytton wrote: 'Let the British public foot the bill for its "cheap sentiment", if it wished to save life at a cost that would bankrupt India.' Cited from Lt Colonel Robert D. Osborn, 'India Under Lord Lytton', *Contemporary Review*, 36, December 1879, pp. 552–73. Also see Lady Beatty Balfour, *The History of Lord Lytton's Indian Administration, 1876 to 1880: Compiled from Letters and Official Papers*, Longmans: London, 1899.

51. Lieut. C.C. Scott-Moncrieff, *Irrigation in Southern Europe: Being the Report of a Tour of Inspection of the Irrigation Works in France, Spain, and Italy Undertaken in 1867-68 for the Government of India*, E. & F. N. Spon: London, 1868, p. v.
52. Ibid., p. vi.
53. Colonel Sir Colin C. Scott-Moncrieff, *Report on the Indian Irrigation Commission, 1901–1903. Commission Appointed to Report on the Irrigation in India as Protection against Famine*, Office of the Superintendent of Government Printing: Calcutta, 1903, p. 2.
54. Cited in Elizabeth Whitcombe, 'Irrigation and Railways', in Tapan Raychaudhuri and Irfan Habib, *The Cambridge Economic History of India: c. 1757–1970*, Orient Longman: New Delhi, 2005, p. 717.
55. David Hall-Matthews, 'Inaccurate Conceptions: Disputed Measures of Nutritional Needs and Famine Deaths in Colonial India', *Modern Asian Studies*, Vol. 42(6), 2008, p. 1201.
56. W. Eric Gustafson and Richard B. Reidinger, 'Delivery of Canal Water in North India and West Pakistan', *Economic and Political Weekly*, December 1971, p. 158.
57. N. Gerald Barrier, 'The Punjab Disturbances of 1907: The Response of the British Government in India to Agrarian Unrest', *Modern Asian Studies*, Vol. 1(4), 1967, p. 355.
58. Sukhdarshan Nat, 'Sardar Ajit Singh Hero of the "Pagdi Sambhal Jatta" Movement', *CPI(M-L) website*, http://archive.cpiml.org/liberation/year_2007/october/Sardaar_ajit_singh.htm. Nat gives a snapshot of the agitation. Also sees, Ajit Singh, *Buried Alive: Autobiography, Speeches and Writings of the Indian Revolutionary Ajit Singh*, Geetanjali: New Delhi, 1984.
59. Barrier, 1967, pp. 353–83.
60. *The Imperial Gazetteer*, Clarendon Press: Oxford, 1909, p. 29.
61. For details of the Triple Canal Project see, Imran Ali, *The Punjab Canal Colonies: 1885–1940*, A thesis, Australian National University: Canberra, 1979, p. 89 and p. 289.
62. Cited in Saiyid Ali Naqvi, *Indus Waters and Social Change: The Evolution and Transition of Agrarian Society in Pakistan*, Oxford University Press: Oxford, 2013, p. 22.
63. Benton, 1915, p. 25.
64. Ibid., p. 29.

65. Naqvi, 2013, p. 22.
66. Zahid Ali Khalid, *State, Society and Environment in the Ex-State of Bahawalpur: A Case Study of the Sutlej Valley Project, 1921–1947*, thesis submitted to University of Sussex, UK, April 2017, p. 60.
67. Quoted in *Completion Report and Schedules, Sirhind Canal, 1893*, Punjab Public Works Department, C & M Gazette Press: Lahore, 1893, p. 62. Captain Baker first drafted a project for irrigating Patiala alone. Colonel Dias thereafter devised a comprehensive project for irrigating British India and the Native States of Patiala, Nabha, Jind. See John G. Laylin, 'Principles of Law Governing the Uses of International Rivers: Contribution from the Indus Basin', *Proceedings of the American Society of International Law at Its Annual Meeting (1921–1969)*, 51, April, 1957, p. 25. Also cited in World Bank Group (WBG) Archives, *The Indus Basin Dispute—International Law—Document 01*, 1787921, Washington D.C., p. 3; and in *Report of The Narmada Water Disputes Tribunal*, Government of India, New Delhi, Vol. III, 1978, p. 85.
68. Cited in Alfred Deakin, *Irrigated India: An Australian View of India and Ceylon, Their Irrigation and Agriculture*, W. Thacker and Co., London, 1893, pp. 197–8. Also see Lady Hope and William Digby, *General Sir Arthur Cotton: His Life and Work*, Kessinger Publishing, 2010. 'I showed then—that was in 1856–1857—that the Corporation of Manchester had, during the preceding fourteen years spent more in public works for the good of its own population, than the East India Company had spent in the same fourteen years throughout the vast territories which were subjected to their care or to their neglect now.'
69. Cited in The Principles of Law Governing the Use of International Rivers, Memorandum of the Department of State prepared by Mr William L. Griffin, Attorney, Office of the Legal Adviser, 21 April 1958, WBG Archives, 1787922, p. 31.
70. Ibid.
71. George Hamilton speech in the House of Commons, 5 August 1897, *Hansard: House of Commons Debate*, Third Series, Vol. 52, column, 435.
72. Ibid., column, 437.
73. Joseph Chamberlain speech at the annual dinner of the Royal Colonial Institute on 31 March 1897. W.D. Handcock (ed.), *English Historical Documents, 1874–1914*, Routledge: London, 1996, p. 389.
74. Wilson, 1903, p. 35. In terms of net revenue, however, Punjab was earning almost half of that of Madras ($18,854,000). It's earning was far less than that of Northwest Province ($15,107,000) and Bengal ($13,066,000) and even Bombay ($9,791,000). Ibid., p. 35.
75. WBG Archives, 1787922, p. 31. Sir Claude Hill surprisingly makes no reference to the 1918 suggestion in his book *India-Stepmother*, William Blackwood & Sons Ltd: Edinburgh and London, 1929.

76. Cited in *Report of The Narmada Water Disputes Tribunal*, Vol. III, 1978, p. 29.

77. Ibid.

78. *Report of the Indian Cotton Committee*, Superintendent Government Printing: Calcutta, 1919, pp. 35–6.

79. Cited in Constitution of India 'Remarks' on the Government of India Act, 1919.

80. Government of India Act, 1919: Rules Thereunder and Government Reports 1920, N.N. Mitter: Calcutta, 1921, p. 126. Under Schedule I Part I Central Subjects 5(c) interestingly makes a reference to inland navigation: 'Inland waterways including shipping and navigation thereon so far as not declared by the Governor General in Council to be central subject as regards inland steam vessels to legislation by the Indian legislature.'

81. See Ministry of Jal Shakti, http://mowr.gov.in/about-us/history

82. View, 'Construction of the Sukkur Barrage', Vintage Movie, Government of India (Railways Department), 1924. Movie link, https://thewaterchannel.tv/videos/the-construction-of-the-sukkur-barrage-vintage-movie/

83. Report of a Committee on Distributions of Water of the Indus and Its Tributaries, Vol. I, Government of Punjab Printing: Lahore, p. 9.

84. In 1918, during the deliberation between Punjab, Bahawalpur and Bikaner, Sir Claude Hill, Chairman of the meeting had suggested this principle which was accepted by the three parties. Cited in *Report of the Indus (Anderson) Committee*, Vol. II, 1935, p. 60.

85. S.C. Mishra, 'Progress of Irrigation during the Period of Maharaja Ganga Singh' in G.S.L. Devra (ed.), *Maharaja Ganga Singhji Centenary Volume 1980*, Centenary Celebration Committee: Bikaner, 1980, p. 39. Also see L.S. Rathore, *The Regal Patriot: Maharaja Ganga Singh of Bikaner*, Roli: New Delhi, 2007.

86. Ibid., p. 38.

87. Ibid.

88. Report of a Committee on Distributions of Water of the Indus and its Tributaries, Vol. I, WBG Archives, 1787860, p. 8.

89. Ibid., p. 9. 'The Government of Bombay had already consented to 500 cusecs being utilized by the Punjab for the Jalalpur pumping scheme and the Committee considered that that discharge might be increased to 1,250 cusecs, as the difference of 750 cusecs was well within the margin of error in discharge observations at Sukkur. The Committee also suggested that if the Government of the Punjab preferred to undertake the Haveli Scheme in preference to the Jalalpur scheme, the 1,250 cusecs allotted in *rabi* to the latter would enable them to do so as there appeared no difficulty in finding the 7,500 cusecs from the 20th of April required for *kharif*.'

90. Ibid., p. 10.

91. Ibid.

92. Ibid., p. 11.
93. Ibid.
94. Ibid., p. 12. 'The Sukkur Barrage Project was completed in 1932, and various discharges were allotted to the canals in accordance with figures contained in the 1919–20 Project. Although those figures were evidently intended to be the authorized maximum withdrawals, which could be utilized at any time in the month concerned, the Sindh authorities did not consider them as maxima and on occasions exceeded those figures. Moreover, the Government of India, in their letter No. I.R.:61 dated June 29th, 1929 (2) laid down on the understanding that no "prescriptive rights" to such excesses were claimed at a later date.'
95. Ibid.
96. Ibid., p.11.
97. Ibid., p. 12. 'The Committee also found that the supplies available at certain periods of the year were far short of requirements for the canals taking off the Sutlej. On the other hand there appeared to be ample water at Panjnad and therefore they recommended the deletion of clause 4. D. 2 of the [Tripartite] Agreement.' The Clause notes: 'For the perennial and non-perennial canals for Bahawalpur from the Panjnad the mean draw off in each crop shall be maintained at the same fraction of their authorized maximum capacity in cusecs as that of the British canals from the Gharra.'
98. Ibid. The interested parties were the Indus basin provinces: Punjab, Bombay (Sindh), North West Frontier Province, Bahawalpur, Khairpur and Bikaner. There were only three non-British as advisers: Gurmukhsingh J. Butani; Rai Bahadur Jai Gopal; Khan Bahadur J. R. Colabawala representing Bombay (Sindh), Bahawalpur and Khairpur States respectively.
99. WBG Archives, 1787860, p. 13.
100. See letter from the Government of India, Public Works Branch, Department of Industries and Labour to the Punjab Public Works Department, Irrigation Branch of 30 March 1937 summing up the 'Distribution of waters on the Indus and its tributaries', WBG Archives, 1787860, pp. 1–2.
101. Rasul Bux Palijo, Sindh–Punjab Water Dispute 1859–2003, p. 12. Copyright © www.panhwar.com
102. WBG Archives, 1787860, pp. 23–4.
103. F.J. Fowler, 'Some Problems of Water between East and West Punjab', Geographical Review, Vol. 40(4), October 1950, p. 583.
104. Text of the Government of India Act, 1935, p. 87. http://www.legislation.gov.uk/ukpga/1935/2/pdfs/ukpga_19350002_en.pdf
105. Report of the Indus (Rau) Commission, 1942.
106. Ibid.
107. David Gilmartin, 'Scientific Empire and Imperial Science: Colonialism and Irrigation Technology in the Indus Basin', The Journal of Asian Studies, 53 (4), November 1994, p. 1139.

108. Ibid., p. 1136. Also see John Broich, *Engineering the Empire: British Water Supply System and Colonial Societies, 1850–1900*, Cambridge University Press online, 21 December 2012, p. 348.

109. Cited in John Black, 'The military influence on engineering education in Britain and India, 1848–1906', *The Indian Economic and Social History Review*, 46(2), 2009, p. 232.

110. These papers are available on Internet archives.

111. Kanwar Sain, *Reminiscences of an Engineer*, Young Asia Publications: New Delhi, 1978, p. 58.

112. Ibid., p. 59.

113. 'Regime channel' occurs 'When an artificial channel is used to convey silty water, both bed and banks scour or fill, changing depth, gradient and width, until a state of balance is attained at which the channel is said to be in regime.' Cited in E.S. Lindley, *Regime Channels*, https://pecongress.org.pk/images/upload/books/Regime-Channels.pdf. A 'Stable channel' design is 'deduced from the condition that, for any given steady flow, total sediment concentration maintains a balanced average in space and time within a stable channel.' Cited in George Griffiths, 'Stable-channel design in alluvial rivers', *Journal of Hydrology*, Vol. 65(4), September 1983, p. 259.

114. Gilmartin, 2015, p. 151. Also see R.G. Kennedy, 'Prevention of Silting in Irrigation Canals', *Minutes of Proceedings*, Inst of C.E, Vol. cxix, 1895, pp. 281–90.

115. Aparajith Ramnath, *Birth of an Indian Profession: Engineers, Industry and State, 1900-1947*, Oxford University Press: New Delhi, 2017, p. 106.

116. A.V. Shankara Rao, 'Mokshagundam Visvesvaraya: Engineer, Statesman and Planner', *Resonance*, May 2002, p. 76.

117. Ibid.

118. See A.N. Khosla, N.K. Bose, Rai Bahadur and E. McKenzie Taylor, *Design of Weirs on Permeable Foundation*, Ashoka Press: Delhi, 1954 (reprint).

119. The Unionist Party was formed by Chhotu Ram, Sir Sikander Hyat Khan, Sir Fazl-i-Husain and Sir Shahab-ud-Din.

120. Cited in Tika Ram, *Sir Chhotu Ram: A Biography*, Centre for Study of Haryana History: Gurgaon, 2008, p. 82.

121. Nehru during the dedication of the Bhakra Dam to the nation, 22 October 1963.

122. Ramnath, 2017, pp. 70–1.

123. Ibid., p. 66.

124. E.S. Lindley, 'Regime Channels, Minutes of Proceedings', *Punjab Engineering Congress*, Vol.7, 1919, p. 74b.

125. Daniel Klingensmith explains this term in his book, *One Valley and a Thousand: Dams, Nationalism and Development*, Oxford University Press: Oxford, 2007, p. 211.

126. 'End of 200-Year-Old British Rule in India', front page headline of
     The Hindustan Times, New Delhi, Saturday, 19 July 1947.

Part IV: Partition *of* Land *and* Rivers

1.   7th paragraph of the 20 February 1947, Statement of Clement Attlee in the
     House of Commons.
2.   Winston Churchill speech in the House of Commons. Hansard House of
     Commons Debate, 6 March 1947, Vol. 434, column. 676.
3.   For full text of the statement see Nicholas Mansergh (ed.), *The Transfer of
     Power, 1942–47*, Vol. 11, 31 May–7 July 1947, London, 1992, pp. 89–94.
4.   Alan Campbell-Johnson, *Mission with Mountbatten*, London: Robert Hale,
     1972, p. 124.
5.   Nicholas Mansergh (ed.), *The Commonwealth Experience from British to
     Multi-Racial Commonwealth, Vol. Two*, Palgrave Macmillan: London, 1982,
     p. 126.
6.   W.H. Morris-Jones, 'Thirty-Six Years Later: The Mixed Legacies of
     Mountbatten's Transfer of Power', *International Affairs*, 59(4), 1983, p. 623.
7.   Note by Mountbatten, 11 February 1947, Mountbatten papers, T.O.P.,
     IX, p. 378. Also see Anita Inder Singh, 'Decolonization in India: The
     Statement of 20 February 1947', *The International History Review*, 6(2),
     1984, pp. 191–209.
8.   Barney White-Spunner, *Partition: The Story of India's Independence and the
     Creation of Pakistan in 1947*, Simon & Schuster: New Delhi, 2017, p. 355.
9.   Mountbatten Papers, India Office Records, London, File No. 206. Cited
     in Latif Ahmed Sherwani, *The Partition of India and Mountbatten*, Atlantic
     Publishers and Distributors: New Delhi, 1989, p. 12.
10. 'Lord Mountbatten on His Viceroyalty', *The Asiatic Review*, XLIV (160),
     October 1948, p. 348.
11. Larry Collins and Dominique Lapierre, *Mountbatten and the Partition of
     India, Vol. 1: March 22–August 15, 1947*, Vikas Publishing House: New
     Delhi, 1982, pp. 44–6. Also see the brilliantly written review article by John
     R. Wood, 'Dividing the Jewel: Mountbatten and the Transfer of Power to
     India and Pakistan', *Pacific Affairs*, 58(4), 1985–6, pp. 653–62.
12. Philip Ziegler, *Mountbatten: The Official Biography*, William Collins:
     London, 1985, pp. 398–9.
13. Aloys Arthur Michel, *The Indus Rivers: The Study of the Effects of the Partition*,
     Yale University Press: New Haven, 1967, p. 29.
14. Laylin, 1957, p. 2. A good account of the partition of land and water is
     explained by Ashutosh Misra, *India-Pakistan: Coming to Terms*, Palgrave
     Macmillan: New York, 2010, pp. 57–80.
15. *A Manual of Irrigation Practice*, Public Works Department, Irrigation Branch,
     Government of Punjab, 1943.

16. The basin included all or part of British Baluchistan, the pre-Partition Indian Provinces of Sindh, the Punjab and the North-West Frontier, the Indian States of Bahawalpur, Jammu and Kashmir, Kapurthala, Khairpur, Patiala and a number of smaller states in Baluchistan, northwest of Jammu and east of the Punjab, and the Gilgit Agency.

17. Text of Jinnah's statement opposing the partition of Punjab and Bengal, 4 May 1947. See National Archives, https://www.nationalarchives.gov.uk/education/resources/the-road-to-partition/jinnah-partition/

18. Rajendra Prasad's reply to Jinnah's statement. Ibid.

19. Campbell-Johnson, 1972, p. 115. The report was largely written by John Christie, Mountbatten's joint private secretary.

20. Cited in Anwesha Sengupta, 'Of Men and Things: The Administrative Consequences of Partition of British India', *Refugee Watch*, 39 and 40, June and December 2012, p. 3. Footnote, Viceroy's Personal Report No. 8, L/PO/ 6/ 123: ff 114–21, p. 163.

21. Ibid, p. 4.

22. Stanley Wolpert, *Jinnah of Pakistan*, Oxford University Press: Oxford, 1997, p. vii.

23. Jinnah's statement on 4 May 1947, I and B Department, India National Archives, FO 371-/63533.

24. Kuldip Nayar, *Scoop! Inside Stories from the Partition to the Present*, Harper Collins, New Delhi, 2006, p. 33.

25. Wayne Wilcox, 'The Economic Consequences of Partition: India and Pakistan', *Journal of International Affairs*, Vol. 18(2), 1964, p. 190.

26. Capt. H. Wilberforce-Well, *The History of Kathiawad: From the Earliest Time*, William Heinemann: London, 1917, p. 3. Wilberforce-Well writes (p. 5), 'At some very remote period Kathiawad was undoubtedly an island. Running almost North and South, and forming a connecting link between the Rann of Kachh and the Gulf of Cambay, is a strip of undulating country known as the "Nal" or "watercourse". There is every indication of its having at one time formed the bed of some mighty river, and there can be little doubt in the conjecture that the Indus River, which has so often changed its course, and whose eccentricities are notorious, once entered the ocean by way of the Gulf of Cambay.'

27. Wilfred Cantwell Smith, *Islam in Modern History*, Princeton University Press: NJ, 1957, fn. 22, pp. 271–2.

28. Nehru's statement cited in *White Paper on India-Pakistan Trade Relations*, *India's News Bulletin*, 13 February 1950, p. 3.

29. Patrick Spens, 'The Arbitral Tribunal in India, 1947–48', *Transaction of the Grotius Society*, 36, 1950, pp. 61–2. Sir Patrick Spens was appointed Chairman of the Arbitral Tribunal.

30. Nayar, 2006, p. 34.

31. Wilcox, 1964, p. 188.

32.   W.H. Auden, 'Partition', in Edward Mendelson (ed.), *Collected Poems by W.H. Auden*, Modern Library Edition: New York, pp. 803–4.

33.   The Boundary Commission met on 21 July 1947. The Commission consisted of four members each from the INC and the Muslim League and was chaired by Radcliffe. According to *The Gazette of India* notification dated 30 June 1947, 'The Boundary Commission is instructed to demarcate the boundaries of the two parts of the Punjab on the basis of ascertaining the contiguous majority areas of Muslims and non-Muslims. In doing so it will take into account other factors.' The notification appointed members of the Punjab Boundary Commission: Justice Din Muhammad; Justice Muhmmad Munir (nominees of the Muslim League); Justice Mehr Chand Mahajan and Justice Teja Singh (nominees of the Congress). It also appointed members of the Bengal Boundary Commission: Justice Bijan Kumar Mukherjea; Justice C.C. Biswas; Justice Abu Saleh Mohamed Akram and Justice S.A. Rahman. During the deliberations of the Bengal Boundary Commission, 'Arguments were presented to the Commission by numerous parties on both sides, but the main cases were presented by counsel on behalf of the Indian National Congress, the Bengal Provincial Hindu Mahasabha and the New Bengal Association on the one hand, and on behalf of the Muslim League on the other.'

34.   Cyril Radcliffe, Report of the Punjab Boundary Commission (6), 12 August 1947.

35.   M.L. Setalvad presented the Congress case before the Commission. He was assisted by a dozen or more lawyers and public men including Bakshi Tek Chand, Jivan Lai Kapur, Harnam Singh, Shiv Shashtri, Thaker Das Bhargava and R.B. Badri Das. The Muslim League was represented by Sir Mohammed Zafrullah who was assisted by Sir Feroz Khan Noon.

36.   V.N. Datta, 'The Punjab Boundary Commission Award', *Proceedings of the Indian History Congress*, 59, 1998, p. 854.

37.   The provisional boundaries indicated in the Appendix were based on district-wise majorities as recorded in the 1941 census. It showed that Muslims were in the majority in three of the five administrative divisions of the Punjab. Rawalpindi Division: Attock, Gujarat, Jhelum, Mianwali, Rawalpindi, Shahpur; Multan Division: Dera Ghazi Khan, Jhang, Lyallpur, Montgomery, Multan, Muzaffargarh; Lahore Division: Gujranwala, Gurdaspur, Lahore, Sheikhupura and Sialkot districts. Amritsar, which belonged to Lahore division, had a non-Muslim majority and was, therefore, not included among the Muslim majority areas in the Appendix. Besides Amritsar district, Hindus and Sikhs were in a majority in the following division and their districts. Jullundur Division: Ludhiana, Ferozepore, Jullundur, Hoshiarpur, Kangra; Ambala Division: Gurgaon, Rothak, Hissar, Karnal, Ambala, Simla.

38.   For details see Kirpal Singh (ed.), *Select Documents on Partition of Punjab, India and Pakistan, 1947*, National Book Shop: Delhi, 1991, pp. 223–4. Cited in

Ilyas Ahmad Chattha, *Partition and Its Aftermath: Violence, Migration and the Role of Refugees in the Socio-Economic Development of Gujranwala and Sialkot Cities, 1947–1961,* Thesis, University of Southampton Research Repository ePrints Soton, 2009, p. 50.

39. H.V. Hodson, *The Great Divide: Britain-India-Pakistan*, Hutchinson and Co.: London, 1969, p. 339.

40. Cyril Radcliffe, Report of the Bengal Boundary Commission, 12 August 1947, The Schedule, Annexure A (5).

41. Joya Chatterji, 'The Fashioning of a Frontier, The Radcliffe Line and Bengal's Border Landscape', *Modern Asian Studies*, 30(1), 1999, p. 222. In the footnote, Chatterji refers to the Mathabhanga issue which was one of those clarified by Justice Bagge in 1950. The starting point of the river was fixed at a point in the Ganges south-west of Jalangi village. 'Decisions given by the Indo-Pakistan Boundary Disputes Tribunal', PP, Vol. VI, p. 321.

42. Ibid., pp. 223–34.

43. Radcliffe, Report of the Punjab Boundary Commission, 12 August 1947, The Schedule, Annexure A (1).

44. Joya Chatterji, 1999, p. 211.

45. Stanley Wolpert, *Shameful Flight: The Last Years of the British Empire in India*, Oxford University Press: Oxford, 2009, p. 167.

46. Muhamad Zafrullah Khan, *Agony of Pakistan*, Kent Publications: Oxford, 1973, p.59. As Zafrullah said about Radcliffe, 'He would approach it with an open and impartial mind. But an empty mind would demand being filled, and the source of sources from which it were filled would not fail to sway it.'

47. Larry Collins and Dominique Lapierre, *Freedom at Midnight*, Vikas Publishing House: New Delhi, 1975, p. 281. Gurdaspur, Batala and Pathankot in the Gurdaspur district on the 'northern extremity of the Punjab' came to India.

48. Radcliffe, Report of the Punjab Boundary Commission (9), 12 August 1947.

49. Ibid.

50. Text of the International Regulation regarding the Use of International Watercourses for Purposes other than Navigation Declaration of Madrid, 20 April 1911, II (7).

51. Leonard Mosley, *The Last Days of the British Raj*, Jaico Publishing House: Bombay, 1960, p. 226.

52. Cited in Mehr Chand Mahajan, *Looking Back: Autobiography of Mehr Chand Mahajan*, Asia Publishing House: New Delhi, 1963, p. 115.

53. Spens, 1950, p. 70.

54. Ibid.

55. Ibid., p. 71.

56. Ibid.

57. F.J. Berber, 'Indus Water Dispute', *Indian Year Book of International Affairs*, Diocesan Press, 1957, p. 3. Also see Tufail Jawed, 'The World Bank and the

Indus Basin Dispute: Background- I', *Pakistan Horizon*, 18(3), 1965, p. 229. Of the fifteen headworks in Pakistan, five were on the Indus at Kalabagh, Taunsa, Guddu, Sukkur and Kotri; two on the Jhelum at Mangla and Rasool; four on the Chenab at Marala, Khanki, Trimmu and Punjnad; two on the Ravi at Balloki and Sidnai and last two on the Sutlej at Suleimanki and Islam.

58. Michel, 1967, pp. 188–9. Also see Gulhati, 1973, p. 57.

59. Sain, 1978, p. 117.

60. Ibid., pp. 117–8.

61. *Mounbattens Visit Bikaner*, 2 February 1948. British Movietone News, Associated Press Archives.

62. Sain, 1978, p. 119.

63. Ibid., p. 122.

64. Nehru in a letter to Vallabbhai Patel describing the Maharaja, 11 April 1948. *Selected Works of Jawaharlal Nehru*, Volume Two, Jawaharlal Nehru Memorial Fund: New Delhi, 1984, p. 311. Nehru had similarly expressed in a letter to Sir B.N. Rau, on the same day as he wrote to Patel, saying that the Maharaja 'has a bee in his bonnet about sovereignty'. See p. 137.

65. The Maharaja of Bikaner and his group of principality states were in favour of joining the Union immediately while the Nawab of Bhopal and the majority of the princes were in favour of 'wait and see'. The Maharaja had walked out of the Standing Committee of the Chamber of Princes in Bombay on 1 April 1947 over differences between the time when the states should join the Constituent Assembly. See R.L. Rathore, *Maharaja Sadul Singh of Bikaner: A Biography*, Books Treasure and Maharaja Ganga Sighji Trust: Jodhpur, 2005, p. 353.

66. The statement of the Maharaja of Bikaner on 24 April 1947 referred to in the letter written by Nehru to the Maharaja on 29 April 1947. *Selected Works of Jawaharlal Nehru*, Volume Two, Jawaharlal Nehru Memorial Fund: New Delhi, 1984, p. 253.

67. Ibid.

68. Sain, 1978, p. 122.

69. Ibid., p. 121.

70. Cited in Wolpert, 2009, p. 167.

71. Collins and Lapierre, 1975, p. 227.

72. Sain, 1978, p. 122.

73. White-Spunner, 2017, p. 219.

74. Collins and Lapierre, 1982, p. 86.

75. Latif Ahmed Sherwani, *The Partition of India and Mountbatten*, Atlantic Publishers and Distributors: New Delhi, 1989, p. 198.

76. Ibid.

77. Jinnah in a broadcast speech from Lahore on 30 October 1947. Cited in G.W. Choudhury, *Pakistan's Relations with India*, Meenakshi Prakashan: Meerut, p. 20.

78. Sher Muhammad Garewal, 'Muslim League's Tacit Acceptance of Radcliffe Award: A Critical Review', *Pakistan Journal of History and Culture*, XXVI (2), 2005, p. 58.
79. Laylin, 1957, pp. 6–7.
80. India and Pakistan had pledged: 'Both Governments [of Bharat and Pakistan] have pledged themselves to accept the awards of the Boundary Commissions, whatever these may be . . . Both Governments will take appropriate steps to allow the Boundary Commission to work without any disturbance and as soon as the awards are announced, both Governments will enforce them impartially and at once.'
81. Sain, 1978, p. 126.
82. Ibid.
83. Ibid., p. 128.
84. Nehru to Sardar Patel, 11 April 1948. *Selected Works of Jawaharlal Nehru*, Second Series, Volume Six, Jawaharlal Nehru Memorial Fund: New Delhi, 1984, p. 311.
85. White-Spunner, 2017, pp. 219–20.
86. Awards of the Arbitral Tribunal on References Nos. 1, 2 and 3 (valuation of canals, Crown wastelands brought under irrigation and irrigated forests taken on the basis of their pre-Partition value when canal water was delivered from upstream areas that became Indian territory), and No. 5 (apportionment of income from seigniorage levied by the Punjab on non-riparian states for irrigation water supplied from the Sutlej).
87. Text of the Stand-still Agreement, Jalandhar, 20 December 1947. See Avtar Singh Bhasin (ed.), *India and Pakistan Relations, 1947–2007, A Documentary Study, Vol. VII*, Geetika Publications: New Delhi, 2012, p. 5578. Also Salman M.A. Salman and Kishor Uprety, *Conflict and Cooperation on South Asia's International Rivers*, Kluwer Law International: The Haque, 2002, p. 42.
88. Ibid.
89. *Dawn*, Karachi, 28 February 1948. In March 1948, a short-term settlement valid until 31 August was reached that India would get 20 bales of Pakistan cotton for each 12 bales of cloth and yarn. Duty on cotton for India was now Rs 60 a bale. India, *Dawn*, Karachi, 13 March 1948.
90. Michel, 1967, p. 195.
91. Salman and Uprety, 2002, p. 43.
92. Cited in Laylin, 1957, p. 8.
93. Stephen C. McCaffrey, 'The Harmon Doctrine One Hundred Years Later: Buried, Not Praised', *Natural Resources Journal*, Fall 1996, p. 725.
94. Keith Pitman, 'The Role of the World Bank in Enhancing Cooperation and Resolving Conflict in International Watercourses: The Case of the Indus Basin', in Salman M. A. Salman and Laurence Boisson de Chazournes (eds.) *International Watercourses: Enhancing Cooperation and Managing Conflict*, World Bank: Washington, 1998, p. 158. Also see Michel, 1967, p. 200.

95. Chaudhri Muhammad Ali argued that 'without water, the canals rather than being assets would merely be dry ditches', Ali, *The Emergence of Pakistan*, Columbia University Press: New York, 1967, p. 320.

96. As informed by the Indian Deputy High Commissioner stationed at Lahore who telegraphically informed the Ministry of External Affairs on 14 April 1948 of the stoppage of the canal waters to West Punjab on expiry of agreement on 1 April. Bhasin, 2012, p. 5582.

97. Alam, 1998, p. 57.

98. Berber, 1957, p. 5.

99. Letter from Chief Secretary East Punjab to Chief Secretary West Punjab, 10 April 1948. Bhasin, 2012, p. 5581.

100. Ibid.

101. Berber, 1957, p. 5.

102. McCaffrey, 'Water, Politics and International Law', in *Water in Crisis: A Guide to the World's Fresh Water Resources*, Peter H. Gleick (ed.), Oxford University Press: Oxford, 1993, p. 95. Also see F.J. Fowler, 'The Indo-Pakistan Water Dispute', *Yearbook of World Affairs*, Vol. IX, London, 1955, p. 101.

103. Gulhati, 1973, pp. 63–4.

104. Ibid., p. 64.

105. Jagat S. Mehta, 'The Indus Water Treaty: A Case Study in the Resolution of an International River Basin Conflict,' *Natural Resources Forum*, 12, 1998, p. 72.

106. *Dawn*, Karachi, 28 April 1948.

107. Telegram from Pakistan Prime Minister Liaquat Ali Khan to Prime Minister Jawaharlal Nehru. Karachi, 28 April 1948, Bhasin, 2012, p. 5592.

108. Telegram from Liaquat Ali Khan to Nehru, 15 April 1948, Ibid., p. 5582.

109. The three-step process was conditional and sequential. In the first step, Pakistan was asked to withdraw all its nationals that entered Kashmir for the sake of fighting. In the second step, India was asked to progressively reduce its forces to the minimum level required for law and order. In the third step, India was asked to appoint a plebiscite administrator nominated by the United Nations who would conduct a free and impartial plebiscite.

110. Letter from Jawaharlal Nehru to Premier of East Punjab Gopichand Bhargava. New Delhi, 28 April 1948. Bhasin, 2012, p. 5592.

111. Nehru's speech at the 55th Session of Indian National Congress at Jaipur on 18 December 1948.

112. Letter from Liaquat Ali to Nehru, 24 April 1948. Bhasin, 2012, p. 5590.

113. Nehru's record of an Interview with Ghulam Mohammad, 3 May 1948. *Selected Works of Jawaharlal Nehru*, Volume Six, Jawaharlal Nehru Memorial Fund: New Delhi, 1987, pp. 63–4.

114. Ibid., p. 64.

115. See the text of the Inter-Dominion Agreement on Punjab Canal Waters Dispute Between East Punjab and West Punjab of 4 May 1948. Bhasin, 2012, p. 5598.

116. Ibid.
117. Ibid.
118. Ibid.
119. Ibid.
120. Nehru's cable to Liaquat Ali Khan on 18 May 1948. Bhasin, 2012, p. 5599.
121. Gulhati, 1973, p. 70.
122. Clause 7 of the Inter-Dominion Agreement, 4 May1948, 'The Dominion Government of India and Pakistan accept the above term and express the hope that a friendly solution will be reached.'
123. Alam, 1998, p. 57.
124. Ibid.
125. Bhasin, 2012, p. XCV.
126. This was an explanatory note in a telegram from Nehru to Liaqat Ali on 18 May 1948. In view of the urgency of the matter, the East Punjab Governor also wrote to his counterpart in Lahore, but the latter informed him that, 'channels of diplomatic correspondence' precluded him 'from answering' his queries and that he had sent a copy of the message to the Government of Pakistan and advised the East Punjab Governor to take up the matter with the Government of India if considered desirable. He said that this matter being 'other than Partition matter, and should, therefore, be discussed and settled at Dominion level only.' Bhasin, 2012, p. 5600.
127. Ibid., p. 5599.
128. Information conveyed on 5 June 1948 by the Deputy High Commissioner in Lahore in a telegram to the Ministry of External Affairs. Explanatory note to the telegram from Jawaharlal Nehru to Pakistan Foreign Minister Zafrullah Khan, 5 June 1948. It prompted Nehru to immediately write to Zafrullah upon hearing the news from the Deputy High Commissioner. Bhasin, 2012, p. 5608.
129. Statement by Baldev Singh, India's defence minister in Poona, quoted in *Tribune*, Simla, 10 May 1948.
130. According to Avtar Singh Bhasin, Nehru's idea of a 'No War Declaration' was that 'the declaration' had become necessary to reduce the tension between the two countries and once that objective was achieved through the medium of 'No War Declaration', the 'ways and means of settling outstanding disputes' could be discussed between the two countries on the merits of each issue, Bhasin, 2012, p. LVI.
131. Anandita Bajpai, *Speaking the Nation: The Oratorical Making of Secular, Neoliberal India*, Oxford University Press: New Delhi, 2018, p. 53.
132. Telegram from Nehru to Sri Prakasa, 18 June 1948. *Selected Works of Jawaharlal Nehru*, Volume Six, Jawaharlal Nehru Memorial Fund: New Delhi, 1987, pp. 74–6. Later in his letter to General Sir Roy Bucher, Nehru wrote, 'Reports both from London and Karachi indicates that a large number, said to be about 400, of Polish aviators, who have specialised in

bombing, have been engaged in England by Pakistan. 30 of these are said to have arrived in Karachi. Other reports state that the Pakistan's army intends starting bombing from January.' *Jawaharlal Nehru Papers*, 23 December 1948.

133. N.V. Gadgil, *Government from Inside*, Meenakshi Prakashan: Meerut, 1968, p. 86.

134. *The Dawn*, Karachi, 27 December 1948.

135. *The Dawn*, Karachi, 23 December 1948. The editorial made these remarks after Sardar Patel's speech at the Jaipur Congress on 17 December 1948. Patel warned Pakistan to either 'create conditions for the peaceful stay of these persons in their own homes' or provide 'additional space for their settlements'. See Bhasin, 2012, p. LIX–LX.

136. At a press conference in Srinagar on 23 May 1944, Jinnah replied to a question on who can join the All India Muslim League. *Tahrik-ihuriyyat-i Kashmir* (History of Independence Movements in Kashmir), *Volume 2, 1936–1945*, Mahafiz Pablikeshanz: Srinagar, 1968, p. 291. For details of the press conference see 'Mr. Jinnah regarded Ahmadis as Muslims', *The Light & Islamic Review*, Vol. 69(1), Jan–Feb 1992, pp. 15–8. It was to be Jinnah's last visit to Kashmir. The Ahmadis were constitutionally declared as 'non-Muslims' in Pakistan in 1974 by Zulfikar Bhutto.

137. Telegram from Nehru to Zafrullah, 5 June 1948. Bhasin, 2012, p. 5605.

138. Ibid., p. 5606.

139. Zafrullah telegram to Nehru, 19 June 1948. Ibid., p. 5611.

140. Ibid.

141. Nehru telegram to Zafrullah, 20 June 1948. Ibid., p. 5612.

142. Telegram from Nehru to Gopichand Bhargava, 20 June 1948. *Selected Works of Jawaharlal Nehru*, Volume Six, Jawaharlal Nehru Memorial Fund: New Delhi, 1987, p. 77.

143. Ibid., p. 78.

144. Shakti Sinha and Himanshu Roy (eds.), *Patel: Political Ideas and Policies*, Sage: New Delhi, 2019, p. ix.

145. Telegram from Zafrullah to Nehru, 6 July 1948. Bhasin, 2012, p. 5613.

146. Statement handed over to India by Pakistan. Karachi, 21 July 1948. Likewise, a statement was handed over to Pakistan by India. Ibid., pp. 5614–5.

147. Ibid., p. 5619.

148. Telegram, from the Pakistan Ministry of Foreign Affairs to the Ministry of External Affairs. Karachi, 15 September 1948. Ibid.

149. Telegram from Ministry of External Affairs to Pakistan Ministry of Foreign Affairs. New Delhi, 18 October 1948. Ibid., p. 5621.

150. Ibid. Also underlined by Nehru's letter to Zafrullah Khan on 13 June 1949. Ibid., pp. 5623–5. In a telegram from the Pakistan Ministry of Foreign Affairs to Ministry of External Affairs, 13 June 1949, West Punjab also transferred to East Punjab 'Rs12,35,000 half of 24,70,000, subject to adjustments when

proper undisputed charges have been ascertained, and as for balance of ad hoc sums specified in your [Ministry of External Affair] letter of April 6th, these will be deposited in Reserve Bank of India in name of West Punjab, all without prejudice to PAKISTAN'S right as heretofore.' Ibid., p. 5626.

151. The 8 March 1949 communication from Pakistan to Nehru cited in Berber, 1957, p. 9.

152. Telegram from the Pakistan Ministry of Foreign Affairs to Ministry of External Affairs, para (7), 13 June 1949. Bhasin, 2012, p. 5627.

153. Note from Pakistan Ministry of Foreign Affairs to the High Commission for India in Pakistan, para (1), 16 June 1949. Ibid., p. 5628.

154. Ibid, para (8), p. 5629.

155. Ibid.

156. Minutes of the Inter-Dominion Conference held on 4, 5 and 6 August 1949 on the Canal Water Dispute, New Delhi, 6 August 1949. It had three Appendix. Ibid., pp. 5632–5.

157. APPENDIX—III Copy of D.O. letter from the Hon'ble Shri N. Gopalaswami Ayyangar, Minister of Transport, Government of India, New Delhi, to Zafrullah Khan, 6 August 1949. Ibid., p. 5637.

158. Pakistan's Draft and Clarification provided by India. Ibid., p. 5640.

159. Note by Prime Minister Jawaharlal Nehru on the Canal Water dispute with Pakistan. New Delhi, 28 September 1949. Ibid., p. 5643.

160. Note from the High Commissioner for India in Pakistan to the Pakistan Ministry of Foreign Affairs. Karachi, 5 October 1949. Ibid., p. 5645.

161. Note from High Commission for India in Pakistan, to Pakistan Ministry of Foreign Affairs. Karachi, 19 December 1949. Ibid., p. 5657.

162. Letter from Jawaharlal Nehru to Liaquat Ali Khan. New Delhi, 18 January 1950. Ibid., p. 5659.

163. Note from the High Commission for India in Pakistan, to the Pakistan Ministry of Foreign Affairs. Karachi, 23 February 1950, Ibid., p. 5668.

164. Letter from Liaquat Ali Khan to Jawaharlal Nehru. Karachi, 23 August 1950. Ibid., p. 5678.

165. Ibid., p. 5679.

166. Note from Pakistan Ministry of Foreign Affairs to High Commission for India in Pakistan. Karachi, 23 August 1950. Ibid., p. 5680.

167. See, Text of UN Charter 10.

168. Letter from Jawaharlal Nehru to Governor of Punjab, C.M. Trivedi. New Delhi, 28 August 1950. Bhasin, 2012, pp. 5684–5.

169. Ibid., p. 5685.

170. Ibid.

171. Letter from C.M. Trivedi to Jawaharlal Nehru, 2 September 1950. Ibid., p. 5688.

172. Letter from C.M. Trivedi to Deputy Prime Minister Sardar Patel, 4 September 1950. Ibid., p. 5689.

173. Letter from Jawaharlal Nehru to Sardar Vallabhbhai Patel, 9 September 1950. Ibid., pp. 5690–1.

174. Ibid., p. 5691.

175. Letter from Sardar Vallabhbhai Patel to Jawaharlal Nehru. Bombay, 11 September 1950. Ibid., p. 5692.

176. Ibid., p. CIII.

177. With Liaquat coming to Delhi for talks with Nehru, in a letter to Nehru, Gopalaswami Ayyangar, Transport Minister, writes, 'The figure of 300 crores as representing Pakistan's capacity to pay was estimated by Deshmukh at my request, but it will be too much to expect that we could, for squaring the amount relating to evacuee property, ask Pakistan to shoulder the whole of this amount as a debt, she would owe to India on account of evacuee property alone. We should be prepared, if there is going to be an *ad hoc* arrangement to accept much less. I think it will be worthwhile to do so in order to end all the trouble we are going through in this connection.' Ibid., p. CIV.

178. Note from Pakistan Ministry of Foreign Affairs to High Commission for India in Pakistan, 23 August 1950. Ibid., pp. 5680–1.

179. The Draft enclosed in the Letter from Jawaharlal Nehru to Sardar Vallabhbhai Patel, New Delhi, 11 September 1950. Ibid., pp. 5695–6.

180. Ibid, p. 5696.

181. Letter from Jawaharlal Nehru to Liaquat Ali Khan, New Delhi, 12 September 1950. Ibid., p.5698. The draft response was communicated by a Note from High Commissioner for India in Pakistan to the Pakistan Ministry of Foreign Affairs. Karachi, 15 September 1950. Ibid., p. 5698.

182. Extract from letter from Jawaharlal Nehru to Liaquat Ali Khan. New Delhi, 8 October 1950, Ibid., p. 5702.

183. Ibid., p. 5703.

184. Letter from Liaquat Ali Khan to Jawaharlal Nehru. Karachi, 18 October 1950. Ibid., p. 5704.

185. Letter from Liaquat Ali Khan to Jawaharlal Nehru, 21 October 1950. Ibid., p. 5706.

186. Ibid. The Indo-Pakistan Boundary Disputes Tribunal also known as the Bagge Tribunal was set up in 1948 to resolve the boundary disputes between East Pakistan and India. It was chaired by Justice Algot Bagge of the Supreme Court of Sweden. See Virender Grover (ed.), *50-Years of India-Pak Relations. The Initial Phase: Partition of India, Indo-Pak Wars, The UNO, Vol.1*, Deep and Deep Publications: New Delhi, 2002.

187. Extract from letter from Liaquat Ali Khan to Jawaharlal Nehru, Karachi, 21 November 1950. Bhasin, 2012, p. 5714.

188. Berber, 1957, p. 9. Also see Gulhati, 1973, p. 322.

189. Ibid., p. 9.

190. Ibid, p. 10.

191. Extract from letter from Nehru to Liaquat Ali Khan, 27 October 1950. Bhasin, 2012, p. 5708.

192. Extract from letter from Liaquat to Nehru, 27 November 1950. Ibid., p. 5719.

193. Jinnah in conversation with Grafftey Smith on 9 December 1947. Smith had sent the conversation with Jinnah to the Commonwealth Office in London on 31 December 1947. Paul Preston and Michael Partridge (eds.), *British Documents on Foreign Affairs, Part IV, January 1947–December 1947*, University Publications of America, 2001, p. 115.

194. Gulhati, 1973, pp. 161–2.

195. Letter to Gopichand Bhargava, 28 April 1948. *Selected Works of Jawaharlal Nehru*, Volume Six, Jawaharlal Nehru Memorial Fund: New Delhi, 1987, p. 62. In another letter to Bhargava on 26 September 1948, Nehru writes, 'But I am quite clear that you should not stop the supply of canal water at this stage or in the future. In the existing circumstances that would be very harmful from many points of view.'

196. Berber, 1957, pp. 3–4.

197. Shri R.K. Chetty, finance minister, on 28 February 1948, while presenting the budget for 1948–9 stated, 'For our balance of payments with Pakistan, I fear it is not possible to make even the roughest estimates. In the half year January to June 1948 we hope to earn through our exports and other sources Rs 208 crores. We expect to spend during the same period Rs 260 crores. We therefore anticipate an overall deficit of Rs 52 crore. Out of our total expenditure during the half year, no less than Rs 61 crore will be spent on the purchase of food.' See *Constituent Assembly of India (Legislative) Debates*, Vol. II, No. 9, 28 February 1948.

198. Ambedkar was also Member of the Reconstruction Committee of the Council and President of the Policy Committee for Irrigation and Power.

199. A.K. Biswas, 'Ambedkar, the Architect of Damodar Valley Corporation', *Mainstream*, LIV (17), 16 April 2016.

200. S.K. Thorat, *Ambedkar's role in Economic Planning and Water Policy*, Shipra Publications: New Delhi, 1998, p. 10.

201. *Dr B.R. Ambedkar Writings and Speeches, Vol. 10*, compiled by Vasant Moon: Bombay, 1991, p. 288. Between 15 November 1943 and 8 November 1945, Ambedkar addressed five conferences, of which two were on the Damodar Valley Project, both held at Calcutta, one on Mahanadi Valley Project and two on electric power.

202. Debate over the DVC Bill, *Constituent Assembly of India (Legislative) Debates*, Vol. III, No. 4, 11 March 1948.

203. The Kosi Project, the Bhakra Project, the Mahanadi Project, the Assam Valley Project and on the Godavari the Ramapada Sagar Project were made reference to in the debate over the DVC Bill, *Constituent Assembly of India (Legislative) Debates*, Vol. III, No.4, 11 March 1948. During the course of

the discussion on the Bill, Rohini Kumar Chaudhuri (Assam: General) told the Constituent Assembly that he hoped the minister N.V. Gadgil 'meant seriously' when the minister had assured him that 'he had nothing but goodwill and future for Assam'. Balakrishna Sharma (UP: General) retorted, 'Is there any Maharatta ever serious in what he says?' Chaudhuri then said in the ongoing discussion, 'My grievance is, sir, that it is difficult to know when and where my honourable friend the Minister is speaking seriously.' The DVC Bill witnessed an extensive debate with many provinces hopeful that once the Bill is approved other projects will follow.

204. Debate over the DVC Bill, *Constituent Assembly of India (Legislative) Debates*, Vol. III, No. 4, 11 March 1948.

205. Ibid.

206. Ibid.

207. Clause 43 (1) and (2) of the Damodar Valley Corporation Act. Act No. XIV of 1948.

208. Giani Gurmukh Singh Musafar (East Punjab: Sikh), Debate over the DVC Bill, *Constituent Assembly of India (Legislative) Debates*, Vol. III, No. 4, 11 March 1948.

209. Subhas Chandra Bose's address to the *Indian Science News Association*, 1938.

210. Sugata Ray and Venugopal Maddipati (eds.) *Water Histories of South Asia: The Materiality of Liquescence*, Routledge: London, 2020, pp. 189–90. Also Santimay Chatterjee and Enakshi Chatterjee, *Meghnad Saha*, National Book Trust: New Delhi, 1984 and S.B. Karmohapatra, *Meghnad Saha*, Publications Division, Govt. of India: New Delhi, 1997.

211. Lilienthal defined hydrology as a combination of machine, technology and science and to allow 'men to work in harmony with the forces of nature'. David E. Lilienthal, *TVA: Democracy on the March*, New York: Pocket Books, 1945, p. xii.

212. Sudhir Sen, *Wanderings: In Search of Solutions of the Problem of Poverty*, Macmillan, 1989.

213. Gilmartin, 2015, p. 204.

214. Haris Gazdar, 'Baglihar and Politics of Water: A Historical Perspective from Pakistan', *Economic and Political Weekly*, 40 (9), 26 February–4 March 2005, p. 814.

215. Bashir Malik, *Indus Waters Treaty in Retrospect*, A.M. Shakoori Publisher: Lahore, pp. 113–4.

216. Ibid., p. 114.

Part V: Making *of* the Indus Waters Treaty

1.   Narendra Singh Sarila, *The Shadow of the Great Game: The Untold Story of India's Partition*, Harper Collins: New Delhi, 2005, p. 371. All the prime ministers of India, starting with Nehru, have had to face the challenges of

cross-border infiltration leaving them often frustrated and angry. Nehru was certain that the invasion 'could not have taken place without 100% assistance of Pakistan authorities'. Cited in Srinath Raghavan, *War and Peace in Modern India*, Permanent Black: Ranikhet, 2010, p. 107.

2. Ibid., 2005, p. 371.

3. Foreign Relations of the United States, 1947, The British Commonwealth, Europe, Vol. III, 29 December 1947, p. 186. Gallman, US *chargé de affairs* in London in a telegram to US secretary of state on 29 December 1947. Gallman was reporting what he heard from Sir Paul Patrick of the British Commonwealth Relations Office.

4. Sarila, 2005, p. 372.

5. *Selected Works of Jawaharlal Nehru*, Volume Four, Jawaharlal Nehru Memorial Fund: New Delhi, 1987, pp. 411–2.

6. Lord Ismay, who handled the Kashmir affairs in New Delhi, strongly favoured the Pakistani raiders in Kashmir, derecognizing the Abdullah government and the UN-supervised plebiscite. Lord Ismay had the trust and confidence of Clement Attlee and the Commonwealth Secretary, Noel-Baker. Ismay's Kashmir propositions were similarly reflected by Noel-Baker in the UN. Even Ernest Bevin, the secretary of state for foreign affairs, had warned the government against displeasing the international Muslim community. See Sarila, 2005, p. 374. Also see Rakesh Ankit, '1948: The Crucial Year in the History of Jammu and Kashmir', *Economic and Political Weekly*, 45(11), 13–9 March 2010, p. 52.

7. 'Setting out the Reasons in Favour of Lord Mountbatten Staying on as Governor General of the Dominion of India' in Lionel Carter (ed.), *Mountbatten's Report on the Last Viceroyalty 22 March–15 August 1947*, Manohar: New Delhi, 2005, p. 357.

8. MB1/E/193, Broadland Archives, Mountbatten Papers Database, University of Southampton. Also cited in Nisid Hajari, *Midnight's Furies: The Deadly Legacy of India's Partition*, Penguin: London, 2015, p. 170.

9. For further reading on Britain's lobbying with the US on Kashmir in early 1948. See Chandrashekar Dasgupta, *War and Diplomacy in Kashmir, 1947–48*, Sage: New Delhi, 2002. Insights of global powers' interest in Kashmir also comes out from letters exchanged on 23 January 1948 between Nehru and Vijaya Lakshmi Pandit, India's representative to the UN, 1946–8 and simultaneously India's ambassador to Moscow, 1947–9. See *Vijaya Lakshmi Pandit Papers, I Instalment*, File No. 54, Nehru Memorial Museum and Library, New Delhi. Also see Rakesh Ankit, 'Britain and Kashmir, 1948: "The Arena of the UN"', *Diplomacy & Statecraft*, Vol. 24(2), 2013, pp. 273–90 and 'Great Britain and Kashmir, 1947–9', *India Review*, Vol. 12(1), 2013, pp. 20–40.

10. 'Exchange of Views with British Representatives with Respect to Kashmir', *Foreign Relations of the United States, 1948, the Near East, South Asia and*

Africa, Vol. V, 27 February 1948, p. 306. The British delegation included: B.R. Curson, B. Cockram and Cecil Griffin from Commonwealth Relations Office and M.E. Bathurst UK delegation member to the UN; the American officials included Dean Rusk, Charles Noyes, Hare, Thurston and Sparks.

11. Ibid.

12. Ibid., p. 311.

13. Nehru statement to Patrick Gordon Walker, under-secretary of state for commonwealth relations, on 28 January 1948. *Selected Works of Jawaharlal Nehru*, Volume Six, Jawaharlal Nehru Memorial Fund: New Delhi, 1987, p. 203.

14. The Security Council Resolution (47) on 21 April 1948 was passed with eight in favour; none against and four abstained. The US along with Argentina, Belgium, Canada, China, France, Syria and UK were in favour. The USSR along with Belgium, Colombia and Ukrainian S.S.R. abstained.

15. Ankit, 2010, pp. 51–2. Mountbatten writes to Attlee, 'India's complaint was passed over at the request of Zafrullah Khan, backed by Noel-Baker on 31 January [1948] to the extent that the cart was put before the horse, i.e., the plebiscite has become the first issue . . . I am at a loss to understand why India who has been brought to her present predominant position in Asia largely through British efforts in the past and which is the only country which is now likely to give a lead in the Far East, is being treated this way.' British officials were split over the Kashmir issue. Mountbatten, Stafford Cripps and Pug Ismay were considerate towards India while Clement Attlee, Ernest Bevin and Philip Noel-Baker were sympathetic towards Pakistan.

16. See Text of the UN Resolution 47 (1948).

17. Ibid.

18. Ibid.

19. Pakistan had denied its regular army involvement in the 1948 war in Kashmir. However, accounts by Maj. Gen. Mohammad Akbar Khan who led the raiders comprising of tribals from NWFP, the Afridis and Mahsuds revealed that Pakistan desired to liberate Kashmir and by May 1948 he had Pakistan's regular troops under his command. See Sisir Gupta, *Kashmir: A Study in India–Pakistan Relations*, Asia Publishing House: New Delhi, 1966, p. 113.

20. Chaudhri Muhammad Ali, 1967, p. 305.

21. Josef Korbel, *Danger in Kashmir*, Oxford University Press: New York, 2002, p. 139.

22. The brainchild of US Secretary of State George C. Marshall, the Marshall Plan enacted in 1948 was a US programme providing a $15-billion aid to Western Europe following the end of World War II.

23. H.W. Brands, 'India and Pakistan in American Strategic Planning, 1947–1954: The Commonwealth as Collaborator', *The Journal of Imperial and Commonwealth History*, 15(1), 1986, p. 41.

24.   Ibid.

25.   Ibid., p. 43.

26.   Robert J. McMahon, 'United States Cold War Strategy in South Asia: Making a Military Commitment to Pakistan, 1947–1954', *The Journal of American History*, 75(3), December 1988, p. 813.

27.   Ibid.

28.   Nehru's speech at the US Congress, 13 October 1949.

29.   Cited in Gulhati, 1973, p. 92.

30.   Betty Miller Unterberger, 'American Views of Mohammad Ali Jinnah and the Pakistan Liberation Movement', *Diplomatic History*, 5(4), 1981, p. 323.

31.   Walter Lippmann's work *Public Opinion* first published in 1922 was a powerful diagnosis of democracy's flaws.

32.   David Lilienthal, *The Journals of David E. Lilienthal*, Vol. 3, Venturesome Years, 1950–55, Harper and Row: New York, 1966. Cited in Asit Biswas, 'Indus Water Treaty: The Negotiating Process', *Water International*, 17(4), 1992, p. 205.

33.   David Lilienthal, 'Are We Losing India?' *Collier's Weekly*, New York, 23 June 1951, pp. 13–15.

34.   Cited in Gulhati, 1973, p. 93.

35.   Gulhati recounts, 'I have a vague idea that I met him [Lilienthal] and showed him a large size relief map of the Indus basin which I had in my room in North Block.' Ibid.

36.   William Drumright, 'His Search for a Viable Middle Ground: A Reappraisal of David E. Lilienthal's TVA—Democracy on the March', *The Princeton University Library Chronicle*, 63(3), 2002, p. 467.

37.   David Lilienthal, *TVA—Democracy on the March*, Harper and Brothers: New York, 1944.

38.   David Lilienthal, 23 June 1951, p. 15.

39.   William Bullitt, 'How We Won the War and Lost the Peace' Part I, *Life*, 30 August 1948 and Part II, 6 September 1948. Also see Robert McMahon, *The Cold War on the Periphery: The United States, India, and Pakistan*, Columbia University Press: New York, 1994, p. 107.

40.   *Washington Post*, 21 February 1992.

41.   David Lilienthal, 'Another "Korea" in the Making', *Collier's Weekly*, New York, 4 August 1951, pp. 22–23.

42.   President Dwight Eisenhower in 1953, to appease the conservative elements in his party, had expressed his view of the TVA as 'creeping socialism' and his administration was virtually split in the middle over the TVA-style development aid to post-colonial countries, with the aid-minded John Foster Dulles and Nelson Rockefeller favouring such an approach against the likes of Herbert Hoover Jr. and George Humphrey, who were strongly opposed to it. David Ekbladh, '"Mr. TVA": Grass-Roots Development, David Lilienthal, and the Rise and Fall of the Tennessee Valley Authority as

a Symbol for U.S. Overseas Development, 1933–1973', *Diplomatic History*, 26 (3), 2002, p. 356.

43. Transcript of interview with Mr Eugene R. Black, President, Brookings Institute, 6 August 1961. The World Bank/IFC Archives, Oral History Program, Folder ID: 78942, Vol. 2, p. 48.

44. The WBG Archives, Records of President Eugene Black Correspondence, Vol.1 (A-L), Folder ID: 1769156, p. 115.

45. Ibid., p. 114.

46. Lilienthal, 4 August 1951, p. 22.

47. Ibid.

48. Henry Trofimenko, 'The Third World and U.S.-Soviet Competition', *Foreign Affairs*, 59(1), Summer 1981, p. 1021.

49. Letter from Eugene Black to Prime Ministers Jawaharlal Nehru and Liaquat Ali Khan, 6 September 1951. WBG Archives, Folder ID: 1787772, Annexure C.

50. Jawaharlal Nehru letter to B.K. Nehru on 22 September 1951. *Selected Works of Jawaharlal Nehru*, Volume Sixteen (II), Jawaharlal Nehru Memorial Fund: New Delhi, 1994, pp. 366–7.

51. Nehru letter of 23 September 1951 to Eugene Black. Ibid., pp. 369–72.

52. Letters from Eugene Black to Prime Ministers Nehru and Liaquat Ali Khan, 8 November 1951. WBG Archives, Correspondence, Folder ID: 1787772, Annexure C.

53. The World Bank signed a $34-million loan to India on 18 August 1949 for railway reconstruction and development. It was signed by Vijaya Lakshmi Pandit, Ambassador to the US. Also present were K.R.K. Menon, Indian Finance Secretary, B.R. Sen, Indian Minister to the US and Eugene Black, *World Bank Notes 61920*, December 1962, p. 8. The World Bank further notes that it was the 'first loan document to be signed by a woman representative', WBG Historical Chronology, WBG Archives, p. 29.

54. Jochen Kraske, 'India and the World Bank', *World Bank, Washington D.C.*, 17 August 1997, p. 2.

55. Eugene Black, *Diplomacy of Economic Development*, Harvard University Press: Boston, 1960, p. 30.

56. Transcript of interview with Eugene R. Black, President, Brookings Institute, 6 August 1961. The World Bank/IFC Archives, Oral History Program, p. 48. On 7 March 1952, a loan project for $27.2 million was signed with Pakistan for the rehabilitation, improvement and modernization of the Pakistan railways. WBG Historical Chronology, WBG Archives, p. 42.

57. Ibid., pp. 48–9

58. Nehru letter of 23 September 1951 to Eugene Black. *Selected Works of Jawaharlal Nehru*, Volume Sixteen (II), Jawaharlal Nehru Memorial Fund: New Delhi, 1994, pp. 368–71.

59. India had approached the World Bank for loans for the construction of the Bhakra-Nangal Multipurpose Project on the Sutlej and the Damodar Valley Project. Pakistan had cited objections to the Bhakra-Nangal Project proposal to the Bank. In 1951, India had also objected to a Pakistani request for financing a barrage at Kotri on the Indus. The bank was aware of the already strained relations between India and Pakistan and was reluctant to make loans for projects that involved any unresolved disputes, not only because the investment was risky, but also because once built, these projects could exacerbate the existing dispute.

60. Lilienthal, 1966, pp. 34–5.

61. Cited in *Dawn*, Karachi, 5 November 1948. This was in response to a question on the Islamic bloc at a press conference in London. In that same press conference, he added, 'As long as the Kashmir dispute is not settled in a fair manner by a plebiscite, it is not possible for Pakistan and India to have close and friendly relations for which the Pakistan people sincerely desire for the common good.'

62. Black's letter to Nehru and Liaquat on 8 November 1951. WBG Archives, Folder ID: 1787772, Annexure C. Also see Press Clipping and Correspondence, Folder ID: 1805183.

63. Jason Scott Smith, 'The Liberal Intervention of the Multinational Corporation: David Lilienthal and Postwar Capitalism', in Kim Phillips-Fein and Julian E. Zelizer (eds.), *What's Good for Business: Business and American Politics since World War II*, Oxford University Press: Oxford, 2012, p. 112.

64. Extracted from Philadelphia Area Archives Research Portal, MC014.

65. Eugene Black's note of 13 March 1952, WBG Archives, Folder ID: 1787772.

66. Gulhati, 1973, p. 101. In a note on this observation, he writes, 'Many years later, I learnt that the Bank was well aware of the unilateral impact of the provision. It was expressed bilaterally not only to give the appearance of impartiality but also because, conceivably, it might have some restraining influence on Pakistan in some of the sensitive situations which, the Bank thought, then existed.'

67. WBG Historical Chronology, WBG Archives, p. 43.

68. Gulhati, 1973, p. 39.

69. Eugene Black's letters to the two prime ministers of India and Pakistan, 13 March 1952. WBG Archives, Folder ID: 1787772, Annexure C. Also see Press Clipping and Correspondence, Folder ID: 1805183.

70. Ibid.

71. Lilienthal's letter to Khosla. Cited in Gulhati, 1973, p. 129.

72. Transcript of interview with Raymond Wheeler, The World Bank/IFC Archives, No. 71948, 14 July 1961, p. 7.

73. *Statesman*, Delhi, 30 January 1953.

74. Gulhati, 1973, p. 113.

75. Quoted in *Civil and Military Gazette*, Lahore, 19 January 1953.
76. Ibid.
77. Letter of Nehru to former Governor General of India Lord Mountbatten. New Delhi, 19 April 1953. *Selected Works of Jawaharlal Nehru*, Volume Twenty-Two, Jawaharlal Nehru Memorial Fund: New Delhi, 1998, p. 316
78. Ayub Khan, *Friends Not Masters: A Political Autobiography*, Oxford University Press: New York, 1967, p. 49.
79. A good example of this was seen when the Pakistan press showed indignation over the opening of the Bhakra Canal in 1954. The *Zamindar* under the heading 'A Fatal Blow' described the inauguration as an act of aggression and added, 'There are now two ways open to Pakistan—either to submit to India and let her economy be ruined or to resort to direct action to secure her just right.' See Gulhati, 1973, pp. 161–2.
80. Extract from the Statement by Prime Minister Jawaharlal Nehru in the House of People (Lok Sabha). New Delhi, 17 March 1953.
81. Letter of Nehru to the chief minister of East Punjab, Bhim Sen Sachar, 18 March 1953. *Selected Works of Jawaharlal Nehru*, Volume Twenty-One, Jawaharlal Nehru Memorial Fund: New Delhi, 1997, p. 509.
82. Ibid. Disappointed and angry over the reduction in flow, Nehru after his inquiry through the Ministry of Irrigation and Power writes, '. . . we have found that the right proportion from the Ferozepore head-works for Pakistan canals should have been 79 per cent of the divisible supplies. Against this, the supply actually made in the Rabi sowing season of 1952, i.e., from October 16 to December 5, 1952 was 69 per cent and that for the Rabi sowing season i.e., from December 5, 1952 to February 12, 1953, was 72 per cent. This was an appreciable reduction over a long period.' Nehru then anguishly expresses, 'Meanwhile, I have made statements in public, in Parliament, etc. denying the fact that we are cutting off canal waters. I am thus put in a most embarrassing position. Will you please enquire into this?'
83. *Statesman*, Delhi, 26 January 1953.
84. Lilienthal, 3 August 1951.
85. The *New York Times*, 16 February 1953.
86. Gulhati, 1973, p. 115.
87. Gulhati, 1973, p. 117.
88. Observation made by George McGhee, the assistant secretary for South Asian Affairs, after having met Nehru in New Delhi in March 1951. The statement was not directly related to the Indus basin, but to the overall impression of India's international approach that included the Soviet Union and China. Cited in H.W. Brands, 'India and Pakistan in American Strategic Planning, 1947–1954: The Commonwealth as Collaborator', *The Journal of Imperial and Commonwealth History*, Vol. 15(1), 1986, p. 49.
89. 'Pakistan: The Struggle for Irrigation Water and Existence', *Embassy of Pakistan*, Washington, D.C., 1 November 1953, p. 9 and p. 2.

90. In his interaction with Lilienthal in Karachi, Liaquat Ali said, 'Kashmir is very important, it is vital to Pakistan's security. Kashmir, as you will see from the map, is like a cap on the head of Pakistan. If I allow India to have this cap on our head, then I am always at the mercy of India . . . The very position, the strategic position of Kashmir, is such that without it Pakistan cannot defend herself against an unscrupulous government that might come in India.' See Lilienthal, 3 August 1951.

91. Summary of the IBRD Ninth Annual Report, 1953–4, Washington, D.C., p. 2.

92. Working Party Meeting in Washington, 6 October 1953.

93. Salman and Uprety, 2002, p. 46.

94. WBG Archives, Folder ID: 1787772, p. 19.

95. Remarks by Zafrullah Khan. Ibid., p. 22.

96. Ibid., p. 21.

97. Zafrullah's letter to Black, 28 July 1954. Ibid., p. 22.

98. Gilmartin, 2015, p. 218.

99. Nehru's letter to World Bank's Vice President, 9 August 1954. WBG Archives, Folder ID: 1787772, p. 123.

100. Gilmartin, 2015, p. 218.

101. John Marshall, US Chief Justice of the Supreme Court on delivering the opinion of the Court, *US Reports: The Exchange V. McFaddon & Others*, Library of Congress, 116, 1812, pp. 136–7.

102. Memorandum of State Department, 21 April 1958, US government: Washington, 1958, p. 87.

103. US Reports: New Jersey v. New York, Library of Congress, 283 US 336, 1931, pp. 342–3.

104. Gulhati, 1973, p. 254.

105. The World Bank, 'Indus Water Treaty', *World Affairs*, Vol. 123(4), Winter, 1960, p. 100.

106. Ibid., p. 101.

107. US Congress House Committee on Appropriations Hearings, University of Michigan Library, 1964, p. 1991.

108. Declassified US National Security Council Paper, NSC 129/1, 24 April 1952 in *Foreign Relations of the United States, 1952-1954, The Near and Middle East*, Vol. IX, Part I, US Government Printing Office: Washington, D.C., 1986.

109. Joint Chiefs of Staff 2099/253, 5 November 1952. For details of the political development of the period, see Walter S. Poole (ed.), *The Joint Chiefs of Staff and National Policy, 1950-1952*, Volume IV, Office of Joint History and Office of the Chairman of the Joint Chiefs of Staff: Washington, D.C., 1998, pp. 171–193.

110. 'Memoranda of Conversations in New Delhi and Elsewhere between Ambassador Bowles and Indian Officials, October 20, 1951–March 20,

1953', folder 392, box 104, Chester Bowles Papers (Sterling Library, Yale University, New Haven, Conn.).

111. The CIA's role was well known but it was in August 2013 that the CIA publicly admitted for the first time its involvement in the 1953 coup against Iran's Prime Minister Mohammad Mossadegh.

112. Robert J. Donovan, *Harry S. Truman, 1949–1953: Tumultuous Years*, University of Missouri Press: Columbia, 1996, p. 69.

113. David Stone, 'The United States and the Negotiations of the Indus Waters Treaty', *USI Journal*, CXL, January–March, 2010, p. 76.

114. Chester Bowles to John Foster Dulles, 30 December 1953, cited in Robert J. McMahon, 'United States Cold War Strategy in South Asia: Making a Military Commitment to Pakistan, 1947–1954', *The Journal of American History*, 75 (3), December 1988, p. 839.

115. Statement by President Eisenhower on Eric Johnston's Mission to the Middle East, 16 October 1953.

116. Ibid.

117. Josepha Ivanka Wessels, 'Playing the Game, identity and perception-of-the-other in water cooperation in the Jordan River Basin', *Hydrological Sciences Journal*, 61(7), 2016, p. 1325.

118. Munther J. Haddadin and Uri Shamir, *Jordan Case Study*, UNESCO Publication, UNESDOC Digital Library, 2003, p. 9.

119. Aaron Wolf, 'Water for Peace in the Jordan River Watershed', *Natural Resources Journal*, 33(3), 1993, p. 804.

120. Points of Agreement in London Discussions of Arab–Israeli Settlement, 10 March 1955. See Document 48 in Carl N. Raether (ed.), *Foreign Relations of the US, 1955–57, Arab-Israeli Dispute 1955*, Vol. XIV, United States Government Printing Office: Washington, D.C., 1989.

121. US Congress Senate Committee on Appropriations Hearings Vol. 5, 1968, p. 216.

122. Taylor Sherman, 'A New Type of Revolution: Socialist Thoughts in India, 1940s–1960s', *Postcolonial Studies*, Vol. 21(4), 2018, p. 487.

123. Ibid.

124. Gulhati writes, 'While the two principal political parties, in opposition, the *Swatantra* and the Communist, welcomed the treaty, other political parties and a section of the media felt that the concessions made by India were not justified by the merits of the claims advanced by Pakistan.' Gulhati, 1973, p. 344.

125. Lok Sabha Debates, Vol. XLVII, Twelfth Session, 16 November 1960, column. 603.

126. Ibid., column. 604.

127. Ibid., column. 605.

128. Ibid., column. 2338.

129. Uttam Kumar Sinha, 'Nehruvian Imprint on Indus Waters Treaty', *The Hindustan Times*, New Delhi, 19 September 2020.

130. Harish Chandra Mathur citing the *The Hindu* and the *Times of India*, Lok Sabha Debates, Vol. XLVIII, Twelfth Session, 30 November 1960, column. 3178.

131. Ibid., column. 3178.

132. Cited by H.C. Mathur. Ibid., column. 3211.

133. Ibid., column. 3177.

134. Ibid., column. 3180.

135. Nehru note to M.J. Desai, the Commonwealth Secretary, New Delhi, 6 April 1958. *Selected Works of Jawaharlal Nehru*, Volume Forty-Two, Jawaharlal Nehru Memorial Fund: New Delhi, 2010, p. 595.

136. Patil's speech in Lok Sabha on 26 March 1958. Ibid., p. 598.

137. Nehru's response on 5 June 1958 to Black's letter. *Selected Works of Jawaharlal Nehru*, Volume Forty-Two, Jawaharlal Nehru Memorial Fund: New Delhi, 2010, p. 598.

138. Lok Sabha Debates, Vol. XLVIII, Twelfth Session, 30 November 1960, column. 3188.

139. Article 253 of the Constitution of India, 1950 says: 'Notwithstanding anything in the provisions of this Chapter, Parliament has power to make any law for the whole or any part of the territory of India for implementing any treaty, agreement or convention with any other country or countries or any decision made at any international conference, association or other body.'

140. Lok Sabha Debates, Vol. XLVIII, Twelfth Session, 30 November 1960, column. 3193.

141. Ibid., column. 3189.

142. Ibid., columns. 3191–2.

143. Ibid., column. 3186.

144. Ibid., column. 3192.

145. Ibid., column. 3215.

146. Khan, 1967, p. 126.

147. Cited in J.N. Dixit, *India-Pakistan in War & Peace*, Books Today: New Delhi, 2002, p. 137.

148. Ibid., p. 137.

149. Ashok Mehta's statement. Lok Sabha Debates, Vol. XLVIII, Twelfth Session, 30 November 1960, column. 3187.

150. Notes from the unpublished diary of India's acting High Commissioner in Pakistan, K.V. Padmanabhan, *The Hindu*, New Delhi, 28 September 2016.

151. Ibid., column. 3187.

152. Ibid., column. 3193.

153. Ibid., column. 3195.

154. Ibid., column. 3196.

155. Ibid., columns. 3198–9.

156. Ibid., columns. 3213–4.

157. Ibid., column. 3192.

158. Ayub Khan, 'Pakistan Perspective', *Foreign Affairs*, Vol. 38 (4), July 1960, p. 555–6.
159. Nehru's press statement on 14 May 1959.
160. K.V. Padmanabhan, 'How the Indus Treaty Was Signed', *The Hindu*, 28 September 2016.
161. Gulhati describes the historic signing of the treaty. Gulhati, 1973, pp. 307–8.
162. T.C.A. Raghavan, *The People Next Door: The Curious History of India's Relations with Pakistan*, C. Hurst and Co.: London, 2019, p. 67.
163. Lok Sabha Debates, Vol. XLVIII, Twelfth Session, 30 November 1960, columns. 3214–5.
164. Violet Alva describing Nehru's conduct in Parliament. See, Subhash Kashyap, *The Political System and Institution Building Under Jawaharlal Nehru*, National Publishing House: New Delhi, 1990, p. 169.
165. Lok Sabha Debates, Vol. XLVIII, Twelfth Session, 30 November 1960, column. 3215.
166. Ibid., column. 3215.
167. Ibid., column. 3216.
168. Ibid.
169. Ibid., column. 3217.
170. Ibid.
171. Ibid., columns. 3217–8.
172. Ibid., column. 3220.
173. Ibid.
174. Nehru's speech at the Asian–African Conference, Bandung, 22 April 1955. See Jawaharlal Nehru's Speeches, Volume Three (1953–7), Publication Division, Government of India, 1983.
175. Lok Sabha Debates, Vol. XLVIII, Twelfth Session, 30 November 1960, column. 3221.
176. Ibid., columns. 3220–1.
177. Ibid., column. 3223.
178. Ibid., column. 3225.
179. Vajpayee's reference to Ayub's statement. Ibid., column. 3228.
180. Gulhati, 1973, p. 273.
181. Ibid., p. 328. It was Zulfikar Bhutto's maiden speech at the UN General Assembly.
182. Salahuddin Khan (ed.), *Speeches, Messages and Statements of Madar-i-Millat Mohtarama Fatima Jinnah (1948–1967)*, Research Society of Pakistan, University of the Punjab, 1976, p. 369.
183. Ibid.
184. Masood Khadarposh mentions the incident in his memoir, *Tashakus Ka Bohran: Batain Masud Khaddarposh Ki* (Identity Crisis: The Views of Masud Khaddarposh), Nigarshat Publications: Lahore, 1988, p. 73.

Postscript

1. Preamble of the Indus Waters Treaty.
2. Statement of Ayub Khan. Cited from Gulhati, 1973, p. 340.
3. Uttam Kumar Sinha, 'Indus Waters Civilization', *The Indian Express*, New Delhi, 22 September 2010.
4. Article III of the Indus Waters Treaty.
5. *FAO Aquastat Report*, 'Transboundary River Basin Overview—Indus', 2011, p. 9.
6. 'Annual flow from China to India in the Indus basin is 181.62 km^3 and it is estimated that the flow generated within India is 50.86 km^3, resulting in a flow from India to Pakistan in this part of 232.48 km^3, of which 170.27 km^3 are reserved for Pakistan and 62.21 km^3 are available for India.' Ibid., p. 3.

Bibliography

Primary Source
Acts and Agreements

Government of India Act, 1919.
Government of India Act, 1935.
Indus (Rau) Commission, 1942.
Indus Basin Development Fund Agreement, 19 September 1960.
Indus Waters Treaty, 19 September 1960.
Inter-Dominion Agreement on Canal Water Dispute, 4 May 1948.
Northern India Canal and Drainage Act, 1873.
Punjab Minor Canal Act, 1905.

Debates

Constituent Assembly of India (Legislative) Debates, 28 February 1948.
Constituent Assembly of India (Legislative) Debates, 11 March 1948.
House of Commons Debate, 3 June 1834.
House of Commons Debate, 23 July 1834.
House of Commons Debate, 6 February 1840.
House of Commons Debate, 13 February 1843.
House of Commons Debate, 8 February 1844.
House of Commons Debate, 5 August 1897.
House of Lords Debate, 12 February 1872.
Lok Sabha Debates, 16 November 1960.
Lok Sabha Debates, 30 November 1960.
US Congress House Committee on Appropriations Hearings, 1964.
US Congress Senate Committee on Appropriations Hearings, 1968.

Records, Reports and Papers

A Manual of Irrigation Practice, Government of Punjab, 1943.

Asiatic Intelligence, The Asiatic Journal and Monthly Register for British, Foreign India, China, and Australasia, 1832.

Asiatic Journal and Monthly Register, September–December 1831.

Chester Bowles Papers, Sterling Library, Yale University.

Completion Report and Schedules, Sirhind Canal, 1893.

East India Company's Records, 1602–1613, 1896.

Food and Agricultural Organisation of the UN Aquastat Report, Version 2011.

IBRD Ninth Annual Report, 1953–4.

India National Archives, FO 371-/63533.

Indian Papers, No. 5, Correspondence Relating to Affghanistan, No. 18, 27 March 1839.

Indian Papers, No. 5: Correspondence Relating to Affghanistan, No.3, 27 March 1839.

Indian Papers, No. 5: Correspondence Relating to Affghanistan, No.7, 27 March 1839.

Irrigation Department Lahore, Report no. C-12, 1998.

Jawaharlal Nehru Papers, Nehru Memorial Museum and Library.

Minutes of the Proceedings of the Institution of Civil Engineers, 1930.

Mountbatten Papers Database, Broadland Archives, University of Southampton.

Nehru Papers, Nehru Memorial Museum and Library, New Delhi.

Proceedings Institution Civil Engineers, 1879.

Proprietors of East India Stock, Summary of the Operations in India with their Results from 13 April 1814 to 31 January 1823.

Philadelphia Area Archives Research Portal, MC014.

Report of the Bengal Boundary Commission, 12 August 1947.

Report of the Indian Cotton Committee, 1919.

Report of the Indus (Anderson) Committee, 1935.

Report of the Punjab Boundary Commission, 12 August 1947.

Report on the Shah Nahr or Hasli, 28 April 1848.

Reports and Papers, Political, Geographical and Commercial Submitted to Government Employed on Missions in the Years 1835–36–37 in Scinde and Afghanistan, and Adjacent Countries, 1839.

The First Punjab Administration Report, 1849–51.

The Punjab Administration Report, 1911–2.

The Imperial Gazetteer of India, 1909.

The Report of Narmada Water Disputes Tribunal, 1978.

US National Council Security Paper 129/1, 24 April 1952.

White Paper on India-Pakistan Trade Relations, 1950.

World Bank Group (WBG) Archives, Washington, D.C.

Indus Basin Dispute Files:
Folder ID: 71948. 14 July 1961.
Folder ID: 1769156. Records of President Eugene R. Black Correspondence, Vol. I (A-L), 20 June 1951–9 August 1960.
Folder ID: 1787772. 1 December 1954–31 December 1954.
Folder ID: 1787860. 1 December 1949–31 December 1953.
Folder ID: 1787921. 1 May 1954–31 October 1958.
Folder ID: 1787922. 1 May 1954–31 October 1958.
Folder ID: 1805183. Press Clipping and Correspondence, 1 August 1951–1 December 1953.
World Bank/IFC Archives, No. 71948, 14 July 1961.
World Bank Group Historical Chronology.
World Bank Notes 61920. December 1962.
World Bank Oral History Program, Folder ID: 78942.

Secondary Source
Books

A.N. Khosla, N.K. Bose, Rai Bahadur and E. McKenzie Taylor, *Design of Weirs on Permeable Foundation*, Ashoka Press: Delhi, 1954 (reprint).
Abdul Fazal Allami, Ain I Akbari, tr. by Col. H.S. Jarrett, Vol. II, Asiatic Society of Bengal: Calcutta, 1891.
Abd al-Malik Isami, *Futuh's Salatin*, tr. by Agha Mahdi Husain, Asia Publishing House: New York, 1967. Abdulla, Tarikh–*i-Daudi*, Vol. IV, Kitab Mahal: Allahabad, 1964.
Ajit Singh, *Buried Alive: Autobiography, Speeches and Writings of the Indian Revolutionary Ajit Singh*, Geetanjali: New Delhi, 1984.
Al Baladhuri, *Kitab Futūh al-Buldān*, Part II, tr. from Arabic by Francis Clark Murgotten, Columbia University Press: New York, 1924.
Alan Campbell-Johnson, *Mission with Mountbatten*, Robert Hale: London, 1972.
Alexander Burnes, *Travels Into Bokhara; Being The Account Of The Journey From India To Cabool, Tartary, and Persia; Also, Narrative Of A Voyage On The Indus, From The Sea To Lahore, With Presents From The King Of Great Britain; Performed Under The Orders Of The Supreme Government Of India, In The Years 1831, 1832, And 1933. In Three Volumes*, John Murray: London, 1834.
Alexander Burnes, *Cabool: A Personal Narrative Of A Journey To, And Residence In That City In The Years 1836–37 and –38*, John Murray: London, 1843.
Alfred Deakin, *Irrigated India: An Australian View of India and Ceylon, Their Irrigation and Agriculture*, W. Thacker and Co.: London, 1893.

Alicia Albinia, *Empires of the Indus: The Story of a River*, John Murray: London, 2008.

Allen F. Isaacman and Richard L. Roberts (eds.), *Cotton, Colonialism, and Social History in Sub–Saharan Africa*, Heinemann: Portsmouth, N.H., 1995.

Aloys Arthur Michel, *The Indus Rivers: A Study of the Effects of Partition*, Yale University Press: New Haven, 1967.

Amar Farooqui, *Smuggling as Subversion: Colonialism, Indian Merchants and the Politics of Opium 1790–1843*, Lexington Books: Lanham, 2005.

Amita Paliwal, *Sindh in the Mughal Empire (1591–1740): A Study of its Administration, Society Economy and Culture*, thesis submitted to Aligarh Muslim University: Aligarh, 2010.

Anandita Bajpai, *Speaking the Nation: The Oratorical Making of Secular, Neoliberal India*, Oxford University Press: New Delhi, 2018.

Andrew Goudie, *Great Desert Explorers*, Silphium Press: London, 2016.

Aparajith Ramnath, *Birth of an Indian Profession: Engineers, Industry and State, 1900–1947*, Oxford University Press: New Delhi, 2017.

Arnold Toynbee, *East to West: A Journey Around the World*, Oxford University Press: New York, 1958.

Arrian's *History of Alexander's Expedition*, Vol. II, tr. from Greek by John Rooke, Allen and Co. and J. Walker and Co.: London, 1814.

Arrian, *The Anabasis of Alexander*, Book VI Chapter XX, tr. by E.J. Chinnock, Hodder and Stoughton: London, 1884.

Ashutosh Misra, *India–Pakistan: Coming to Terms*, Palgrave Macmillan: New York, 2010.

Avtar Singh Bhasin (ed.), *India-Pakistan Relations, 1947–2007*, Vol. I, Geetika Publishers and the Public Diplomacy Division, Ministry of External Affairs: New Delhi, 2012.

Ayub Khan, *Friends Not Masters: A Political Autobiography*, Oxford University Press: London, 1967.

Babur-Nama, (Memoirs of Babur), tr. from the Original Turkish text of Zahiru'd-din Muhammad Babar Padshah Ghazi by Annette Susannah Beveridge. Two Volumes Bound in One, Low Price Publications: Delhi, 1921.

Barney White-Spunner, *Partition: The Story of India's Independence and the Creation of Pakistan in 1947*, Simon & Schuster: New Delhi, 2017.

Baron de Montesquieu, *The Spirit of the Laws*, tr. by Thomas Nugent, Hafner Publishing: New York, 1949.

Bashir Malik, *Indus Waters Treaty in Retrospect*, Shareef Printers: Lahore, 2005.

Ben Macintyre, *The Man Who Would Be King: The First American in Afghanistan*, Farrar Straus Giroux: New York, 2004.

Bina Shah, *A Season of Martyrs*, Speaking Tiger Books: New Delhi, 2014.

Buzurg Ibn Shahriyar, *The Book of the Marvels of India: Arabian Travellers' Tales*, tr. from Arabic by L. Marcel Devic, George Routledge & Sons, Ltd.: London, 1928.

C.A. Bayly, *Imperial Meridian. The British Empire and the World, 1780–1830*, Longman: London, 1989.

Capt. H. Wilberforce-Well, *The History of Kathiawad: From the Earliest Time*, William Heinemann: London, 1917.

Carl N. Raether (ed.), *Foreign Relations of the US, 1955–57, Arab-Israeli Dispute 1955*, Vol. XIV, United States Government Printing Office: Washington, D.C., 1989.

Chandrashekhar Dasgupta, *War and Diplomacy in Kashmir, 1947–48*, Sage: New Delhi, 2002.

Charles Masson, *Narrative of Various Journeys in Balochistan, Afghanistan, Punjab, and Kalat, Vol. III*, Richard Bentley: London, 1844.

Charles Miller, *Khyber, British India's North West Frontier: The Story of an Imperial Migraine*, Macmillan: New York, 1977.

Chaudhri Muhammad Ali, *The Emergence of Pakistan*, Columbia University Press: New York, 1967.

Colonel Sir Colin C. Scott-Moncrieff, *Report of the Indian Irrigation Commission, 1901–1903.Commission Appointed to Report on the Irrigation in India as a Protection against Famine*, Office of the Superintendent of Government Printing: Calcutta, 1903.

Craig Murray, *Sikunder Burnes: Master of the Great Game*, Birlinn Ltd.: Edinburgh, 2016.

D.G. Harris, *Irrigation in India*, Humphrey Milford, Oxford University Press: London, 1923.

Daniel Klingensmith, *One Valley and a Thousand: Dams, Nationalism and Development*, Oxford University Press: Oxford, 2007.

David E. Lilienthal, *The Journals of David E. Lilienthal*, Vol. 3, Venturesome Years, 1950–55, Harper and Row: New York, 1966.

David E. Lilienthal, *TVA-Democracy on the March*, Harper and Brothers: New York, 1944; reprint, 1953.

David Gilmartin, *Blood and Water: The Indus River Basin in Modern History*, University of California Press: California, 2015.

Divyabhanusinh, Ashok Kumar Das and Shibani Bose, *The Story of India's Unicorn*, Marg Foundation: Mumbai, 2018.

Edward C. Sachau, *Alberuni's India, Vol. I*, Kegan Paul, Trench, Trubner and Co. Ltd: London, 1910.

Edward Gibbon, *The History of the Decline and Fall of the Roman Empire*, Vol. I, Fred de Pau and Company: New York, 1776.

Edward Gibbon, *The History of the Decline and Fall of the Roman Empire*, Vol.6, chapter LXXI, Fred de Pau and Company: New York, 1788.

Edward Thompson, *The Making of the Indian Princes*, Oxford University Press: London, 1943.

Edward Thornton, *A Gazetteer of the Countries Adjacent to India on the North–West; Including Sinde, Afghanistan, Beloochistan, Punjab and the Neighbouring States, In Two Volumes*, W.H. Allen: London, 1844.

Edwin Arnold, *The Marquis of Dalhousie's Administration of British India*, Vol. I, Saunders Otley & Co.: London, 1862.

El–Mas'ūdi's, *Historical Encyclopaedia Entitled 'Meadows of Gold and Mines of Gems', Vol. I*, tr. by Aloys Sprenger, W.H. Allen and Co.: London, 1841.

Eugene Black, *Diplomacy of Economic Development*, Harvard University Press: Boston, 1960.

F. & C. Grey (eds.), *Tales of Our Grandfather or India Since 1856*, Smith, Elder and Co.: London, 1912.

Finbarr B. Flood, *Objects of Translation: Material, Culture and Medieval 'Hindu-Muslim' Encounter*, Princeton University Press; Princeton, 2009.

Ganda Singh, *Ahmad Shah Durrani: Father of Modern Afghanistan*, Asia Publishing House: London, 1959.

George Frederick Fitzclarence, *Journal of a Route Across India, Through Egypt, to England, in the latter end of the year 1817, and the Beginning of 1818*, John Murray: London, 1819.

Golam W. Choudhury, *Pakistan's Relations with India 1947–1966*, Meenakshi Prakashan: Meerut, 1971.

H. Caldwell Lipsett, *Lord Curzon in India, 1898–1901*, Messrs Everett & Co.: London, 1903.

H.C. Verma, *Harvesting Water and Rationalization of Agriculture in North Medieval India*, Anamika Publishers: New Delhi, 2001.

H.M. Vibart, *Richard Baird Smith. Leader of the Delhi Heroes in 1857. Private Correspondence of the Commanding Engineer During the Siege, and Other Interesting Letters Hitherto Unpublished*, Archibald Constable and Co.: Westminster, 1897.

H.V. Hodson, *The Great Divide: Britain–India–Pakistan*, Hutchinson and Co.: London, 1969.

Halford L. Hoskins, *British Routes to India*, Longmans, Green and Co.: London, 1928.

Harish Jain, *The Making of Punjab*, Unistar Books: Chandigarh, 2003.

Hazrat Syed Yaqoob Bazmi, *Muqaddama-E-Sirajul Absar*, Vol. Two, tr. by Syed Sharief Khundmiri, Trafford Publishing: Victoria, Canada, 2013.

Henry M. Elliot, *The History of India, as Told by Its Own Historians: The Muhammadan Period*, Vol. I, Trubner and Co.: London, 1867.

Henry M. Elliot, *The History of India, as Told by Its Own Historians. The Muhammadan Period*, Vol. V, Trubner and Co.: London, 1872.

Henry Pottinger, *Travels in Beloochistan and Sinde*, accompanied by a Geographical and Historical Account of Those Countries, With a Map, Longman, Hurst, Rees, Orme, and Brown: London, 1816.

Herbert Edwardes and Herman Merivale, *Life of Sir Henry Lawrence*, Macmillan: New York, 1873.

Herbert M. Wilson, *Irrigation in India*, U.S. Geological Survey: Washington, 1903 (Second Edition).

Ian Stone, *Canal Irrigation in British India: Perspectives on a Technological Change in a Peasant Economy*, Cambridge University Press: Cambridge, 1984.

Ibn Battuta Travels in Asia and Africa, Book III, tr. by H.A.R. Gibb, Routledge and Kegan Paul: London, 1929.

Ilyas Ahmad Chattha, *Partition and Its Aftermath: Violence, Migration and the Role of Refugees in the Socio-Economic Development of Gujranwala and Sialkot Cities, 1947–1961*, thesis, University of Southampton Research Repository ePrints Soton, 2009.

Imran Ali, *The Punjab Canal Colonies: 1885–1940*, a thesis, Australian National University: Canberra, 1979.

Imran Ali, *The Punjab under Imperialism, 1885–1947*, Princeton University Press: New York, 1988.

Iqbal Ahmed Siddiqui, 'History of Water Laws in India' in Chhatrapati Singh (ed.), *Water Law in India*, Indian Law Institute: New Delhi, 1992.

Iqtidar Hussain Siddiqui, *Authority and Kingship under the Sultans of Delhi: Thirteenth–Fourteenth Centuries*, Manohar: New Delhi, 2006.

Irfan Habib, *Economic History of Medieval India 1200–1500*, Pearson Longman: New Delhi, 2011.

J.A. Norris, *The First Afghan War 1838–1842*, Cambridge University Press: Cambridge, 1967.

J.N. Dixit, *India-Pakistan in War & Peace*, Books Today: New Delhi, 2002.

Jagmohan, *My Frozen Turbulence in Kashmir*, Allied Publishers: New Delhi, 1991.

James Burnes, *Narrative of a Visit to the Court of Sinde at Hyderabad on the Indus; Illustrated with Plates and a Map; With a Sketch of the History of Cutch and an Appendix*, Longman and Co.: London, 1839.

James Outram, *The Conquest of Scinde: A Commentary*, Part II, William Blackwood and Sons: Edinburgh and London, 1846.

James R. Penn, *Rivers of the World: A Social, Geographical and Environmental Sourcebook*, ABC-CLIO: Santa Barbara, LA, 2001.

Jawaharlal Nehru's Speeches, Volume Three (March 1953–August 1957), Publications Division, Government of India, 1983.

Jeremiah Curtin, *The Mongols: A History*, Little Brown and Company: Boston, 1908.

John Andrew Hamilton, 'Edward Law, Earl of Ellenborough (1790-1871)' in Sidney Lee (ed.), *Dictionary of National Biography*, Vol. XXXI, Macmillan and Co.: New York, 1892.

John Bright, *Selected Speeches of Rt. Hon. John Bright M.P. on Public Questions*, J.M. Dent & Co.: London, 1853.

John Broich, *Engineering the Empire: British Water Supply System and Colonial Societies, 1850–1900*, Cambridge University Press online, 21 December 2012.

John Brunton, *John Brunton 1812–1899, Memoirs of An Engineer*, Cambridge University Press: Cambridge, 1939.

John James Hood Gordon, *The Sikhs*, William Blackwood and Sons: London, 1904.

John Marshall (ed.), *Mohenjo-daro and the Indus Civilization*, Being an official account of Archaeological Excavations at Mohenjo-daro carried out by the Government of India between the years 1922 and 1927, Volume I and II, Arthur Probsthain: London, 1931.

John Martineau, *Life and Correspondence of Sir Bartle Frere*, Vol. 1, Cambridge University Press: Cambridge, 1895.

John William Kaye, *The Life and Correspondence of Charles, Lord Metcalfe*, Vol. I, Smith, Elder and Co.: London, 1858.

Jos Gommans, *The Indian Frontier: Horse and Warband in the Making of Empires*, Manohar: Delhi, 2018.

Josef Korbel, *Danger in Kashmir*, Oxford University Press, New York, 2002.

Josiah Harlan, *Memoir of India and Avghanistaun*, J. Dobson: Philadelphia, 1842.

K.C. Sagar, *Foreign Influence on Ancient India*, Northern Book Centre: New Delhi, 1992.

Kalhana's Rajatarangini: A Chronicle of the Kings of Kashmir, Vol. II, tr. by M.A. Stein, Motilal Banarsidass Publication: New Delhi, 1900.

Kanwar Sain, *Reminiscences of an Engineer*, Young Asia Publications: New Delhi, 1978.

Karl Wittfogel, *Oriental Despotism: A Comparative Study of Total Power*, Yale University Press: New Haven, 1957.

Kaushik Roy and Peter Lodge (eds.), *Chinese and Indian Warfare—From the Classic Age to 1870*, Routledge: London, 2015.

Keith Pitman, 'The Role of the World Bank in Enhancing Cooperation and Resolving Conflict in International Watercourses: The Case of the Indus Basin', in Salman M. A. Salman and Laurence Boisson de Chazournes (eds.), *International Watercourses: Enhancing Cooperation and Managing Conflict*, World Bank: Washington, 1998.

Kelcie Daniels, Hannah Michael-Schwartz and Nick Spring, 'The Grand Manifesto of Alexander I', Napoleon Translations, *The Institutional Repository at DePaul University*, Chicago, 2011.

Kim Phillips-Fein and Julian E. Zelizer (eds.), *What's Good for Business: Business and American Politics since World War II*, Oxford University Press: Oxford, 2012.

Kirpal Singh (ed.), *Selected Documents on Partition of Punjab, India and Pakistan, 1947*, National Book Shop: Delhi, 1991.

Kuldip Nayar, *Scoop! Inside Stories from the Partition to the Present*, Harper Collins, New Delhi, 2006.

L.S. Rathore, *The Regal Patriot: Maharaja Ganga Singh of Bikaner*, Roli: New Delhi, 2007.

Lady Beatty Balfour, *The History of Lord Lytton's Indian Administration, 1876 to 1880: Compiled from Letters and Official Papers*, Longmans: London, 1899.

Lady Hope and William Digby, *General Sir Arthur Cotton: His Life and Work*, Kessinger Publishing: Whitefish, Montana, 2010.

Larry Collins and Dominique Lapierre, *Freedom at Midnight*, Vikas Publishing House: New Delhi, 1975.

Larry Collins and Dominique Lapierre, *Mountbatten and the Partition of India*, Vol. 1: *March 22–August 15, 1947*, Vikas Publishing House: New Delhi, 1982.

Latif Ahmed Sherwani, *The Partition of India and Mountbatten*, Atlantic Publishers and Distributors: New Delhi, 1989.

Leonard Mosley, *The Last Days of the British Raj*, Jaico Publishing House: Bombay, 1960.

Lieut. C.C. Scott-Moncrieff, *Irrigation in Southern Europe: Being the Report of a Tour of Inspection of the Irrigation Works in France, Spain, and Italy, Undertaken in 1867-68 for the Government of India*, E. & F. N. Spon: London, 1868.

Lionel Carter (ed.), *Mountbatten's Report on the Last Viceroyalty 22 March–15 August 1947*, Manohar: New Delhi, 2005.

Manan Ahmed Asif, *A Book of Conquest: The Chachnama and Muslim Origins in South Asia*, Harvard University Press: Boston, 2016.

Masood Khadarposh mentions the incident in his memoir, *Tashakus Ka Bohran: Batain Masud Khaddarposh Ki* (Identity Crisis: The Views of Masud Khaddarposh), Nigarshat Publications: Lahore, 1988.

Meenakshi Jain (ed.), *The India They Saw: Foreign Accounts, 8th–15th Centuries*, Ocean Books: New Delhi, 2011.

Mehr Chand Mahajan, *Looking Back: Autobiography of Mehr Chand Mahajan*, Asia Publishing House: New Delhi, 1963.

Michael Edwardes, *Asia in the European Age*, Praeger: New York, 1963.

Michael Edwardes, *British India: 1772–1947*, Rupa: New Delhi, 1993.

Michael H. Fisher, *A Short History of the Mughal Empire*, I.B. Tauris: London, 2016.

Mikhail Volodarsky, *Soviet Union and Its Southern Neighbours: Iran and Afghanistan, 1917–1933*, Routledge: London, 1994.

Mohan Lal, *Travels in the Panjab, Afghanistan and Turkistan to Balk, Bukhara, and Herat; and a Visit to Great Britain and Germany*, Allen and Co.: London, 1846.

Mountstuart Elphinstone, *Account of the Kingdom of Caubul, and Its Dependencies in Persia, Tartary, and India: Comprising a View of the Afghaun Nation, and a History of the Dooraunee Monarchy*, Vol. 1, Longman, Hurst, Rees, Orme and Brown, and J. Murray: London, 1819.

Mountstuart Elphinstone, *An Account of the Kingdom of Caubul, and its dependencies in Persia, Tartary and India; Comprising a view of the Afghaun Nation, and the History of the Dooraunee Monarchy*, Vol. II, Richard Bentley: London, 1842.

Muhamad Zafrullah Khan, *Agony of Pakistan*, Kent Publications: Oxford, 1973.

Munther J. Haddadin and Uri Shamir, Jordan Case Study, UNESCO Publication, UNESDOC Digital Library, 2003.

N.V. Gadgil, *Government from Inside*, Meenakshi Prakashan: Meerut, 1968.

Narendra Singh Sarila, *The Shadow of the Great Game: The Untold Story of India's Partition*, Harper Collins, New Delhi, 2005.

Nayanjot Lahiri, *Finding Forgotten Cities: How the Indus Civilization Was Discovered*, Seagull Book: New York, 2006.

Nazer Aziz Anjum, *Economy of Transport in Mughal India*, Unpublished Thesis, Aligarh Muslim University, Aligarh, 2010.

Nicholas Mansergh (ed.), *The Commonwealth Experience from British to Multiracial Commonwealth*, Vol. Two, Palgrave Macmillan: London, 1982.

Nicholas Mansergh (ed.), *The Transfer of Power, 1942–7. Vol. XI: The Mountbatten Viceroyalty Announcement and Reception of the 3 June Plan 31 May–7 July 1947*, Her Majesty's Stationery Office: London, 1982.

Niranjan D. Gulhati, *Indus Waters Treaty: An Exercise in International Mediation*, Allied Publishers: Bombay, 1973.

Nisid Hajari, *Midnight Furies: The Deadly Legacy of India's Partition*, Penguin: London, 2015.

Olli Varis, Cecilia Tortajada and Asit Biswas (eds.), *Management of Transboundary Rivers and Lakes*, Springer–Verlag: Berlin, 2008.

P.N. Chopra, B.N. Puri, M.N. Das and A.C. Pradhan, *A Comprehensive History of Medieval India*, Sterling Publishers: New Delhi, 2003.

Paul Preston and Michael Partridge (eds.), *British Documents on Foreign Affairs, Part IV, January 1947–December 1947*, University Publications of America: Frederick, Maryland, 2001.

Percy Sykes, *A History of Afghanistan, Vol. 1*, Macmillan and Co. Ltd.: London, 1940.

Philip Ziegler, *Mountbatten: The Official Biography*, William Collins: London, 1985.

Pir Ghulam Hussain Koyahami, *Tarikh-i-Hasan*, Urdu tr. by Shams-ud-din, Shams-ut-Tawarikh: Srinagar, 2003.

Proby T. Cautley, 'Canals of Irrigation in the North Western Provinces', *The Calcutta Review*, XII, 1849.

Proby T. Cautley, *Report on the Ganges Canal Works, from their commencement until the opening of the canal in 1854*, Smith, Elder and Co.: London, 1860.

Qazi Nur Mohammadin, *Jang Namah*, tr. and summarized by Ganda Singh, Sikh Historical Research Foundation: Amritsar, 1939.

R. Bosworth Smith, *The Life of Lord Lawrence*, Vol. 2, Smith, Elder & Co.: London, 1885.

R.C. Dutt, *Famines and Land Assessments in India*, Kegan Paul: London, 1900.

R.B. Buckley, *Irrigation Works in India and Egypt*, E. & F.N. Spon: London, 1893.

R.L. Rathore, *Maharaja Sadul Singh of Bikaner: A Biography*, Books Treasure and Maharaja Ganga Sighji Trust: Jodhpur, 2005.

T.R.E. Holmes, *Sir Charles Napier*, Reproduced by Sani H. Panhwar, California, 2009.

Rasul Bux Palijo, Sindh–Punjab Water Dispute 1859–2003, Copyright © www.panhwar.com

Richard A. Gabriel, *The Madness of Alexander the Great: The Myth of Military Genius*, Pen and Sword: Barnsley, Yorkshire, 2015.

Rita P. Wright, *The Ancient Indus: Urbanism, Economy and Society*, Cambridge University Press: New York, 2009.

Robert J. Donovan, *Harry S. Truman, 1949–1953: Tumultuous Years*, University of Missouri Press: Columbia, 1996.

Robert McMahon, *The Cold War on the Periphery: The United States, India, and Pakistan*, Columbia University Press: New York, 1994.

S.A.A. Rizvi, *The Wonder That Was India*, Vol. II, Picador India: New Delhi, 2005.

S.B. Karmahapatra, *Meghnad Saha*, Publications Division, Govt. of India: New Delhi, 1997.

S.C. Mishra, 'Progress of Irrigation during the Period of Maharaja Ganga Singh' in G.S.L. Devra (ed.), *Maharaja Ganga Singhji Centenary Volume 1980*, Centenary Celebration Committee: Bikaner, 1980.

S.K. Thorat, *Ambedkar's Role in Economic Planning and Water Policy*, Shipra Publications: New Delhi, 1998.

S.M. Jaffar, *The Mughal Empire from Babur to Aurangzeb*, reprint, S. Muhammad Sadiq Khan: Peshawar, 1936.

S.P. Gupta, *The 'Lost' Sarasvati and the Indus Civilization*, Kusumanjali Prakashan: Jodhpur, 1995.

S.S. Thorburn, *Musalmans and Moneylenders in the Punjab*, William Blackwood and Sons: London and Edinburgh, 1886.

Saiyid Ali Naqvi, *Indus Waters and Social Change: The Evolution and Transition of Agrarian Society in Pakistan*, Oxford University Press: Karachi, 2013.

Salahuddin Khan (ed.), *Speeches, Messages and Statements of Madar-i-Millat Mohtarama Fatima Jinnah (1948–1967)*, Research Society of Pakistan, University of the Punjab, 1976.

Salman M.A. Salman and Kishor Uprety, *Conflict and Cooperation on South Asia's Rivers: A Legal Perspective*, The World Bank: Washington D.C., 2002.

Santimay Chatterjee and Enakshi Chatterjee, *Meghnad Saha*, National Book Trust: New Delhi, 1984.

Selected Works of Jawaharlal Nehru, Volume Two, Jawaharlal Nehru Memorial Fund, 1984.

...., Volume Six, Jawaharlal Nehru Memorial Fund, 1987.

...., Volume Four, Jawaharlal Nehru Memorial Fund, 1987.

...., Volume Five, Jawaharlal Nehru Memorial Fund, 1987.

...., Volume Sixteen (II), Jawaharlal Nehru Memorial Fund, 1994.

...., Volume Twenty-One, Jawaharlal Nehru Memorial Fund, 1997.

...., Volume Twenty-Two, Jawaharlal Nehru Memorial Fund, 1998.

...., Volume Forty-Two, Jawaharlal Nehru Memorial Fund, 2010.

Shah Mahmoud Hanifi (ed.), *Mountstuart Elphinstone in South Asia: Pioneer of British Colonial Rule*, Oxford University Press: New York, 2019.

Shakti Sinha and Himanshu Roy (eds.), *Patel: Political Ideas and Policies*, Sage: New Delhi, 2019.

Sir Charles Napier, *Lights and Shades of Military Life, Vol. I*, Henry Colburn: London, 1840.

Sisir Gupta, *Kashmir: A Study in India–Pakistan Relations*, Asia Publishing House: New Delhi, 1966.

Speeches and Writings of Mr. Jinnah, Vol. II, Shaikh Muhammad Ashraf: Lahore, 1947.

Srinath Raghavan, *War and Peace in Modern India*, Permanent Black: Ranikhet, 2010.

Srivara, *Jaina-Rajatarangini*, tr. by Jogesh Chunder Dutt, Calcutta, 1879.

Stanley Lane–Poole, *Medieval India Under Mohammedan Rule, 712–1764*, G.P. Putnam's Sons: London, 1903.

Stanley Wolpert, *Jinnah of Pakistan*, Oxford University Press: Oxford, 1997.

Stantley Wolpert, *Shameful Flight: The Last years of the British Empire in India*, Oxford University Press: Oxford, 2009.

Stephen C. McCaffrey, 'Water, Politics and International Law', in *Water in Crisis: A Guide to the World's Fresh Water Resources*, Peter H. Gleick (ed.), Oxford University Press: Oxford, 1993.

Subhas Kashyap, *The Political System and Institution Building Under Jawaharlal Nehru*, National Publishing House: New Delhi, 1990.

Sudhir Sen, *Wanderings: In Search of Solutions of the Problem of Poverty*, Macmillan: Madras, 1989.

Sugata Ray and Venugopal Maddipati (eds.), *Water Histories of South Asia: The Materiality of Liquescense*, Routledge: London, 2020.

Sunil Amrith, *Unruly Waters: How Mountain Rivers and Monsoon Have Shaped South Asia's History*, Basic Books: New York, 2018.

T.C.A. Raghavan, *The People Next Door: The Curious History of India's Relations with Pakistan*, C. Hurst and Co.: London, 2019.

Tarikh-i-Firishta, *Rise of Mahomedan Power in India*, till the year A.D. 612, tr. by John Briggs, Longman, Rees, Orme, Brown & Green: London, 1829.

Tahrik-i huriyyat-i Kashmir (History of Independence Movements in Kashmir), *Volume 2, 1936–1945*, Mahafiz Pablikeshanz: Srinagar, 1968.

Tapan Raychaudhuri and Irfan Habib (eds.), *The Cambridge Economic History of India: c. 1757–1970*, Orient Longman: New Delhi, 2005.

Teja Singh and Ganda Singh, *Short History of the Sikhs, Vol. One (1469–1765)*, Publication Bureau Punjabi University: Patiala, 2006.

The Chachnamah, An Ancient History of Sind, tr. from Persian by Mirza Kalichbeg Fredunbeg, Sind Commissioners Press: Karachi, 1900.

The Farewell Addresses of the Inhabitants of Jamaica, To the Right Honourable Sir Charles Theophilus Metcalfe, Governor of the Island, Jordan, and Osborn: Kingston, 1842.

The Jahangirnama: Memoirs of Jahangir, Emperor of India, tr. by Wheeler Thackston, Oxford University Press: Oxford, 1999.

The Travels and Adventures of the Turkish Admiral Sidi Ali Reis: In India, Afghanistan, Central Asia and Persia during the Years 1553–1556, tr. from the Turkish by A. Vambery, London, 1899.

The Tuzuk-i-Jahangiri or Memoirs of Jahangir, tr. by Alexander Rogers, Royal Asiatic Society: London, 1909.

Tika Ram, *Sir Chhotu Ram: A Biography*, Centre for Study of Haryana History: Gurgaon, 2008.

Timothy D. Haines, '*Building the Empire Building the Nation: Water, Land and the Politics of River Development in Sind, 1898–1969*', thesis submitted to the Royal Holloway College, University of London, 2011.

Travels of Ibn Batuta, tr. from the Abridged Arabic Manuscript Copies by the Rev. Samuel Lee, the Oriental Translation Committee: London, 1829.

Undala Alam, *Water Rationality: Mediating the Indus Waters Treaty*, Unpublished thesis, University of Durham: UK, 1998.

Urgunge Onon, *The Secret History of the Mongols: The Life and Times of Chinggis Khan*, Routledge Curzon: London, 2001.

V.P. Menon, *The Story of the Integration of the Indian States*, Orient Longmans Ltd.: Calcutta, 1956.

V.S. Naipaul, *Among the Believers: An Islamic Journey*, Andre Deutsch Limited: London, 1981.

Virender Grover (ed.), *50 Years of India-Pak Relations. The Initial Phase: Partition of India, Indo-Pak Wars, The UNO*, Vol.1, Deep and Deep Publications: New Delhi, 2002.

W.D. Handcock (ed.), *English Historical Documents, 1874–1914*, Routledge: London, 1996.

W.H. Auden, 'Partition', in Edward Mendelson (ed.), *Collected Poems by W.H. Auden*, Modern Library Edition: New York, 2007.

W.W. Hunter, *A Life of the Earl of Mayo: Fourth Viceroy of India*, Vol. II, Smith, Elder and Co: London, 1876.

Walter R. Lawrence, *The Valley of Kashmir*, Henry Frowde: London, 1895.

Walter S. Poole (ed.), *The Joint Chiefs of Staff and National Policy, 1950-1952*, Volume IV, Office of Joint History and Office of the Chairman of the Joint Chiefs of Staff: Washington, D.C., 1998.

Wilfred Cantwell Smith, *Islam in Modern History*, Princeton University Press: NJ, 1957.

William Darlymple, *Return of a King: The Battle of Afghanistan, 1839–42*, Bloomsbury: London, 2014.

William Foster (ed.), *Early Travels in India: 1583-1619*, Oxford University Press: London, 1921.

William Foster, *The English Factories in India, 1634-1636: A Calendar of Documents in the India Office, British Museum and Public Record Office*, The Clarendon Press: Oxford, 1911.

William Foster, *The English Factories in India, 1637-1641: A Calendar of Documents in the India Office, British Museum and Public Record Office*, The Clarendon Press: Oxford, 1912. Winifred Bamforth, *British Interest in the Tigris-Euphrates Valley: 1856–1888*, M.A. thesis May 1948, ProQuest: An Arbor, MI, 2016.

Zahid Ali Khalid, *State, Society and Environment in the Ex–State of Bahawalpur: A Case Study of the Sutlej Valley Project, 1921–1947*, thesis submitted to University of Sussex, UK, April 2017.

Articles and Essays

A.K. Biswas, 'Ambedkar, the Architect of Damodar Valley Corporation', *Mainstream*, LIV (17), 16 April 2016.

A.V. Shankara Rao, 'MokshagundamVisvesvaraya: Engineer, Statesman and Planner', *Resonance*, May 2002.

Aaron Wolf, 'Water for Peace in the Jordan River Watershed', *Natural Resources Journal*, 33(3), 1993.

Abraham M. Hirsch, 'From the Indus to the Jordan: Characteristics of Middle East International River Disputes', *Political Science Quarterly*, 71(2), June 1956.

Anita Inder Singh, 'Decolonization in India: The Statement of 20 February 1947', *The International History Review*, 6(2), 1984.

Anwesha Sengupta, 'Of Men and Things: The Administrative Consequences of Partition of British India', *Refugee Watch*, 39 and 40, June and December 2012.

Asiatic Intelligence, *The Asiatic Journal and Monthly Register for British, Foreign India, China, and Australasia*, Vol. VIII, 1832.

Asiatic Journal and Monthly Register, New Series Vol. VI, part II, September–December 1831.

Ayub Khan, 'Pakistan Perspective', *Foreign Affairs*, Vol. 38(4), July 1960.

Betty Miller Unterberger, 'American Views of Mohammad Ali Jinnah and the Pakistan Liberation Movement', *Diplomatic History*, Vol. 5(4), 1981.

Bijan Omrani, 'The Durand Line: History and Problems of the Afghan–Pakistan Border', *Asian Affairs*, Vol. XL(II), July 2009.

C.H. Buck, 'Canal Irrigation in the Punjab', *The Geographical Journal*, 27 January 1906.

The Calcutta Review, Vol. XII, 1849.

David Ekbladh, 'Mr. TVA: Grass–Roots Development, David Lilienthal, and the Rise and Fall of the Tennessee Valley Authority as a Symbol for U.S. Overseas Development, 1933–1973', *Diplomatic History*, Vol. 26(3), 2002.

David Gilmartin, 'Scientific Empire and Imperial Science: Colonialism and Irrigation Technology in the Indus Basin', *The Journal of Asian Studies*, Vol. 53(4), November 1994.

David Hall–Matthews, 'Inaccurate Conceptions: Disputed Measures of Nutritional Needs and Famine Deaths in Colonial India', *Modern Asian Studies*, Vol. 42(6), 2008.

David Stone, 'The United States and the Negotiations of the Indus Waters Treaty', *USI Journal*, CXL, January–March 2010.

E.S. Lindley, 'Regime Channels, Minutes of Proceedings', *Punjab Engineering Congress*, Vol. 7, 1919.

Elizabeth Moynihan, 'The Lotus Garden Palace of Zahir al–Din Muhammad Babur', in *Muqarnas*, Vol. 5, 1988.

F.J. Berber, 'Indus Water Dispute', *Indian Year Book of International Affairs*, Diocesan Press, 1957.

F.J. Fowler, 'The Indo–Pakistan Water Dispute,' *Yearbook of World Affairs*, Vol. IX, 1955.

F.J. Fowler, 'Some Problems of Water between East and West Punjab', *Geographical Review*, Vol. 40(4), October 1950.

George Griffiths, 'Stable–channel design in alluvial rivers', *Journal of Hydrology*, Vol. 65(4), September 1983.

George W. Briggs, 'The Indian Rhinoceros as a Sacred Animal', *Journal of the American Oriental Society*, Vol. 51(3), September 1931.

Ghulam Rasool Nahami, 'Suyya: The Brain Behind the Idea to Counter Kashmir Floods, Part V', *Kashmir Watch*, 5 October 2014.

H. Donaldson Jordan, 'Lord Ellenborough: A Biography of Edward Law, Earl of Ellenborough, Governor General of India, Book Review', *The American Historical Review*, Vol. 46(3), April 1941.

H.W. Brands, 'India and Pakistan in American Strategic Planning, 1947–1954: The Commonwealth as Collaborator', *The Journal of Imperial and Commonwealth History*, Vol. 15(1), 1986.

Haris Gazdar, 'Baglihar and Politics of Water: A Historical Perspective from Pakistan', *Economic and Political Weekly*, 40(9), 26 February–4 March 2005.

Helen James, 'The Assassination of Lord Mayo: The "First Jihad"?' *International Journal of Asia Pacific Studies*, Vol. 5(2), July 2009.

Henry Trofimenko, 'The Third World and U.S.–Soviet Competition', *Foreign Affairs*, Vol. 59(1), Summer 1981.

Ian Talbot, 'The Punjab under Colonialism: Order and Transformation in British India', *Journal of Punjab Studies*, 14(1), 2007.

Iqbal Chawla, 'Wavell's Breakdown Plan, 1945–47: an Appraisal', *Journal of Punjabi Studies*, Vol. 16(2), 2009.

J.P. Parry, 'Steam Power and British Influence in Baghdad', *The Historical Journal*, Vol. 56(1), March 2013.

Jagat S. Mehta, 'The Indus Water Treaty: A Case Study in the Resolution of an International River Basin Conflict', *Natural Resources Forum*, Vol. 12, 1998.

Jagjeet Lally, 'Beyond Tribal Breakout: Afghan in the History of Empire, ca. 1747–1818', *Journal of World History*, Vol. 29(3), September 2018.

James Wescoat, 'Early water systems in Mughal India', *Environmental Design*, Vol. 2, January 1985.

Jochen Kraske, 'India and the World Bank', *World Bank*, 17 August 1997.

John Black, 'The military influence on engineering education in Britain and India, 1848–1906', *Indian Economic and Social History Review*, Vol. 46(2), 2009.

John K. Galbraith, '"The Turbulent Frontier." As a Factor in British Expansion', *Comparative Studies in Society and History*, Vol. 2(2), 1960.

John F. Richards, 'The Economic History of the Lodi Period: 1451–1526', *Journal of the Economic and Social History of the Orient*, Vol. 8(1), August 1965.

John G. Laylin, 'Principles of Law Governing the Uses of International Rivers: Contribution from the Indus Basin', *Proceedings of the American Society of International Law at its Annual Meeting (1921–1969)*, Vol. 51, April 1957.

John R. Wood, 'Dividing the Jewel: Mountbatten and the Transfer of Power to India and Pakistan', *Pacific Affairs*, Vol. 58(4), 1985–6.

Josepha Ivanka Wessels, 'Playing the Game, identity and perception-of-the-other in water cooperation in the Jordan River Basin', *Hydrological Sciences Journal*, Vol. 61(7), 2016.

Joya Chatterji, 'The Fashioning of a Frontier, The Radcliffe Line and Bengal's Border Landscape', *Modern Asian Studies*, Vol. 30(1), 1999.

Latika Chaudhary and Anand V. Swamy, 'A Policy of Credit Disruption: The Punjab Land Alienation Act 1900', *Semantic Scholar*, October 2008.

Lieut. Colonel Robert D. Osborn, 'India Under Lord Lytton', *Contemporary Review*, Vol. 36, December 1879.

Lieut. Yule, 'Canal Act of Emperor Akbar with some notes and remarks on the History of the Western Jumna Canals', *The Journal of the Asiatic Society*, Vol. XV, 1846.

Liuvu Giosan, et. al., 'Fluvial landscapes of the Harappan civilization', *Proceedings of the National Academy of Sciences*, 29 May 2012.

Lord Mountbatten, 'Lord Mountbatten on His Viceroyalty', *The Asiatic Review*, XLIV (160), October 1948.

M.A. Yapp, 'British Perceptions of the Russian Threat to India', *Modern Asian Studies*, Vol. 24 (1), October 1987.

Muhammad Afzal Khan, 'Ali Mardan Khan: The Great Iranian Noble of Shah Jahan', *Proceedings of the Indian History Congress*, Vol. 44, 1983.

Muhammad Fazle Karim Khan and Muhammad Nawaz, 'Karez Irrigation in Punjab', *GeoJournal*, Vol. 37(1), 1995.

N. Gerald Barrier, 'The Punjab Disturbances of 1907: The Response of the British Government in India to Agrarian Unrest', *Modern Asian Studies*, Vol. 1(4), 1967.

Neha Gupta, 'Why the Social Context of Archaeology Matters in the Study of the Indus Valley Civilization: Insight on Banerji's Pre–Buddhist Period at Mohenjodaro', *Heritage: Journal of Multidisciplinary Studies in Archaeology*, Vol. 1, 2013.

Owen Lattimore, 'The Geography of Chingis Khan', *The Geographical Journal*, Vol. 129(1), March 1963.

Patrick McGinn, *Capital, Development and Canal Irrigation in Colonial India*, Working Paper 209, Institute for Social and Economic Change, 2009.

Proby T. Cautley, 'Canals of Irrigation in the North Western Provinces', *The Calcutta Review*, Vol. XII, 1849.

R. Bernbeck and S. Pollock, 'Ayodhya, Archaeology, and Identity', *Current Anthropology*, Vol. 37(1), 1996.

R.D. Buckley, 'Keeping Irrigation Canals Clear of Silt', *Proceedings Institution Civil Engineers*, 58, 1879.

R.G. Kennedy, 'Prevention of Silting in Irrigation Canals', *Minutes of Proceedings*, Inst. of C.E., Vol. CXIX, 1895.

Rakesh Ankit, '1948: The Crucial Year in the History of Jammu and Kashmir', *Economic and Political Weekly*, 45(11), 13–19 March 2010.

Rakesh Ankit, 'Britain and Kashmir, 1948: "The Arena of the UN"', *Diplomacy & Statecraft*, Vol. 24(2), 2013.

Robert J. McMahon, 'United States Cold War Strategy in South Asia: Making a Military Commitment to Pakistan, 1947–1954', *The Journal of American History*, Vol. 75(3), December 1988.

Rohan D'Souza, 'Water in British India: The Making of a Colonial Hydrology', *History Compass*, Vol. 4(4), 2006.

Sher Muhammad Garewal, 'Muslim League's Tacit Acceptance of Radcliffe Award: A Critical Review', *Pakistan Journal of History and Culture*, Vol. XXVI(2), 2005.

Silky Agarwal, et. al., 'Archaeological studies at Dholavira using GPR', *Current Science*, Vol. 114(4), February 2018.

Sir John Benton, 'The Punjab Triple Canal System', Paper No. 4137, *Minutes of Proceedings*, 16 November 1915, University of Sussex.

Sir Patrick Spens, 'The Arbitral Tribunal in India, 1947–48', *Transaction of the Grotius Society*, Vol. 36, 1950.

Stephen C. McCaffrey, 'The Harmon Doctrine One Hundred Years Later: Buried, Not Praised', *Natural Resources Journal*, Fall 1996.

Sukhwant Singh, 'Agricultural Science and Technology in the Punjab in the Nineteenth Century', *Indian Journal of History of Science*, Vol. 17(2), 1982.

T.T. Jones, 'The Genesis of Military River Operations: Alexander the Great at the Hydaspes River', *The Military Engineer*, Vol. 56(374), November–December 1964.

Taylor Sherman, 'A New Type of Revolution: Socialist Thoughts in India, 1940s–1960s', *Postcolonial Studies*, Vol. 21(4), 2018.

The Asiatic Annual Register, Vol. XI, 1809.

The Asiatic Journal and Monthly Register for British, Foreign India, China, and Australasia, Vol. VIII, 1832.

The Asiatic Journal, Vol. XVII, New Series, May–August 1835.

The Asiatic Review, XLIV (160), October 1948.

The Calcutta Review, Vol. LIX(CXVII), 1874.

The Calcutta Review, Vol. LX(CXX), 1875

The Journal of the Asiatic Society, Vol. XV, 1846.

The Light & Islamic Review, Vol. 69(1), Jan–Feb 1992.

The World Bank, 'Indus Water Treaty', *World Affairs*, Vol. 123(4), Winter 1960.

Tripta Wahi, 'Shah Nahar: Its History, Technology and Socio-Political Implications', *Proceedings of the Indian National Congress*, Vol. 74, 2013.

Tufail Jawed, 'The World Bank and the Indus Basin Dispute: Background-I', *Pakistan Horizon*, Vol. 18(3), 1965.

V.N. Datta, 'The Punjab Boundary Commission Award', *Proceedings of the Indian History Congress*, Vol. 59, 1998.

W. Ainsworth, 'A Narrative of the Visit to the Court of Sinde by James Burnes', *The Journal of the Royal Geographical Society of London, Vol. I*, John Murray: London, 1832.

W. Eric Gustafson and Richard B. Reidinger, 'Delivery of Canal Water in North India and West Pakistan', *Economic and Political Weekly*, December 1971.

W.H. Morris–Jones, 'Thirty–Six Years Later: The Mixed Legacies of Mountbatten's Transfer of Power', *International Affairs*, Vol. 59(4), 1983.

Wayne Wilcox, 'The Economic Consequences of Partition: India and Pakistan', *Journal of International Affairs*, Vol. 18(2), 1964.

William Drumright, 'His Search for a Viable Middle Ground: A Reappraisal of David E. Lilienthal's TVA—Democracy on the March', *The Princeton University Library Chronicle*, 63(3), 2002.

William T. Everall, 'The Reconstruction of the Attock Bridge across the River Indus on the North Western Railway, India', *Minutes of the Proceedings of the Institution of Civil Engineers*, Vol. 230(1930), 1930.

Yoginder Sikand, 'Hazrat Bulbul Shah: The First Known Muslim Missionary in Kashmir', *The Journal of Muslim Minority Affairs*, Vol. 20(2), 2010.

Newspapers/News Magazines/Websites

A.G. Noorani, 'Chasing the vision', *Frontline*, Chennai, 2–15 June 2012.

Bombay Courier, Bombay, 15 November 1832.

British Movietone News, 'Mounbattens Visit Maharaja of Bikaner', 2 February 1948.

Civil and Military Gazette, Lahore, 19 January 1953.

David Lilienthal, 'Are We Losing India?', *Collier's Weekly*, New York, 23 June 1951.

David Lilienthal, 'Another Korea in the Making', *Collier's Weekly*, New York, 4 August 1951.

Dawn, Karachi, 28 April 1948.

Dawn, Karachi, 23 December 1948

Dawn, Karachi, 27 December 1948.

Dawn, Karachi, 28 February 1948.

Dawn, Karachi, 13 March 1948.

Dawn, Karachi, 5 November 1948.

Dublin Review, London, 1841.

E.S. Lindley, *Regime Channels*, https://pecongress.org.pk/images/upload/books/ Regime–Channels.pdf

Ghulam Rasool Nahami, 'Suyya: The Brain Behind the Idea to Counter Kashmir Floods, Part V', *Kashmir Watch*, 5 October 2014, https://kashmirwatch.com/ suyya-the-brain-behind-the-idea-to-counter-kashmir-floods-v/

K.V. Padmanabhan, 'How the Indus Treaty was Signed,' *The Hindu*, New Delhi, 28 September, 2016.

Manu S. Pillai, 'Sir Arthur Cotton, the engineer and his rice bowl', *Mint*, New Delhi, 12 August 2017.

Ministry of Jal Shakti, http://mowr.gov.in/about–us/history

Salman Rashid, 'Jalaluddin Khwarazm', *The Express Tribune*, Karachi, 27 January 2012.

Sukhdarshan Nat, 'Sardar Ajit Singh Hero of the 'Pagdi Sambhal Jatta' Movement', *CPI(M-L) website*, http://archive.cpiml.org/liberation/year_2007/october/ Sardaar_ajit_singh.htm

The Athenaeum, No. 823, London, 5 August 1843.

The Hindustan Times, New Delhi, 19 July 1947.

The New York Times, 16 February 1953.

The Pakistan Times, Simla, 19 August 1947.

The Statesman, Calcutta, 19 August 1947.

The Statesman, Delhi, 26 January 1953.

The Statesman, Delhi, 30 January 1953.

The Tribune, Simla, 26 April 1960.

The Tribune, Simla, 10 May 1948.

The Washington Post, 21 February 1992.

Uttam Kumar Sinha, 'Nehruvian Imprint to Indus Treaty', *The Hindustan Times*, New Delhi, 19 September 2020.

Uttam Kumar Sinha, 'Indus waters civilization', *The Indian Express*, New Delhi, 22 September 2010.

Vintage Movie, 'Construction of the Sukkur Barrage', Government of India (Railways Department), 1924.

William Bullitt, 'How We Won the War and Lost the Peace', Part I, *Life*, New York, 30 August 1948 and Part II, 6 September 1948.